KNOWLEDGE REPRESENTATION AND DEFEASIBLE REASONING

STUDIES IN COGNITIVE SYSTEMS

VOLUME 5

James H. Fetzer
University of Minnesota, Duluth
Editor

KNOWLEDGE REPRESENTATION AND DEFEASIBLE REASONING

Edited by

HENRY E. KYBURG, Jr.

Departments of Philosophy and Computer Science,
University of Rochester, U.S.A.

RONALD P. LOUI

Department of Computer Science,
Washington University, U.S.A.

and

GREG N. CARLSON

Department of Foreign Languages,
University of Rochester, U.S.A.

KLUWER ACADEMIC PUBLISHERS

DORDRECHT / BOSTON / LONDON

Library of Congress Cataloging in Publication Data

```
Knowledge representation and defeasible reasoning / [edited by] Henry
    E. Kyburg, Jr., Ronald P. Loui, and Greg N. Carlson.
        p.   cm. -- (Studies in cognitive systems)
    Includes bibliographical references.
    ISBN 0-7923-0677-5 (alk. paper)
    1. Artificial intelligence. 2. Knowledge, Theory of.
  3. Reasoning. 4. Frames (Information theory)   I. Kyburg, Henry
  Ely, 1928-    . II. Loui, Ronald P. III. Carlson, Greg N., 1948-
  . IV. Series.
  Q335.K578   1990
  006.3--dc20                                          90-30971
```

ISBN 0-7923-0677-5

Published by Kluwer Academic Publishers,
P.O. Box 17, 3300 AA Dordrecht, The Netherlands.

Kluwer Academic Publishers incorporates
the publishing programmes of
D. Reidel, Martinus Nijhoff, Dr W. Junk and MTP Press.

Sold and distributed in the U.S.A. and Canada
by Kluwer Academic Publishers,
101 Philip Drive, Norwell, MA 02061, U.S.A.

In all other countries, sold and distributed
by Kluwer Academic Publishers Group,
P.O. Box 322, 3300 AH Dordrecht, The Netherlands.

Printed on acid-free paper

Printed in the Netherlands

TABLE OF CONTENTS

PART III / INFERENCE RULES AND BELIEF REVISION

PART IV / LOGICAL PROBLEMS IN REPRESENTING
KNOWLEDGE

SERIES PREFACE

This series will include monographs and collections of studies devoted to the investigation and exploration of knowledge, information, and data-processing systems of all kinds, no matter whether human, (other) animal, or machine. Its scope is intended to span the full range of interests from classical problems in the philosophy of mind and philosophical psychology through issues in cognitive psychology and sociobiology (concerning the mental capabilities of other species) to ideas related to artificial intelligence and computer science. While primary emphasis will be placed upon theoretical, conceptual, and epistemological aspects of these problems and domains, empirical, experimental, and methodological studies will also appear from time to time.

The present volume provides a collection of studies that focus on some of the central problems within the domain of artificial intelligence. These difficulties fall into four principal areas: defeasible reasoning (including the frame problem as a part), ordinary language (and the representation problems that it generates), the revision of beliefs (and its rules of inference), and knowledge representation (and the logical problems that are encountered there). These papers make original contributions to each of these areas of inquiry and should be of special interest to those who understand the crucial role that is played by questions of logical form. They vividly illustrate the benefits that can emerge from collaborative efforts involving scholars from linguistics, philosophy, computer science, and AI.

J. H. F.

INTRODUCTION

Artificial intelligence and certain kinds of philosophy have a lot in common: a concern with logic and language, a faith that progress in understanding intelligence is possible, and the belief that a community of scholars, working together, is the best method of achieving this progress. There is another link: both groups find in computer science a useful methodology. Computational linguistics is another discipline that involves both traditional and modern approaches to language.

Representatives of these three groups met in Rochester in the spring of 1987 under the aegis of the Society for Exact Philosophy. The Society for Exact Philosophy is a descendent of the famous Vienna and Berlin Circles.[1] The movement called "Logical Positivism" began in the 1920's, and had issued its manifesto in 1929. It flourished until the rise of Nazism, at which point its members scattered, many to the United States and Britain.

There was no doctrine to which members of this movement were supposed to adhere; there was rather a faith that the methods of science would lead to truth, and that truth was cumulative and scientific inquiry progressive. There was a common, but not doctrinaire, supposition that many of the ills of the world — war, nationalism, *etc.* — were due to the careless and improper use of language. The language of science could be made precise; the formalism of Russell and Whitehead's *Principia Mathematica* could decisively distinguish good from bad arguments; careful attention to the language of ethics, for example, would throw light on moral argument and prevent its misuse. Both attention to science, and attention to logic and language were central.

Although there is no doctrinaire relation between the Society for Exact Philosophy and the Vienna and Berlin Circles, there is a clear indebtedness. Many of the attitudes seem the same. There is the respect for empirical evidence; the concern with and sensitivity to language. There is above all a desire to achieve permanent progress — to achieve results, whether empirical or analytical, that will survive until they are surpassed. There is the faith in scientific progress. Along with these attitudes goes a distrust of grand schemes, of grandiose language, and of *a priori* claims that cannot be defended by careful reasoning.

---

[1]It is said that it was invented in a Beerstübe in Vienna by Mario Bunge and Richard Montague.

The relation between philosophy of this sort and artificial intelligence is a natural one. From the beginning of exact philosophy there has been concern with exact and explicit definition of concepts. With the advent of fast digital computers, the concern has shifted to a concern with computability. Thus philosophical ideas (for example, concerning the structure of language, the measurement of confirmation, the propagation of uncertainty in a field of propositions, the representation of knowledge) that could only be conjectural a few decades ago can now be tested.

From the other direction, artificial intelligence has developed partly in response to the demand for systems that will represent and employ knowledge in the real world. To do this, one must think about what knowledge is, how it is to be used, how it can be represented in language, how a system embodying knowledge can be communicated with, and so on. It is obvious (at least in retrospect) that these are traditional philosophical questions, and it is not surprising that many of the early efforts of artificial intelligence were primarily devoted to reinventing the wheel.

Artificial intelligence has matured. In its maturity it has discovered that philosophers have often had useful things to say.[2] Linguistics, similarly, has discovered that philosophical logic, semantics, and the formalization of language, have useful things to contribute to the understanding of ordinary language. And to complete the circle, one of the concerns of artificial intelligence has always been the project of enhancing communication between speakers of binary code and the speakers of ordinary language.

The idea behind the meeting from which these papers come was to bring all three groups together for the purpose not merely of exchanging ideas (though that is always fun) but for the purpose of exchanging technology, theorems, axioms — the stuff of which substantive, permanent, scientific progress is made.

Defeasible reasoning is the newest area of active interdisciplinary work between philosophy and AI. Defeasible reasoning is called non-monotonic by the computer scientists. This adjective, non-monotonic, highlights the possibility of adding axioms while losing theorems. The philosophers' term, defeasibility, focuses instead on disallowing putative inferences. But the two are essentially the same, and both points of view are useful.

The Frame Problem and its variant, the Yale Shooting Problem have become benchmarks for works on defeasible reasoning. It is only a small exaggeration to say that non-monotonic reasoning was invented to deal with the

---

[2] It always knew they weren't always right!

Frame Problem. When Hanks and McDermott discovered the Yale Shooting Problem, essentially the weaving together of two frame problems, it presented new challenges for defeasible reasoning systems. Some thought that it further challenged our best representations for actions and events. But none of the papers here indulge that opinion; they focus instead on the problem's relation to defeasible reasoning.

In addition to the Yale Shooting Problem, defeasible reasoning has been affected by fallout from David Touretzky's inheritance system. Touretzky argued that there is more to choosing one defeasible reason over another than just the order in which they were considered, or the number of steps in each. A story had to be given about what rules were really in conflict, and how that conflict should be resolved. In fact, a number of stories could be given, and this led to a "clash of intuitions."

It is possible that the *cognoscenti* could be satisfied if Donald Nute's paper were the only paper on the Yale Shooting Problem; there may now be fifty lesser papers on the problem. Nute's motives are two-fold: first, to present a new version of his original defeasible reasoning system, *LDR*; second, to demonstrate its effectiveness on the Yale Shooting Problem. Nute's original system, *LDR*, contained the first explicit statement that one non-monotonic rule is better than another if their consequents are contradictories and one's antecedent is logically stronger than the other's. This had been intuitive to many. Some may claim it was implicit in contemporaneous work by David Poole. Most thought the rule was the natural generalization of Touretzky's (and others') rule for choosing defaults from more specific classes. If Pollock is right that this generalization is incorrect, then Nute is the first to hang. Still, at the moment, most agree that the generalization is appropriate.

Since *LDR* was targeted for easy implementation in PROLOG, it was based on a relatively inexpressive language, with a weak sense of negation. Nute's paper augments that language. Once augmented, all kinds of problems have to be addressed, such as how to treat counter-arguments, what to do about directness defeat, and how non-monotonic rules can come into conflict without being direct contradictories. These are problems with which other authors on defeasible reasoning had been grappling, and here Nute joins them. Interestingly, his system remains the only defeasible reasoning system that defines defeasible entailments in terms of how lines can be added to a proof.

Len Schubert's paper is even more ambitious than the one he gave at the meeting. He is interested in demonstrating that the situation calculus, contrary to popular belief, never did rule out concurrency of actions. He introduces functions to express the situation that results from co-starting concurrent actions in a situation.

But the Frame Problem raises its grotesque head again. It has been hard to extend the solution of the frame problem to this "concurrent" situation calculus. In general, actions have pre- and co-requisites, and to deduce that a proof works, one needs to show that the pre- and co-requisites are satisfied. Often, the reason they're satisfied is that they've persisted from an earlier situation. This approach needs to be generalized to deal with concurrent actions. The main technical problem is that actions can overlap in various ways; hence, we can no longer ignore the internal structure of actions. Actions must be viewed in terms of a continuum of states, composed of parts. Moreover, this requires closure axioms about the parts-structure of actions to establish that most overlapping actions do not change most fluents.

The paper by Hector Geffner and Judea Pearl attempts to ground most of the intuitively desirable inference rules in a logic of high probability of the kind Ernest Adams studied two decades ago. Not all of the desired behavior can be grounded in this way. But adding one ostensibly simple axiom on "irrelevance by convention" reveals what is missing. The axiom's simplicity is a bit misleading, however, since there are issues about the best form of "implicit irrelevance," on which the axiom relies. There may yet be a clash over Geffner's intuitions.

The last paper on the frame problem is by J. Michael Dunn. His paper is a brief and pointed rejoinder to Fodor, who had attacked McDermott, and Pat Hayes, one of the originators of the problem. Fodor deserves rebuttal on a number of points, but Dunn is particularly concerned with the allegation that the frame problem is unsolved because the relevance problem is unsolved. Dunn claims that he has a formalism that determines relevance. Regardless of whether it helps to solve the frame problem, it counters Fodor's rhetoric.

One of the concerns of the early positivists was to be faithful to ordinary language, as well as to attempt to improve ordinary language by formalizing it. If we think of natural language as being a precise tool for the conveying of thoughts, we at once notice that it has a number of disagreeable properties. For instance, there are a lot of vague terms (such as the term "a lot") whose precise meanings are difficult to pin down, even in a single given context. Worse yet, their meanings appear to vary with context in ways that are not easy to explicate. Natural language is ambiguous, both lexically ("ruler," "bank," "bit," *etc.*), and constructionally ("The chicken is ready to eat"). Furthermore, natural language fails to express faithfully how the meanings of the expressions are actually built up — the "logical form" of natural language is often different from the surface form (reflect momentarily on what a logical form for "The first man landed on the Moon in 1969" might look like). And, natural language often includes elements which are meaningful in some contexts, but in others appear devoid of that meaning (*e.g.*, the plural in "scissors"), or are redundant ("Men, women and children" means the same as "Men and women and children"). Natural language is also context-dependent, in very obvious ways ("I am here now," "The bread is in the left-hand drawer"), and a variety of more subtle ways (— "more subtle" than what?). Thus viewed by philosophers wishing to express themselves precisely, it is not hard to make a *prima facie* case for the unsuitability of natural language.

It is natural then that some might seek to substitute a less problematic means for expressing thoughts, and turning to formal logic provides one insightful means of doing this. Frege and Russell both made very influential proposals for how certain meanings expressed in natural language might be analyzed in a logical system, and provided much of the groundwork for subsequent developments in this vein. Later developments in modal logic (*e.g.*, Carnap, C. Lewis), and the theory of truth (Tarski) advanced this approach, again with at least some special attention paid to natural language. However, the idea that natural language itself should be considered a formal system does not appear to have gained currency until after the work of Chomsky (in syntax), and such people as Bar-Hillel, Montague, and Cresswell (in semantics), and others, became more widely known and understood, ultimately during the 1970's. There has since been a large body of research devoted to understanding natural language phenomena, including the traditional problems of context-dependency. During this period, too, natural language work from a computational perspective has blossomed, a field of research which incorporates at its very foundations the idea that natural language might be gainfully viewed as an explicit computational system.

Many of these developments took place within a context provided by somewhat less logic-based approaches, but which gave natural language central status nonetheless. Wittgenstein, for instance, tried to make the point that a solid understanding of natural language was essential for understanding the way out of certain philosophical problems. Then Austin, Searle, and Grice sought to explain how human interaction is carried out with (mere) words.

The papers in the natural language section of this volume illustrate a variety of approaches to the use and study of natural language. Don Perlis' contribution, "Thing and Thought," takes a computational perspective on the traditional philosophical problem of self-reference, focusing on its consequences for the area of artificial intelligence. The basic problem Perlis considers is the nature of thoughts. On the one hand, thoughts can be about objects (as in having a thought about this morning's paper), or thoughts can be about other thoughts (and those resulting thoughts themselves can then be the object of yet other thoughts). Thus, there is a need for an agent to be able to represent as a formal object its own behavior, and so it appears that thoughts need to be reified. Perlis proceeds to examine three frameworks in which such reification is commonly achieved — what he calls the "ideal", the "pseudo-ideal", and "situated" systems — and discusses the problems inherent in each for dealing with problems of self-representation of one's own thoughts and knowledge. The work ends with some speculative remarks on "aboutness," suggesting that it is a much more internal phenomenon than normally believed.

But other tools can be applied to natural language as an object, with the result that natural language itself is more completely understood as a system. One means is to employ standard truth-conditional semantic analysis which characterizes meanings in terms of independently understood and formally characterized logical systems. Brendan Gillon's paper is an excellent example of this approach. He is interested in evaluating arguments presented by Greg Carlson (in a 1977 publication) according to which so-called "bare plural" noun phrases (*e.g.*, "cats" in a sentence like "John chased cats off his doorstep") should not be analyzed as plural indefinites, paralleling the singular indefinite marked by the determiner '$a(n)$' (as in "a cat"). A large and informative portion of the paper is dedicated to the evaluation of certain presumptions that Carlson makes in his arguments, chiefly about the logical analysis of plurality. Gillon shows quite conclusively that these presumptions are in need of a more sophisticated replacement that he outlines in detail, using a set-theoretic framework to formulate his alternative and to guide the thinking about natural language meaning. Gillon also presents other criticisms which at least one of the present editors urges readers to consider the potential validity of very carefully, and in light of appropriate background reading. This article comes the closest to exemplifying the methodology in natural language semantics among certain linguists and philosophers that has resulted from the work spawned by Montague's contributions in the early 1970's.

The most 'traditional' of the papers, Nuel Belnap and Michael Perloff's contribution, takes natural language itself as the means of insight into a philosophical question, namely, what constitutes an action? In this case, language is being taken as the tool for the investigation of a philosophical problem, and is not taken to be the object of the inquiry. The strategy Belnap and Perloff pursue is to seek a natural language expression which serves as necessary and sufficient canonical form for demarcating actions (that is, for anything that constitutes an action describable in a natural language, that action may be described in that canonical way, though perhaps other ways are also available). The title of the paper, "Seeing to it that ...", states at the outset what that natural language construction is. Separating actions from non-actions in this way, one can then examine the character of the two classes, and reflect more precisely on what differentiates the two from each other. In this case, it is the tool of natural language itself that lends precision to the enterprise.

Like the paper by Perlis, that by Andrew McCafferty represents a computational approach to dealing with problems that arise in understanding natural language. But he deals with quite different problems, in quite a different way. McCafferty is interested in characterizing the ingredients necessary for a successful computational treatment of discourse. In many cases, appropriateness (and hence, meaningfulness) of a response may critically depend on information not overtly present in the semantic characterization of a previous sentence. For instance, if one proposes, "Let's go to the movies tonight" and this is responded to by saying, "I have to study for an exam," the response is taken to be a "no" while at the same time giving a reason for declining the invitation, even though there is nothing in the meaning of either sentence to suggest this. In McCafferty's paper, it is proposed that a successful characterization of a discourse requires knowledge not only of sentence meanings, but also proper recognition of the speaker's plan that led to his or her uttering a particular sentence in that discourse, as well as knowledge of "domain plans", which is real-world script-like knowledge that encodes the customary ways of achieving some end (such as seeing a movie or taking a plane trip). The role of each of these is defended and elaborated on in this work.

It is clear that the background of knowledge and belief we bring to a decision problem bears directly on principles according to which we will come to a decision. Some writers (Cheeseman, Jeffrey) claim that "background knowledge" is just a casual way of referring to the set of statements to which we assign high probabilities. Others (McCarthy, Reiter) suggest that probabilities are only relevant in highly specialized circumstances, and that for modifying background knowledge in the face of new information we require a non-monotonic logic. Most writers think there is a place for both considerations. We are thus interested in both changing background knowledge and in updating probabilities.

Non-monotonic logic requires us to reject statements that are part of our background knowledge in the light of new evidence. For example, if I have a body of beliefs that implies a predictive observation statement, and I observe something contrary to that statement, I will be led to reject at least one of the premises of the implication. But which one? That is a problem often referred to in philosophy as the problem of theory change (changing background knowledge in the face of uncooperative experience) and often referred to in AI as the problem of non-monotonicity. One sophisticated approach to this problem has been initiated by Peter Gärdenfors. A careful analysis of this suggestion leads, according to Charles Cross, to a contrary conclusion: rather than sacrificing the Ramsey principle that indicative conditional propositions accepted as background knowledge record an agent's dispositions to revise beliefs, one should sacrifice the preservation principle, according to which one should give up beliefs only when new beliefs actually contradict the old.

Updating probabilities — or, more generally, uncertainties — has been of central concern in both AI and philosophy for a long time. From the beginnings of the probability calculus as a way of representing or guiding beliefs, it has been assumed that one should modify one's degrees of belief in accord with conditionalization. If your belief is given by a probability function $P(\ .\ )$, and you get a new piece of evidence E to which you assign the probability 1, then your belief function should be changed to $P(\ .\ |\ E)$.

But a number of questions have been raised. One question concerns the problem of uncertain evidence. If you obtain new evidence E, but are not warranted in assigning it probability 1, how should your beliefs be modified? There is a rule that has been offered: Jeffrey's rule (Richard Jeffrey), but this rule has been criticized by many. Judea Pearl explores the conditions under which Jeffrey's rule provides a correct updating mechanism.

Even given updated probabilities, however, there is still a gap to be filled: to agree on an action, we must agree about what to pursue as well as about probabilities. These two considerations come together, with discouraging consequences, in the paper by Seidenfeld.

Probability and decision have long been associated. The early development of the theory of probability arose from the concerns of intellectual gamblers, and the discipline of decision theory is intimately associated with probability. One modern tradition in the interpretation of probability stems from the work of Frank P. Ramsey. Ramsey's idea was that probabilities should reflect degrees of belief, and that one's degrees of belief should be revealed by one's choices. The upshot is that probability and decision, on this view, are wedded from the outset.

One problem that remains is that of exploring the problem of extending the norms of rationality from individuals to groups. There are well known difficulties in the case of non-probabilistic (voting) decision procedures (Arrow's "paradox"). Seidenfeld explores similar problems that arise in the equally important case of combining uncertainty and utility judgements of different experts. The problems he reveals are ominous.

Another question is tied to the idea that conditionals indicate how one's beliefs should change in the light of new evidence. This is captured in the catch question of whether or not the probabilities of conditionals should be conditional probabilities — *i.e.*, whether the probability of $(X\ a\ Y)$ should be the conditional probability $P(X \mid Y)$ for some interesting conditional connective a.

This question was answered in the negative for a number of conditionals by Lewis who showed that one could only have a couple of values of probabilities if this thesis was to be answered in the affirmative. A more general set of results is established by Leblanc and Roeper in their trivialization theorems. It is hard to see how any interesting thesis connecting conditionals and conditional probabilities can survive.

Rich Thomason's paper at the meeting summarized past and proposed research conducted jointly at Pittsburgh and Carnegie-Mellon in collaboration with computer scientist Touretzky, philosopher Jeff Horty, and one of non-monotonicity's pioneers, computer scientist Jon Doyle. The paper that appears in this volume is co-authored by Rob Carpenter, a computational linguist working with Thomason. So this paper is an especially valuable review of pioneering work for newcomers to the area of inheritance hierarchies, and their connection to non-monotonic reasoning.

Artificial intelligence has long recognized the need to deal with uncertainty, and has long been involved in devising systems to provide advice to decision-makers. The problems of uncertainty and decision thus come together both in philosophy, in the general domain of practical reason, and in artificial intelligence, in both the domain of knowledge representation and the domain of expert systems.

Ron Loui's paper attempts to use defeasible reasoning instead of arguing about it. Too many people have presumed that planning and decision theory can very simply be put together. The fact that no one had done so was assumed to be due to a conflict of cultures, not a reflection of some technical difficulty.

If the states in a decision analysis are described by sets of logical formulae, then the description of a state that results from action or the occurrence of an event requires theorem-proving. If we cannot expect all this theorem-proving to be completed in the available deliberation time, then we must be able to assess utilities on partially described states. The better the description of states, the better the reasoning about preferences among actions. The technical achievement is the simple axiomatization of this intuition in a logic for defeasible reasoning. The general philosophical point is that decision analysis ought to proceed as defeasible reasoning, through the process of argument, counter-argument, and rebuttal.

The papers presented here cover a wide range of topics within the general area of belief and decision. As central to the problem of decision making under uncertainty as measures of degrees of belief are measures of utility. Problems of vagueness and imprecision are endemic in classical logic, and central when we are concerned with making decisions in the face of uncertainty. Robin Giles attempts to meet these problems head on by devising a novel logic of assertions.

Despite all the work that has been done in philosophy over the past seventy-five years on the foundations and interpretation of probability, and the even more intense examination of uncertainty that became possible with the advent of economies of computation, the fundamental questions about probability and uncertainty are still unsettled. Romas Aleliunas, in "A New Normative Theory of Probabilistic Logic," attempts to provide a very general framework in which these questions can be addressed and perhaps, in some cases, answered definitively.

Although these four selections are diverse, they are no broader than the general topic — decision in the face of uncertainty — that they address. And that topic, itself, is so pervasive in everyday life as well as in expert and professional judgment, that any number of angles and points of view can shed light.

Philosophy is often thought to be concerned with large and pervasive questions. Exact philosophy is concerned with getting exact, scientifically and logically defensible, answers to a few of those big questions. The question of practical reason — given what we know about the world, and what we value in the world, how should we rationally try to go about getting what we value — is a question that lends itself easily to both the analytic resources of exact philosopy and to the analytic and computational resources of artificial intelligence. We believe this present selection of essays provides evidence of the fruitfulness of the cooperation between certain kinds of philosophy and artificial intelligence.

ACKNOWLEDGEMENTS

In the spring of 1988, when the Lilacs were in bloom, the Society for Exact Philosophy held its annual meeting at the University of Rochester. The meeting was dedicated to an unusual confluence of linguistics, artificial intelligence, and decision theory. We think we may say that the meeting was a success. But this does not convey the enthusiasm and dedication of the group. Perhaps even more important, it does not convey how much fun we had. All of this — the enthusiasm and the fun — is largely to be credited to the individuals who attended the meeting. It is also due to the quality of the questions asked and the discussions offered at the official sessions, and also to the general conversation to which every participant contributed during meals, receptions, and late at night. It is to everyone who attended that the success of this meeting is due.

More than their share was contributed by the graduate students, Mariam Thalos, Abahya Nayak, Josh Tenenberg, and Jay Weber. Financial support was contributed by the American Association for Artificial Intelligence, the Rochester's University Committee for Interdisciplinary Studies, the Departments of Linguistics, Computer Science, and Philosophy, and the program for cognitive science at the University of Rochester. Anna Harrison, then on the staff of the department of Philosophy, helped enormously with the logistics.

Christine Sharp saw fit to help with typing, arranging figures, and typesetting this manuscript. This copy would never have taken shape in our five few weeks if Gene Johnson hadn't shown me how to make text *move*. We apologize to Michelle Pearl for re-pasting her wonderful figures because of our inadequate technology.

H. E. K.
R. P. L.
G. N. C.

Authors' Affiliations

Romas Aleliunas, *School of Computing Science, Simon Fraser University, Burnaby, Canada*

Charles Cross, *Department of Philosophy, Reed College, Portland, Oregon*

Nuel Belnap, *Department of Philosophy, University of Pittsburgh, Pennsylvania*

Greg Carlson, *Department of Linguistics, University of Rochester, New York*

Bob Carpenter, *Intelligent Systems Program, University of Pittsburgh, Pennsylvania*

Charles Cross, *Department of Philosophy, Reed College, Portland, Oregon*

J. Michael Dunn, *Departments of Philosophy and Computer Science, Indiana University, Bloomington*

Hector Geffner, *Department of Computer Science, University of California at Los Angeles*

Robin Giles, *Department of Mathematics, Queens University, Kingston, Ontario, Canada*

Brendan Gillon, *University of Toronto, Ontario, Canada*

Henry Kyburg, Jr., *Department of Computer Science, University Rochester, New York*

Hugues LeBlanc, *Department of Philosophy, Temple University, Philadelphia, Pennsylvania*

Ronald Loui, *Department of Computer Science, Washington University, St. Louis, Missouri*

Andrew McCafferty, *Department of Philosophy, LSU, Baton Rouge*

Donald Nute, *Department of Philosophy, Artificial Intelligence Program, University of Georgia, Athens*

Judea Pearl, *Cognitive Systems Laboratory, Computer Science Department, University of California at Los Angeles*

Donald Perlis, *Computer Science Department and Institute for Advanced Computer Studies, University of Maryland, College Park, and Computer Science Department, University of Rochester, New York*

Michael Perloff, *Department of Philosophy, University of Pittsburgh, Pennsylvania*

Peter Roeper, *Department of Philosophy, The Australian National University*

Len Schubert, *Department of Computer Science, University Rochester, New York*

Teddy Seidenfeld, *Departments of Philosophy and Statistics, Carnegie Mellon University, Pittsburgh, Pennsylvania*

Richmond Thomason, *Department of Philosophy, University of Pittsburgh, Pennsylvania*

Part I.
Defeasible Reasoning and the Frame Problem :

Defeasible Logic and The Frame Problem

Donald Nute /- GA-Q

1 Introduction

McCarthy and Hayes [McCarthy&Hayes69] originally applied the term "frame problem" to a specific puzzle about knowledge representation. Hayes [Hayes87] distinguished the original frame problem from a growing number of related problems that have been called the frame problem:

> One feels that there should be some economical and principled way of succinctly saying what changes an action makes, without having to explicitly list all the things it doesn't change as well; yet there doesn't seem to be any other way to do it. That is the frame problem. If there are 100 actions, and 500 labile properties and relations, then we might need 50,000 of these silly 'frame axioms' ....(p. 125)

Wherever I use the expression "the frame problem" in the rest of this paper, I will have this original version of the problem in mind.

This paper defends the use of a particular non-monotonic formalism to solve the frame problem. A version of the proposal I will defend appeared in [McDermott87]. McDermott's suggestion was

> ... to condense all the frame axioms into one:

> 'If a fact is true in a situation, and it cannot be proven that it is untrue in the situation resulting from an event, then it is still true.' (p. 115)

McDermott declares that solving the frame problem is of little importance, although it raises interesting issues for non-monotonic logic. McDermott quickly abandoned this position [Hanks&McDermott86]; in fact, we notice that the publication date for the paper in which his non-monotonic solution is rejected is earlier than that of the paper in which it was proposed.

3

H.E. Kyburg, Jr. et al. (eds.), Knowledge Representation and Defeasible Reasoning, 3–21.
© 1990 *Kluwer Academic Publishers. Printed in the Netherlands.*

Hanks and McDermott indict three of the best known non-monotonic logics by presenting a simple frame problem example (since called the Yale Shooting Problem (*YSP*)) that these formalisms get wrong. A longer paper [Hanks&McDermott87] includes responses to claims that modifications of these three formalisms or that other non-monotonic formalisms get the *YSP* right.

What I will argue here is that there are natural and simple non-monotonic formalisms for which the original McDermott solution to the frame problem remains plausible. In particular, defeasible logic [Nute88a] is a non-monotonic system that escapes the *YSP*. I will review the *YSP*. Then I will present an independent case for defeasible logic. After outlining the formal system, I will show how defeasible logic can properly represent the *YSP* and other familiar examples which often cause problems for non-monotonic systems. I will defend defeasible logic and some kindred systems against a counter-charge leveled by Hanks and McDermott. Finally, I will sketch a semantics and describe some extensions and applications of defeasible logic.

2   The Yale Shooting Problem

Hanks and McDermott use the situation calculus [McDermott82] to represent their simple example. A statement of the form $T(p, s)$ indicates that proposition p is true of situation s. An event is something that occurs in a situation. As a result of an event occurring, we have a new situation. We will use $RESULT(e, s)$ to refer to the new situation that results from the occurrence of event e in situation s.

The *YSP* involves only one initial fact and three events. The initial fact is that some particular individual, call him Fred, is alive. If we let s_0 be the initial situation of the example, we can represent this initial fact as $T(alive, s_0)$. The three events in the example are *load*, *wait*, and *shoot*. Causal principles are associated with *load* and *shoot*. If *load* occurs in any situation, a certain gun is loaded in the resulting situation:

(Rule L) $T(loaded, RESULT(load, s))$.

If *shoot* occurs in any situation, then the same gun is pointed at Fred and fired. If *shoot* occurs when the gun is loaded, then Fred is not alive in the resulting situation:

(Rule S) $T(loaded, s) \rightarrow T(\neg alive, RESULT(shoot, s))$.

wait has no consequences except that enough time has passed that we have a new situation.

Our assumption about the persistence of circumstances through time says roughly that for any proposition p, situation s, and event e, if $T(p, s)$, then $T(p, RESULT(e, s))$ unless something interferes. The problem, of course, is to represent this principle properly. If we start with $T(alive, s_0)$, is Fred alive after the events *load*, *wait*, and *shoot* occur in succession? That is, can we derive either of

(*YSP1*) $T(alive, RESULT(shoot, RESULT(wait, RESULT(load, s_0))))$

(*YSP2*) $T(\neg alive, RESULT(shoot, RESULT(wait, RESULT(load, s_0))))$

in our non-monotonic logic? Intuitively, (*YSP2*) is correct. Our persistence principle or frame axiom (FA) and $T(alive, s_0)$ yield

$T(alive, RESULT(load, s_0))$.

Rule L and the above yield

$T(loaded, RESULT(load, s_0))$.

Since *wait* has no consequences, FA and the above yield

$T(alive, RESULT(wait, RESULT(load, s_0)))$

and

$T(loaded, RESULT(wait, RESULT(load, s_0)))$.

But then Rule S and the above yield (*YSP2*), interfering with the result FA would otherwise give us.

This result is not assured in the non-monotonic formalisms of McCarthy, McDermott, and Reiter. Each of these systems represents FA with a rule that has a special kind of condition. For McCarthy's [McCarthy80] circumscription we have

(FAc) $T(p, s)\ \&\ \neg AB(e, p, s)\ \rightarrow\ T(p, RESULT(e, s))$

where $AB(p, e, s)$ says "event e is abnormal with respect to proposition p persisting in situation s". McCarthy then circumscribes the predicate AB to produce a new first order theory from the original theory in which the example is represented. I will not describe the circumscription procedure in detail, but it basically adds sentences to the theory that allow us to show that the circumscribed predicate does not apply in any case where it could not be proved that it applied in the original theory. In McDermott's non-monotonic logic [McDermott&Doyle80] FA becomes

(FAn) $T(p, s)$ & $M(T(p, RESULT(e, s))) \rightarrow T(p, RESULT(e, s))$

where M is a unary operator used to say that something is consistent with the theory. Reiter's [80] default rule uses a similar operator and resembles McDermott's formulation:

(FAd) $$\frac{T(p, s) : M(T(p, RESULT(e, s)))}{T(p, RESULT(e, s))}$$

There are important differences between these three approaches, but they share one crucial feature: the proof procedure for each system is linked to a notion of a minimal set of formulae satisfying certain closure conditions for a theory of the system (minimal models for McCarthy, fixed points for McDermott, default extensions for Reiter). The *YSP* has two "minimal extensions" (to use a single phrase) of the required sort in each of the three logics: one that includes (*YSP1*) but not (*YSP2*), and one that includes (*YSP2*) but not (*YSP1*). Since both McCarthy and McDermott count something as derivable from a theory only if it is in every minimal extension of the theory, we can derive neither (*YSP1*) nor (*YSP2*). Reiter on the other hand says that any minimal extension of a default theory is "believable" and provides no further criteria for choosing. Hanks and McDermott rightly complain that "A logic that generates one intuitive extension and one unintuitive extension does not provide an adequate representation of the problem, since there is no way to distinguish between the two interpretations." (p. 329)

To see what goes wrong, we need to look at the role of the frame axiom FA in the example. If the gun is loaded, then we wait, then the gun is fired, some proposition true in some situation cannot persist to the next situation without violating one of our other two rules. The intuitive way to resolve this conflict results in Fred's death. On this account, Fred is alive at the next to last situation, and FA is violated when we move to the last situation. But we could countermand FA at some earlier point in the example. When *wait* occurs, going from the second to the third state, we could allow that the gun ceases to be loaded. If the gun is not loaded when it is fired, the fact that Fred is alive can persist without violating Rule L or Rule S. We must interfere with FA at least once in the example, but there are two accounts of what happens that violate neither of the other two rules and countermand FA only once. There are other minimal extensions, but these two illustrate the problem.

The *YSP* shows that the inference procedure(s) we use must involve more than generating minimal extensions of the *YSP*. At the very least, some one extension must be selected. I propose that when people think about these kinds of examples only one set of conclusions is ever generated in the first place. This set of conclusions may or may not be identical to one of the minimal extensions generated by one of the three non-monotonic formalisms we have discussed. The resources used in generating this correct answer need not be very great, but we need to concentrate on proof theory rather than model theory to see how this happens.

3   Defeasible Logic

Linking proof theory to minimal extensions makes the various formulations of FA absolute. There can be no circumstance where the condition of the rule is true and the consequent is false. Oversimplifying (particularly for the case of circumscription), non-monotonicity arises because the answer to the question whether or not the peculiar condition of a rule is satisfied depends on which other rules we have already used. This gives rise to the multiple extensions that cause McCarthy, McDermott, and Reiter problems with the *YSP* and other examples.

Rather than absolute rules with peculiar abnormality or consistency conditions, what is needed are peculiar rules and a well-defined procedure for applying them. Such "other things being equal" rules apply to the normal or typical cases, but in abnormal or special cases they are defeated and do not apply. In these cases, the condition of the defeasible rule is true but the conclusion is false.

Defeasible rules are those rules-of-thumb that make up so much of common knowledge. When their conditions are satisfied, we (often unthinkingly) act as though their consequents were true unless something goes wrong. What can go wrong is that we acquire information about a case that indicates the rule may not apply to it. Then the rule is defeated. A defeasible rule might be defeated by another defeasible rule, but it might also be defeated by a strict rule or by a weaker kind of rule called a defeater.

A strict rule is a rule that can't be defeated by additional information. A rule might be strict because it is grounded in some scheme of categories we use to organize the world, because it depends on a definition, because it expresses a well-confirmed scientific principle or "fact", or because it reflects some geographical or temporal invariance. Here are examples of each of these kinds of strict rules:

Penguins are birds.

Vixens are female.
Gold is heavier than iron.
Anything in Atlanta is in Georgia.

This list is not intended to be exhaustive, and there are other kinds of strict rules.

A defeater is a very weak kind of rule that says what might be the case. Examples are 'A sick bird might not fly' and 'A damp match might not burn if it were struck'. These rules do not allow us to conclude that a sick bird will not fly or that a damp match will not burn. They are too weak to ever justify any conclusion. Rather their role is to prevent us from tentatively concluding that a bird flies when we discover it is sick, or that a match will burn when we discover that it is damp. Of course, since 'Birds fly' is itself a defeasible rule, we know that any bird might not fly. But being a bird is not a reason for thinking that it might not fly. Being a sick bird is. We only voice a defeater when we want to draw attention to a reason for thinking that we may be dealing with some special or abnormal case in which the usual rule-of-thumb may not apply.

A proper proof theory for defeasible rules will indicate when they are defeated and how conflicts between competing rules are resolved. This resolution of conflicts between rules is extremely important since this is what guarantees that a theory has a single closure or minimal extension no matter in what order the rules are applied. And this, in turn, is what produces a single, intuitively correct outcome for the *YSP*.

We will look at a propositional version of defeasible logic for the sake of simplicity. Current versions of defeasible logic resemble Horn clause logic in ways that will become apparent. This simplifies both the theoretical development and the implementation of the system. This is particularly important since, unlike many non-monotonic systems, there exists a relatively simple implementation of defeasible logic as an extension of the logic programming language PROLOG.

We assume a countably infinite set P_1, P_2, P_3, *etc.*, of propositional constants, a negation symbol $\neg$, and a monadic sentence operator E. A literal is a propositional constant or the negation of a propositional constant. Thus the literals are P_1, $\neg P_1$, P_2, $\neg P_2$, *etc.* For every propositional constant P_i, we define P_i and $\neg P_i$ to be the complements of each other. We will denote the complement of any literal p as $\neg p$. A sentence is a literal or an expression of the form Ep where p is a literal. We read Ep as 'Evidently, p'. Neither $\neg$ nor E may occur more than once in a sentence, and $\neg$ cannot occur before (to the left of) E in a sentence.

A rule is a license to draw an inference. It has a set of conditions represented by a set of literals and a consequent represented by a single literal. We use the symbols $\rightarrow$, $\Rightarrow$, and $\twoheadrightarrow$ to represent our rules. Where $A \cup \{p\}$ is a finite set of literals, $A \rightarrow p$ is a strict rule, $A \Rightarrow p$ is a defeasible rule, and $A \twoheadrightarrow p$ is a defeater. These three kinds of rules play different roles in our proof theory, have different formal semantics, and correspond to different kinds of regulatory principles in our speech and thought.

In the most general formulation of defeasible logic, a defeasible theory is an ordered triple $<R, K, \leq>$ where R is a set of rules, K is a set of literals, and $\leq$ is a partial order on R. Where r_1 and r_2 are in R, we say r_1 is superior to r_2 just in case $r_2 \leq r_1$ and $r_2 \not\leq r_1$. Every strict rule will be superior to every defeasible rule. The basic idea behind our proof theory is that we can infer Ep from a defeasible rule $A \Rightarrow p$ only if every member of A is evident and the rule $A \Rightarrow p$ is superior to every competing rule. A competing rule is a rule whose consequent is $\neg p$ and whose set of conditions is also evident.

We must sometimes show that something is not provable in order to show that some defeasible rule is not defeated. A formal proof should reflect this fact. We will use $+$ or $-$ in each line of a proof to indicate whether the sentence displayed in the line is proved or disproved. Looking for the moment only at finite theories that contain no strict rules or defeaters, we can define a proof of Ep from a theory $<K, R, \leq>$ quite simply as a finite sequence of lines of the form $<Eq, v>$, where q is a literal and v is either $+$ or $-$. The last line in the proof must be $<Ep, + >$, and for every line L in the proof one of the following must hold:

D1. a. $L = <Eq, + >$ and
    b. $q \in K$.

D2. a. $L = <Eq, + >$,
    b. $\neg q \notin K$, and
    c. there is an $A \Rightarrow q \in R$ such that
       i. $<Ea, + >$ is an earlier line for each $a \in A$ and
       ii. for each $B \Rightarrow \neg q \in R$, either $A \Rightarrow q$ is superior to $B \Rightarrow \neg q$ or there is a $b \in B$ such that $<Eb, - >$ is an earlier line.

D3. a. $L = <Eq, ->$,
   b. $q \notin K$, and
   c. for every $A \Rightarrow q \in R$, either
      i. there is some $a \in A$ such that $<Ea, ->$ is an earlier
         line, or
      ii. there is a $B \Rightarrow \neg q \in R$ such that $A \Rightarrow q$ is not
          superior to $B \Rightarrow \neg q$ and $<Eb, +>$ is an earlier line
          for each $b \in B$.

Notice that condition D3 insures that we cannot satisfy condition D1 or D2
for Eq.

The most interesting defeasible theories are those where the partial order
on the set of rules is generated by some natural principle. Specificity is one
natural order on rules. One rule is superior to another if its antecedent is
more specific than the antecedent of the other. If we can define specificity
in terms of the rules in the theory, then perhaps we can incorporate into our
proof a demonstration that one rule is superior to another. Then we can
dispense with explicit mention of the partial order. In the remainder of this
paper, I use 'defeasible theory' to denote structures of the form $<R, K>$
where the partial order is incorporated into the proof theory.

The familiar Tweety example suggests one way the rules in a defeasible
theory can be used to determine a partial ordering of the rules. We know
that all penguins are birds, which gives us the strict rule;

(Rule PB) $\{penguin(Tweety)\} \rightarrow bird(Tweety)$

We also know that birds normally fly and that penguins normally don't:

(Rule B) $\{bird(Tweety)\} \rightarrow flies(Tweety)$

(Rule P) $\{penguin(Tweety)\} \rightarrow \neg flies(Tweety)$

Knowing that $penguin(Tweety)$, we infer that $bird(Tweety)$. The question,
then, is does Tweety fly? The intuitively correct answer is that he does not.
How can we explain this given our two defeasible rules with contradictory
consequents?

Remember that defeasible rules are supposed to be rules-of-thumb that apply in the normal or typical case. Do we have any evidence that Tweety is a special kind of penguin or bird? Indeed, we do. Our strict rule tells us Tweety is a special kind of bird. So rules about penguins are more specific than rules about birds and should be superior to rules about birds. Thus Rule P is superior to Rule B and, just as we would expect, Tweety does not fly.

Another way of looking at this example is that we always want to use as much of the possibly incomplete information available to us as we can. Only then can we hope to reach the best conclusion that can be reached on the information we have. But different rules have conditions that take into account more or less of the available information. Our penguin rule uses more information than our bird rule. What measurement of information are we using in making this judgment? Simply that given the rules available to us, we can infer being a bird from being a penguin, but we can't make the converse inference.

This example suggests the following natural principle for partially ordering rules in a defeasible theory: a defeasible rule $A \implies p$ or defeater $A \multimap\!\!\!\!\gg p$ is superior to another defeasible rule $B \implies q$ or defeater $B \multimap\!\!\!\!\gg q$ in a defeasible theory $<R, K>$ if and only if we can derive every member of B from A using rules in R, but there is some member of A that we cannot derive from B using only the rules in R.

The question immediately arises, which rules do we use in determining specificity? Certainly we should use the strict rules as we did in the Tweety example. But do we use defeasible rules? We probably do. If a smoker stops smoking, his health improves. If a smoker develops emphysema, he stops smoking. If a smoker develops emphysema, his health does not improve. All of these are defeasible, yet we would readily use the second rule to justify the claim that the third rule is more specific than and superior to the first.

Unfortunately, using defeasible rules to establish specificity raises other questions. Suppose Carl is dating two girls, Alice and Betty. Alice and Betty don't know each other, and each believes that she is Carl's only girl friend. David knows and likes both Alice and Betty. He also knows and dislikes Carl. With this background, we form four plausible rules for when Alice, Betty, Carl, and David would normally attend a party. If Alice attends, then normally Carl attends; but if Alice and Betty both attend, then normally Carl stays far away. If Alice and Betty both attend, then David normally attends; but if Carl attends, then David normally doesn't. We symbolize these as:

(1.1) $\{attends(Alice,\ X)\}\ \Rightarrow\ attends(Carl,\ X)$

(1.2) $\{attends(Alice,\ X),\ attends(Betty,\ X)\}\ \Rightarrow\ \neg attends(Carl,\ X)$

(1.3) $\{attends(Alice,\ X),\ attends(Betty,\ X)\}\ \Rightarrow\ attends(David,\ X)$

(1.4) $\{attends(Carl,\ X)\}\ \Rightarrow\ \neg attends(David,\ X)$

Now suppose, contrary to our expectations, that Alice, Betty, and Carl all attend a certain party. Does David attend or not? In this case, no answer is the intuitively correct answer.

What does our logic say about this case if we use defeasible rules to determine specificity? That depends on whether 1.3 is defeated, and that depends on whether 1.3 is more specific than 1.4. Rule 1.1 would let us derive $attends(Carl,\ Party)$ from $\{attends(Alice,\ Party),\ attends(Betty,\ Party)\}$ if we used defeasible rules, but 1.1 is itself defeated by 1.2. However, 1.2 is clearly violated in this particular case since Alice and Betty went to the party, but Carl also went. If we use 1.1 to establish the superiority of 1.3 over 1.4, then we conclude that David went to the party when our intuitions say that we cannot tell. Appealing to 1.2 saves us from drawing an unintuitive conclusion, but appealing to a rule that is violated by the case at hand should raise some eyebrows.

We will call the use of both strict and defeasible rules to determine the specificity of rules defeasible specificity and call the use of strict rules only strict specificity. Our party example suggests that there could be different versions of defeasible specificity. We do not need defeasible specificity to resolve the frame problem, and only strict specificity will be assumed in the proof theory developed below. We will call the proofs defined by this theory *SDL* proofs.

SDL proofs look very much like the proofs we defined earlier, except that we now incorporate into our proofs demonstrations that some defeasible rules are superior to (more specific than) other defeasible rules or defeaters. To do this, we derive the antecedent conditions of one rule from those of another. When we do this, we cannot appeal to any literals in the theory that are not also part of the antecedent of the superior rule. To see what this means, reconsider the Tweety example. If we add the antecedent of Rule B to the defeasible theory, we can derive the antecedent of Rule P since it is already in the theory. So Rule B is at least as specific as Rule P, the two rules defeat each other, and we can draw no conclusion. What this shows is that we have used the wrong method for determining specificity. What we want to know is whether we can derive *penguin(Tweety)* from *bird(Tweety)* using only *bird(Tweety)* and the strict rules of the theory.

A consequence of this constraint is that we must always keep track of the support set of lines in our proofs. In some lines of an *SDL* proof, we can appeal to all the literals in the theory; in other lines, we can appeal only to the literals in the antecedent of a particular rule. So in each line of the proof, we must record the set of literals that is available to us. This is a necessary complication if we are to demonstrate the superiority of certain rules within the proof itself.

An *SDL* proof of a sentence p from a defeasible theory $<R, K>$, then, is a finite list of triples $<q, v, A>$ such that q is a sentence, v is $+$ or $-$, and A is a set of literals (the support set for that line). The last line of the proof must be $<p, +, K>$, and every line L of the proof must satisfy one of these conditions:

C1. a. $L = <q, +, A>$ and
　　b. $q \in A$.

C2. a. $L = <q, +, A>$ and
　　b. there is a $B \rightarrow q \in R$ such that $<b, +, A>$ is an earlier line for each $b \in B$.

C3. a. $L = <q, -, A>$,
　　b. q is a literal,
　　c. $q \notin A$, and
　　d. for every $B \rightarrow q \in R$ there is a $b \in B$ such that $<b, -, A>$ is an earlier line.

C4. a. $L = <Eq, +, K>$ and
　　b. $<q, +, K>$ is an earlier line.

C5. a. $L = <Eq, +, K>$,
　　b. $<\neg q, -, K>$ is an earlier line,
　　c. there is a $B \rightarrow q \in R$ such that $<Eb, +, K>$ is an earlier line for each $b \in B$, and
　　d. for every $C \rightarrow \neg q \in R$, there is a $c \in C$ such that

$<Ec, -, K>$ is an earlier line.

C6. a. $L = <Eq, +, K>$,
  b. $<\neg q, -, K>$ is an earlier line,
  c. there is a $B \Rightarrow q \in R$ such that $<Eb, +, K>$ is an earlier line for each $b \in B$,
  d. for every $C \rightarrow \neg q \in R$, there is a $c \in C$ such that $<Ec, -, K>$ is an earlier line, and
  e. for every $C \Rightarrow \neg q \in R$ or $C \Rrightarrow \neg q \in R$, either $<c, -, K>$ is an earlier line for some $c \in C$, or $<b, -, C>$ is an earlier line for some $b \in B$ and $<c, +, B>$ is an earlier line for each $c \in C$.

C7. a. $L = <Eq, -, K>$,
  b. $<q, -, K>$ is an earlier line, and
  c. $<\neg q, +, K>$ is an earlier line.

C8. a. $L = <Eq, -, K>$;
  b. $<q, -, K>$ is an earlier line;
  c. for every $B \rightarrow q \in R$, either
    i. $<Eb, -, K>$ is an earlier line for some $b \in B$, or
    ii. there is a $C \rightarrow \neg q \in R$ such that $<Ec, +, K>$ is an earlier line for each $c \in C$; and
  d. for every $B \Rightarrow q \in R$ either
    i. $<Eb, -, K>$ is an earlier line for some $b \in B$, or
    ii. there is a $C \rightarrow \neg q \in R$ such that $<Ec, +, K>$ is an earlier line for each $c \in C$, or
    iii. there is a $C \Rightarrow \neg q \in R$ or a $C \Rrightarrow \neg q \in R$ such that
      $<c, +, K>$ is an earlier line for each $c \in C$, and
      $<c, -, B>$ is an earlier line for some $c \in C$ or
      $<b, +, C>$ is an earlier line for each $b \in B$.

C1 – C3 explain what it means for a literal to follow or to not follow from a set of premises strictly. C4 says that a literal follows defeasibly or is evident from a set of premises if it follows from them strictly. C5 says that the consequent of a strict rule is evident from a set of premises if its condition is evident, the complement of its consequent is not strictly derivable, and it is not defeated by another strict rule. This is a difference between *SDL* proofs and the proofs in [Nute88] where strict rules could not defeat each other even when their antecedents are only evident. C6 specifies when the consequent of a defeasible rule is evident from a set of premises, and C7 and C8 tell us when a literal is not evident from some set of premises.

Notice that defeasible theories contain only rules and literals. They do not contain sentences of the form Ep. They may, however, contain defeasible rules with empty condition sets, *i.e.*, rules of the forms $\{\} \implies p$. A defeasible rule with an empty condition set is called a presumption. A sentence of the form Ep represents a tentative conclusion that will be rejected if we acquire some new information that defeats a defeasible rule on which Ep depends. Thus, we don't want to put Ep itself into our theory. If we do, we can never get rid of it. For tentative initial assumptions, we use presumptions. From $\{\} \implies p$ we immediately derive Ep unless the presumption is defeated.

Here is an *SDL* proof that $E(\neg flies(Tweety))$ is provable from $<R, \{penguin(Tweety)\}>$, where R contains Rules PB, B, and P.

1. $<flies(Tweety), -, K>$ C3
2. $<penguin(Tweety), +, K>$ C1; Rule PB
3. $<penguin(Tweety), +, \{penguin(Tweety)\}>$ C1
4. $<bird(Tweety), +, \{penguin(Tweety)\}>$ C2; Rule PB; line 3
5. $<penguin(Tweety), -, \{bird(Tweety)\}>$ C3
6. $<E(\neg flies(Tweety)), +, K>$ C6; Rule P; lines 1,2,4,5

The only line in this proof that is at all difficult is the last line. Line 1 satisfies C6b. Rule P and line 2 satisfy C6c. Since there are no strict rules in R that have $flies(Tweety)$ as consequent, C6d is satisfied vacuously. Finally, Rule B is the only defeasible rule or defeater in R with $flies(Tweety)$ as its consequent. Line 5 shows that Rule P is superior to Rule B, satisfying C6e.

The Tweety example is as important for evaluating non-monotonic systems as the *YSP*. It also has two fixed-points (McDermott), minimal models (McCarthy), or default extensions (Reiter), one in which Tweety flies and one in which he doesn't. McDermott's and McCarthy's systems allow us to derive neither result, and Reiter's default logic lets us take our pick.

4   The Yale Shooting Problem Revisited

Although we have presented a propositional version of defeasible logic for the sake of simplicity, we will want to represent the *YSP* using quantification. We have three rules:

(FA) $\{T(f, s)\} \implies T(f, RESULT(e, s))$

(Rule L) $T(loaded, RESULT(load, s))$

(Rule S¬) $\{T(alive, s), T(loaded, s)\} \implies T(\neg alive, RESULT(shoot, s))$

We will treat our rule-forming operators as binding all variables in their scope with universal strength. Rule S is defeasible, like all causal rules. We also need two consistency rules to guarantee that when a literal is true in a situation, then its complement is not:

$$\{T(p, s)\} \implies \neg T(\neg p, s)$$

$$\{T(\neg p, s)\} \implies \neg T(p, s)$$

Where R contains these rules and $K = \{T(alive, s_0)\}$, we can produce an *SDL* proof from $<R, K>$ containing both

$$<E(T(\neg alive, RESULT(shoot, RESULT(wait, RESULT(load))))), + , K>$$

and

$$<E(T(alive, RESULT(shoot, RESULT(wait, RESULT(load))))), - , K>.$$

This proof is not reproduced here because of its length. Since we can show that for no defeasible theory $<R, K>$ and literal p it is possible to construct proofs containing both $<Ep, + , K>$ and $<Ep, - , K>$, this amounts to showing that *YSP2* is defeasibly provable from our representation of the *YSP* and that *YSP1* is not.

Causal rules produce changes. Thus, we include $T(alive, s)$ in the antecedent of Rule S¬. In the presence of the frame axiom FA, Rule S¬ is tantamount to an "even-if" conditional, that is, 'Even if Fred is alive before the gun is shot, he is not alive afterward.' Technically, this antecedent condition is necessary for us to show that Rule S¬ is superior to or more specific than our frame axiom FA. In the general defeasible logic, we can accomplish the same end by making all causal rules superior to the frame axiom in the explicit superiority relation.

Ronald Loui [87] offers a solution to the *YSP* which he compares with the solution proposed here and with an analysis due to David Poole [85]. Loui's solution would be very similar although not identical to using defeasible logic with defeasible specificity. He also modifies Rule S by adding the condition that the victim is alive in the situation where the shooting event occurs. He says each rule comes with a natural set of "unless" conditions and another natural set of "even if" conditions. "The antecedent of the defeasible rule could be specialized in any of a number of ways, while still allowing the consequent. In particular, being *alive*@1 (Loui's notation) does not interfere with the reported association (between *fired*@1 and *not-alive*@2)."

Hanks and McDermott object that Loui offers no way of knowing that $T(alive, s)$ is the right condition to add to Rule S. Since Fred would be dead even if it were raining, why not add $T(rain, s)$ to Rule S?

Loui has suggested the right solution, but his explanation of why it's the right solution has clouded the issue. It is unimportant that there are many natural "unless" and "even if" conditions for Rule S. We don't want to make these explicit in any case since this would defeat the whole purpose of defeasible reasoning: once these conditions are added, we would have to know which of them were satisfied before we could apply the rule. There is one and only one condition to add to Rule S, and that is the condition that the victim is alive at the time of the shooting. This condition is syntactically determined by the consequent of Rule S. A rough English paraphrase of Rule S is, "Shooting someone with a loaded gun normally kills them (causes them to cease living)." But of course, shooting someone would not kill them if they were already dead. An event cannot cause a circumstance that already existed prior to the event, although it may cause the circumstance to persist. Most causal events have a potential to change things. If our situation has certain features before the event, these features will be changed. Thus, we should expect the antecedent of a causal rule to contain the complement of its consequent.

5 Final Observations

Perhaps it is a mistake to think of rules as having truth values or to try to provide them with truth conditional semantics. Rules regulate belief formation and revision. They require a compliance semantics where the meaning of a rule is the set of restrictions placed upon any epistemic agent who accepts the rule. An agent who does not comply with these restrictions either does not understand the rule or does not accept it. Since defeasible rules and defeaters interact in complex ways, it is easier to describe compliance conditions for a set of rules than for an individual rule. We can think of an agent's belief state as the set of propositions he firmly holds together with the set of propositions he tentatively accepts. Compliance with a set of rules should restrict the possible belief states that an agent could be in. A semantics of this sort is developed for an earlier version of defeasible logic in [Nute88]. Shoham and Moses [Shoham&Moses89] take a different approach and use the notion of defeasibility in the analysis of belief.

The proof theory presented here works well enough for finite theories, but infinite theories require modification. We could have infinitely many competitors for a defeasible rule, and yet the rule could be superior to all of them. Of course, we cannot have infinitely many earlier lines in a proof showing that none of these competitors actually defeats our defeasible rule. But we could develop proofs as trees rather than as finite lists. The conclusion to be proved is at the top of the tree. A node in the tree might have infinitely many immediate daughter nodes where all the challengers to a defeasible rule used in reaching that node are discounted. Thus, such a proof tree might be infinitely wide. Then there are two plausible restrictions we might place on such proof trees: either the weak restriction that each branch must be of finite length, or the strong restriction that there must be some integer n such that each branch is of length n or less.

The formal language for defeasible logic used here has a distinct syntactic similarity to Horn clause logic. More to the point, the language is very PROLOG-like. This, of course, is no accident. The language was designed to facilitate implementation of a sound but incomplete defeasible theorem prover in PROLOG [Nute88a]. Defeasible logic has also been incorporated into PROLOG to produce an extension of the PROLOG inference engine called d-PROLOG [Nute&Lewis86]. d-PROLOG stands in much the same relation to defeasible logic as PROLOG does to Horn clause logic except that d-PROLOG rejects as ill-formed rules containing disjunction, cut, or negation-as-failure. It has restrictions similar to those of PROLOG on its ability to find proofs (namely looping), which is the price paid for other kinds of efficiency. d-PROLOG provides the control structure of a prototype system for selecting business forecasting models [Nute *et al.*88].

Defeasible logic enjoys intuitive motivation independently of the *YSP*.

Yet it gives intuitively correct results for this example and for other troublesome but simple examples like the Tweety example. Its defeaters provide a device for representing knowledge of a kind that cannot be represented in other well-known non-monotonic systems. It is easily implemented as an extension of PROLOG. At the very least, it disarms the strong suggestion by Hanks and McDermott that non-monotonic logic cannot offer any relief for the frame problem. The specific version described here should be valuable as a general framework for temporal reasoning, representing hierarchies with exceptions [Billington *et al.*89], reasoning with inconsistent theories, and other applications. The general characterization of a defeasible logic in terms of a partial ordering of the rules provides opportunities to explore other ways of determining the superiority relation for a set of rules.

6   Bibliography

Billington, D., De Coster, K., and Nute, D. "A modular translation from defeasible nets to defeasible logics," Computing and Information Technology Research Report 31, Brisbane, Queensland, Australia: Griffeth University. Also appears as Artificial Intelligence Programs Research Report AI-1989-05, Athens, Georgia: The University of Georgia, 1989.

Hanks, S., and McDermott, D. "Default reasoning, non-monotonic logics, and the frame problem," *Proceedings of the National Conference on Artificial Intelligence*, Morgan–Kaufman, pp. 328–333, 1986.

Hanks, S., and McDermott, D. "Default logic and temporal projection," *Artificial Intelligence 33*, pp. 379–413, 1987.

Hayes, P. "What the frame problem is and isn't," *The Robot's Dilemma: The Frame Problem in Artificial Intelligence*, Z. Pylyshyn, ed., Ablex, pp. 123–138, 1987.

Loui, R. "Response to Hanks and McDermott: temporal evolution of beliefs and beliefs about temporal evolution." *Cognitive Science 11*, pp. 303–317, 1987.

McCarthy, J. "Circumscription – a form of non-monotonic reasoning," *Artificial Intelligence 13*, pp. 27–39, 1980.

McCarthy, J., and Hayes, P. "Some philosophical problems from the standpoint of artificial intelligence," *Machine Intelligence 4*, B. Meltzer and D. Michie, ed., Edinburgh University Press, pp. 463–502, 1969.

McDermott, D. "A temporal logic for reasoning about processes and plans," *Cognitive Science 6*, pp. 101–155, 1982.

McDermott, D. "We've been framed: or, why AI is innocent of the frame problem," *The Robot's Dilemma: The Frame Problem in Artificial Intelligence*, Z. Pylyshyn, ed., Ablex , pp. 113–122, 1987.

McDermott, D., and J. Doyle. "Non-monotonic logic I," *Artificial Intelligence 13*, pp. 41–72, 1980.

Nute, D. "Defeasible reasoning and decision support systems," *Decision Support Systems: The International Journal 4*, pp. 97–110, 1988.

Nute, D. "Defeasible reasoning: a philosophical analysis in Prolog," in J. Fetzer, ed., *Aspects of Artificial Intelligence*, Kluwer, pp. 251–288, 1988a.

Nute, D., and M. Lewis. "A user's manual for d-Prolog," ACMC Research Report 01-0016, Athens, Georgia: The University of Georgia, 1986.

Nute, D., Mann, R., and B. Brewer. "Using defeasible logic to control selection of a business forecasting method," *Proceedings of the 21st Hawaii International Conference on System Science*, Washington: IEEE Computer Society, pp. 437–444, 1988.

Poole, D. "On the comparison of theories: preferring the most specific explanation," *IJCAI-85: Proceedings of the Ninth International Joint Conference on Artificial Intelligence*, Los Angeles, Morgan-Kaufmann, pp. 144–147, 1985.

Reiter, R. "A logic for default reasoning," *Artificial Intelligence 13*, pp. 81–132, 1980.

Monotonic Solution of The Frame Problem in The Situation Calculus:

An Efficient Method for Worlds with Fully Specified Actions

Lenhart Schubert I- RCT- C

1   Introduction

"One feels that there should be some economical and principled way of succinctly saying what changes an action makes, without having to explicitly list all the things it doesn't change as well; yet there doesn't seem to be any other way to do it. *That* is the frame problem."

— Pat Hayes [Hayes87; p. 125]

The frame problem originally surfaced within McCarthy's Situation Calculus [McCarthy68], when [McCarthy&Hayes69] applied it to reasoning about goal achievement. To illustrate their approach, they considered the problem of initiating a telephone conversation. They began by writing down plausible axioms which seemed to characterize the preconditions and effects of looking up a person's telephone number and dialling that number. However, they found that they were still unable to prove that the plan "look up the number and dial it" would work, even if all the initial conditions were right (*i.e.*, that the caller had a telephone and a telephone book, that the intended party was home, *etc.*). For example, the axioms provided no assurance that looking up the number would not make the caller's telephone disappear, thus voiding a precondition for dialling.

At this point, McCarthy and Hayes made a move which set the stage for all subsequent discussions of the frame problem, and proposals to solve it: they augmented their axiom for the effects of looking up a phone number, so that it asserted that the action does *not* make the caller's possessions disappear, and does *not* change the intended party's location. These, of course, are the sorts of axioms known as frame axioms.

H.E. Kyburg, Jr. et al. (eds.), Knowledge Representation and Defeasible Reasoning, 23–67.

They apparently viewed their strategy of specifying the relationships *not* changed by an action as the only one available within the Situation Calculus proper, though they deplored both its *ad hoc* character and the proliferation of axioms to which it leads:

> "If we had a number of actions to be performed in sequence we would have quite a number of conditions to write down that certain actions do not change the values of certain fluents [properties and relationships]. In fact with n actions and m fluents, we might have to write down mn such conditions."

One might add that these conditions are rather implausible in a world with multiple agents (like the one we live in). For instance, there is no assurance in real life that either the intended party, or all one's possessions will stay put while one is consulting a phone book.

Virtually all later discussions of the frame problem reiterate McCarthy and Hayes' line of reasoning, without questioning the need for frame axioms of the type suggested by them, at least within the Situation Calculus and perhaps within any classical logical framework.[1]

Yet another sort of move is available, which entirely avoids frame axioms. This is to introduce axioms about what actions are *required* to produce given types of changes. This approach was proposed for a serial world by Andrew Haas [Haas87].[2] An example is the following axiom (where $holding(R, x, s)$ means that the robot is holding object x in situation s, $Result(a, s)$ is the situation resulting from carrying out action a in situation s, and $Putdown(R, x)$ is the action of R putting down x, regarded as an abstract individual; as usual, a "situation" is thought of as a possible "state of the universe"):[3]

$$(\forall a, x, s, s')[[holding(R, x, s) \land \neg holding(R, x, s') \land s' = Result(a, s)]$$
$$\rightarrow a = Putdown(R, x)];$$

---

[1] See, for example, the preface and articles in [Pylyshyn87] and [Brown87].

[2] Similar proposals have been made by [Lansky87] and [Georgeff87]. The latter suggests that "the combinatorics [of specifying what fluents are independent of what events] can be substantially reduced by explicitly specifying *all* the events that could possibly affect each fluent". However, Georgeff's approach is non-functional and less direct than Haas', in its reliance on a notion of *independence* (which remains somewhat unclear).

[3] I will consistently use lower-case identifiers for predicates and variables, and capitalized identifiers for individual constants and functions.

i.e., if the robot ceases to hold an object x between situations s and s', and situation s' was obtained from situation s by act a, then a must have been the act of putting down x. (For a more versatile robot, the right-hand side of the axiom might have allowed $a = Drop(R, x)$, and perhaps one or two other actions, as an alternative to $a = Putdown(R, x)$). Thus, given that in a certain situation the robot holds some specific object B, and in that situation performs some action *other* than $Putdown(R, B)$, we can infer from the contrapositive that the robot still holds B after that action. I will give details and argue the succinctness and other advantages of the approach in §2.

Haas termed his axioms "domain-specific frame axioms." I will instead call axioms which specify the actions needed to produce a given type of change *explanation-closure* axioms. This reflects the fact that they supply complete sets of possible explanations for given types of change. As such (I will suggest) they are important in other areas of AI, such as story understanding. It is true that the contrapositive of an axiom like the above predicts a non-change, and in that sense resembles a "frame axiom." However, it does so on the basis of the *non-occurrence*, rather than the occurrence, of certain specific actions, and it is clear that this is not what McCarthy and Hayes, or any of the many commentators on the frame problem since then, meant by frame axioms. As I will try to show, explanation closure axioms have important advantages over (traditional) frame axioms.

In §3, I will provide a more complete illustration of how primitive actions in a serial world can be axiomatized using explanation closure. I will include an illustration that confronts the problem of *implicit effects*. An example of an implicit effect is the change in the location of the topmost object in a stack, when the base of the stack is moved; though the effect is causally direct, its detection may require any number of inference steps. I will give examples of what can and cannot be inferred in this world, contrasting this with the more usual approaches.

Despite the emphasis in the Hayes quote on succinctness, computational efficiency is of obvious importance in reasoning about change and non-change. In §4, I will show that a default strategy which is essentially the "sleeping dog" strategy of STRIPS is deductively sound when appropriately based on explanation closure. This refutes a common assumption that monotonic solutions to the frame problem are the slowest, and that the STRIPS strategy lies somehow beyond the pale of ordinary logic.

In §5, I will briefly explore the potential of the Situation Calculus, and the present approach to the frame problem, with respect to external events, continuous change, action composition using sequencing, conditionals and iteration, and most of all, concurrency. Note that the earlier inference about persistence of *holding* depended on the assumption that actions cannot be concurrent, so that performance of one action cannot produce changes that require other actions. Extensions to worlds with concurrent actions are possible using parallel composition of actions, along with a modified form of Haas' axioms and general axioms about the primitive parts of complex actions.

An example of a composite action is ($Costart(\ Walk(R,L_0,L_1),\ Walk(H,L_2, L_3)$)) which represents concurrent walks by R and H starting simultaneously and finishing whenever both walks are done (not necessarily simultaneously). Just as in the serial case, the *Result* function is interpreted as yielding the unique new state which results if *only* the action specified by its first argument takes place. By maintaining this functional view of actions, we preserve an important property of the original Situation Calculus (exploited by [Green69]: plans are terms, and can be extracted deductively from existence proofs. On the other hand, the approach may not be systematically extensible to cases where reasoning about a given situation occurs against the backdrop of a large world knowledge base. The difficulty lies in the lack of uniform principles for identifying the relevant agents and the "boundaries" of the given situation in a way that will make a functional view of action, and explanation closure, consistent with the background knowledge.

2   Explanation Closure: A Simple Illustration and Preliminary Assessment

> "A weapon has been used to crush a man's skull and it is not found at the scene of the crime. The only alternative is that it has been carried away."
>
> — Isaac Asimov, *The Naked Sun*

Let us begin by going through the earlier example, adapted from Haas [Haas87], in more detail. We are assuming a robot's world in which the robot can walk about, paint or dye objects, pick them up and put them down or drop them, *etc.* He cannot perform any of these primitive actions simultaneously.[4] The immediate consequences of actions are expressed by

---

[4] *Primitive* actions are immediately executable, requiring no further elaboration or decomposition into lower-level actions (though they may require execution monitoring to see whether, in fact, they run their course as expected). All practical planning systems seem

effect axioms such as

A1. $(\forall x, y, s, s')[[at(R, x, s) \land s' = Result(Walk(R, x, y), s)]$
$\rightarrow at(R, y, s')]$

Note that the fluent literal $at(R, x, s)$ functions as a (sufficient) precondition for the success of *Walk*.

We assume that in the initial situation S_0, the robot is at location L_0 holding an object B:

$at(R, L_0, S_0)$
$holding(R, B, S_0)$

We are interested in the situation S_1 resulting from R's walking from L_0 to L_1:

$S_1 = Result(Walk(R, L_0, L_1), S_0)$

Specifically, we wish to show that R is still holding B in S_1:

G1. $holding(R, B, S_1)$

The possible explanations for cessation of holding are that the robot put down or dropped the object:

A2. $(\forall a, x, s, s')[[holding(R, x, s) \land \neg holding(R, x, s') \land s' = Result(a, s)]$
$\rightarrow a \in \{Putdown(R, x), Drop(R, x)\}]$,

where $a \in \{a_1, \cdots, a_n\}$ abbreviates $a = a_1 \lor \cdots \lor a = a_n$. To prove G1, we assume its negation

$\neg holding(R, B, S_1)$,

and use (A2) along with the initial conditions and the definition of S_1 to obtain

$Walk(R, L_0, L_1) \in \{Putdown(R, B), Drop(R, B)\}$.

But syntactically distinct primitive actions are not the same:

---

to recognize such a level of primitive actions, even though the choice of where to "draw the line" is rather arbitrary.

A3 *(Inequality schemas).* If α and β are distinct m-place and n-place function symbols ($m, n \geq 1$) representing primitive actions, then
$$(\forall x_1, \cdots, x_m, y_1, \cdots, y_n)\, \alpha(x_1, \cdots, x_m) \neq \beta(y_1, \cdots, y_n),\ \text{and}$$
$$(\forall x_1, \cdots, x_m, y_1, \cdots, y_n)[\alpha(x_1, \cdots, x_m) \neq \alpha(y_1, \cdots, y_m) \vee$$
$$(x_1 = y_1 \wedge \cdots \wedge x_m = y_m)].$$

Appropriate instances of these schemas deny that a *Walk* is identifiable with a *Putdown* or a *Drop*, and this contradiction establishes the desired conclusion G1.

Note that the traditional approach would have used a set of frame axioms including

$$(\forall a, x, y, z, s, s')[[holding(R, x, s) \wedge s' = Result(Walk(R, x, z), s)]$$
$$\to holding(R, x, s')]$$

and similar ones for every other action which does not affect *holding*, in place of (A2). Explanation closure axioms are more succinct than sets of such frame axioms because there are typically few actions that change a given fluent, but many fluents that are unaffected by a given action.[5] Besides, (as suggested earlier) frame axioms do not generalize to worlds with *concurrent* actions. For example, in a world in which a robot can *simultaneously* walk and drop an object, there is no guarantee that an object held at the beginning of a walk is still held at the end.

The preceding succinctness claim for explanation closure axioms is quite vague. It is unlikely that it can be made fully precise, since it amounts to a claim about the structure of "natural" theories of action for real-world domains. A "natural" theory should be intuitively understandable, extensible, and effectively usable for inference. But such desiderata are hard, if not impossible, to reduce to *syntactic* constraints.

Nevertheless, the claim can be made rather plausible, if formulated *relative* to the complexity of the axiomatization of effects. The following argument is an intuitive and empirical one, in its tacit appeal to the form which effect axioms "naturally" take (in the sorts of axiomatizations familiar to AI researchers). It assumes a primitive, serial world with "explicit effects". In the next section, I will attempt a slight generalization.

Succinctness Claim 1 (for explanation closure in a primitive, serial

---

[5]However, as Kowalski [Kowalski79; p. 135] showed, sets of frame axioms specifying all fluents unaffected by a given action can be collapsed by reifying fluents and quantifying over them.

world with explicit effects). In a natural axiomatization of a world in terms of a set of fluents and a set of nonconcurrent primitive actions, where the axioms specifying the effects of an action explicitly state which fluents become true and which ones become false, it is possible to axiomatize non-change using explanation closure axioms whose overall complexity is of the same order as that of the effect axioms.

Argument. To see the intuition behind the claim, think of the effect axioms as conditionals of form "fluent p changes if action a_1, or $a_2, \cdots$, or a_k occurs" (this may require some slight syntactic rearrangements); *e.g.*,

- an object changes color if it is painted or dyed (with a new color); (note that this statement may collapse two axioms, one for the effect of painting and one for the effect of dyeing);

- an object ceases to be *on* another if the robot picks it up;

- the robot changes location if he takes a walk or pushes an object; (this might again correspond to two effect axioms); *etc.*

Now, roughly speaking, the addition of explanation closure axioms is just a matter of changing all the "if"s to "if and only if"s. At least this is so if each of the effect axioms states *all* fluent changes engendered by the actions. The addition of the "only if" axioms clearly will not increase the overall complexity by more than a constant factor.

I hasten to add that this is an oversimplification. Explanation closure does, in general, differ from a strict "biconditionalization" of the effect axioms — indeed, I am about to argue that this is an advantage it has over circumscriptive or nonmonotonic approaches. Nevertheless, an explanation closure axiom in a world with explicit effects typically supplies those actions as alternative explanations of a change which *produce* that change according to the effect axioms. □

One could further argue that such *relative* succinctness assures a storage complexity well below $O(mn)$, since the complexity of the effect axioms presumably lies below this.[6] Note also that if effect axioms do not involve unboundedly many fluents for each action, their complexity should be $O(n)$,

---

[6] If it did not, McCarthy and Hayes would hardly have had grounds for complaining about the potential $o(mn)$ complexity of frame axioms!

and if a fluent is not referenced in unboundedly many effect axioms, it should be $O(m)$.[7]

Being succinct, the explanation closure approach offers a viable alternative to nonmonotonic and circumscriptive approaches. Unlike nonmonotonic approaches, it does not jeopardize effective provability. Unlike circumscription, it does not create subtle problems about what to circumscribe. As Hanks and McDermott [Hanks&McDermott87] remark, finding the "right" circumscriptive theory invariably hinges on already knowing the preferred model it should deliver. I would suggest that explanation closure axioms are a natural way to express our preferences directly, at least in simple worlds.[8]

Another crucial advantage of the approach is that it avoids overly strong persistence inferences. This point was made briefly by Haas [Haas87], but deserves detailed reiteration. Suppose, for example, that we want to allow for the possibility that when the robot drops an object it might break, without insisting that this will be the outcome. A natural way to approximate this situation is to make the outcome dependent on how fragile the object is, without assuming that we *know* whether it is fragile enough to break. So the effect axiom might be:

A4. $(\forall x, s, s')[[holding(R, x, s) \land s' = Result(Drop((R, x), s)]$
$\rightarrow [\neg holding(R, x, s') \land [fragile(x, s) \rightarrow broken(x, s')]]]$

Although we won't be able to infer breakage without knowledge of fragility, we still want to assert that if an object breaks, it was dropped. This can be straightforwardly expressed by the explanation closure axiom

A5. $(\forall a, x, s, s')[[\neg broken(x, s) \land broken(x, s') \land s' = Result(a, s)]$
$\rightarrow a = Drop(R, x)]$

Note that here (A5) cannot be derived from the corresponding effect axiom (A4) by some systematic "biconditionalization", or any other general principle. It is essentially a domain fact.[9] So, given the particulars

---

[7] It would be nice to be able to replace such tentative arguments with a hard-and-fast theoretical argument to the effect that (a) the logical structure of causation is such that for the "right" choice of formal terminology (*i.e.*, the "right" fluents and actions), effect axioms *will not* involve more than a few fluents on average; and perhaps even that (b) there is an effective procedure allowing an agent interacting with the world to converge toward such a "right" choice of terminology. Fodor [Fodor87] seems to demand all this and more of any genuine solution to the frame problem; however, most AI researchers take a more practical view.

[8] I argue below for their naturalness.

[9] In a more realistic world, we would allow for some additional ways of breaking, such as being struck or crushed.

$\neg broken(C, S_0)$, $holding(R, C, S_0)$ and $S_1 = Result(Drop(R, C), S_0)$,

we can infer neither $broken(C, S_1)$ nor $\neg broken(C, S_1)$, and that is as it should be.

By contrast, a circumscriptive approach that minimizes the amount of "abnormality" engendered by an action [McCarthy84], or its causal efficacy [Lifschitz87], would predict $\neg broken(C, S_1)$ and hence $\neg fragile(C, S_0)$. Similarly nonmonotonic methods [Reiter80] would sanction this unwarranted inference. Moreover, if we are given the particulars

$$\neg broken(C, S_0),\ broken(C, S_1),\ \text{and}\ S = Result(A, S_0),$$

the explanation closure approach yields the reasonable conclusion $A = Drop(R, C)$, whereas circumscriptive and nonmonotonic approaches are silent about A (given axiom (A4) but not (A5)).

Areas of uncertainty or ignorance like that concerning breakage are hard to avoid in domain theories of practical magnitude. A familiar instance of this is the "*next-to*" problem: it is hard to provide effect axioms which will supply *all* changes in *next-to* relations (without appeal to some overly precise geometrical representation). Yet circumscriptive and nonmonotonic approaches will treat the axioms as if they supplied all such changes, and as a result sanction unwarranted persistence inferences. I will return to the *next-to* problem in the next section, which contains a more elaborate "robot's world."

Finally, I claim that encoding non-change via explanation closure axioms is principled and natural, in the sense that there are reasons independent of the frame problem for invoking them. One such reason is the observation that people can come up with small sets of plausible explanations for changes of state almost instantaneously, at least in familiar domains. For example, if the grass got wet, perhaps it rained, or the sprinkler was on, or dew formed overnight, or some snow melted — and that just about covers the most likely explanations.[10] Endowing machines with comparable abilities would seem to require some quite direct encoding of the connection between various phenomena and their immediate causes. Furthermore, research in natural language understanding has shown that the ability to infer actions

---

[10]Similarly consider, "How did the wall come to be blue?", "Why is the sun no longer shining?", "How did John's location get changed from the ground floor to the 17th floor of his apartment building?", "How did John learn about the earthquake in Italy while having breakfast alone in his New York apartment?", "How did John gain possession of the hamburger he is eating?", "What is causing John's nose to be runny?", *etc.*

that accomplish given state changes is extremely important, and has led to postulation of knowledge structures very similar to explanation-closure axioms. For example, Schank and Abelson [Schank&Abelson77; p. 75] suggest that state changes deliberately brought about by human agents are associated with sets of possible actions (in their terms, sets of "plan boxes") that achieve those state changes. They assume that if a story leads to the inference that an agent will try to accomplish a state change, the further inference is warranted that he will attempt one of the associated actions. Clearly this involves a tacit closure assumption that a deliberately caused state change is normally brought about by one of a fixed set of actions.

To be sure, examples of "real-world" explanation closure are generally subtler than (A2) or (A5). They vary in level of detail (scale or "grain size") and level of abstraction (see §5), and most importantly, are "defeasible" — the standard explanations occasionally *do* fail. However, my primary concern here is with causally insulated, predictable worlds, free of booby-trapped boxes and meteor strikes. Everything of interest that occurs will be attributable to known agents. In such a setting, (non-defeasible) explanation closure works remarkably well.

3   Explanation closure in a world with implicit effects

In case of *holding*, the cessation of this relation can be directly attributed to a *Putdown* or *Drop*. Based on such examples, the "explicit effects" assumption required direct axiomatic connections from actions to all affected fluents. This requirement is hard to enforce in nontrivial worlds. For instance, suppose that a robot is regarded as "carrying" its own integral parts, anything "riding" in or on it, and anything those "riders", in turn, are carrying (*cf.* the "assemblies" of [Haas87]). This is a useful notion, because an object "carried" by another changes location with it. Now in axiomatizing actions like *Walk* or *Pickup*, we do not want to explicitly specify *all* effects on objects carried (and left behind). Rather, we want these changes to follow from axiomatic connections between *holding, in, on, etc.*, and *carrying*.

The following partial theory of a world with implicit effects serves several purposes. First, it shows that the explanation closure approach to the frame problem extends readily to such worlds.[11] Second, it provides a nontrivial setting for illustrating inference based on explanation closure. Finally, it provides the background for further discussion of the succinctness claim and

---

[11] The new closure axioms are (A16–A20).

the "*next-to*" problem.

A6. An object "carries" its integral parts, its riders, anything carried by its riders, and nothing else.[12]

$$(\forall x, y, s)[carries(x, y, s) \leftrightarrow [integral\text{-}part(y, x) \lor rider(y, x, s)\lor$$
$$(\exists z)[rider(z, x, s) \land carries(z, y, s)]]]$$

A7. "*Carries*" is irreflexive (so that by A6 and A9, *integral-part, rider, in, on* and *holding* are also irreflexive).

$$(\forall x, y, s)[carries(x, y, s) \to \neg carries(y, x, s)]$$

A8. An object carried by another is at the same place as its carrier.

$$(\forall x, y, z, s)[[carries(x, y, s) \land at(x, z, s)] \to at(y, z, s)]$$

A9. An object is a rider on another iff it is in, on, or held by it.

$$(\forall x, y, s)[rider(y, x, s) \leftrightarrow [in(y, x, s) \lor on(y, x, s) \lor holding(x, y, s)]]$$

A10. "*in*" corresponds to one or more nested in_0's.

$$(\forall x, z, s)[in(x, z, s) \leftrightarrow [in_0(x, z, s) \lor (\exists y)[in(x, y, s) \land in_0(y, z, s)]]]$$

A11. *Paint* has the expected effect, if the robot is next to a paintbrush, paint of the right hue, and the object to be painted, and isn't holding anything.

$$(\forall x, b, c, p, s, s')[[next\text{-}to(R, x, s) \land next\text{-}to(R, b, s) \land next\text{-}to(R, p, s)\land$$
$$brush(b) \land paint(p) \land hue(p, c)\land \neg(\exists y)holding(R, y, s)\land$$
$$s' = Result(Paint(R, x, c), s)] \to color(x, c, s')]$$

A12. *Dye* has the expected effect — much like (A11).

A13. *Putdown* has the expected effect, if the robot is holding the object.[13]

---

[12] Nonintegral parts, such as a computer remotely controlling a robot, need not be carried by it.

[13] To illustrate less direct effects, effects on *in* and *on* are also included.

$$(\forall x, y, s, s')[[holding(R, x, s) \wedge s' = Result(Putdown(R, x), x)]$$
$$\rightarrow \neg holding(R, x, s') \wedge [above(x, y, s) \rightarrow$$
$$[[container(y) \wedge smaller(x, y) \rightarrow in(x, y, s')] \wedge$$
$$[\neg container(y) \vee \neg smaller(x, y) \rightarrow on(x, y, s')]]]]]$$

A14. *Pickup* has the expected effect on *holding*, if the robot is next to the object and the object is liftable.[14]

$$(\forall x, s, s')[[next\text{-}to(R, x, s) \wedge liftable(x) \wedge \neg(\exists z)holding(R, z, s) \wedge$$
$$s' = Result(Pickup(R, x), s)] \rightarrow holding(R, x, s')]$$

A15. As in the case of (A13), we might have included additional effects of *Pickup* in (A14). Alternatively, we can state additional effects separately, as in the following axiom about (successful) *Pickup*s being able to undo *carries* relations:

$$(\forall x, y, s, s')[[next\text{-}to(R, x, s) \wedge liftable(x) \wedge \neg(\exists z)holding(R, z, s) \wedge$$
$$s' = Result(Pickup(R, x), s)]$$
$$\rightarrow [[carries(y, x, s) \wedge \neg carries(y, R, s)] \rightarrow \neg carries(y, x, s')]]$$

A16. If an object ceases to be of some color y, it was painted or dyed with some color z.

$$(\forall a, x, y, s, s')[[color(x, y, s) \wedge \neg color(x, y, s') \wedge s' = Result(a, s)]$$
$$\rightarrow (\exists z)a \in \{Paint(R, x, z), Dye(R, x, z)\}]$$

A17. A change from *not holding* an object to *holding* it requires a *Pickup* action.

$$(\forall a, x, y, s, s')[[\neg holding(x, y, s) \wedge holding(x, y, s') \wedge s' = Result(a, s)]$$
$$\rightarrow a = Pickup(x, y)]$$

A18. If an object ceases to be *in* a container, then the robot must have picked up the object, or picked up something in the container carrying the object.

---

[14] *liftable* is here treated as independent of the agent and the given situation (*e.g.*, whether there are "riders" on the object), but could easily be made dependent on them.

$$(\forall a, x, y, s, s')[[in(x, y, s) \land \neg in(x, y, s') \land s' = Result(a, s)]$$
$$\rightarrow [a = Pickup(R, x)\lor$$
$$(\exists z)[a = Pickup(R, z) \land in(z, y, s) \land carry(z, x, s)]]]]$$

A19. If an object x comes to be *in* a container, then the robot must have put down or dropped an object z it was holding above the container, where z is smaller than the container, and either *is* x or was carrying it:

$$(\forall a, x, y, s, s')[[\neg in(x, y, s) \land in(x, y, s') \land s' = Result(a, s)]$$
$$\rightarrow (\exists z)[[z = x \lor carries(z, x, s)] \land holding(R, z, s) \land$$
$$above(z, y, s) \land smaller(z, y) \land$$
$$[a = Putdown(R, z) \lor a = Drop(R, z)]]]]$$

A20. If an object ceases to be *at* a location, then the robot took a *Walk* to some place, and either the robot is that object, or was carrying that object.

$$(\forall a, x, y, s, s')[[at(x, y, s) \land \neg at(x, y, s') \land s' = Result(a, s)]$$
$$\rightarrow (\exists z)[a = Walk(R, y, z) \land [R = x \lor carries(R, x, s)]]]$$

This partial axiomatization lacks axioms for *on* and *next-to*, explanations for *color* or *at* becoming true, *etc.* While further axioms would be needed in any practical application, it is significant that even a partial axiomatization allows many reasonable conclusions about change and non-change to be drawn, as the following examples show (see also §4). The problem of unwarranted persistence inferences, which attends circumscriptive and non-monotonic closure of incomplete theories, does not arise (at least not within settings with fully specified actions; limitations are discussed in §5).

The following example describes initial conditions in the robot's world in which the robot is at location L_0, and is next to a blue box B containing a cup C (and perhaps other objects). In addition, there is a doormat D at location L_1, which is distinct from L_0. The problem is to show that if the robot picks up the box and walks to a location L_2, the location of the cup is changed but not the color of the box or the location of the doormat.[15]

---

[15]The descriptions "box", "cup", and "doormat" are not actually encoded in the premises, but are used for mnemonic reasons.

Proposition 1. Given axioms (A1–A20), along with initial conditions

$at(R, L_0, S_0)$, $next$-$to(R, B, S_0)$, $in_0(C, B, S_0)$, $liftable(B)$,
$color(B, Blue, S_0)$, $at(D, L_1, S_0)$, $L_1 \neq L_0$,
$\neg(\exists z)holding(R, z, S_0)$

and plan

$S_1 = Result(Pickup(R, B), S_0)$,
$S_2 = Result(Walk(R, L_0, L_2), S_1)$

then

(a) $color(B, Blue, S_2)$, (b) $at(D, L_1, S_2)$, (c) $at(C, L_2, S_2)$.

Proof sketch.

(a): If the color of box B were not blue in situation S_1, then by (A16) the *Pickup* action which led to the situation would have had to equal a *Paint* or *Dye* action, which is impossible by (A3). Similarly we infer the persistence of B's color through the *Walk*.

(b): We assume that the doormat does *not* stay at L_1. Then by explanation closure for cessation of *at* (A20), the robot walked from L_1 to some location and either is D or carried D. But this is impossible, because the *Pickup* was no *Walk*, and the *Walk* was from L_0, which differs from L_1.[16]

(c): To prove the cup ends up at L_2, we first show that the robot ends up there, by (A1). Next, we show he ends up *holding* the box B, since the *Pickup* in the first step succeeds by (A14) and the *holding* persists through the *Walk* (by explanation axiom (A2) for cessation of holding, and the inequality schemas). Hence, we deduce by (A8) that the box ends up *at* L_2 (via the *rider* and *carries* relations, (A5) and (A6)). Next we infer by (A10) that since cup C is in_0 the box, it is *in* it, and that this relation persists through the *Pickup* and the *Walk*, using explanation axiom (A18) for cessation of *in*.[17] Finally, with the box at L_2 and the cup in it, we infer by (A8) that the cup is at L_2 (via the *rider* and *carries* relations). □

So non-change, as well as change, can be straightforwardly deduced in our robot's world, without appeal to nonstandard methods. As well, it is relevant to consider what sorts of things *cannot* be inferred in this world.

---

[16] Besides, the robot is not D, and didn't carry D, because the locations of D and the robot in situation S_0 are distinct.

[17] The former inference requires use of irreflexivity for *in* (A6, A7, A9), to rule out the possibility that in picking up the box, the robot lifted the cup *out* of the box along with the box!

Suppose, for instance, we add an assumption that there is a video camera at the robot's location at the outset, *i.e.*, $at(VC, L_0, S_0)$. We can deduce neither $at(VC, L_0, S_2)$ nor its negation, and that is as we would want. After all, the camera may or may not be attached to (or carried by) the robot.

Is the succinctness claim still tenable in such worlds with implicit effects? I submit that it is, although the evidence, even more than before, must be sought in examples (such as the one just presented) and in our intuitions about "natural" axiomatic theories.

Succinctness Claim 2 (for explanation closure in a primitive, serial world with implicit effects). In a natural axiomatization of an intuitively comprehensible dynamic world in terms of a set of situational fluents and a set of (nonconcurrent) primitive actions, it is possible to axiomatize non-change using explanation closure axioms whose overall complexity is of the same order as that of the effect axioms *plus* the axioms relating primary fluents (those explicitly connected to actions) to secondary ones.

Argument. In this case, "biconditionalizing" effect axioms of form "fluent p changes if action a_1, or $a_2, \cdots$, or a_k occurs" will provide explanation closure axioms for the primary fluents only (in approximate form). Do we also need closure axioms for secondary fluents? The preceding example suggests that secondary fluents will often have *definitions* in terms of primary ones (see *carries* and *rider* in (A6) and (A9)). Changes in such fluents are fully determined by — as well as explained by — changes in the relevant primary fluents. For example, if an object ceases to be a rider on another, we can infer from (A9) that if it was previously *in*, *on* or held by the other object, that relationship ceased; hence we can infer what action (or possible actions) must have occurred. So it appears that separate closure axioms will often be redundant for secondary fluents.

But even where such axioms turn out to be necessary or convenient, the overall complexity of closure should not exceed that of other axioms. After all, for each secondary fluent at least one axiom must already be present which introduces that fluent and relates it to others. As long as explanation closure axioms do not get arbitrarily more complicated than these relational ones, the succinctness claim remains true.

Examples suggest they will not get arbitrarily more complicated. For instance, although explanation closure axioms are theoretically redundant for the *carries* and *rider* fluents of our illustration, it is convenient to have them. For explaining how a *carries* relation comes about for the robot and an object x, and how it ceases, we might say:

A21. $(\forall a, x, s, s')[[\neg carries(R, x, s) \land carries(R, x, s') \land s' = Result(a, s)]$
$\rightarrow (\exists y)[[y = x \lor carries(y, x)] \land a = Pickup(R, y)]]$

A22. $(\forall a, x, s, s')[[carries(R, x, s) \land \neg carries(R, x, s') \land s' = Result(a, s)]$
$\rightarrow (\exists y)[[y = x \lor carries(y, x)] \land$
$[a = Putdown(R, y) \lor a = Drop(R, y)]]]$

These are no more complicated than the closure axioms suggested for primary fluents like *holding* and *in*.

Indeed, it seems unlikely that a natural set of concepts for describing an *intuitively comprehensible* domain would include fluents whose changes, even under ordinary conditions, cannot be explained (at any level) in terms of a few simple alternative causes. In other words, it seems to me that having simple explanation and prediction rules for a dynamic world is what *makes* it intuitively comprehensible. □

Finally, let us return to the *next-to* problem, whose relevance to practical robot problem solving makes it a touchstone for putative solutions to the frame problem. Essentially the problem is that neither persistence nor change of *next-to* relations can be reliably inferred for all pairs of objects. For example, suppose that our robot's world contains two adjacent windows W_1, W_2 and (for whatever reason) the robot is interested in the goal

$(\exists s)next\text{-}to(R, W_1, s) \land \neg next\text{-}to(R, W_2, s).$

Suppose also that the robot has a *Go-next-to* action, which is capable of taking him next to either window.[18] But if he walks next to W_1, will he be next to W_2? Perhaps so, if the execution routines choose a place between the windows, and perhaps not, if they choose a place next to W_1 but on the far side from W_2. In such a case we do *not* want the robot to think he can achieve the above goal by starting at a place *not* next to W_2, and going next to W_1, with the conviction that $\neg next\text{-}to(R, W_2, S_0)$ will persist. Rather, he might decide the problem is not amenable to reliable solution, or he might know some facts which will allow him to overcome the problem (*e.g.*, he might just happen to know that if he goes next to the left portion

---

[18] Assume for this discussion that *Go-next-to* replaces *Walk*, though it wouldn't be hard to allow for both.

of a window's frame, he will be next to the window but not next to any windows or doors to its right).[19]

Similarly, it would be risky to assume (as STRIPS-style robots typically do) that when the robot walks, it ceases to be *next-to* whatever stationary objects it was *next-to* at the start. After all, it may only have travelled a short distance, or along a trajectory parallel to an object (*e.g.*, alongside a table).

One possible way of dealing with the *next-to* problem is to rely on an exact geometrical model (*e.g.*, one which divides up the floor space into tiles, and deduces *next-to* or ¬*next-to* from which tiles are occupied). For this to permit the construction of reliable plans involving *next-to*, however, we have to insist that all actions available to the robot *precisely* and *predictably* determine his location. But this is just not a tenable assumption in a realistic, reasonably complex world.

Now the challenge is this: how do we avoid unsound persistence and change inferences, such as those above, while still obtaining those that *are* sound? For instance, we *do* want to infer that the robot's *next-to* relations don't change, say when he picks up, puts down, or paints an object (under a "horizontal" interpretation of *next-to*); and we *do* want to infer that *nonmoving* objects maintain their *next-to* and ¬*next-to* relations.

This challenge, ostensibly a very serious one for nonmonotonic and circumscriptive approaches, is easily met by explanation closure. For instance, we can state that $next\text{-}to(R, x, s')$ becomes true only if the robot goes *next-to* an object y (possibly x itself) which is not remote from x (where, say, *remote* means beyond four times the maximum distance for being *next-to*):

A23. $(\forall a, x, s, s')[[\neg next\text{-}to(R, x, s) \wedge next\text{-}to(R, x, s') \wedge s' = Result(a, s)]$
$\rightarrow (\exists y)[a = Go\text{-}next\text{-}to(R, y) \wedge \neg remote(x, y, s)]]$

This does *not* require exhaustive knowledge of what's remote from what, but if we *do* happen to know that the object the robot went to is remote from x, we can exclude x from the set of objects the robot may now be next to. Note that the axiom also permits inference of persistence of ¬$next\text{-}to(R, x, s)$ if the robot did something *other* than a *Go-next-to*. Similarly we can add closure axioms for $next\text{-}to(R, x, s)$ becoming false, and for $next\text{-}to(x, y, s)$ becoming

---

[19] Anyone inclined to think the robot ought to just make some default assumption, such as that he'll not be next to W_2, should imagine a situation in which W_1 has its blinds drawn but W_2 does not, and the robot is aware of a sniper across the street, bent on his destruction!

true or false for objects x, y other than the robot.[20] These will capture just
the persistences that are intuitively warranted by our conception of *next-to*.

The next section describes a practical and deductively sound way in
which explanation closure axioms can be "translated" into efficient, STRIPS-
like persistence inference methods.

4 STRIPS revisited: explanation closure meets the sleeping dog

The practical problem of efficiently inferring change and non-change has
been discussed by many writers on the frame problem (B. Raphael [Raphael71],
being an early example). Ideally, we would like to match the *constant-time*
inference of non-change achieved by STRIPS-like systems [Fikes&Nilsson71].
These employ the "sleeping dog" strategy: fluents referenced by the add-
lists and delete-lists of operators are updated, and the rest are assumed to
remain unchanged.

The idea in the following is to emulate STRIPS within the Situation Calculus by working out certain effects of plan steps, and inferring persistence
via default rules. The default rules treat the "most recent" values of fluents
as still correct in the current situation. One novelty is that explanation
closure axioms are used to guard against overly strong persistence inferences (by flagging certain fluents as "questionable"). The default inferences
are deductively sound (and in special cases, complete) relative to a domain
theory which includes the explanation closure axioms.

I will first illustrate these techniques for a specific set of fluents in a
slightly curtailed version of the previous "robot's world." In this case no
flagging of fluents is needed, and the rules are not only sound, but also
complete for fluents of form $(\neg)holding(R, \beta, \sigma)$, relative to any "certifiable"
plan — one whose steps have provably true preconditions. Further, they
permit constant-time persistence inference when suitably implemented.

I will then abstract from this example, and provide a general method for
using explanation closure axioms as "sentries" which watch for actions that
may change a given fluent. This enables flagging fluents so as to pave the
way for sound (but not in general complete) default inferences.

In order to look up the "most recent" value of a fluent one needs to have
worked out the relevant values at each step of a plan. Consequently, any
formal claims about such strategies must rely on some formalized notion of

---

[20]They will be much like the *at*-closure axiom, (A20).

the updating process.

In the *holding* example, this is accomplished by defining an initial "world" (theory) D_0 and a succession of augmented worlds $D_1, D_2, \cdots$, where each D_i incorporates D_{i-1}, a new plan step, and some logical consequences of the step. In practice, one would expect each D_i to be derived by some "forward inference" process from D_{i-1} and the ith plan step. In the example, the forward inferences have been judiciously chosen to provide explicit preconditions for any subsequent *Pickup, Putdown,* or *Drop* step, and formulas of the right sort for making sound and complete persistence inferences.

Our domain axioms will essentially be (A2) – (A19). By leaving out the *Walk*-axiom (A1) and explanation axiom for changes in *at*, (A20), we have changed the robot from a rover to a stationary manipulator. This allows us to avoid *next-to* reasoning; in fact, we can drop the situation argument from *next-to*, so that *next-to*(R, x) is permanently true, or permanently false, for any object x.

As another practical measure we invoke the "unique names assumption"; *i.e.,* all constants of our theory are drawn from a set *Names*, where these are interpreted (much as in the case of action names) as having distinct denotations. This could be expressed by axiom schema $\alpha \neq \beta$, where α, β are distinct names.

An initial world description D_0 consists of (A2) – (A19) (with *next-to* changed as discussed) along with $\neg(\exists x)holding(R, x, S_0)$, any number of additional formulas which can be consistently added, and all instances of *liftable*(β) and *next-to*(R, β) entailed by the rest of D_0 for constants β occurring in D_0. A plan is a set of formulas

$$S_i = Result(\alpha, S_{i-1}) \ , \quad i = 1, \cdots, N,$$

where each $\alpha \in \{Pickup(R, \beta), Putdown(R, \beta), Drop(R, \beta), Paint(R, \beta, \gamma),$ $Dye(R, \beta, \gamma)\}$ for some $\beta \in$ *Names* and $S_1, \cdots, S_N$ are constants distinct from each other and from all constants occurring in D_0. The augmented descriptions relative to such a plan are given (for $1 \leq i \leq N$) by

1. for $S_i = Result(Pickup(R, \beta), S_{i-1})$, $\beta \in$ *Names*, and
   $\{next\text{-}to(R, \beta), liftable(\beta), \neg(\exists z)holding(R, z, S_{i-1})\} \subset D_{i-1}$,

   let $D_i = D_{i-1} \cup \{S_i = Result(Pickup(R, \beta), S_{i-1}), holding(R, \beta, S_i)\}$;

2. for $S_i = Result(Putdown(R, \beta), S_{i-1})$, $\beta \in$ *Names*, and
   $holding(R, \beta, S_{i-1}) \in D_{i-1}$,

let $D_i = D_{i-1} \cup \{S_i = Result(Putdown(R,\beta), S_{i-1}), \neg holding(R,\beta,S_i),$
$\neg(\exists z)holding(R,z,S_i)\};$

3. same as (2), with *Drop* replacing *Putdown*;

4. for α a *Paint* or *Dye* action (whose effects can be left implicit, since only *holding* relations are to be inferred by default),

let $D_i = D_{i-1} \cup \{S_i = Result(\alpha, S_{i-1})\}.$

Note that in essence, each of (1) – (3) "checks" the preconditions of the action, and adds appropriate postconditions (effects). These follow logically from D_{i-1} together with the new step. For instance in (2), $\neg holding(R,\beta,S_i)$ is added as a logical consequence of the effect axiom (A13) for *Putdown*. $\neg(\exists z)holding(R,z,S_i)$ is also a consequence, though not an obvious one: it follows from the presence of $\neg(\exists z)holding(R,z,S_0)$ in D_0 (and hence D_i) and from the explanation axiom (A17) for *holding* becoming true (an inductive proof is required). It would not ordinarily be found by forward inference, but is included to secure completeness in the "sleeping-dog" proposition to follow.

Evidently, D_i does not exist if the preconditions of some step aren't provable. However, D_i exists *whenever* the preconditions for *Pickup, Putdown,* or *Drop* actions are provable (because (4) is indifferent to the preconditions of *Paint* and *Dye* steps). I will term such plans *certifiable* (relative to D_0).

As a final preliminary we note the following way of applying explanation closure axioms to multistep plans (expressed as *Result*-equations):

Serial Plan Lemma. Given an explanation closure axiom

$$(\forall a, x_1, \cdots, x_k, s, s')[[\pi(x_1, \cdots, x_k, s) \wedge \overline{\pi}(x_1, \cdots, x_k, s') \wedge$$
$$s' = Result(a,s)] \rightarrow \varphi(a)],$$

where π is a negated or unnegated predicate and $\overline{\pi}$ its complement and $\varphi(a)$ a formula containing a, and a plan

$$S_i = Result(\alpha_i, S_{i-1}), \quad i = 1, \cdots, N,$$

such that $\pi(\tau_1, \cdots, \tau_k, S_0)$ and $\overline{\pi}(\tau_1, \cdots, \tau_k, S_N)$ hold (where $\tau_1, \cdots, \tau_k$ are terms), we can conclude that for some i ($1 \leq i \leq N$), $\varphi(\alpha_i)$.

Proof. Obviously $\pi(\tau_1, \cdots, \tau_k, S_{i-1})$ and $\overline{\pi}(\tau_1, \cdots, \tau_k, S_i)$ must hold for some

i, allowing application of the closure axiom. $\square$

Sleeping-dog proposition for *holding*. Let D_N be a theory (*i.e.*, domain theory and plan) as defined above. Then the following default rules are sound and complete for conclusions of form $holding(R, \beta, S_k)$ and $\neg holding(R, \beta, S_k)$, where $\beta \in Names$ and $0 < k \leq N$:

$$\frac{holding(R, \beta, S_i)}{holding(R, \beta, S_k)} \quad , \quad \frac{\neg holding(R, \beta, S_i)}{\neg holding(R, \beta, S_k)} \quad , \quad \frac{\neg (\exists z) holding(R, z, S_i)}{\neg holding(R, \beta, S_k)}$$

where i is the largest integer $\leq k$ such that at least one of $holding(R, \beta, S_i)$, $\neg holding(R, \beta, S_i)$, and $\neg (\exists z) holding(R, z, S_i) \in D_k$.

Proof.
Soundness: We need to show that if i (as defined) exists for a given $\beta \in Names$, then D_k entails whichever conclusions are given by the default rules. Suppose otherwise, *i.e.*, there are β, i satisfying the premises for which a default rule gives a conclusion whose negation follows from D_k, or neither the conclusion nor its negation follows from D_k. Consider the case where $holding(R, \beta, S_i) \in D_k$ and $D_k \vdash \neg holding(R, \beta, S_k)$. Then by (A2) (explanation for *holding* becoming false) and the Serial Plan Lemma, there was a step $S_j = Result(\alpha, S_{j-1})$ with $\alpha \in \{Putdown(R, \beta), Drop(R, \beta)\}$ and $i < j \leq k$. By the unique-names assumption and inequality schemas (A3), this step must appear in D_k in precisely this form, *i.e.*, as jth step of the plan. But then by (2) and (3), $\neg holding(R, \beta, S_j) \in D_k$, contrary to the definition of i. Next consider the case where $\neg holding(R, \beta, S_j) \in D_k$ and $D_k \vdash holding(R, \beta, S_k)$. Then a contradiction is derived just as before, using (A17) (explanation for *holding* becoming true) and (1). Third, consider the case where $\neg (\exists z) holding(R, z, S_i) \in D_k$ and $D_k \vdash holding(R, \beta, S_k)$. Then the contradiction follows just as in the previous case, except for use of the fact that $\neg (\exists z) holding(R, z, S_i) \vdash \neg holding(R, \beta, S_i)$.

Now suppose β, i are such that neither the conclusion of the applicable default rule, nor its negation, follows from D_k. Consider the case where $holding(R, \beta, S_i) \in D_k$. Since $D_k \not\vdash holding(R, \beta, S_k)$, we can consistently form $D'_k = D_k \cup \{\neg holding(R, \beta, S_k)\}$. Then in this theory we can prove that there was a step $S_j = Result(\alpha, S_{j-1})$ with $\alpha \in \{Putdown(R, \beta), Drop(R, \beta)\}$ and $i < j \leq k$, and that this step must appear explicitly in D'_k, and hence in D_k, by exactly the same line of argument as before (*i.e.*, using the Serial Plan Lemma, unique names, and (A3)); thus we arrive at a contradiction as before. We can derive contradictions from the remaining two cases (for $\neg holding(R, \beta, S_i)$ or $\neg(\exists z)holding(R, z, S_i) \in D_k$) in an exactly analogous manner.

Completeness: Assume first that $D_k \vdash holding(R, \beta, S_k)$ for some $\beta \in$ Names. We need to show that i exists as defined and $holding(R, \beta, S_i) \in D_k$ (so that default inference yields $holding(R, \beta, S_k)$).[21] By the premises of the proposition, $\neg(\exists z)holding(R, z, S_0) \in D_0$, so i certainly exists. Now suppose $holding(R, \beta, S_i) \notin D_i$. Then (by the definition of i) either $\neg holding(R, \beta, S_i) \in D_i$ or $\neg(\exists z)holding(R, z, S_i) \in D_i$. In either case, by (A17) there is a step $S_j = Result(Pickup(R, \beta), S_{j-1})$ for some j ($i < j \leq k$) and this must be explicitly in D_k by the unique-names assumption and inequality schemas. By (1), applied to D_j, this contradicts the definition of i. Second, assume that $D_k \vdash \neg holding(R, \beta, S_i)$ for some $\beta \in$ Names; we show i exists as defined and either $\neg holding(R, \beta, S_i) \in D_k$ or $\neg(\exists z)holding(R, z, S_i) \in D_k$ (so that default inference yields $\neg holding(R, \beta, S_k)$). The denial of this disjunction leads to $holding(R, \beta, S_i) \in D_k$, and a contradiction follows as before. $\square$

These default rules clearly give us a fast method of inferring non-change for *holding* (or $\neg holding$), when we are working out the effects of a plan step-by-step. In fact, we can ensure the inferences will be made in constant time (on average). We store the initial and inferred instances of literals of form $holding(R, \beta, \sigma)$, $\neg holding(R, \beta, \sigma)$, $\neg(\exists z)holding(R, z, \sigma)$, where $\beta, \sigma \in$ Names, in a common hash table with complex key (*holding*, β).[22] Note that σ (the situation constant) is ignored in the key, so that as we progress through the plan, a list of entries will be formed for each key in chronological order. The literal needed for default inference will always be at the front of the list, allowing constant-time access.

So this provides a detailed and concrete example of efficient, STRIPS-like inference in the Situation Calculus, with the additional advantage of soundness and completeness (for a certain class of formulas) relative to the underlying domain theory. Moreover, the structure of the soundness and completeness proofs suggests that such proofs will be possible for many fluents in many applications.

Nevertheless, such default propositions are not entirely trivial to formulate (in particular, with regard to what "effect inferences" should be

---

[21] Of course, if i happens to be k, the "default inference" gives nothing new.

[22] We include *holding* as part of the key for generality, *i.e.*, for cases where other fluents are "tracked" as well.

included in the D_i) and to prove. We would much prefer to have a *general* methodology for exploiting closure axioms for STRIPS-like default inferences.

Now it turns out that the main source of difficulty in formulating and proving sleeping-dog propositions is the goal of completeness, *i.e.*, having the default rules cover all persistence inferences of a certain form. But it is acceptable, and ultimately necessary, to relax this constraint. It is acceptable because losing a few of the fast persistence inferences need not seriously degrade average performance. It is ultimately necessary in an unrestricted first-order theory because the forward inferences (from actions to resultant changes) needed to support subsequent default inferences may become arbitrarily hard. Clearly deducing change by forward inferencing is worthwhile only to the extent that its costs do not exceed the resultant savings in deducing non-change. It is unclear how to trade these off in general, so I will leave the issue open in the following, concentrating instead on the issue of soundness.

As soon as we consider incomplete inference of change, the risk of overly strong persistence inference arises: if at some point a change in a fluent occurred, but we failed to infer and register it, our default rules might mistakenly give us the old, outdated value as the current one. Fortunately, explanation closure axioms can be used to safeguard against such errors. Roughly the idea is to set them up as "sentries" on fluents, and "trigger" them when an action that may account for a change in those fluents occurs. Brief attempts to prove change or non-change are then made, and where both fail, the fluent is flagged as "questionable." This flagging blocks unsound default inferences. Since the flagging is essentially confined to "old" fluent literals referenced by explanation closure axioms and not subsequently updated using effect axioms, the total computational effort arguably remains modest.

In more detail, we begin with an initial world description D_0, including fluent formulas describing initial situation S_0. I will write an unspecified fluent formula for a particular situation S_i resulting from the ith step of a plan as $\varphi(S_i)$. S_i is understood to be the *only* constant situational argument occurring in $\varphi(S_i)$. $\varphi(S_k)$ is the result of uniformly substituting S_k for S_i. $\overline{\varphi}(S_i)$ is the negation of $\varphi(S_i)$ (with double negations eliminated). $?\varphi(S_i)$ is $\varphi(S_i)$ prefixed with "?", after removal of the negation, if any. We also define the *essential* fluents as some algorithmically recognizable class of fluent formulas for whose changes we have explanation closure axioms. For instance, these might be all formulas of form $(\neg)\pi(\beta_1, \cdots, \beta_k, S_i)$, where π is a primary fluent predicate (used in the axiomatization of the direct effects of actions), and $\beta_1, \cdots, \beta_k$ are constants. We now apply the following procedure.[23]

Plan Tracking Procedure. We take account of the steps of a given plan $S_k = Result(\alpha_k, S_{k-1})$, $k = 1, \cdots, N$, expanding D_{k-1} to D_k for each k as follows. Note that for $k > 1$, D_{k-1} may contain "questioned" fluents.

1. Initialize D_k to D_{k-1}

2. Add $S_k = Result(\alpha_k, S_{k-1})$ to D_k

3. Apply effect axioms to this plan step in an algorithmically bounded way, adding new fluents $\varphi(S_k)$ to D_k. Some implicit effects may be deduced as well, as long as the computation is guaranteed to terminate. Preconditions of effect axioms at situation S_{k-1} may be verified in part by default rules, to be described.

4. Determine a subset V of the "visible" essential fluents. A fluent formula $\varphi(S_i)$ $(0 \leq i \leq k)$ is visible if none of $\varphi(S_j)$, $\overline{\varphi}(S_j)$, $?\varphi(S_j)$ are present for any $j > i$ (these would "conceal" $\varphi(S_i)$). V must include any visible, essential $\varphi(S_i)$ for which $\varphi(S_k)$ is not provable (*i.e.*, for which $D_0 \cup \{S_j = Result(\alpha_j, S_{j-1}) \mid j = 1, \cdots, k\} \not\vdash \varphi(S_k)$). (Note that we must have $i < k$). In other words, it must include the essential fluents whose persistence has not been proved, or cannot be proved. [24]

5. For each $\varphi(S_j) \in V$, initiate concurrent proof attempts for $\varphi(S_k)$ and $\overline{\varphi}(S_k)$, basing the former on relevant explanation closure axioms and the latter on relevant effect axioms. Again, conditions at situation S_{k-1} may be established with the aid of default rules. Terminate the computations by some algorithmic bound $T(\varphi(S_k), D_k)$. If the proof of $\varphi(S_k)$ succeeded, proceed to the next element of V (*i.e.*, $\varphi(S_i)$ need *not* be concealed). If the proof $\overline{\varphi}(S_k)$ succeeded, add $\overline{\varphi}(S_k)$ to D_k. If both attempts failed, add $?\varphi(S_k)$ to D_k.

Having tracked a plan to step N, we would attempt to prove the goals of the plan, in the same manner as we prove preconditions in step (3). Of

---

[23]The role of explanation closure axioms as "sentries" in step (4) is left implicit for the moment.

[24]This can be guaranteed by including *all* visible essential fluents, but this would defeat our purposes; more on this later.

course, in a bounded proof attempt in unrestricted Situation Calculus, step (3) and the goal proof attempt may both terminate before a target formula is confirmed, even though it may be provable in principle. However, in the event of failed precondition or goal proofs we might well use some systematic way of increasing the computational effort in steps (3) and (5) (and the final goal proof). If our underlying proof procedures are complete, this will ensure that we will *eventually* prove the preconditions and goals, if indeed they are provable.

All this presupposes that the procedure as stated is deductively sound. This hinges entirely on the soundness of the default rules employed in steps (3) and (5). We now turn to these.

Default Lemma. For each $k \in \{i, \cdots, N\}$, at the end of step (5) of the Plan Tracking Procedure, the following default rule

$$\frac{\varphi(S_i)}{\varphi(S_k)}$$

is sound for any essential fluent formula $\varphi(S_i)$ visible in D_k, *i.e.*, $D_0 \cup \{S_j = Result(\alpha_j, S_{j-1}) \mid j = 1, \cdots, k\} \vdash \varphi(S_k)$.

Proof. By induction on k. The proposition is true for $k = 0$, since then all visible formulas are $\in D_0$. Assume it is true for all $k \leq k' - 1$ ($k' > 0$). Then the first $k' - 1$ cycles through steps (1) – (5) clearly add only logical consequences of $D_0 \cup \{S_j = Result(\alpha_j, S_{j-1}) \mid j = 1, \cdots, k' - 1\}$ to $D_{k'-1}$ (aside from questioned fluents). At the k'-th cycle, the use of default rules in steps (3) and (5) to derive essential fluents $\varphi(S_{k'-1})$ is also sound by hypothesis. In step (5), by the definition of V every essential fluent $\varphi(S_i)$ such that $\varphi(S_{k'})$ is *not* deducible is concealed. Hence no such $\varphi(S_{k'})$ can be unsoundly obtained by default rules after step (4). □

Soundness is a minimal requirement if the plan tracking procedure is to provide an interesting alternative to STRIPS-like or other nonmonotonic methods. The other requirement is efficiency. How does the efficiency of the procedure compare to that of STRIPS-like methods? And does the use of the default rule provide gains over ordinary proofs based on explanation closure, like that of Proposition 1?

I don't think either of these imprecise questions can be made precise without confining oneself to some specific domain. That is an exercise we have already gone through (in the sleeping-dog proposition for *holding*), so my answers will not aspire to theoremhood. It appears that plan tracking can be roughly constant-time per plan step in STRIPS. This assumes that true preconditions can be confirmed in constant time on average (*i.e.*, preconditions do not depend on "deeply implicit" effects), and that the fluents matched by add-list and delete-list patterns do not become arbitrarily numerous. How close does the plan tracking procedure come to this level of efficiency?

Steps (1) – (3) closely resemble precondition and effect computations for STRIPS operators, and so can reasonably be expected to be of comparably low complexity. This assumes that essential fluents correspond closely to fluents that would be referenced in STRIPS operators. It also assumes that default determination of precondition fluents will usually succeed in step (3) when it succeeds via the STRIPS (persistence) assumption; and *that* depends on steps (4) and (5), so let us turn to these.

The key question is whether in step (4), V is an *easily found, small* subset of the visible, essential fluents. If V does not become arbitrarily large (even when the number of essential fluents "tracked" becomes arbitrarily large) or arbitrarily hard to find, then step (5) will also have bounded complexity — provided that the bound T is sufficiently tight. Furthermore, if V remains small, then there will be few failures in step (3) to infer essential precondition fluents by default.

The first observation about the size of V is that it is sometimes 0. That was the point of the sleeping-dog proposition for *holding*. Essentially this was made possible by the biconditional nature of the combined effect and explanation axioms: *holding* begins iff the robot (successfully) picks something up, and ceases iff he (successfully) puts down or drops something.

But exploiting this fact required a definition of $D_1, D_2, \cdots$ tailored to the domain. How is D to be determined in general? The answer is to be sought in the explanation closure axioms. V consists of essential fluents which *may* have changed as a result of the last plan step, but have not been proved to do so. But if we have an explanation closure axiom for such a fluent, we know that the only way it *could* have changed is through the occurrence of one of the actions specified in the explanation. *This immediately rules out all the essential fluents for which the known types of explanations for change do not match the action which occurred.* This should eliminate the great majority of candidates.

Knowing that only a fraction of the visible essential fluents are candidates for V is no immediate guarantee that we can avoid sifting through them all. However, if we accept the action inequality schemas (3) and the unique-names assumption (so that "action instances that don't look the same denote distinct actions"), we can use the following sort of indexing scheme to compile V effortlessly. (i) We store (names of) explanation closure axioms in a static table with the type of fluent whose change they explain as key. (ii) We also store them in another static table with the types of actions they invoke as explanations as keys (with separate storage under each alternative explanation). (iii) Finally, we maintain a dynamic table which for each explanation closure axiom contains a list of those visible, essential fluents whose change, if it occurs, would be explained by the axiom.[25] When a new essential fluent is asserted, we delete any fluent in table (iii) concealed by the new fluent (using back pointers from the fluents to the table). We look up the closure axiom relevant to the fluent in table (i), and hence store the fluent in table (iii). We can then implement step (4) of the plan tracking procedure by indexing into table (ii) for the new action α_k; we thus find the relevant "sentries" (closure axioms involving explanations which the new action instantiates), and hence retrieve the visible essential fluents potentially affected by the action from table (iii) (where we can restrict attention to those $\varphi(S_i)$ with $i < k$, as indicated in step (4)). This makes plausible the claim that STRIPS-like efficiency can be achieved, while retaining soundness.

A brief return to the *next-to* problem may help to clarify the differences between the inferences made by a STRIPS-like approach and those made by the present procedure. Let us treat fluents of form $(\neg)next\text{-}to(R, \beta, \alpha)$ (where β and σ are constants) as essential. We already have (A23) as possible explanation closure axiom for *next-to* becoming true, to which we might add:

A24. $(\forall a, x, s, s')[[next\text{-}to(R, x, s) \land \neg next\text{-}to(R, x, s') \land s' = Result(a, s)]$
$\quad \rightarrow (\exists y)[a = Go\text{-}next\text{-}to(R, y) \land \neg next\text{-}to(x, y, s)]]$

Also, the effect axiom is

A25. $(\forall a, x, s, s')[[\neg next\text{-}to(R, x, s) \land s' = Result(Go\text{-}next\text{-}to(R, x), s)]$
$\quad \rightarrow next\text{-}to(R, x, s')]$

We take (A3) and (A23) – (A25) as our *only* general axioms here, and assume initial situation S_0 such that

$\neg next\text{-}to(R, W_1, S_0), \quad \neg next\text{-}to(R, W_2, S_0), \quad remote(Door, W_1, S_0),$
$\neg next\text{-}to(R, Door, S_0), \quad next\text{-}to(W_1, W_2, S_0)$

---

[25] These are the fluents for which the axiom serves as "sentry".

Now we track the effect of "plan" $S_1 = Result(Go\text{-}next\text{-}to(R, W_1), S_0)$. Applying effect axiom (A25):

$next\text{-}to(R, W_1, S_1)$

At this point, $next\text{-}to(R, W_1, S_1)$, $\neg next\text{-}to(R, W_2, S_0)$, and $\neg next\text{-}to(R, Door, S_0)$ are visible, essential fluents. [26] The first is not in V (see step (4) of procedure) since it is a current fluent ($i = k$). $\neg next\text{-}to(R, W_2, S_0)$ leads to concurrent proof attempts for $next\text{-}to(R, W_2, S_1)$ and $\neg next\text{-}to(R, W_2, S_1)$, the former via effect axiom (A25) (which fails), and the latter via explanation axiom (A23). One way the proof strategy might proceed is by assuming $next\text{-}to(R, W_2, S1)$ and attempting to derive a contradiction from (A23). This yields

$$(\exists y)[Go\text{-}next\text{-}to(R, W_1) = Go\text{-}next\text{-}to(R, y) \wedge \neg remote(W_2, y, S_0)].$$

By inequality schemas (A3), $W_1 = y$, so

$$\neg remote(W_2, W_1, S_0).$$

This does not lead to contradiction; so since both proof attempts failed, the questioned fluent $?next\text{-}to(R, W_2, S_1)$ is posted.

Similarly $\neg next\text{-}to(R, Door, S_0)$ leads to concurrent proof attempts for $next\text{-}to(R, Door, S_1)$ and $\neg next\text{-}to(R, Door, S_1)$. The former fails. The latter may again be attempted by assuming $next\text{-}to(R, Door, S_1)$ and trying to derive a contradiction from (A23). This yields

$$(\exists y)[Go\text{-}next\text{-}to(R, W_1) = Go\text{-}next\text{-}to(R, y) \wedge \neg remote(Door, y, S_0)].$$

By schemas (A3), $W_1 = y$, so

$$\neg remote(Door, W_1, S_0),$$

---

[26] $next\text{-}to(W_1, W_2, S_0)$ is not essential as we have supplied no explanation closure axioms that apply; $W_1 \neq R$ by the unique-names assumption.

contrary to a given fact. Since persistence of the robot's not being next to the door has thus been confirmed, nothing further is done: $\neg next\text{-}to(R, Door, S_0)$ will stay visible in world description D_1 and will thus be available for default inference of $\neg next\text{-}to(R, Door, S_1)$.

Of course, since the example only recognizes one type of essential fluent, and this is the one affected by the assumed action, it cannot serve to illustrate the claim that only a small fraction of the visible essential fluents will typically fall into subset V. What it does illustrate is the distinction the approach makes between warranted and unwarranted persistence inferences — it correctly recognizes the persistence of $\neg next\text{-}to(R, Door, S_0)$, and correctly "questions" the persistence of $\neg next\text{-}to(R, W_2, S_0)$. STRIPS-like, circumscriptive, and nonmonotonic approaches would fail to make this distinction.

This still leaves the question of whether the Plan Tracking Procedure, with its reliance on default inference, provides significant gains over proofs in the style of Proposition 1.

Here the answer appears to be "not necessarily" — only in special cases. Consider how one might try to argue the affirmative. One might, for instance, point to tasks such as letter carrying. Repetitive tasks of this type may well be of considerable interest in robotic domains. Now one might argue that a nondefault approach would have to prove after each delivery that the mail bag is still at hand, and the undelivered letters still in it. But such an argument would be erroneous. A goal-directed approach that performs inferences as needed would ignore the question of where the letters are until it was time to deliver the letter x to address y. At this point the reasoner would note that x was in the bag at the outset, that only "delivering x" can change this fact, that this action did not occur, and hence that x is still in the bag. If actions are suitably indexed (*e.g.*, via keys like (*Deliver, Letter41*)), this inference process is a constant-time one, and hence cannot be significantly worse (in terms of order of complexity) than the default method.

Still, the default method has the advantage that in cases like the above even less work (*viz.*, a look-up) is needed; in other words, the constant is smaller. Also, the greater explicitness of world descriptions in the default-based approach may facilitate "mental perception" processes, such as recognition of opportunities and threats. For instance, a robot planning to change a lightbulb and to hang up a calendar might "observe himself" passing close to the tool shelf in imagining his excursion to the basement to fetch a bulb. This might prompt him to obtain a hammer and nail on the same trip.

"Observing" his proximity to the tool shelf requires maintenance of an up-to-date world model, one which reflects both change (his own location) and persistence (the tool shelf location). The STRIPS-inspired Plan Tracking Procedure seems well-suited to this kind of mental perception; for instance, one can imagine using "demons" which watch for opportune circumstances (relative to current goals). It would be harder to trigger such demons if the circumstances of interest could only be brought to light through persistence inference, however efficiently.

5 Possible extensions and probable limitations

Its supposed impotence *vis-à-vis* the frame problem is not the only deficiency commonly attributed to the Situation Calculus. It is also alleged to rule out concurrent actions, an independently changing world (external events), continuous change, nonprimitive and hierarchically structured actions, and other complex actions such as conditional and iterative ones.

While this range of topics is too broad for detailed consideration here, I will attempt a brief exculpation, with emphasis on the issue of concurrency. However, an interesting weakness that does emerge is that there is a kind of tension between the predicative language of propositional fluents, and the functional language of actions and *Result*. The former provides a simple means for describing change in any desired aspect of the world. The latter is *in principle* compatible with a broadly changing world, but is useful only to the extent that one adopts a localized view centered around one or a few agents. In particular, the rest of the world poses a hazard to consistency of the functional view. So the overall picture is that the Situation Calculus is in principle much more expressive than generally assumed, but is hampered in practise by the "parochialism" of the *Result* function.

To see that the Situation Calculus does not rule out external events and agencies, think of the situations $S' = Result(A, S)$ as being the result of A *and* situation S (rather than just the result of A *in* situation S). In other words, S may be a dynamic situation, which is headed for change no matter *what* actions are initiated in it. This view allows for any sort of deterministic external change we care to describe, such as that the sun will have risen by 8:00 O'clock on any day, no matter what:

$$(\forall a, d, s, s')[[day(d) \land contains(d, s) \land contains(d, s') \land$$
$$\neg risen(Sun, s) \land Clock\text{-}time(s') > 8 \land s' = Result(a, s)]$$
$$\rightarrow risen(Sun, s')]$$

We can even accommodate animate agencies of change, as in the arrival of buses at a bus stop. Here we might use a *Wait-for-bus* action whose "result" — thanks to the transit agency and drivers — is the presence of a bus.

However, external agencies of change do become a problem if they alter criterial fluents (those on which planned actions and goals depend) unpredictably. In such a case both effect axioms and explanation closure axioms may be invalidated. For example, if traffic on the bus route may jam, or the drivers may strike, then being at the bus stop with the fare at hand is no longer a sufficient condition for success of *Wait-for-bus*.[27] Similarly, if the money in my pocket may be arbitrarily lost or stolen, I cannot assert an axiom that its depletion requires an expenditure. Thus, I will be unable to prove the financial preconditions for boarding the bus. It would not help to include loss and theft among the possible explanations for depletion of funds, since the occurrence of these events cannot be ruled out on the grounds that some other event occurred, such as *Wait-for-bus* (or to put it differently, they weren't part of the plan).

This inability to deal effectively with a larger, more capricious world was implicit even in the earlier, sharply delimited robot's world: the closure axioms used there have highly implausible consequences if applied to the world at large. For instance, (A20), the closure axiom for cessation of *at*, together with a simple action like $S_1 = Result(Pickup(R, B), S_0)$ and the inequality schemas (A3), entails that

$$\neg(\exists x, y)\ [at(x, y, S_0) \land \neg at(x, y, S_1)],$$

i.e., nothing moved (horizontally) between S_0 and S_1. While this is a reasonable conclusion within a restricted robot's world, it is not reasonable in a world where numerous external agencies are active concurrently with the agent of interest. One way of achieving greater realism would be to place restrictions on the variables of the closure axioms. For instance, we might say that when any one of a *certain set of objects* (nondiminutive ones within the setting of interest) ceases to be *at* a location, then the robot walked, and is that object or carried it. However, it is unclear in general how to formulate such variable restrictions in a principled, uniform manner. Even agents physically remote from an object may be able to affect it (*cf.* [Georgeff87]).

Despite these limitations, the fact remains that the Situation Calculus in principle admits external events.

---

[27] In other words, we encounter the *qualification problem*.

Before moving on the the next supposed deficiency of the Situation Calculus, let us recall that it subsumes first-order logic. As such it allows the formation of complex action terms from simpler ones. This compositional potential has generally been overlooked (but see [Kowalski86], [Kowalski&Sergot86]). All of my remaining suggestions hinge on modifying or combining actions by means of functions.

In the standard "robot's world" examples (including the ones herein) change occurs in quantum jumps. However, in formalizations based on the Situation Calculus, this is not due to a limitation of the formalism (in contrast with STRIPS, for instance), but only to tradition. We can readily attain a continuous view of what goes on during an action, using a function such as $Trunc(a, t)$ for "cutting short" action a after t seconds, if it would otherwise have taken longer. The properties of truncated actions can be axiomatized using a *Time* function on situations which is real-valued and one-to-one on any set of situations constituting a "possible history of the universe" (*cf.*, [McDermott82], [Allen84]). *Trunc* allows us to say, for example, that at all situations s'' during $Walk(R, x, y)$ starting in situation s and ending in s', the fluent formula $moving\text{-}toward(R, y, s'')$ holds. Moreover, a slight generalization of explanation closure axioms allows us to extend persistence reasoning to ongoing actions. For example, we can modify (A2) appropriately by stating that the only primitive actions whose *initial segments* can lead to cessation of *holding* are *Putdown* and *Drop*.

Another simple use to which functions on actions can be put is to form *sequences* of actions.[28] In particular, we can employ a binary *Seq* function with the obvious definition

$$(\forall a, b, s) \ Result(Seq(a, b), s) = Result(b, Result(a, s)).$$

Axioms to distinguish primitive from composite actions are easily formulated, using predicates *prim* and *comp*. Another slight amendment of explanation closure axioms will then preserve their utility: in axioms like (A16) – (A24), we include the qualification $prim(a)$ in the antecedent.

Now what makes sequences of actions interesting is the possibility of using them as "macros" (larger-scale actions) in plan reasoning. For this to be profitable, however, both effect axioms and explanation closure axioms need to be formulated at the level of composite actions. Both turn out to

---

[28]McCarthy and Hayes modelled sequencing and other control regimes by inserting expressions of the Situation Calculus into sc algol programs, rather than attempting composition within the Situation Calculus.

be possible, at least within limits. For effect axioms, we can use "lemmas" about their net effect based on effects of constituent primitive actions. For explanation closure, where there are just two levels (*prim* and *comp*) of stratification, we can use entirely separate closure axioms at the *comp* level, with actions qualified as *comp(a)* in the antecedent. For instance, suppose we have defined *Move-object* as a 3-step macro (involving *Pickup*, *Walk*, and *Putdown*), along with "stationary" macros like *Empty-into*, *Open-blind*, *Unlock*, and so on. Then we can state that if an object changes location *via a comp action*, the action must be a *Move-object* (and the relocated object must be the argument, or carried by it, or is the robot, or something the robot was already carrying at the start).

Generalizing beyond two levels of stratification is certainly desirable but at this point an open problem. We need to move from the two predicates *prim* and *comp* toward a general taxonomy of actions, allowing for both composition (constructing larger-scale actions out of smaller-scale ones) and abstraction (classifying a given set of actions as being of the same abstract type). As an example of abstraction, running, walking, crawling and hopping (by humans) can all be classified as types of unmechanized travel, where the latter is in turn subsumed under (mechanized and unmechanized) travel. Preliminary research suggests that persistence reasoning based on explanation closure axioms carries over to this setting, with the requirement that "action inequality reasoning" based on schemas (A3) be replaced by "action exclusion reasoning" (*e.g.*, the incompatibility of running and walking).

One possible weakness of the Situation Calculus that emerges from a consideration of action abstraction is its somewhat counterintuitive distinction between "deterministic actions" — those (reified) actions which lead to a unique successor state via *Result* — and abstract actions — those describable only by *predicates* over (reified) actions. This problem apparently cannot be solved without substantial reformulation of the calculus (*e.g.*, in terms of a result — *relation* over actions and pairs of situations) or without losing the advantage of having plans expressed as terms, allowing their deductive extraction in the manner of Green.

Conditional actions and iteration can also be introduced with the aid of composition functions such as *If*(*test, action*) and *While*(*test, action*). The details would take us too far afield, but three things are worth pointing out. First, *test* cannot be simply construed as a reified description of a situation, since that would entail an assumption of omniscience, and perhaps even lead to paradox; consider, for instance, *If*(*Goldbach-conjecture*, *Say-yes*(*R*)) or *If*(*Committed-to-saying-yes*(*R*), *Say-no*(*R*)) (*cf.*, [Manna&Waldinger87]).

Nevertheless, tests *are* dependent on reified description of situations and that leads to the second point: such reified descriptions appear to call for duplicating the entire logic within its functional notation, including quantifiers and connectives (*e.g.*, consider "test whether there is a blue cup in every box"). This is feasible [McCarthy79], but to my mind not very attractive. The third point is that at least if we limit ourselves to "tests" which fit into our taxonomy of actions (*e.g.*, *prim* and *comp* in simple cases), explanation closure can be used to prove persistence through conditionals and loops — though naturally both change and nonchange inference can become quite complicated in proofs by cases or by induction.

Finally, I will consider concurrency at somewhat greater length. As before, the key is action composition, in this case by a parallel combinator. I will restrict myself to one for the moment, $Costart(a_1, a_2)$ which is the action consisting of simultaneously started actions a_1, a_2, and which terminates as soon as both are done (not necessarily at the same time). a_1 and a_2 need not be independent of each other, *i.e.*, the effect of each may depend upon the co-occurrence of the other (as for example, in cooperative lifting and carrying of a sofa). However, I will not concern myself with reasoning about independent actions here.

It is important to understand the intuitive interpretation of the expression

$$Result(Costart(a_1, a_2), s).$$

Just as in the case of $Result(a, s)$, this is the resultant situation when *only* the action specified by the first argument (in this case, $Costart(a_1, a_2)$) takes place. This incidently does *not* preclude external change any more than in the serial case. The notation simply says that the concurrent actions a_1 and a_2 are the only ones carried out by the agents of interest — those who from our chosen perspective generate the space of possible future histories (while any other sources of change can only be accommodated predictively).

The following example will serve to illustrate reasoning about persistence (and change) in a world with concurrent actions. In a room containing a man, a robot and a cat as the only potential agents, the only actions are that the man walks from one place to another, while the robot picks up a box containing the (inactive) cat and walks to another place. So the initial conditions (in part) and the plan are as follows:

$at(R, L_1, S_0)$, $next\text{-}to(R, B, S_0)$, $in_0(C, B, S_0)$, $liftable(B)$,
$color(C, Ginger, S_0)$, $at(H, L_0, S_0)$, $\neg(\exists z)holding(R, z, S_0)$

$$H plan = Walk(H, L_0, L_3)$$
$$R plan = Seq(Pickup(R, B), Walk(R, L_1, L_2))$$
$$Plan = Costart(H plan, R plan)$$
$$S_3 = Result(Plan, S_0)$$

Our goal is to show that the cat retains its ginger color:

(a) $\qquad color(C, Ginger, S_3)$

Since we will need to reason about the primitive parts of composite actions, we will use the following postulates.

A25. *Walk, Pickup, etc.* are primitive:

> for α an n-place function $\in \{$ *Walk, Pickup, Paint,* ...$\}$,
> $(\forall x_1, \cdots, x_n) \ prim(\alpha(x_1, \cdots, x_n))$

A26. A primitive part of two concurrent actions is a primitive part of one or the other.

$$(\forall x, y, z)[\ prim\text{-}part(x, \ Costart(y, z))$$
$$\rightarrow [prim\text{-}part(x, y) \lor prim\text{-}part(x, z)]]$$

A27. Similarly for sequences of actions

$$(\forall x, y, z)[\ prim\text{-}part(x, \ Seq(y, z))$$
$$\rightarrow [prim\text{-}part(x, y) \lor prim\text{-}part(x, z)]]$$

A28. A primitive part of a primitive action is identical with it.

$$(\forall x, y)[[prim\text{-}part(x, y) \land prim(y)] \rightarrow \ x = y]$$

To prove color persistence, we will use the following variant of closure axiom (A16):

A29. If an object ceases to be of color v in the course of a plan, that plan contains a primitive part which is the action of painting or dyeing the object some color w.

$$(\forall p, y, v, s, s')[[color(y, v, s) \land \neg color(y, v, s') \land s' = Result(p, s)]$$
$$\rightarrow (\exists x, a, w)[a \in \{Paint(x, y, w), Dye(x, y, w)\} \land$$
$$prim\text{-}part(a, p)]]$$

We can now prove our goal (a) by assuming it is false and applying (A29) with s' and p instantiated to S_3 and *Plan* respectively. We infer that for some agent x, x painted or dyed the cat and this action is a primitive part of *Plan*. Then this action is also a primitive part of *Hplan* or *Rplan* by (A26). Hence it is a primitive part of $Walk(H, L_0, L_3)$, $Pickup(R, B)$, or $Walk(R, L_1, L_2)$ by (A27). By (A25) and (A28) the painting or dyeing action is identical with one of these three actions, contrary to the inequality schemas.

This proof (and its axiomatic basis) is very simple, and that is the primary point of the illustration. However, we would also like to confirm that *change* can be inferred in such a setting, based on reasonable success criteria for the concurrent actions involved. As in the case of serial worlds, this is a little harder than inferring persistence.

For actions which have their usual preconditions satisfied, I will take spatiotemporal disjointness of their "projected paths" as a sufficient condition for their successful concurrent execution.[29] $Path(a, s)$ can be thought of as a time-varying spatial region, namely the region which the agent of action a and all the objects it "carries" is expected to occupy from $Time(s)$ onward, if a is the *only* action initiated in situation s or beyond. Projected paths are assumed to be adhered to in the performance of an action as long as any actions concurrent with it are independent of it.

To state these assumptions formally, we need to think of situations (and time) as changing continuously throughout actions, and to provide a way of referring to portions of plans preceding or following some intermediate situation at which a component action ends. For the preceding portion, we define $Costart_1(p, q)$ as the action which consists of running p to completion while running q concurrently, cutting it off if it has not yet finished when p is done.[30] We will later define $Remainder(p, q, s)$ as the "left-over" portion of p.[31]

Let us prove that the cat ends up in the same final location as the robot; *i.e.*,

---

[29] Spatiotemporal disjointness is a special case of disjoint "resource" use, if one conceives of resources broadly as including occupiable regions of space. Disjoint resource use is often a sufficient condition for compatibility of concurrent actions, though not a necessary one.

[30] As in the case of *Trunc*, this does not necessarily entail an actual cutoff, but just that *Result* applied to this action will return the situation at the point where p finishes.

[31] In the same vein, one can delay, vacuously extend, and truncate actions, using a vacuous action $Passtime(t)$ in $Seq(Passtime(t), p)$, $Costart(Passtime(t), p)$, and $Costart_1(Passtime(t), p)$.

(b) $at(C, L_2, S_3)$

introducing further axioms as needed. We begin by showing that R's *Pickup* succeeds. The modified effect axiom for *Pickup* is

A30. $(\forall a, x, y, p, s, s')[[next\text{-}to(x, y, s) \wedge liftable(y) \wedge \neg(\exists z)holding(x, z, s)$
$\wedge\ a = Pickup(x, y) \wedge compatible(a, p) \wedge$
$s' = Result(Costart_1(a, p), s)]$
$\rightarrow\ holding(x, y, s')]$

This illustrates the generalization of effect axioms to worlds with concurrent actions. Note that the result of the action is considered in the context of an arbitrary concurrent plan p.

To apply this axiom to the robot's *Pickup* action in the context of the man's *Walk*, we need to establish the compatibility of the two actions. To minimize geometrical complexities, let us assume that we are able to calculate "action corridors" for $Pickup(R, B)$ and $Walk(H, L_1, L_2)$ independently of the situation in which they are attempted, except for being given the location of R in the *Pickup* (*i.e.*, L_1). This is plausible if corridors are "generously" defined so as to allow for "elbow room" and as large a collection of objects as R or H are capable of carrying.[32] By definition the projected path of any *Pickup* feasible in isolation will be confined to the *Corridor* for that *Pickup*, and similarly for the projected path of a *Walk*:

A31. $(\forall a, u, x, y, s)[[at(x, u, s) \wedge next\text{-}to(x, y, s) \wedge liftable(y) \wedge$
$\neg(\exists z)holding(x, z, s) \wedge a = Pickup(x, y)]$
$\rightarrow\ confined\text{-}to(Path(a, s), Corridor(a, u))]$
$(\forall a, x, y, z, s)[[at(x, y, s) \wedge a = Walk(x, y, z)]$
$\rightarrow\ confined\text{-}to(Path(a, s), Corridor(a, y))]$

Call the relevant action corridors *Corridor-R-Pickup* and *Corridor-H-Walk*, and assume they are disjoint regions of space:

A32. $Corridor(Pickup(R, B), L_0) = Corridor\text{-}R\text{-}Pickup$
$Corridor(Walk(H, L_0, L_3), L_0) = Corridor\text{-}H\text{-}Walk$
$disjoint(Corridor\text{-}R\text{-}Pickup, Corridor\text{-}H\text{-}Walk)$

Clearly the antecedents in (A31) are satisfied by $a = Pickup(R, B)$ and $a = Walk(H, L_0, L_3)$ respectively, and so we can conclude with the aid

---

[32] In practice the corridors might be generalized cylinders based on the geometry of the room and the agents, plus clearance.

of (A32) that their projected paths are confined to the above-mentioned corridors. This finally puts us in a position to infer their compatibility, using

A33. $(\forall a_1, a_2, c_1, c_2, s)[[confined\text{-}to(Path(a_1, s), c_1) \land$
$confined\text{-}to(Path(a_2, s), c_2) \land disjoint(c_1, c_2)]$
$\rightarrow compatible(a_1, a_2, s)]$

The conclusion is $compatible(Pickup(R, B), Walk(H, L_0, L_3), S_0)$, and so we can instantiate (A30) and conclude that the $Pickup$ succeeds, *i.e.*, *holding* (R, B, S_1), where $S_1 = Result(Costart_1(Pickup(R, B), Walk(H, L_0, L_3)), S_0)$
To show that the robot's $Walk$, initiated right after the $Pickup$, succeeds, we begin by defining $Remainder(p, q, s)$ as a function which returns the part of p "left over" if $Costart_1(q, p)$ is executed in situation s; *i.e.*,[33]

A34. $(\forall p, q, s)\ Result(Costart(p, q),\ s) =$
$Result(Seq(Costart_1(q, p),\ Remainder(p, q, s)),\ s)$

The reason for having a situation argument in the $Remainder$ function is that the part of p left over when q finishes in general depends on initial conditions. In addition, a $Tail$ function will serve to return the remainder of a path, starting at a specified time. Then a required axiom about conformity between actual and projected paths, in the case of compatible concurrent actions, can be stated as follows:

A35. $(\forall p, q, r, s_0, s)[[compatible(p, q, s_0) \land r = Remainder(p, q, s_0) \land$
$s = Result(Costart_1(q, p), s_0)]$
$\rightarrow [Path(r, s) = Tail(Path(p, s),\ Time(s))]]$

This says that if a plan p has been partially executed concurrently with another *compatible* plan till the latter was done, then the projected path for the remainder of p is unchanged from the original projection (apart from the absence of the initial path segment already completed). Thus we can use the previously inferred compatibility of R's $Pickup$ and H's $Walk$ to calculate the projected remainder of H's $Walk$, namely,

$Tail(Path(Walk(H, L_0, L_3),\ S_0),\ Time(S_1))$.

---

[33]A suitable null element can be used when nothing is left over.

We assume that a situation reached from another via an action is temporally later, so this "tail" path will be a part of the complete *Walk*-path. Since the latter is confined to *Corridor-H-Walk*, it is clear (without going into further detail) that the former is also. So, assuming

A36. $Corridor(Walk(R, L_1, L_2), L_1) = Corridor\text{-}R\text{-}Walk$
$disjoint(Corridor\text{-}R\text{-}Walk, Corridor\text{-}H\text{-}Walk),$

we can confirm the preconditions for R's *Walk*, in

A37. $(\forall a, x, y, z, p, s, s')[[at(x, y, s) \ \wedge \ a = Walk(x, y, z) \ \wedge$
$compatible(a, p) \ \wedge \ s' = Result(Costart_1(a, p), s)]$
$\rightarrow \ at(x, z, s')]$

At least, we will be able to confirm those preconditions if we can derive the persistence of the robot's location during the *Pickup*, i.e., $at(R, L_1, S_1)$. But this follows easily from a closure axiom for change in at similar to (A29) and the primitive-part axioms (A26) and (A28).

It then remains to track the location of the cat as it gets picked up and moved along with the box. This need not detain us, since it is completely analogous to the proof of Proposition 1(c). (Of course, all additional effect axioms and explanation axioms need to allow for concurrent plans in the manner of (A29), (A30) and (A37). Also, some axioms are needed for relating alternative ways of decomposing composite plans in terms of *Costart*, *Costart*$_1$, *Seq*, and *Remainder*). □

Clearly, the main complication in tracking change has been the establishment of compatibility between concurrent actions. This was done by the rather crude device of assuming that action paths are confined to disjoint "corridors". Even that was a little tedious, suggesting (unsurprisingly) that the Situation Calculus is not well-suited to reasoning about detailed geometrical and kinematic relationships — at least not without supplementation by specialized data structures and algorithms.

My main objective, however, has been to demonstrate the ease of proving non-change, using explanation closure in a world with concurrent actions. Generalization of STRIPS-like plan tracking methods to worlds with concurrent actions remains an open problem. However, I see no serious obstacle to doing so at least in the cases where the chronological ordering of the start and end points of the set of concurrent actions can be inferred, and concurrent actions are independent of each other.

Finally, a few words are in order on McCarthy and Hayes' telephone problem, with which I started. In a sense, this is simpler than my robot-and-the-cat problem, since it involves no concurrency (look up the number and then dial it) and hence requires no action-compatibility reasoning. If we are prepared to posit such "primitive" actions as *Lookup-number*(x, y), *Dial-number*(x, y), *Carry-off*(x, y), and *Leave-home*(x), providing effect and closure axioms in terms of these actions for fluents like *know-number*(x, y, s), *has*(x, y, s), *at-home*(x, s), and *in-conversation*(x, y, s), we will have no trouble with the problem.

However, the same caveats apply as in the discussion of external agencies of change at the beginning of this section. If we are not careful about the way we qualify success conditions for actions, or variable restrictions in explanation closure axioms, our axioms will be patently false in the world at large. This is certainly something to be avoided in a general "commonsense reasoner," yet we do not at this point have a general, principled method of doing so.

I believe that the most promising research avenue in dealing with this difficulty lies in the application of probabilistic methods such as those of [Pearl88], [Bacchus88], [Kyburg88], [Dean&Kanazawa88], and [Weber89]. These methods allow one to give expression to the "statistical" aspect of our experience and knowledge of the world. For instance, people know that a penny left on the sidewalk is much more likely to stay put for a day than a dollar bill, that a car parked at night on a residential street will stay in place much longer on average than one parked on a weekday at a supermarket, and so on. In part, this knowledge is due to direct or linguistically transmitted observation, and in part it derives from related knowledge about *why*, and *how often*, people or other agents do the things which account for change. The dollar bill illustrates both aspects: we have a pretty good idea from direct observation about the density of pedestrian traffic on various kinds of streets at various times, and we also know that few people would fail to notice a dollar bill on the sidewalk, and having noticed it, fail to retrieve it. As well, we know about winds and their effects. Such "statistical" knowledge is absolutely indispensable in coping with a complex and more or less capricious world. It may even constitute the bulk of our general knowledge.

The role of this knowledge with respect to the frame problem is that it provides a stable, yet pliable base on which we can superimpose our episodic knowledge. Since this base merely supplies statistical priors, it yields to the pressure of event reports that run against the odds, replacing probable persistence with known change. So, at least, one hopes it will be in a comprehensive probabilistic representation of knowledge. Effect axioms and explanation closure axioms would be recast probabilistically in such a representation, and supplemented with direct empirical probabilities for various kinds of change. If we regard the success of an action as a mere likelihood, given that the major preconditions are met, we avoid a futile quest for perfectly reliable preconditions. If we regard certain actions capable of effecting change as merely improbable, rather than as assuredly absent, we avoid unfounded beliefs about the lack of change in the world at large, and about the inevitable success of our plans.

Of course, the nonmonotonic theorists can reasonably claim to be striving toward just this kind of resilient, yet amendable knowledge base. There is, however, a fundamental difference between probabilistic and nonmonotonic methods of inferring persistence. According to the former, McCarthy and Hayes' phone stays put, in the absence of information to the contrary, because we know perfectly well that phones very rarely get moved (and indeed, we know *why* they don't). According to the latter, it stays put in the absence of information to the contrary simply because there *is* no information to the contrary. The former is sensitive to the statistical facts of the world (such as that the phone is much less likely to depart than the intended party at the other end), while the latter is turned entirely inwards.

6 Conclusions

I have provided evidence that explanation closure axioms provide a succinct encoding of nonchange in serial worlds with fully specified actions, and a basis for STRIPS-like, but monotonic inference of change and nonchange in such worlds. As such, they are certainly preferable to frame axioms; they also offer advantages over circumscriptive and nonmonotonic approaches, in that they relate nonchange to intuitively transparent explanations for change, retain an effective proof theory, and avoid unwarranted persistence inferences.

Furthermore, unlike frame axioms, explanation closure axioms generalize to worlds with concurrent actions. I led up to an illustration of this claim by enumerating some generally unknown capabilities of the Situation Calculus with respect to external events, continuous change, and composite actions, all of which seem compatible with explanation closure. Throughout, I adhered to the original *Result*-formalism, so as to retain the treatment of plans as terms, and hence the possibility of extracting plans from proofs.

Limitations of the Situation Calculus I noted along the way were the tediousness of reasoning about simple spatiotemporal relationships (without special methods), and more importantly, the parochial view of the world enforced by the *Result*-formalism. It works well only for domains in which the actions capable of effecting salient change are fully and reliably known. I suggested that probabilistic methods offer the best hope of overcoming this limitation.

Directions for further research are generalizations of the results (especially the "sleeping dog" strategy) to more complex theories of the world (with external events, continuous change, higher-level actions, and concurrency), investigation of planning (as opposed to mere "plan tracking") using deductive or other methods, and the study of all of these issues within a probabilistic framework.

Acknowledgements I am grateful to Scott Goodwin and Randy Goebel for providing astute criticisms and important pointers to the literature when this work was in the early stages. Others who provided valuable comments and suggestions were James Allen and several members of a graduate class at the University of Rochester, especially Jay Weber and Hans Koomen. The paper would have languished in semicompleted state without the generous and timely help of Chung Hee Hwang on many aspects of the paper, both small and large. The initial research was supported by the Natural Sciences and Engineering Research Council of Canada under Operating Grant A8818.

7 Bibliography

Allen, J. F. "Towards a general theory of action and time," *Artificial Intelligence 23*, 1984.

Bacchus, F. "Statistically founded degrees of belief," Proceedings of the Seventh Biennial Conference of the Canadian Society for Computational Studies of Intelligence (CSCSI '88), June 6–10, Edmonton, Alberta 1988.

Brown, F. M., ed. *The Frame Problem in Artificial Intelligence*, Morgan Kaufmann, 1987.

Dean, J. and K. Kanazawa. "Probabilistic Causal Reasoning," Proceedings of the Seventh Biennial Conference of the Canadian Society for Computational Studies of Intelligence (CSCSI '88), June 6–10, Edmonton, Alberta 1988.

Fikes, R. E. and N. J. Nilsson. "STRIPS: A new approach to the application of theorem-proving to problem-solving," *Proceedings of the Second International Joint Conference on AI (IJCAI '71)*, Morgan Kaufmann, 1971.

Fodor, J. A. "Modules, frames, fridgeons, sleeping dogs, and the music of the spheres," *The Robot's Dilemma: The Frame Problem in Artificial Intelligence*, Pylyshyn, Z. W., ed., Ablex, 1987.

Georgeff, M. P. and A. M. Lansky. *Reasoning about Actions and Plans*, Morgan Kaufmann, 1987.

Georgeff, M. P. "Actions, processes, causality," *Reasoning about Actions and Plans*, Georgeff, M. P. and A. M. Lansky, eds., Morgan Kaufmann, 1987.

Green, C. "Application of theorem proving to problem solving," *Proceedings of the International Joint Conference on AI (IJCAI '69)*, Morgan Kaufmann, 1969.

Haas, A. R. "The case for domain-specific frame axioms," *The Frame Problem in Artificial Intelligence*, Brown, F. M., ed., Morgan Kaufmann, 1987.

Hanks, S. and D. McDermott. "Nonmonotonic logic and temporal projection," *Artificial Intelligence 33*, 1987.

Hayes, P. J., "What the frame problem is and isn't," *The Robot's Dilemma: The Frame Problem in Artificial Intelligence*, Pylyshyn, Z. W., ed., Ablex Publishing Corp., 1987.

Kowalski, R. A. "Logic for Problem Solving," *Artificial Intelligence Series 7*, Elsevier, 1979.

Kowalski, R. A. "Database updates in the event calculus," Dept. of Computing, Imperial College, July, DOC 86/12, London, England, 1986.

Kowalski, R. A. and M. J. Sergot. "A logic-based calculus of events," *New Generation Computing 4*, 1986.

Kyburg, H. "Probabilistic inference and probabilistic reasoning," Proceedings of The Fourth Workshop on Uncertainty in AI, Philadelphia, PA, 1988.

Lansky, A. L. "A representation of parallel activity based on events, structure, and causality," *Reasoning about Actions and Plans*, Georgeff, M. P. and A. M. Lansky, eds., Morgan Kaufmann, 1987.

Lifschitz, V. "Formal theories of action," *The Frame Problem in Artificial Intelligence*, Brown, F. M., ed., Morgan Kaufmann, 1987.

Manna, Z. and R. Waldinger. "A theory of plans," *Reasoning about Actions and Plans*, Georgeff, M. P. and A. M. Lansky, eds., Morgan Kaufmann, 1987.

McCarthy, J. "Programs with common sense," *Semantic Information Processing*, M. Minsky, MIT Press, 1968.

McCarthy, J. "First-order theories of individual concepts and propositions," *Machine Intelligence 9*, D. Michie, ed., Edinburgh University Press, 1979.

McCarthy, J. "Circumscription – a form of non-monotonic reasoning," *Artificial Intelligence 13*, 1980.

McCarthy, J. "Applications of circumscription to formalizing commonsense knowledge," Proceedings of the Nonmonotonic Reasoning Workshop, New Paltz, NY Oct. 17–19, 1986.

McCarthy, J. and P. J. Hayes. "Some philiosophical problems from the standpoint of artificial intelligence, " *Machine Intelligence 4*, B. Meltzer and D. Michie, eds., Edinburgh University Press, 1969.

McDermott, D., "A temporal logic for reasoning about processes and plans," *Cognitive Science 6*, 1982.

Pearl, J. *Probabilistic Reasoning in Intelligent Systems*, Morgan Kaufmann, 1988.

Pylyshyn, Z. W. *The Robot's Dilemma: The Frame Problem in Artificial Intelligence*, Ablex, 1987.

Raphael, B. "The frame problem in problem solving systems," *Artificial Intelligence and Heuristic Programming*, N. V. Findler and B. Meltzer, eds., Edinburgh, 1971.

Reiter, R. "A logic for default reasoning," *Artificial Intelligence 13*, 1980.

Schank, R. C. and R. P. Abelson. *Scripts, Plans, Goals and Understanding*, Erlbaum, 1977.

Weber, J. "Statistical inference and causal reasoning," *Proceedings Eleventh International Joint Conference on AI (IJCAI '89)*, Morgan Kaufmann, 1989.

A Framework for Reasoning with Defaults

*I-UCLA-C*Hector Geffner and Judea Pearl *I-UCLA-CG*

1 Motivation

Belief commitment and belief revision are two distinctive characteristics of common sense reasoning which have so far resisted satisfactory formal accounts. Classical logic for instance, cannot accommodate belief revision: new information can only add new theorems. Probability theory, on the other hand, has difficulties in accommodating belief commitment: propositions are believed only to a certain degree which dynamically changes with the acquisition of new information.

Recent years have witnessed a renovated effort to enhance both formalisms in order to overcome these limitations. Those working within the probabilistic framework have tried to devise 'acceptance rules' to work on top of a body of probabilistic knowledge, as to create a body of believed, though defeasible, set of propositions (see [Loui87a] for a review). Those working within the logic framework have developed 'non-monotonic' inference systems [AI Journal80] based on classical logic, in which old 'theorems' can be defeated by new 'axioms'.

In comparison, the probabilistic approach has enjoyed a significant advantage over the logical approach. A body of probabilistic knowledge together with an acceptance rule uniquely determines the conclusions that can be derived. Both the probabilistic knowledge base and the acceptance rule can be modified so as to capture those conclusions which appear reasonable. Non-monotonic logics, on the other hand, have lacked such *clear semantics*. Not only it has been difficult to tune the set of defeasible rules so as to 'entail' the desired conclusions (*e.g.*, [Hanks&McDermott86]), but it has even been difficult to characterize what the conclusions sanctioned by a body of defaults ought to be (see, for instance, [Touretzky *et al.*87], "A clash of intuitions ...").

On the positive side, as noted by [Glymour&Thomason84] and [Loui87a], the logical approach has shown that a *qualitative* account of non-monotonic reasoning which does not require either 'acceptance rules' or the expense

69

H.E. Kyburg, Jr. et al. (eds.), Knowledge Representation and Defeasible Reasoning, 69–87.
© 1990 Kluwer Academic Publishers. Printed in the Netherlands.

and precision of computing with numbers, might be possible, and has even suggested ways in which such an account can be constructed.

In this paper we attempt to show that it is possible to combine the best of both worlds. We present a system of defeasible inference which operates very much like natural deduction systems in logic and, yet, can be justified on probabilistic grounds. The resulting system is closely related to the logic of conditionals developed by Adams [Adams66], as we interpret defaults of the form $p \rightarrow q$ as constraining the conditional probability of q given p to be infinitesimally close to one. On the other hand, the appeal to a notion of relevance in our formulation bears a close relationship to those approaches in AI which investigate defeasible reasoning as resulting from the interaction of competing arguments (*e.g.*, [Touretzky86], [Poole85], [Nute86], [Horty *et al.*87], [Loui87b]).

The structure of the paper is as follows. In §2 we define the core of the system, discuss the need for providing an account of the notion of irrelevance, and present such an account. In §3 we illustrate the behavior of the system on a number of standard examples. Related work is discussed §4 and we conclude, in §5, with a summary of the main contributions.

2   A System of Defeasible Inference

2.1   The Core

The logic we shall present will be referred as **L** and will be characterized by a set of rules of inference in the style of natural deduction systems. The goal of **L** is to sanction as theorems the highly likely consequences that follow from a given context. A context $\Gamma = E_K$ is defined by a background context K, which expresses generic knowledge relevant to the domain of discourse, and an evidence set E, which expresses the particular facts which characterize the particular situation of interest. A background context K, $K = \langle L, D \rangle$, is built from a set of closed wffs L and a set D of defaults. Defaults are denoted by meta-linguistic expressions of the form $p \rightarrow q$, where p and q are closed wffs. We use default schemas of the form $p(x) \rightarrow q(x)$, where p and q are wffs with free variables among those of $x = \{x_1, \ldots, x_n\}$, to represent the infinite collection of defaults that results from substituting the variables x_i by ground terms of the language.

The system of inference implicitly defines the set of conclusions h that follow from a given context E_K, with $K = \langle L, D \rangle$. We write $E \vdash_K p$ to denote that sentence p is derivable from context E_K in L. Likewise, $E, \{q\} \vdash_K p$, abbreviated $E, q \mathrel{\vdash\mkern-9mu\sim}_K p$, states that p is derivable from the context that results from adding the sentence q to E. We use the notation $\vdash$ to stand for derivability in classical first order logic.

The initial set of rules we consider is the following:

Rule 1 (Defaults) If $p \rightarrow q \in D$ then $p \mathrel{\vdash\mkern-9mu\sim}_K q$

Rule 2 (Deduction) If $L, E \vdash p$ then $E \mathrel{\vdash\mkern-9mu\sim}_K p$

Rule 3 (Augmentation) If $E \mathrel{\vdash\mkern-9mu\sim}_K p$ and $E \mathrel{\vdash\mkern-9mu\sim}_K q$ then $E, p \mathrel{\vdash\mkern-9mu\sim}_K q$

Rule 4 (Reduction) If $E \mathrel{\vdash\mkern-9mu\sim}_K p$ and $E, p \mathrel{\vdash\mkern-9mu\sim}_K q$ then $E \mathrel{\vdash\mkern-9mu\sim}_K q$

Rule 5 (Disjunction) If $E, p \mathrel{\vdash\mkern-9mu\sim}_K r$ and $E, q \mathrel{\vdash\mkern-9mu\sim}_K r$ then $E, p \vee q \mathrel{\vdash\mkern-9mu\sim}_K r$

Rule 1 permits us to conclude the consequent of a default when its antecedent is all that has been learned. Rule 2 states that theorems that logically follow from a set of formulas can be concluded in any context containing those formulas. Rule 3 permits the incorporation of an established conclusion to the current evidence set, without affecting the status of any other derived conclusions. Rule 4 says that any conclusion that follows from a context whose evidence set was augmented with a conclusion established in that context, also follows from the original context alone. Finally, Rule 5 permits reasoning by cases.

Rules 2–5 can be shown to share the inferential power of the system of rules proposed by [Adams66] for deriving what he calls the probabilistic consequences of a given set of conditionals. They also appear, in a different form, in several logics of conditionals (see [Nute84]). Interestingly, in the context of non-monotonic logics, Gabbay [Gabbay85] proposed a minimal set of rules which includes Rules 3 and 4 above.

We proceed now to investigate some of the properties of the system of defeasible inference defined by Rules 1–5. Later on, we shall discuss some of its limitations as we enhance the system with a sixth rule motivated by the goal of capturing irrelevance conditions.

2.1.1 Some Meta-Theorems

Theorem 1 (Deductive Closure) If $E \mathrel{\vdash\mkern-9mu\sim}_K p'$, $E \mathrel{\vdash\mkern-9mu\sim}_K p''$, and $E, p', p'' \vdash p$, then $E \mathrel{\vdash\mkern-9mu\sim}_K p$.

By *augmentation* we obtain $E, p' \mathrel{\mid\!\sim}_K p''$ and by *deduction* we get $E, p', p'' \mathrel{\mid\!\sim}_K p$. Applying *reduction* twice, the theorem follows.

Theorem 2 (Context equivalence) If $E, p \mathrel{\mid\!\sim}_K r$ and $p \equiv q$ then $E, q \mathrel{\mid\!\sim}_K r$.

By *deduction* we can obtain both $E, p \mathrel{\mid\!\sim}_K q$ and $E, q \mathrel{\mid\!\sim}_K p$. We can therefore augment $E, p \mathrel{\mid\!\sim}_K r$ to get $E, p, q \mathrel{\mid\!\sim}_K r$, which can then be *reduced* to obtain $E, q \mathrel{\mid\!\sim}_K r$.

Theorem 3 (Presuppositions) If $E \mathrel{\mid\!\sim}_K p$ and $E, q \mathrel{\mid\!\sim}_K \neg p$ then $E \mathrel{\mid\!\sim}_K \neg q$.

From $E, q \mathrel{\mid\!\sim}_K \neg p$, we can obtain by *deductive closure* both $E, q \mathrel{\mid\!\sim}_K \neg p \vee \neg q$ and $E, \neg q \mathrel{\mid\!\sim}_K \neg p \vee \neg q$. Then, by *disjunction* and *context equivalence*, $E \mathrel{\mid\!\sim}_K \neg p \vee \neg q$ follows. Finally, since $E \mathrel{\mid\!\sim}_K p$, we get $E \mathrel{\mid\!\sim}_K \neg q$ by *deductive closure*.

Theorem 4 (Parallel Reduction) If $E, p, q \mathrel{\mid\!\sim}_K r$, $E \mathrel{\mid\!\sim}_K p$, and $E \mathrel{\mid\!\sim}_K q$, then $E \mathrel{\mid\!\sim}_K r$.

By *augmentation*, $E, p \mathrel{\mid\!\sim}_K q$ follows. As a result, by *reduction* we get $E, p \mathrel{\mid\!\sim}_K r$ and by a further *reduction* $E \mathrel{\mid\!\sim}_K r$.

Some non-theorems:

$E \vdash p$ and $p \mathrel{\mid\!\sim}_K q$ do necessarily imply $E \mathrel{\mid\!\sim}_K q$

$E \mathrel{\mid\!\sim}_K p$ and $E' \mathrel{\mid\!\sim}_K p$ do not necessarily imply $E, E' \mathrel{\mid\!\sim}_K p$

Note that the first non-theorem is clearly undesirable. If accepted, it would endow our system with monotonic characteristics of classical logic, precluding exceptions like non-flying birds, *etc.* The second one would incorrectly authorize to conclude for instance, that John will be happy when married to both a Jane and Mary, on the grounds that he will be happy when married to either one of them.

As we shall see later, the system of Rules 1–5 defines an extremely conservative non-monotonic logic. In fact, the inferences sanctioned by these rules do no involve any type of assumptions regarding information absent from the background context. To illustrate this fact, let $K = \langle L, D \rangle$ and $K' = \langle L', D' \rangle$ denote two background contexts, such that $K \subseteq K'$, *i.e.*, $L \subseteq L'$ and $D \subseteq D'$. We have the following theorem:

Theorem 5 (K-monotonicity) If $E \vdash_K p$ and $K \subseteq K'$ then $E \vdash_{K'} p$.

This theorem easily follows by induction on the minimal length n of the derivation of $E \vdash_K p$. If $n = 1$, it means that h was derived from E in K either by Rule 1 or by Rule 2. In either case it is easy to show that h can be derived from E in K'. Let us assume now that h is derivable from E in K in n steps, $n > 1$, and that the theorem holds for all the proofs with length $m < n$. Clearly the last step in the derivation must involve one of the Rules 3–5. In any case, the antecedents of such rule must be derivable in a number of steps smaller than n and, therefore, by the inductive assumption, they are also derivable in K', from which it follows that, using the same rule, h is also derivable from E in K'.

Finally, Rules 1–5 can be shown to be *probabilistically sound*. That is, for a background context $K = \langle L, D \rangle$, a set of formulas E and a formula p, such that $E \vdash_K p$ holds, it can be shown that any probability distribution $P_K(\cdot)$ which makes $P_K(L) = 1$, yields $P_K(p \mid E)$ as close to unity as desired, short of actually being one, if it constraints the conditional probability of the default instances $q \to r$ in D to be sufficiently close to one.[1] We omit the proof here, and refer the interested reader to [Adams66].

Example 1 (Specificity).
The system of Rules 1–5 defines a conservative non-monotonic system capable of accounting for some simple patterns of default reasoning. Consider for instance a background context K comprising the following expressions involving birds (B), red birds (RB), penguins (P) and flying things (F) (see Figure 1):[2]

$$L = \{ \text{P}(x) \Rightarrow \text{B}(x),\ \text{RB}(x) \Rightarrow \text{B}(x)\}$$
$$D = \{ \text{B}(x) \to \text{F}(x),\ \text{P}(x) \to \neg\text{F}(x)\}$$

We can then simply prove that an arbitrary bird, say tim, is likely to fly:

1. $\text{B}(\text{tim}) \vdash_K \text{F}(\text{tim})$; Defaults

by virtue of Rule 1. On the same grounds, we can also prove that an arbitrary penguin is likely not to fly:

---

[1] Actually it is sufficient for $P_K(\cdot)$ to constraint the default instances used in the proof of $E \vdash_K p$ only, rather than all the default instances in D.

[2] Let us recall that expressions of the form $p(x) \to q(x)$ stand for default schemas. Well formed formulas $P(x)$ with free variables among those of x, stand for closed universal sentences of the form $\forall x.\, P(x)$. '$\Rightarrow$' denotes material implication.

$$L = \{ P(x) \Rightarrow B(x),\ RB(x) \Rightarrow B(x) \}$$
$$D = \{ B(x) \rightarrow F(x),\ P(x) \rightarrow \neg F(x) \}$$

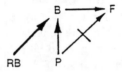

Figure 1: Example 1: Background Context

2. $P(\text{tim}) \mathrel{\vdash\!\!\!\sim}_K \neg F(\text{tim})$; Defaults

Note that there is no contradiction in permitting both conclusions to follow; we have two different conclusions — $F(\text{tim})$ and $\neg F(\text{tim})$ — in two different contexts: $\{B(\text{tim})\}_K$ and $\{P(\text{tim})\}_K$.

Nonetheless, it is not difficult to notice that the latter context subsumes the former one. That is, since penguins are known to be birds, we have by means of Rule 2 that:

3. $P(\text{tim}) \mathrel{\vdash\!\!\!\sim}_K B(\text{tim})$; Deduction

which, by virtue of Rule 3, permits us to assimilate $B(\text{tim})$ in the context $\{P(\text{tim})\}_K$ to yield:

4. $P(\text{tim}), B(\text{tim}) \mathrel{\vdash\!\!\!\sim}_K \neg F(\text{tim})$; Augmentation 2,3

Note that unlike default logic or circumscription, the 'exceptionality' of subclasses does not need to be explicated in order to obtain the expected behavior. Such behavior automatically emerges from the probabilistic interpretation embodied in the rules, and the distinction they make between formulas in the background context K from those in the evidence set E. The reader can verify, for instance, that the behavior we have just illustrated would no be follow if we had included the fact that 'penguins are birds' in E rather than in K. Defaults in K presume the information in the background context. Information in the evidence set, on the other hand, represents evidence that needs to be assimilated in order to reach a conclusion.

While the interpretation of defaults embedded in Rules 1–5 captures certain pattern of reasoning that escape more traditional formulations, it falls short in other important aspects. Consider for instance that we want to derive than an arbitrary red bird flies. Intuitively, we would expect this conclusion to follow from the information given in K. Nonetheless, such conclusion fails to be sanctioned as the rules above cannot maintain derived conclusions in the presence of irrelevant information. So, while we can derive that a bird flies, $B(\text{tim}) \mathrel{\vdash\!\!\!\sim}_K F(\text{tim})$, there is no way to prove that a *red* bird flies: $RB(\text{tim}), B(\text{tim}) \mathrel{\vdash\!\!\!\sim}_K F(\text{tim})$.

What the interpretation of defaults embodied in Rules 1–5 misses is the common sense convention by which a default is expected to "hold" in the absence of conflicting evidence. That is, given a default $p \rightarrow q$ in D, we

expect $E, p \not\vdash_K q$ to hold whenever the body of evidence E does not provide
support for $\neg q$.

In the example above for instance, we expect the default B(tim) $\rightarrow$
F(tim) to hold upon learning RB(tim), since there is no reason to suspect
"color" to be related to "not flying."

A different situation would arise if we consider the evidence P(tim) instead of RB(tim). In this case, a conflict between the defaults B(tim) $\rightarrow$
F(tim) and P(tim) $\rightarrow$ ¬F(tim) arises and the status of the proposition F(tim)
may be affected.

We will say in the first case that RB(tim) is *irrelevant* to the default
B(tim) $\rightarrow$ F(tim) and write $I_K(\text{B(tim)} \rightarrow \text{F(tim)} \mid \text{RB(tim)})$. In the sec-
ond case, on the other hand, we say that P(tim) is *relevant* to the default
B(tim) $\rightarrow$ F(tim). Rule 6, the last of rule of **L**, makes use of these irrelevance
conditions. When a body of evidence E is irrelevant to a default $p \rightarrow q$,
Rule 6 permits to conclude q from both p and E:

Rule 6 (Irrelevance)
   If $p \rightarrow q \in K$ and $I_K(p \rightarrow q \mid E)$ then $E, p \vdash_K q$

Probabilistically, the predicate $I_K(p \rightarrow q \mid E)$ encodes an assumption
about conditional independence by which $P_K(q \mid E, p)$ is regarded to be
approximately equal to $P_K(q \mid p)$. In the next subsection we will focus on
the details concerning the characterization of $I_K(p \rightarrow q \mid E)$. The following
derivation illustrates its use in establishing that a red bird is likely to fly, in
the above background context:

1. $I_K(\text{B(tim)} \rightarrow \neg\text{F(tim)} \mid \text{RB(tim)})$; Definition of $I_K(\cdot)$, below.
2. RB(tim), B(tim) $\vdash_K$ F(tim)   ; Irrelevance 1
3. RB(tim) $\vdash_K$ B(tim)   ; Deduction
4. RB(tim) $\vdash_K$ F(tim)   ; Reduction 2,3. $\square$

Note that the irrelevance rule relaxes Rule 1 above, permitting to assert
a default consequent given *both* the default antecedent *and* an irrelevant
body of evidence. Thus, in this example we can now conclude that a bird –
Tim – flies, "even" if it is a red bird (step 3). The rest of the proof simply
relies on the fact that red birds are birds, making it possible to reduce B(tim)
from the premises.

2.2   Irrelevance

The common interpretation of defaults of the type $p \to q$ is in the form of a disposition to believe q when p is believed and no reason for not doing so is apparent. This reading has two implications we need to be concerned with: one which requires conclusions to be retractable in the light of new refuting evidence; the second which requires conclusions to persist in the light of new but irrelevant evidence. The probabilistic rules 1–5 excel at the first task: their soundness prevents preserving a conclusion in a context in which its high probability cannot be guaranteed. In Example 1 we have shown, for instance, that while birds can be assumed to fly, birds known to be penguins cannot. On the other hand, as we have seen, the same body of rules fails badly in the second aspect. We have seen that while we can conclude that an arbitrary bird flies, we are not authorized to conclude that a red bird flies, even though there is no evidence relating "color" to "not flying".

This 'conservatism' is a consequence of the probabilistic soundness of Rules 1–5. Indeed, while there is no reason to believe that 'redness' could affect the likelihood of flying, that situation is perfectly consistent, and since a sound conclusion must hold in *every* probabilistic model of K, the conclusion $RB(\texttt{tim}), B(\texttt{tim}) \mathrel{\vdash\!\!\!\!\sim}_K F(\texttt{tim})$ is not probabilistically sound and, therefore, it is not derivable from Rules 1–5.

Clearly, if we want to capture these inferences we need to restrict the family of probabilistic models relative to which a given conclusion must be tested for acceptance. We want those models to embed the assumption that no conclusion should be retracted when there is no reason for doing so. The account of the irrelevance conditions below is built around this intuition.

First of all, we associate to each default $p \to q$ in K a sentence $p \Rightarrow q$ obtained by replacing the meta-linguistic default connective by material implication. We refer to the sentences so obtained as *assumptions*. Furthermore, we define an *argument* to be a pair $\langle E, AS \rangle$, where E is a body of evidence and AS is a set of assumptions logically consistent with E and K. This set of assumptions is called the argument *support*. We say then that a proposition p is *arguable* in a context E_K, if there is an argument $\langle E, AS \rangle$ for p, i.e., if $E, K, AS \vdash p$.

The notion of "arguability" provides an upper bound characterization of the conclusions that can be accepted in a given context. As a first approximation this suggests to regard a body of evidence E as relevant to a default $p \to q$, when an argument for $\neg q$ can be constructed from E and p. That characterization, however, turns out to be too weak. Often, certain assumptions are expected not to be applicable in certain contexts. For instance, the assumption bird(tim) $\Rightarrow$ fly(tim) is expected not to be applicable when tim is known to be a penguin. Thus in testing relevance we do not want to consider all possible arguments, but only those arguments which are supported by admissible sets of assumptions. We refer to non-admissible sets of assumptions as *dominated* assumption sets, and define them as follows.

We say that a set of assumptions AS is *dominated* by a default $p \to q$ in K, if $p \vdash_{\overline{K}} \neg AS$, where $\neg AS$ stands for the negation of the conjunction of assumptions in AS. In that case we also say that $p \to q$ dominates all the arguments supported by AS.

As an illustration, in the example above, the default P(tim) $\to \neg$F(tim) dominates the assumption set $AS = \{$B(tim) $\Rightarrow$ F(tim)$\}$, as we can derive P(tim) $\vdash_{\overline{K}}$ B(Tim) $\wedge \neg$F(tim), and therefore, by deductive closure, P(tim) $\vdash_{\overline{K}} \neg AS$. It follows then that arguments supported by AS will be dominated by the default P(tim) $\to \neg$F(tim).

The definition of irrelevance below refines the tentative definition above concerning the relevance of evidence E to a default $p \to q$, by excluding from consideration those arguments which are dominated by $p \to q$.

Thus, we say that a body of evidence E is *irrelevant* to a default $p \to q$, written $I_K(p \to q \mid E)$, if $p \to q$ dominates every argument $\langle E \cup \{p\}, AS \rangle$ for $\neg q$. Otherwise, we say that E is *relevant* to $p \to q$.

In the Example 1 above, for instance, RB(tim) turns out to be irrelevant to the default B(tim) $\to$ F(tim), in virtue of the absence of arguments in support of the proposition $\neg$F(tim) in the context $\{$RB(tim), B(tim)$\}_K$. We have, therefore, that the irrelevance assertion $I_K(\text{B(tim)} \to \text{F(tim)} \mid \text{RB(tim)})$ holds. In the same example though, the irrelevance assertion $I_K(\text{B(tim)} \to \text{F(tim)} \mid \text{P(}$ does not hold, due to the presence of an argument for $\neg$F(tim) with a support $AS = \{$P(tim) $\Rightarrow \neg$F(Tim)$\}$, which is not dominated by the default B(Tim) $\to$ F(tim).

The definition of irrelevance above has a convenient graphical interpretation in those default theories, like inheritance hierarchies, in which strict and default rules can be represented as directed graph structures. In those cases, arguments correspond to (hyper) paths in the graph, and the irrelevance criterion, to a form of graph separation. Furthermore, arguments which are dominated by a default $p \to q$ appear as paths leading to $\neg q$ 'going through' some defeasible consequence of p (see Figure 2).

Figure 2: An argument for ~q dominated by the default p → q

$$L = \{ \, A(x) \wedge Y(x) \Rightarrow USt(x) \, \}$$
$$D = \{ \, A(x) \rightarrow W(x), \; USt(x) \rightarrow A(x), \; USt(x) \rightarrow \neg W(x) \, \}$$

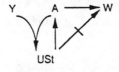

Figure 3: Example 2: Background Context

Such an interpretation suggests for instance (see Figure 1), that RB(tim) is irrelevant to the default P(tim) → ¬F(tim), as the only path which connects RB(tim) with F(tim) contains a proposition B(tim) which follows from P(tim).

Formally, I_K(P(tim) → ¬F(tim) | RB(tim)) can be shown to hold, since we can derive P(tim) $\vdash_{\widetilde{K}}$ B(tim) ∧ ¬F(Tim), and therefore, that the default P(tim) → ¬F(tim) dominates the assumption B(tim) ⇒ F(tim) and any argument supported by it.

It follows then, by means of the irrelevance rule, that a penguin which also happens to be a (strange) red bird will still be expected not to fly, *i.e.*, RB(tim), P(tim) $\vdash_{\widetilde{K}}$ ¬F(tim) .

3   Examples

In this section we illustrate the behavior of the system of defeasible inference determined by Rules 1–6 on a number of examples.

Example 2. (Default Preferences). Let the background context K contain the following defaults : "adults (A) work (W)", "university students (USt) are adults but do not work", and "adults which are young (Y) are university students", expressed as (Figure 3):

$$L \;=\; \{\, A(x) \land Y(x) \Rightarrow USt(x) \,\}$$
$$D \;=\; \{\, A(x) \to W(x),\; USt(x) \to A(x),\; USt(x) \to \neg W(x) \,\}$$

We want to show in K that a young adult, say Ken (k), is likely not to work, *i.e.*, A(k), Y(k) $\vdash_{\widetilde{K}}$ ¬W(k). The proof proceeds as follows:

1.	USt(k) $\vdash_{\widetilde{K}}$ ¬W(k)	; Defaults
2.	USt(k) $\vdash_{\widetilde{K}}$ A(k)	; Defaults
3.	USt(k) $\vdash_{\widetilde{K}}$ ¬(A(k) ⇒ W(k))	; Deductive Closure 1,2
4.	I_K(USt(k) → ¬W(k)	A(k), Y(k))	; No non-dominated argument fo
5.	A(k), Y(k), USt(k) $\vdash_{\widetilde{K}}$ ¬W(k)	; Irrelevance 4
6.	A(k), Y(k) $\vdash_{\widetilde{K}}$ USt(k)	; Defaults
7.	A(k), Y(k) $\vdash_{\widetilde{K}}$ ¬W(k)	; Reduction 5,6.

It is interesting to note that in the same background context, an adult is expected not to be a student:

8.	A(k) $\vdash_{\widetilde{K}}$ W(k)	; Defaults
9.	A(k), USt(k) $\vdash_{\widetilde{K}}$ ¬W(k)	; Augmentation 1,2
10.	A(k) $\vdash_{\widetilde{K}}$ ¬USt(k)	; Presuppositions (Thm 3) 8,9

That is, since we are willing to jump to the conclusion that an adults works, and to the opposite conclusion when an adult is known to be a university student then, in the first case, it is presumed that the adult is not a university student. Such presupposition clearly vanishes when a reason to believe the adult to be a university student (*e.g.*, Ken is young) becomes available.

Example 3 (No coupling). Consider now the background context with defaults as depicted in Figure 4.

The goal is to derive that A's are likely to be F's. The proof for $A(a) \vdash_K F(a)$ can be constructed as follows:

1. $I_K(C(a) \to F(a) \mid A(a), \neg G(a))$; No arguments for $\neg F(a)$
2. $A(a), \neg G(a), C(a) \vdash_K F(a)$; Irrelevance 1
3. $I_K(B(a) \to C(a) \mid A(a), \neg G(a))$; No arguments for $\neg C(a)$
4. $A(a), B(a), \neg G(a) \vdash_K C(a)$; Irrelevance 3
5. $A(a) \vdash_K \neg G(a)$; Defaults
6. $A(a) \vdash_K B(a)$; Defaults
7. $A(a) \vdash_K C(a)$; Parallel Reduction 4,5,6
8. $A(a) \vdash_K F(a)$; Parallel Reduction 2,5,7. $\square$

Note that $B(a) \not\vdash_K F(a)$ even though B is a 'parent' of A. In terms of [Touretzky *et al.*87], thus, there is no coupling in **L** between the property of a class and the properties of its superclasses.

Example 4 (Cases).[3] Let us consider now a background context K with defaults "quakers (q) are doves (d)," "republicans (r) are hawks (h)" and "both doves and hawks are politically motivated (p)," together with the fact that nobody is both a hawk and a dove (Figure 5):

$$L = \{ \neg(d(x) \land h(x)) \}$$
$$D = \{ q(x) \to d(x), \ r(x) \to h(x), \ d(x) \to p(x), \ h(x) \to p(x) \}$$

We want to show that somebody, say Nixon (n), that is both a quaker and a republican is likely to be politically motivated. The proof requires reasoning by cases (Rule 5). First we need to show $q(n), r(n) \vdash_K d(n) \lor h(n)$. The first part, $q(n), r(n), d(n) \vdash_K d(n) \lor h(n)$ follows trivially by *deduction*. The second part, $q(n), r(n), \neg d(n) \vdash_K d(n) \lor h(n)$ requires the *irrelevance* of $E = \{q(n), \neg d(n)\}$ to $r(n) \to h(n)$. Finally, since by *irrelevance* and *disjunction* we get $q(n), r(n), d(n) \lor h(n) \vdash_K p(n)$, the target conclusion follows by *reduction*. Note however that neither $q(n), r(n) \vdash_K d(n)$ nor $q(n), r(n) \vdash_K h(n)$ are

---

[3] Due to Matt Ginsberg.

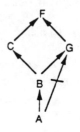

Figure 4: Example 3: A's are F's but B's are not

$$L = \{ \neg(d(x) \wedge h(x)) \}$$
$$D = \{ q(x) \rightarrow d(x),\ r(x) \rightarrow h(x),\ d(x) \rightarrow p(x),\ h(x) \rightarrow p(x) \}$$

Figure 5: Is Nixon politically motivated?

sanctioned by **L**, as the required irrelevance conditions $I_K(\mathtt{q(n)} \to \mathtt{d(n)} \mid \mathtt{r(n)})$ and $I_K(\mathtt{r(n)} \to \mathtt{h(n)} \mid \mathtt{q(n)})$ do not hold.

Example 5 (Inconsistency). Defaults in **L** may sometimes give rise to inconsistent conclusions. For instance, a background containing two defaults "birds fly" and "birds do not fly" will give rise to two contradictory conclusions $\mathtt{bird(tim)} \mathrel{\vphantom{|}\smash{\mathop{\sim}\limits_{K}}} \mathtt{fly(tim)}$ and $\mathtt{bird(tim)} \mathrel{\vphantom{|}\smash{\mathop{\sim}\limits_{K}}} \neg\mathtt{fly(tim)}$. This behavior does not arise in most default reasoning frameworks as these defaults are regarded as conflicting rather than as inconsistent. **L** makes a distinction between conflict and inconsistency. This distinction is useful as, usually, inconsistent default theories reveal something wrong about the encoding. Defaults $p \to q$, $p \wedge q \to r$ and $p \to \neg r$ constitute another example of inconsistent defaults.

4 Related Work

Most non-monotonic logics proposed in AI require the addition of a number of preferences in order to produce the expected behavior from a set of interacting defaults. In recent years, several novel systems of defeasible inference have been proposed which appeal to specificity considerations in order to avoid the need for explicating some of these preferences. In this section we briefly review some of these systems and compare them to **L**.

The formalism for defeasible reasoning closest to **L**, is perhaps the one proposed by [Pollock88]. Pollock also combines probabilities and arguments, though in a different manner. He regards defaults of the form 'most A's are B's' as constraints on the conditional probability relating the *general properties* A and B. Pollock relates defeasible inference to what philosophers have called direct inference: that is, the inference of the *definite probabilities* relating members of certain classes, from the *indefinite probabilities* relating the classes themselves. He regards a conditional indefinite probability $P(B \mid A) \geq r$, for some r reasonably high, together with a given instance a of A, as constituting a *prima facie reason* (*i.e.*, defeasible reason) for believing a to be a B, with a strength which depends on r. *Prima facie* reasons combine to form arguments, and undefeated arguments support what he calls warranted conclusions. The rest of his account is concerned with the conditions for defeat.

The main feature that distinguishes **L** from Pollock's framework, is the form it takes. **L** is a *calculus* of defeasible inference; obtaining a calculus from Pollock's principles, on the other hand, does not appear to be an easy task. Indeed, the complexity associated with the many different kinds of defeat Pollock introduces contrasts sharply with the simplicity of **L**. This simplicity arises both from the different probabilistic semantics that underlies **L**, in which we are only interested in the qualitative behavior that emerges when the relevant probabilities are considered to be arbitrary high or low, and from the limited use of arguments for identifying admissible conditional independence assumptions only. Additionally, as Pollock does not distinguish 'primitive' defaults from 'derived' defaults, he finds himself in the need of an account of the complex notion of projectibility [Pollock88].

A system close in form to the one proposed here is Delgrande's [Delgrande87]. As the core of **L** can be put in correspondence with the logic of indicative conditionals developed by Adams [Adams66], Delgrande's system share its core with a variation of the logic of counterfactuals developed by Stalnaker and Lewis. Delgrande's default logic is thus grounded on a possible world semantics rather than on probabilities. The possible world semantics however does not circumvent the need for supplementing the system core with assumptions about irrelevance. In this regard, while we characterize the notion of irrelevance in terms of arguments and embed it in the meta-predicate $I_K(\cdot)$, Delgrande appeals to fixed point constructions, which he uses to generate an additional numbers of defaults and assertions which are added to the original set. Likewise, Delgrande's system is able to capture more inferences than **L**, as our notion of "defeasible consequence" forms part of Delgrande's object language. It is not clear, however, whether the expressivity gained with such powerful language justifies its associated complexity.

In Loui's [87b] system, default reasoning emerges from dialectical argumentation. A set of rules are used to evaluate arguments in terms of several syntactic attributes, like 'has more evidence', 'is more specific', *etc.* This set of rules appears to embed most of the inference rules that define our system and can be mostly justified in terms of them. Still, it is possible to find some differences. One such difference is that Loui's system is not (deductively) closed. It is possible to believe propositions A and B, and still fail to believe $A \wedge B$ [Loui87b]. In our scheme, on the other, the deductive closure of believed propositions is established by Theorem 1. In particular, if the arguments for A and B in a given theory are completely symmetric, and $A \wedge B$ does not follow for some reason (like conflicting evidence), then neither A nor B will follow. Another difference arises due to the absolute preference given by his system to arguments based on 'more evidence'. This preference leads sometimes to changes in belief originated in the assimilation of propositions which are expected to hold, in contradiction to our augmentation rule.

The system reported by Touretzky [Touretzky86] was motivated by the goal of providing a semantics for inheritance hierarchies with exceptions, capable of avoiding the problems of redundant paths which troubled shortest-path inheritance reasoners. In that work, Touretzky pioneered the approach in which specificity relations embedded in inheritance hierarchies are used to filter spurious ambiguities. Rather than a calculus of defeasible inference however, Touretzky's inferential distance can be regarded as a refinement of Reiter's default logic (see [Etherington88]). As such, in order to determine whether a proposition follows from a network, it is necessary to test whether the proposition holds in all the remaining extensions. Similar observations apply to Poole's [Poole85] specificity selection criterion.

Unlike Loui's, Touretzky's and Poole's systems, Nute [Nute86] and Horty *et al.* [Horty *et al.*87] define the set of defeasible consequences inductively. Specificity considerations play a central role in these definitions. Horty *et al.* define an 'skeptical inheritance' algorithm for homogeneous (defaults only) inheritance hierarchies; Nute's system deals with a larger superset of linear arguments, comprising both defeasible and undefeasible rules. L differs from Horty's *et al.* scheme in the treatment of ambiguity, and from Nute's, in the use of defaults in the determination of specificity. Likewise, L rests on a different semantic basis.

5 Summary

The main contribution of the proposed framework for defeasible inference is the emergence of a more precise proof-theoretic and semantic account of defaults. A default $p \rightarrow q$ in a background context K, represents a clear-cut constraint on states of affairs, stating that, if p is *all* that has been learned, then q can be concluded. We appealed to probability theory to uncover the logic that governs this type of context dependent implications.

Additionally, we have introduced a notion of irrelevance as a set of sufficient conditions under which belief in the consequent of a given default can be preserved upon acquiring new information. This notion plays a role similar to frame axioms in AI: we assume defaults to hold upon acquiring a new piece of evidence E, as long as the evidence does not provide a reason for not doing so.[4]

---

[4] We have not discussed here the semantic basis for the irrelevance account nor the

The proposed scheme avoids the problem of multiple, spurious extensions that often arise in default logic. Moreover, it does not require to consider the different extensions in order to prove that a given proposition follows from a given theory. Proofs proceed 'inside the logic', and look very much like proofs constructed in natural deduction systems.

The system is also clean: the only appeal to 'non-provability' occurs in determining when a proposition can be safely assumed to be irrelevant to a given default. But, in contrast to most non-monotonic logics, the definition of non-monotonic provability is not circular. The irrelevance predicate used for constructing proofs can be inferred syntactically in terms of arguments.

Acknowledgment   We wish to thank E. Adams, F. Bacchus, D. Etherington, M. Ginsberg, P. Hayes, H. Kyburg, R. Loui and D. Poole for useful comments on earlier versions of this paper. We also wish to thank Michelle Pearl for drawing the figures.

---

conditions under which it can be shown to be consistent. This and related issues will be considered elsewhere.

6 Bibliography

———, Special Issue on Non-Monotonic Logics, *AI Journal 13*, 1980.

Adams, E. "Probability and the logic of conditionals," in *Aspects of Inductive Logic*, J. Hintikka and P. Suppes, eds., Elsevier, 1966.

Delgrande, J. "An approach to default reasoning based on a first-order conditional logic," *Proceedings AAAI—87*, 1987.

Etherington, D. *Reasoning with Incomplete Information*, Pitman, 1988.

Gabbay, D. M. "Theoretical foundations for non-monotonic reasoning in expert systems," *Logics and Models of Concurrent Systems*, K. R. Apt, ed., Springer-Verlag, 1985.

Glymour, C., and R. Thomason. "Default reasoning and the logic of theory perturbation," *Proceedings Non-Monotonic Reasoning Workshop*, New Paltz, 1984.

Hanks, S., and D. McDermott. "Default reasoning, non-monotonic logics, and the frame problem," *Proceedings of the AAAI-86*, Philadelphia, PA, pp. 328–333, 1986.

Loui, R. P. "Real rules of inference," *Communication and Cognition – AI 5*, 1988.

Loui, R. P. "Defeat among arguments: a system of defeasible inference," *Computational Intelligence*, 1987.

Nute, D. "Conditional logic," *Handbook of Philosophical Logic 2*, D. Gabbay and F. Guenthner, eds., pp. 387–439.

Nute, D. "LDR: a logic for defeasible reasoning," ACMC Research Report 01–0013, University of Georgia, Athens, 1986.

Pollock, J. "Defeasible reasoning and the statistical syllogism," Unpublished manuscript, 1988.

Poole, D. "On the comparison of theories: preferring the most specific explanation," *Proceedings of the IJCAI-85*, Los Angeles, 1985.

Reiter, R. "A logic for default Reasoning," *AI Journal 13*, pp. 81–132, 1980.

Touretzky, D. *The Mathematics of Inheritance Systems*, Pitman, 1986.

Touretzky, D., Horty, J., and R. Thomason. "A clash of intuitions: the current state of non-monotonic multiple inheritance systems," *Proceedings of the IJCAI-87*, Milano, Italy, 1987.

1131294

The Frame Problem and Relevant Predication

J. Michael Dunn

The "frame problem" is, if one may use the term about so new a field, a "perennial problem" for AI.[1] Like the perennial problems of philosophy, it is most likely not one single problem, but rather a matrix of problems. I would not dare myself to say just what "*the* frame problem" is. But it has commonly been interpreted as explaining how it is that our belief systems rest on a "frame" of default assumptions, and how it is that this frame has a certain resiliency, in that changes in our beliefs do not seem to necessitate wholesale changes in this frame.[2]

Fodor [Fodor87] raises a certain obstacle to those who would seek to say that the frame problem is not a real problem. He does this by way of an invented property, being a "fridgeon." We shall look into the details below, but I want to quote one possible objection that Fodor raises against himself, and his answer. Objection: "Being a fridgeon isn't a real property. Answer: I'll be damned if I see why not, but have it your way. The frame problem is now the problem of saying what a 'real property' is."

Now I suspect that Fodor overstated his case for the sake of rhetoric. The frame problem may not be *just* the problem of saying what a "real property" is. But Fodor does argue persuasively that this is at least part of the frame problem. I find this very exciting, for [Dunn87] purports to give

[1]I wish to thank Jeff Horty for seeing the "relevance" of [Fodor87] to the theory of relevant predication. and for bringing Fodor's paper to my attention. A version of this paper was presented to a meeting of the Society for Exact Philosophy in May, 1988, at the University of Rochester, and at the Automated Reasoning Project at the Australian National University in July, 1988. I wish to thank the organizer of the SEP Meeting, Henry Kyburg, and the coordinators of the ARP, Michael McRobbie and Robert Meyer, for their support and for giving me the occasions to try out this paper. Also it should be mentioned that [Glymour87] mentions a possible connection between the frame problem and Anderson and Belnap's relevant implication, but not I think with the particular application in mind which I discuss here.

[2]The frame problem was originally introduced by [McCarthy&Hayes69] and there it clearly had to do with the problem of describing what remains unchanged by an event. When an event occurs, this necessitates changes in our beliefs about the world. But changes in our beliefs about the world may come about for other reasons, and this is why "the frame problem" as described above is more general.

H.E. Kyburg, Jr. et al. (eds.), Knowledge Representation and Defeasible Reasoning, 89–95.

the apparatus which (at least read in an ontological tone of voice) does says what a "real property" is. Now we turn to details.

Fodor's immediate interlocutor is McDermott [McDermott87], who says that the frame problem is avoided in practice by what he labels "the sleeping dog strategy." The idea is that AI systems, "to reason about result (s, e) (*i.e.*, about the result of an event in a situation), compute all the effects of e in situation s, make those changes, and leave the rest of s (the 'sleeping dogs') alone."

Fodor [Fodor87] replies that the sleeping dog strategy does not solve the problem. "What it does is to convert the frame problem FROM A PROBLEM ABOUT BELIEF FIXATION INTO A PROBLEM ABOUT ONTOLOGY (or, what comes to much the same thing for present purposes, from a problem about belief fixation into a problem about canonical notation)."[3]

Going on, Fodor explains that "the sleeping dog strategy depends on assuming that most of the facts don't change from one event to the next. And the trouble with that assumption is that WHETHER IT'S TRUE DEPENDS ON HOW YOU INDIVIDUATE FACTS. Or, to put it a little more in the formal mode, if you want to use a sleeping dog algorithm to update your database, you must first devise a system of canonical representation for the facts; (algorithms — of course — work on facts AS REPRESENTED)."

Fodor then poses the following conundrum, which we will label "The Fridgeon Effect." Thus Fodor says that "it has got to work out on any acceptable model that when I turn the refrigerator on, certain of my beliefs about the refrigerator — and about other things, of course — become candidates for getting updated ....On the other hand, it should also fall out of a solution of the frame problem that a lot of my beliefs — indeed, MOST of my beliefs — do NOT become candidates for updating ...."

He then goes on. "Consider a certain relational property that physical particles have from time to time: the property of BEING A FRIDGEON. I define 'x is a fridgeon at t' as follows: *x is a fridgeon at t iff x is a particle at t and my fridge is on at t.* It is of course a consequence of this definition that, when I turn my fridge on, I CHANGE THE STATE OF EVERY PHYSICAL PARTICLE IN THE UNIVERSE; namely, every physical particle becomes a fridgeon."

Fodor goes on to say "that the sleeping dog strategy is EMPTY unless we have, together with the strategy, some idea of what is to count as a fact for the purposes at hand. Moreover, this notion — of, as we might call it, a

---

[3]Caps here, and in other quotations, are Fodor's.

COMPUTATIONALLY RELEVANT fact — will have to be FORMALIZED
if we propose to implement the sleeping dog strategy as a computational algorithm. ...So if we want to keep the kooky facts out of the data base, and
keep the computationally relevant facts, we will have to find a way of distinguishing kooky facts from computationally relevant ones IN VIRTUE OF
THE FORM OF THEIR CANONICAL REPRESENTATIONS. The frame
problem, in its current guise, is the problem of formalizing this distinction."

Now Dunn [Dunn87] presents just such a formalization through its notion of "relevant predication." It should perhaps be mentioned that the
choice of the word "relevant" by both Fodor and myself is a matter of
serendipity — neither was under the influence of the other. My choice was
of course motivated by the fact that my formalization occurs in the context
of the Anderson-Belnap relevance logics. Fodor's choice was undoubtedly
motivated by the natural meaning of the word (as was undoubtedly the
Anderson-Belnap choice that was the ancestor of mine).

The idea of [Dunn87] is that one can define relevant predication so that

$$(1) \qquad [\rho x \ \phi x](a) =_{def} \forall x(x = a \to \phi x),$$

where $\to$ stands for relevant implication in the Anderson-Belnap system **R**.
The motive is to avoid what [Dunn87] calls "hokey" properties, which seem
to be same kind of thing that Fodor calls "kooky" properties. The key
motivating example was to rule out it's being a property of say Reagan that
Socrates is wise, *i.e.*, in symbols

$$(2) \qquad [\rho x \ Q](a),$$

which when spelled out using the definition above, amounts to the irrelevant
implication

$$(3) \qquad \forall x(x = a \to Q).$$

Now let us consider the so-called property of being a fridgeon. To say
that an object a has this as a relevant property then is

$$(4) \qquad [\rho x(Pxt \land Fbt)](a).$$

One of the results of [Dunn87] is that even when a formula Gx is of the
kind that determines relevant properties, a compound formula having Gx
as a component need not be. In particular it is easy to see that a formula
of the form $Gx \land Q$ need not determine a relevant property of a even when
Ga and Q are both true. To show this, we use "Fact 4" of [Dunn87], to
wit that relevant properties are closed under relevant implication (an easy
consequence of the definition). And so if

(5) $[\rho x(Gx \wedge Q)](a)$,

then (since in general $P \wedge Q \to Q$ is a theorem of **R**)

(6) $[\rho x\ Q](a)$,

when clearly this last need not be so.

The application to the so-called property of being a fridgeon should now be clear. The formulae $Pxt \wedge Fbt$ need not determine a relevant property of an object a, even though Pxt does and Fbt holds as well (to facilitate discussion we assume t fixed here). If it did determine a relevant property of a, then (by the move from (5) to (6) above), Fbt would as well, but this last is absurd. Fodor's fridge being on is as clear an example of an irrelevant property as one could wish for. Indeed, clearly the whole force of his conundrum derives from this intuition.

Now something should be clarified about my approach to forestall possible objections. I can imagine someone replying that my formalization does not tell us that Fodor's fridge being on is not a relevant property of some particle somewhere, say on Mars. This is our intuition, but (i) our intuition may be wrong, and (ii) even if the intuition is right, my approach does nothing about telling us why it is right.

Both of these points are essentially correct. With respect to (i), I must admit that there are strange things in the world of physics. Bell-type phenomena have been used by some to argue for action at a distance, and it is entirely possible that there is some yet to be discovered connection that links Fodor's refrigerator to particles throughout the universe in some tight physical way. But of course this unlikely eventuality causes no problems for our formalism. It just turns out then that, much to our amazement, (2) is true after all, and it is a relevant property of the particle on Mars that Fodor's refrigerator is on. Of course Fodor's puzzle is now no longer a "mere philosophical problem," to be solved by some appropriate formalism. It is a real problem. And if "The Fridgeon Effect" is not an isolated phenomenon, but widely shared by appliances and other furniture of the universe, it looks as if the universe has conspired against AI.

With respect to (ii), it is acknowledged in [Dunn87] that relevance logic can no more tell us which are the relevant atomic properties, than can classical logic tells us which are the true atomic propositions. Classical logic does not tell us what the truths are (excepting some important limiting cases, the logically valid ones). But it does tell you that if you accept such-and-such propositions as true, then you must accept certain others as true as well, but not necessarily all propositions thus follow. Similarly all the theory of relevant predication can do is to tell you that if such-and-such are relevant properties, then these others must be too, but not necessarily those "kooky" ones.

It is presently the job of a database creator to decide what atomic predicates should be used in representing facts, and which facts and rules should be put into the database. Using relevance logic as the logic of the database, so as to provide the tool of relevant predication, would further add to the job description of the database creator that he or she must decide which predicates are relevant and add that information to the database. Indeed, one strategy might be to use only relevant atomic predicates, but this still would not have all compound formulas determining relevant properties.

It is tempting to end the paper here and simply await the arrival of the Turing Award for having solved the frame problem (or at least some consulting job with a local startup software firm on "the By-pass"). But candor compels me to add two remarks. First, although I think that relevant predication may well provide a solution to Fodor's problem, I am not sure in my own mind how relevant Fodor's problem is to the frame problem.[4] Of course, as I said initially, *the* frame problem is many things to many people, so I shall rephrase this. I am not sure how relevant Fodor's problem is to any interesting problem about updating belief systems.

After all, forgetting the business about relevant predication, the fact that the particle *a* on Mars is a fridgeon, understood as just meaning "*a* is a particle and Fodor's fridge is on," is deducible from facts already in the database (assuming it has the information that *a* is a particle) plus the new fact that Fodor's fridge is on. It is scarcely surprising that when a new fact is added to a database that a large number of new deductive

---

[4] In this I share some of the reservations of Hayes [Hayes 7]. However obviously I do not share Hayes' "of course" in his saying "now, *of course*, there will never be a notation, in this sense, which has the miraculous property that only cognitively useful concepts can be expressed in it; a notation whose very grammar distinguishes between kosher and kooky concepts." Indeed, I propose the notation of relevant predication to mark just such distinctions, though as I acknowledge above, it is up to the database creator to decide which predicates are relevant. Thus I agree with Hayes in his fundamental conclusion that one "can make such distinctions, using both global structural properties of the set of beliefs and direct advice in in the form of beliefs about the relevance of other beliefs," and propose the apparatus of relevant predication as a device to mark the distinctions that Hayes thinks can be made. I believe that Hayes thinks that these distinctions would be shown and not said, but a distinction worth making is a distinction worth having a notation for.

consequences result. Indeed, if $p_1, p_2, \ldots$ are distinct propositions, there are the consequences: Fodor's fridge is on or p_1, Fodor's fridge is on for p_2, $\ldots$. But surely those new deductive consequences do not need to be explicitly updated. The logic will take care of that.

The second remark that I need to make is that using relevance logic for databases is largely an unproven enterprise, and I have no idea how computationally feasible it is. One might think that it is computationally very unfeasible, for Urquhart [Urquhart84] has shown that the logic **R** is undecidable even in its propositional logic fragment (and with relevant predication we are using quantifiers and identity as well). But this consideration is not as compelling as it may first appear.

For one thing, the fact that classical propositional logic is decidable is not as useful in practice as it may seem. Tautological inferences from databases in even a modest number of atomic propositions appear computationally intractable. It could be that relevance logic behaves better computationally with real life applications than does classical logic. The requirement that there be some connection of relevance between premises and conclusion would seem to be a kind of built-in heuristics. Conceivably one would spend less time in the search tree looking up paths that look irrelevant to the putative conclusion, but just might lead to a contradiction (from which in classical logic, of course everything follows, no matter how irrelevant it looks).

The Automated Reasoning Project in Canberra is actively exploring the strategy of using relevance logic in database applications (*cf.* McRobbie, Thistlewaite, and Meyer [McRobbie *et al.*82], and Thistlewaite, McRobbie, and Meyer [Thistlewaite *et al.*88]), and although it is too early I think to make any predictions, they have nonetheless obtained respectable results in terms of speed. And there are other reasons to prefer relevance logic as well. The best known of these to date has to do with the problem of inconsistent databases (one would not want some profound consequence drawn from some piddling contradiction) — *cf.* [Belnap78]. But it could be that Fodor has pointed his finger in the direction of another.

1 Bibliography

Belnap, N. "A useful four-valued logic," *Modern Uses of Multiple-Valued Logic*, J.M. Dunn and G. Epstein, eds., Reidel, pp. 8–37, 1978.

Dunn, J.M. "Relevant predication 1: the formal theory," *Journal of Philosophical Logic 16*, pp. 347–381, 1987.

Fodor, J. "Modules, frames, fridgeons, sleeping dogs, and the music of the spheres," *The Robot's Dilemma*, Z. Pylyshyn, ed., Ablex, pp. 139–149, 1987.

Glymour, C. "Android epistemology and the frame problem comments on Dennett's 'cognitive wheels'," *The Robot's Dilemma*, Z. Pylyshyn, ed., Ablex, pp. 65–75, 1987.

Hayes, P. 1987, "What the frame problem is and isn't," *The Robot's Dilemma*, Z. Pylyshyn, ed., Ablex, pp. 123–137, 1987.

McCarthy, J. and P. Hayes. "Some philosophical problems from the standpoint of artificial intelligence," *Machine Intelligence*, B. and D. Michie, eds., Elsevier, pp. 463–502, 1969.

McDermott, D. 1987, "We've Been Framed, Or Why AI Is Innocent of the Frame Problem," *The Robot's Dilemma*, Z. Pylyshyn, ed., Ablex, pp. 113–122, 1987.

McRobbie, M., Thistlewaite, P., and R. Meyer. "A mechanized decision procedure for non-Classical logics: the program KRIPKE," *The Journal of Symbolic Logic 47*, p. 717 (abstract), 1982.

Thistlewaite, P., Meyer, R., and M. McRobbie. *Automated Theorem-proving in Non-classical Logics, Research Notes in Theoretical Computer Science*, Wiley, 1988.

Urquhart, A. "The undecidability of entailment and relevant implication," *The Journal of Symbolic Logic 49*, pp. 1059–1073, 1984.

Part II.
Representation Problems and Ordinary Language:

11.31295

Thing and Thought

Don Perlis I-MD-C

Self-reference or self-applicability is an important theme throughout Computer Science, from recursive programs to undecidability results, from bootstrapping to program semantics. A relative latecomer to this list is Artificial Intelligence, for only recently has self-reference been seen as an important attribute of intelligent systems. This paper will give a bird's-eye (and personal) overview of some of the issues surrounding self-reference in AI, especially those related to non-monotonicity, reification, and intentionality.

0   Introduction

A thought can be about (other) thoughts. Non-monotonic reasoning (NMR) is a hot-bed of examples of this. When we use NMR, we employ a knowledge modality. What are the objects to which such a modality applies? Some say they are abstract propositions, supposedly rather ethereal entities like thoughts. Now thoughts are usually regarded as taking objects (one thinks about X) and this in turn presents us with two sets of issues: one the one hand, thoughts themselves are often the objects X of (other) thoughts, and as such become reified into things (of sorts); and on the other hand, thoughts do have objects (of which we say the thoughts are 'about'). Both of these ideas are problematic, as we shall see.

I find it convenient to think that the former (reification) has taken three complementary directions, which I will style as ideal reasoning, pseudo-ideal reasoning, and situated reasoning. The first involves traditional concerns with consistent formal foundations for deduction in general, including most formal approaches to commonsense reasoning, in which a single formal fixed theory is the end result. The second makes small concessions on this framework in order to capture some computational power, especially with respect to consistency. The third emphasizes the inconsistent and real-time nature of reasoning in a complex environment and seeks ways to deal with these issues as part of a general 'finitary' intelligence mechanism[1]

---

[1]See references by Barwise&Perry, Elgot-Drapkin, (Elgot-)Drapkin&Perlis, Rosen-schein&Kaelbling, and Suchman.

H.E. Kyburg, Jr. et al. (eds.), Knowledge Representation and Defeasible Reasoning, 99–117.
© 1990 Kluwer Academic Publishers. Printed in the Netherlands.

While I have called these complementary, there is an important sense of progression, in which one goes from envisioning reasoning as a once-and-for-all affair (ideal), to a matter of some adjustments (pseudo-ideal), and then to embracing change as the very life-blood of reasoning (situated). This will become clearer as we proceed. I will present these themes largely with illustrations from my own work, simply because I feel much more confident in discussing my efforts. But many others have made major strides in these areas, and I have tried to indicate this throughout.

In all three approaches, the focus has largely emphasized the topics of self-reference and reification, *i.e.*, the study of mechanisms that explicitly represent as formal syntactic objects much of the agent's own behavior. This has as its motivation the observation that much intelligent behavior seems to involve an ability to model ones environment including oneself and ones reasoning, and especially to perform introspective reasoning such as judging that one does now know a certain fact. In other words, a principal aim is to give the agent reasoned control of its own reasoning.

It turns out that there are difficulties in formally representing self-reference. Much work has approached this problem in terms of first-order logic and the paradoxes of self-reference. In ideal and pseudo-ideal settings, consistency is a principal concern; in situated settings, concern centers on the ability to correct inconsistencies when they are observed. We will begin by presented some rather general ideas about self-reference in regard to the beliefs or thoughts a reasoner may have.

In §1 we present classical reification issues from logic, especially some of the famous paradoxes. In §2–4, we consider related difficulties in common-sense reasoning with respect to ideal, pseudo-ideal, and situated reasoning. Finally, in §5 we briefly return to the theme of aboutness.

1   Reification: Relations as Objects

Consider the sentence "I WAS WRONG BUT I DIDN'T LIE." In more formal dress, this might be written as

$$(\exists x)(Said(I, x) \ \& \ \neg True(x) \ \& \ \neg Know(I, \neg True(x)))$$

Here an unstated proposition x has been reified as argument to *Said* and *True*, and in turn $\neg True(x)$ has been reified as argument to *Know*. Thus nested reifications are a commonplace in natural language, although this is not always apparent until formalized.

Now, the syntactic status of these reified arguments has been left open. Are they arguments to predicates *Said, True, Know*, or are the latter modal operators applied directly to propositions? In a sense this seems a mere quibble, although much has been made of the difference. We will return to this later. First, we illustrate some standard concerns and uses of reification in the following three 'problems' from artificial intelligence.

Brother Problem (Moore): Let B be the proposition that I have a brother. Then the following represents a sound inference, where we abbreviate $Know$ to K:

$$B \rightarrow KB$$

$$\neg KB$$

$$\neg B$$

Moore [Moore83] pointed this out as an example of 'autoepistemic' reasoning. Here $B \rightarrow KB$ is taken to be a piece of general information people tend to accept: If I have a brother then I will know it. But to be applied as shown, also $\neg KB$ must be known or accepted. How is this determined — *i.e.*, how does a reasoner decide that he or she does not know whether (or that) he/she has a brother. It cannot be general information, since many people DO have brothers. In the example, it is intended that, by some introspective mechanism, a person is able to tell that he or she does not have knowledge of a brother, and from this the rest (the conclusion $\neg B$) follows. We will return to this example briefly later.

Reagan Problem (McCarthy): McCarthy (private communication) has presented a pair of problems. The first is as follows: How do we know that we do not know whether Ronald Reagan is (at this moment) seated or standing? Note that this, like the Brother problem, hinges on deciding that we do *not* have certain information.

Gorbachev Problem (McCarthy):   The companion problem to the above:
How do we know that Gorbachev does not know whether Ronald Reagan is
(at this moment) seated or standing? This problem is more subtle, for we
are to assess not our own lack of information, but rather that of someone
else.

We shall not dwell on these problems now. Rather they are intended
here to illustrate the importance of thoughts and sentences as themselves
being objects of thought. We will briefly reconsider them later.

McCarthy [McCarthy79] has emphasized the importance of reification
for commonsense reasoning. One underlying problem is that when concepts
are reified into formal objects, certain paradoxical statements may become
expressible. The desired solution would be to defuse the paradoxes while
retaining a broadly expressive formalism.

The table below presents a brief overview of a small portion of the history
of efforts to deal with reification in mathematical logic, along with parallel
and analogous developments on the study of program semantics. The text
indicates some of the highlights. We use T in place of *True*.

What is indicated is that expressiveness can lead (via reification) to
paradoxes. Gilmore and Kripke found similar promising approaches using iterations based on simple non-paradoxical cases, that happily stop
short of contradictions (shown as L in the table). Some of the earliest
technical work on reification arose in relation to self-reference, especially
in an effort to come to terms with the Liar paradox (which is a kind
of reification problem). This was found to have connections with many
foundational issues, including principles of set formation (Russell's paradox) which in turn seem to have some bearing on commonsense reasoning.

	REIFICATION DIFFICUL-TIES		PROGRAM SE-MANTICS
Expressive Power	α		prog
Reification axioms	$T\alpha \leftrightarrow \alpha$		prog(prog)
Diagonal anomalies	$L \leftrightarrow \neg T(L)$	Russell 1903 Tarski 1936	paradoxical combinator of Curry
Iteration to fixed point with gap	$t_1, t_2, \ldots, L$ $f_1, f2, \ldots, L$	Gilmore 1974 Kripke 1975	Scott's fixed point construction
Axiomatize iterations in theory (incl. gap)	$\neg T(L)$ $\neg T(\neg L)$ $T\alpha \leftrightarrow \alpha*$	Feferman 1984 Perlis 1985	axioms?

One way to state the problem is that the formal 'Tarskian' schema

$$True(`\alpha') \leftrightarrow \alpha$$

is inconsistent with any reasonably expressive theory. Here 'α' is a constant (reified name) for the sentence α. We will routinely leave quotes off, however. A breakthrough occurred in Paul Gilmore's work, which was given further impact by Kripke's paper on truth definitions. It turns out that Gilmore's work provided a way to turn Kripke's informal (semantic) insights into a formal (syntactic) theory of self-referential properties. This was noticed independently by Feferman and myself.[2]

The new approach was to combine ideas of Gilmore [Gilmore74] for set theory and Kripke [Kripke75] for truth semantics, ending up again with a formal schema like Tarski's but modified to look like

$$T(\alpha) \leftrightarrow \alpha^*$$

where α^* is a simple syntactic variant on α.[3]

We showed this allows consistent reification of arbitrary first-order properties (*i.e.*, their defining wffs α) into first-order objects 'α' so that the two

---

[2] Whether a similar syntactic approach can be given for program semantics remains open.

[3] Feferman uses different notation. Our papers were submitted almost simultaneously, his in March 1982 and mine in February 1982, although Feferman recently sent me notes on this written as early as 1976 whereas my own work was begun in 1979.

can be formally related via the predicate T. Moreover, these will have the expected behavior except in occasional self-referential cases, where the behavior departs only slightly from Tarski's schema.

Without going into formal details, the essence of the *-operator is illustrated in the following equivalence:

$$(\ldots \neg T\alpha \ldots)* \leftrightarrow (\ldots T\neg\alpha \ldots)$$

That is, the * has the effect of passing negations signs through the T predicate. Then we do not quite get the Tarski schema; there are cases, such as the Liar sentence L, in which $T(L)$ is not equivalent to L under the *-schema. But these are unusual cases. To see the * in action in an ordinary case, consider the successive uses of the operator below.

$$T(\neg T(1 = 2))$$

iff

$$(\neg T(1 = 2))*$$

iff

$$T(\neg 1 = 2)$$

iff

$$(\neg 1 = 2)*$$

iff

$$\neg 1 = 2$$

We see that the intuitive result, $\neg 1 = 2$, is arrived at with little more effort than one might have used informally. However, with a Liar sentence L, one ends up with a slight switch, that prevents an outright contradiction. One is able to prove $\neg T(L)$ and also $\neg T(\neg L)$, *i.e.*, neither L nor $\neg L$ is true, which has a certain satisfying feel: after all, L is a slippery beast when it comes to truth.

Does this then leave us in a satisfactory state with regard to providing a consistent formalization of commonsense reasoning in first-order logic? Unfortunately the answer is no, as we now examine.

2   Ideal Approaches (to Knowledge)

Studies of ideal reasoning focus on the total set of conclusions that a reasoning agent will ultimately derive, given certain information, viewed apart from consideration of the specific situation and processes that may generate it. The idea is that the given information and reasoning are adequate if the conclusions are appropriate to the problem at hand. Much work in artificial intelligence falls within this area, including much of the work in default reasoning and knowledge representation. Key to this approach is the idea of a single fixed theory in which the reasoning is to be performed.

If we go beyond truth-value (of a reified sentence), to a 'belief-value', *i.e.*, conditions under which a sentence α can be consistently ascribed as a belief $Bel(\alpha)$ of a reasoning agent, it is surprising that rather intuitive axioms for this run into paradox in a classical first-order context. If we define knowledge of α, $K(\alpha)$, as $T(\alpha)$ & $Bel(\alpha)$, then under fairly general conditions the first-order axiom schema $K(\alpha) \rightarrow \alpha$ conflicts with the rule to infer $K(\alpha)$ from α. I have shown that modal logics are on no firmer ground than classical first-order ones when equally endowed with substitutive self-reference, and also that there still are remedies. One remedy allows replacement of the above inference rule with the following: infer $K(\alpha)$ from α^*. Another draws a distinction between 'dynamic' and 'static' notions of provability and belief, and isolates three classes of autoepistemic formulas for further study based on ideas of Moore.

Let us adopt the following abbreviations for the indicated inference rules:

PosInt: infer $K\alpha$ from α.
NegInt: infer $\neg K\alpha$ if α is not inferred.

SCHEMA T: $K\alpha \rightarrow \alpha$.

FULLY INTROSPECTIVE: PosInt & NegInt.

Then we have the following 'impossibility' results:

Theorem (Montague 1963. *The Knower's Paradox*): In a standard arithmetical setting, schema T is inconsistent with rule *PosInt*.

Theorem (Thomason 1980. *The Believer's Paradox*): A predicate Bel applying to (suitable) arithmetic and obeying

$$Bel(\alpha) \rightarrow Bel(Bel(\alpha))$$

$$Bel(Bel(\alpha) \to \alpha)$$

$Bel(\alpha)$ for all valid α

$$Bel(\alpha \to \beta) \to (Bel(\alpha) \to Bel(\beta))$$

also applies to all wffs.

Discussion: It can be urged that propositions as abstract entities avoid the syntactic problems of self-reference that are found in a sentential representation of thoughts. For instance, the above two theorems are false when applied in a direct way to their modal counterparts. However, this will not do, since we express thoughts by sentences, whether or not the thoughts themselves are regarded as sentences. For instance, when we say we can (or can't) prove B, and thus that $\neg B$ (say), we refer to syntactic entities, at least as CARRIERS of propositions. For proof is a syntactic notion, and also we communicate by means of syntax, with substitutional structure. Then we are led to the following negative result:

Theorem (Perlis 1986): Modal versions are also inconsistent if referenceable (substitutive).

Finally we have:

Theorem (Perlis 1987): There is no consistent fully introspective theory in a standard arithmetical setting.

Proof sketch: Let $BB \leftrightarrow \neg KBB$. If $\vdash BB$ then also KBB, and also $\neg KBB$. But if $\nvdash BB$ then also $\neg KBB$ and so BB, hence KBB.

Set theories are, of course, the most wildly reificational theories around, for they turn virtually everything into an object (called a set). In [Perlis 87a] it is argued that sets can play an important role in circumscription's ability to deal in a general way with certain aspects of commonsense reasoning. This also can be viewed as taking reification another step, since sets allow the expression of (even infinitely many) axioms as a single term. I give a single first-order axiom for circumscribing in the language of set theory. A by-product is that the entire circumscription scheme (or second-order axiom) can be made into a defining axiom for minimization, which has no effect until it is proven that any particular formula is to be minimized. For instance, one can assert as a general axiom that $Minimized(p) \to Circum(p)$ where $Circum$ is defined by a single axiom. This opens up the possibility circumscribing p can be a decision made by an agent faced with a particular problem (*i.e.*, by proving $Minimized(p)$) rather than a mechanism externally put in place for each use. Note that here again reification comes into play, in that p is an object term rather than a predicate.

In [Perlis88c] is proposed a set theory called CST_2. This is an attempt to combine a theory like that of A [Ackermann56] (a somewhat traditional hierarchical notion of set built up in stages from previously constructed entities) with one allowing self-reference along Gilmore-Kripkean (GK) lines. One way to think about this is that someone (in the role of GK) postulates an abstract entity, and someone else (in the role of A) shows that it is concretely present. This is indeed a familiar form of rational experience, both in scientific investigations and also in everyday deliberations. Put differently, GK provides a sort of philosophical architecture, and A some constructive engineering techniques, for sets. I conjecture that this has close ties to commonsense in that we dance a fine line between intensions and extensions in our reasoning, as witness the famous *de dicto/de re* distinction.

Some positive results regarding self-reference in commonsense reasoning, especially with regard to the notions of belief and knowledge, have been found despite the earlier negative ones. A few of these are given below:

Theorem (Des Rivieres & Levesque 1985): A first-order language can be suitably restricted so as to disallow contradictory wffs in Montague's axiomatization.

Theorem (Perlis 1985): The α^* technique can be used with K (instead of T) to defuse contradictions and still allow the full language in a variant of Montague's axiomatization.

3 Pseudo-Ideal Approaches

One source of the difficulties in the approaches we have been considering is their insistence on a single fixed theory whose theorems are to represent all the conclusions of a rational (ideal) agent. Another way to envision the situation is to consider that as an agent introspects, the theory undergoes a change and is no longer the same theory. This in fact is a common way of viewing theories designed for non-monotonic forms of inference. Minsky [Minsky75] was the first to point out the need for a new way of thinking about commonsense kinds of inference, and he in fact coined the expression 'non-monotonic'. Although he regarded this as evidence that logical formalisms are inappropriate for commonsense reasoning, others have taken it as a challenge to revise or extend existing formalisms to incorporate this further kind of reasoning (NMR).

One way to view the new approaches is to say that one needs $\neg K\alpha$, rather than a device such as the *-operator. That is, avoiding inconsistency is not the only consideration. Now it becomes important to be able to decide unprovability (of α, for example, so that $\neg K\alpha$ can be asserted). While overall consistency of the reasoning is still one desideratum, the focus is on means to test or characterize unprovability. Now, to be sure, this involves consistency issues, for the unprovability of α is precisely the same thing as the consistency of $\neg \alpha$ (with respect to a given theory). But instead of seeking to guarantee consistency as before, now the focus is on finding out potential consistencies so as to justify a default (NMR) conclusion such as $\neg K\alpha$. Of course, at the same time, one wishes the overall reasoning to remain consistent as well. This then is the essence of the pseudo-ideal approach. It is pseudo-ideal, rather than ideal, because under fairly general circumstances it has been shown that consistency-checking (or, equivalently, unprovability-checking) is not performable within the very theory under question. This was shown by Gödel [Gödel31] and Löb [Löb55].[4] Thus one cannot hope to determine results such as $\neg K\alpha$ within a fixed theory, if K refers to what is established in that same theory. We must then move outside the given theory, perhaps extend it somehow. This is what the various approaches to NMR do.

Of the major approaches to NMR ([Reiter80], [McDermott&Doyle80], [Moore83], and [McCarthy80]), only McCarthy's — circumscription — provides a fairly general *mechanism* to decide unprovability. That is, unlike the others, circumscription is semi-decidable (at least in its proof-theoretic forms). Of course, by the above, it cannot be complete, for that would violate the undecidability constraint; and it cannot be performed within a fixed theory, for that would violate the Gödel-Löb result. Hence it involves extending a given theory by adjoining new axioms; however, it does so in a very general way, which we summarize now.

One version of McCarthy's circumscription schema is as follows: $R[P]$ is a given set of axioms involving the predicate letters P. The idea, roughly, is to minimize the true instances of a supposedly rare property P_0, *i.e.*, to require P_0 to be false whenever possible. Formally

$$R[Z] \ \& \ ((\forall x)(Z_0 x \rightarrow P_0 x) \ \& \ \neg Z_0 y \ .\rightarrow. \ \neg P_0 y$$

---

[4]In fact, even worse, consistency-checking usually is not even decidable!

where the antecedent can be regarded as saying that Z_0 is a possible interpretation of P_0, as far as is known from $R[P]$, which does not introduce any new (rare) P_0-objects, and such that y is not a Z_0-object. The conclusion then is that y (in all likelihood) is also not a P_0-object.

In response to the problem of consistency-checking, it is tempting to weaken $\neg P_0$ to $\neg K P_0$, so as to record the unprovability without committing ourselves to the truth or falsity of P_0 itself. This was done in [Perlis88b], and is called autocircumscription.

We let AUTO[R] be the revised schema:

$$R[Z] \ \& \ (\forall x)(Z_0 x \rightarrow P_0 x) \ \& \ \neg Z_0 y \ .\rightarrow. \ \neg K(P_0 y)$$

Here the conclusion, $\neg K(P_0 y)$, is not a default — it is a truth about the reasoner's set of theorems, namely that $P_0 y$ is not one of those theorems. Moreover, consistency is guaranteed under fairly mild conditions.

Thus autocircumscription provides a partial decision procedure for consistency. It also can solve the Reagan problem and certain forms of the Brother problem. We illustrate with the Reagan problem. Let A be the theory:

$Seated(Bill)$

$\neg Seated(Sue)$

$Seated(x) \leftrightarrow \neg Standing(x)$

$Reagan \neq Bill$

$Reagan \neq Sue$

Then

$$A + AUTO[A] \ \vdash \ \neg K(Seated(Reagan))$$

To see this, let $Z_0(x)$ be $x = Bill$, and $Z_1(x)$ be $x \neq Bill$. Then we easily verify $A[Z_0, Z_1]$ and $Z_0(x) \rightarrow Seated(x)$. Therefore from AUTO[A]: $\neg Z_0(x) \rightarrow \neg K(Seated(x))$, we conclude $\neg K(Seated(x))$. Similarly we can show $\neg K(Standing(x))$.

4   A Situated Approach

Pseudo-ideal approaches, especially NMR approaches, acknowledge that reasoning is often tentative and changing. This is reflected in their two-tiered
character, in which a base theory is augmented by a non-monotonic part.
However, to do justice to this idea, one should envision an endless series of
theory adjustments. Thus, one conclusion of this survey can be summarized
as "one, two, ... many theories". Situated reasoning has to do with taking
account of the fact that reasoning does not go on in a vacuum but rather
surrounded by features in space and time.

In a sense then this addresses somewhat more practical issues of on-
going reasoning in an intelligent agent situated in an active environment.
Aspects of situated reasoning have been studied by many, including [Bar-
wise&Perry83], [Levesque84], [Fagin&Halpern85], [Suchman85], and [Rosen-
schein-Kaelbling87]. This too can involve a kind of self-reference, in that the
agent is to formulate sentences referring to the agent's own situation within
the environment, thereby making the agent's on-going reasoning process itself explicitly represented in the agent's reasoning. This line of research
has focussed on the observation that reasoning in a complex environment
often goes on while the environment is changing. Nilsson has used the
phrase 'computer individual' to describe much the same problem. It places
an unusual set of constraints on the reasoning; in particular, it must be
self-referential in a way somewhat different from that considered in earlier
sections. For example, the reasoning should take into account that *time is
being used* by that very act of reasoning. Thus another item must be made
explicit, namely the on-going time taken as the reasoning proceeds. Also,
the very real possibility of error must be accounted for, whether it is error
of observation or otherwise.

This suggests a view of reasoning as always unfinished and tentative and
taking account of its own progress, in contrast to other approaches in which
a kind of deductive closure is invoked (whether of full logical inference or
some weakened form). One idea here is that concepts often are confused or
vague, so that the agent must be able to alter them to fit a given situation.
Logic is a useful tool for this, both to determine that there is confusion, and
to amend it. However, some special features are desirable for such a logic: it
should allow reification so that poor concepts can be syntactically identified,
and it should proceed in a step-like fashion so that its own progress can be
modelled internally.

A schematic illustration of this approach is below:

0	...
1	...
2	...
...	...
i	$\dots \alpha \dots$
$i+1$	$\dots \alpha \dots \alpha \rightarrow \beta \dots$
$i+2$	$\dots \alpha \dots \alpha \rightarrow \beta \dots \beta \dots$
...	...

Here each numerical index on the left represents a moment in time, and the wffs to the right of an index are the (finitely many) beliefs held by the reasoner at that time.

One feature of this is that inconsistencies are now OK. That is, in passing from one step (index) to the next, only one level of inference is performed, so that an inconsistency will not necessarily produce a large number of undesired conclusions, and moreover, there is time left in later steps to take corrective action if such undesired conclusions to arise. However, a more subtle feature is that the time indices themselves are allowed in the agent wffs appearing on each line. That is, there is a notion of 'Now' which changes as the reasoning proceeds.

An example that has motivated some of this work is again the Brother problem, which in 'step logic' takes roughly the following form (simplified for ease of illustration. Here step $i+1$ is of especial interest, since it illustrates the conclusion $\neg K(i,B)$, that at time i the agent did not know B. In an ordinary (ideal) setting this would be unattainable, since there is no available sense there of what is known *so far*. The finiteness of each step set of wffs, together with the non-deductively-closed notion of K, makes this a simple look-up; see [Elgot-Drapkin88] for details):

i	$\dots Now(i) \dots B \rightarrow K(i-1,B) \dots$
$i+1$	$\dots Now(i+1) \dots B \rightarrow K(i,B) \dots \neg K(i,B) \dots$
$i+2$	$\dots Now(i+2) \dots B \rightarrow K(i+1,B) \dots \neg K(i,B) \dots \neg B$

It may be worth mentioning one additional sample problem: Three-wisemen problem: this classical problem has served as a good test for a number of theoretical efforts in AI. [Elgot-Drapkin88] presents one solution in step-logic.

5 Speculations on Aboutness

Finally, we return to the 'other' theme produced by our questioning the nature of thoughts as things, namely, what is it for a thought to be *about* something? That is, how is reference possible at all? This is a traditional philosophical problem (of intentionality, meaning, or aboutness) which has more recently become of interest to researchers in artificial intelligence. In short, how can internal symbols (to a reasoning agent) refer to anything outside the agent? There are many positions on this. See [Dennett78], [Stich84], [Churchland84], and [Pylyshyn84] for a general account of much of the literature. One approach I wish to explore here is based on the idea is that a chief role of thought is to delineate possible situations distinguished from the supposed real situation. On this view, to think about X is to contrast a particular representation of X (the presumed actual one) with alternative representations (*e.g.*, conjectural or goal representations). Thus there will be at least two internal symbolic structures, X and X', where X' is about X (or X' is a possible state of X, *etc.*). Since X and X' are both internal to the agent, reference (so viewed) avoids some of the traditional difficulties. This also bears on the problem of identifying poor or confused concepts mentioned above. Related suggestions have been made in [Perlis&Hall86], [Perlis86b,87b], [Rapaport88], [Minsky68], [Sloman86], [Steels86].

What I have in mind here is that a belief is something believed to be *true,* and that therefore the concept of a representational structure being *true or false* is relevant. This leads into the second point, for in order to take the stand that a certain structure is, say, false, one must distinguish it from what it supposedly is about. This is much like saying a word is different from what it stands for, and can even be misused. If I mention the dog by the tree and you say it isn't a dog but rather a wolf, you have recognized the word 'dog' as having being misapplied to the creature by the tree, rather than thinking some dog by the tree is also a wolf or has been replaced by or changed into a wolf.

But why bother to have two notational tokens? An answer is to distinguish what is from what isn't. For instance, I may change my mind that I have seen a dog, but to use this fact (that I have changed my mind), I recall that I used 'dog' inappropriately, or that I entertained the sentence "there is a dog present". Quotes (or words as such) allow us to entertain possibilities, even ones we think are false. By 'quotes' I mean simply names; I refer to the capacity for creating structures to manipulate *vis-a-vis* one another. This can apply to images or any other structures. But crucial to this is a mechanism for relating name and named, essentially a truth-predicate (or reality-predicate): the dog-image is of a dog, or 'dog' stands for a dog. Then we can choose between hedging (maybe that isn't a dog) or going for it (that is a dog) where 'that' is some other internal entity such as an image. The main point though is that not only 'that' but also the considered reference (dog) is internal to the system, even if it is not quoted. To draw out the illustration further, a dog 'becomes' (under suitable circumstances) 'dog' and then may not be a dog after all. This strange statement may seem less so when taken with the further claim that, as far as meaning goes, all is imag-inal. As long as thinking works, we use it, but possibly there are no 'firm' dogs at all.[5]

How do we avoid the criticism that then we never think about *real* things? Well, here we can borrow from the adverbial theory of perception, which maintains, for instance, that Macbeth was "perceiving dagger-ly" in the famous scene in which he seems to see a dagger before him. By way of analogy, we may think 'aboutly', that is, when I think about a dog, I really am thinking in an 'about dog-ly' fashion, or better put, I 'refer dog-ly'. That is, I have (at least) a pair of tokens, such as 'dog' and ' "dog" ', in my head, that I am using to form hypotheses, to reason concerning what is or isn't. In effect, when we (say we) think about an external object, we are contrasting internal entities, often happily in conjunction with the actual presence of corresponding external objects. See [Perlis87b] and [Rapaport88] for more detail.

Now, whether or not tokens *are* 'real' (externally), *i.e.*, whether or not there is a (natural) external referent for the internal tokens, becomes contingent, much as in the adverbial theory of perception. We may refer 'unicorn-ly' and yet have no external referent; the same for a dog which may be referred to in error (if there is really no dog that is the object of ones thought). This suggests that reference is much more an internal phenomenon than has generally been acknowledged. However, it is by no means clear that such an account can be made to work in a general way, so that much remains to be investigated here.

---

[5]This is reminiscent of natural kinds, which often defy definition.

6   Conclusions

To return to our overall themes, we have seen that thoughts present us
with two sets of issues: one the one hand, thoughts themselves are often
the objects X of (other) thoughts, and as such become reified into things
(of sorts); and on the other hand, thoughts do have objects (of which we
say the thoughts are 'about'). We have seen that both of these ideas are
problematic. The former is largely a formal issue in mathematical logic;
the latter is a philosophical and cognitive one about the how words have
meanings. While final words are not in on either of these, it appears that
the greater burden now is on the latter problem.

Acknowledgement   I would like to thank Greg Carlson and Nat Martin
for helpful comments.

This research has been supported in part by the U. S. Army Research
Office (DAAL03–88–K0087), by NSF Coordinated Experimental Research
grant #DCR–8320136, and by ONR/DARPA research contract #N00014–
82–K–0193.

7 Bibliography

Ackermann, W. "Zur axiomatik der mengenlehre," *Mathematische Annalen 131* pp. 336–345, 1956.

Barwise, J. and J. Perry. *Situations and Attitudes*, MIT Press, 1983.

Churchland, P. *Matter and Consciousness*, MIT Press, 1984.

Dennett, D. *Brainstorms*, Bradford Books, 1978.

des Rivieres, J. and H. Levesque. "The consistency of syntactical treatments of knowledge," *Proceedings of the Conference on Theoretical Aspects of Reasoning About Knowledge*, Monterey, October 1986.

Drapkin, J. and D. Perlis. "Step-logics: an alternative approach to limited reasoning," *Proceedings, 7th European Conference on Artificial Intelligence*, Brighton, England, July 1986.

Drapkin, J. and D. Perlis. "A preliminary excursion into step logics," *Proceedings, International Symposium on Methodologies for Intelligent Systems*, Knoxville, Tennessee, October 1986.

Elgot-Drapkin, J. and D. Perlis. "Reasoning situated in time," submitted to *Artificial Intelligence*, 1988.

Elgot-Drapkin, J. Ph.D. Dissertation, University of Maryland, 1988.

Fagin, R. and J. Halpern. "Belief, awareness, and limited reasoning: preliminary report," *IJCAI 85*, pp. 491–501, 1985.

Feferman, S. "Toward useful type-free theories, I," *Journal of Symbolic Logic 49*, 75–111, 1984.

Gilmore, P. "The consistency of partial set theory without extensionality," *Axiomatic Set Theory*, T. Jech, ed., American Mathematical Society, pp. 147–153, 1974.

Gödel, K. "Uber formal unentscheidbare Satze der Principia Mathematica und verwandter Systeme I," *Monatschrifte Mathematische Physik 38*, pp. 173–198, 1931.

Kripke, S. "Outline of a theory of truth," *Journal of Philosophy 72*, pp. 690–716, 1975.

Kripke, S. "A puzzle about belief," *Meaning and Use*, A. Margalit, ed., Dordrecht, pp. 234–283, 1979.

Levesque, H. "A logic of implicit and explicit belief," *Proceedings 3rd National Conference on Artificial Intelligence*, pp. 198–202, 1984.

Löb, M. "Solution of a problem of Leon Henkin," *Journal of Symbolic Logic 20*, pp. 115–118, 1955.

McCarthy, J. "First order theories of individual concepts and propositions," *Machine Intelligence 9*, pp. 129–147, 1979.

McCarthy, J. "Circumscription–a form of non-monotonic reasoning," *Artificial Intelligence 13*, pp. 27–39, 1980.

McCarthy, J. "Applications of circumscription to formalizing common-sense knowledge," *Artificial Intelligence 28*, pp. 89–118, 1986.

McDermott, D. and J. Doyle. "Non-monotonic logic I," *Artificial Intelligence 13*, pp. 41–72, 1980.

Minsky, M. "Matter, mind, and models," *Semantic Information Processing*, M. Minsky, ed., MIT Press, pp. 425–432, 1968.

Montague, R. "Syntactical treatments of modality, with corollaries on reflexion principles and finite axiomatizability," *Acta Philosophica Fennica 16*, pp. 153–167, 1963.

Moore, R. "Semantical considerations on nonmonotonic logic," *IJCAI 83*, 1983.

Perlis, D. "Languages with self-reference I: foundations," *Artificial Intelligence 25*, pp. 301–322, 1985.

Perlis, D. "On the consistency of commonsense reasoning," *Computational Intelligence 2*, pp. 180–190, reprinted in M. Ginsberg, ed., *Non-Monotonic Reasoning*, Morgan Kaufmann, pp. 56–66, 1987.

Perlis, D. "What is and what isn't," *Symposium on Intentionality*, Society for Philosophy and Psychology, Johns Hopkins University, 1986b.

Perlis, D. "Circumscribing with sets," *Artificial Intelligence 31*, pp. 201–211, 1987a.

Perlis, D. "How can a program mean?" *Proceedings International Joint Conference on Artificial Intelligence,* Milan, August, 1987.

Perlis, D. "Languages with self-reference II: knowledge, belief, and modality," *Artificial Intelligence 34*, pp. 179–212, 1988a.

Perlis, D. "Autocircumscription," *Artificial Intelligence 36*, pp. 223–236, 1988b.

Perlis, D. "Commonsense set theory," *Meta-Level Architectures and Architectures*, P. Maes and D. Nardi, eds., Elsevier, 1988c.

Perlis, D. and R. Hall. "Intentionality as internality," *Behavioral and Brain Sciences, 9(1)*, pp. 151–152, 1986.

Pylyshyn, Z. *Computation and Cognition*, MIT Press, 1984.

Rapaport, W. "Syntactic semantics: foundations of computational natural-language understanding," *Aspects of Artificial Intelligence*, J. Fetzer, ed., Kluwer, pp. 81–131, 1988.

Reiter, R. "A logic for default reasoning" *Artificial Intelligence 13*, pp. 81–132, 1980.

Rosenschein, S. and L. Kaelbling. "The synthesis of digital machines with provable epistemic properties," SRI Technical Report 412, 1987.

Sloman, A. "Reference without causal links," *Proceedings 7th ECAI*, July 21–25, 1986, Brighton, UK., pp. 369–381, 1986.

Steels, L. "The explicit representation of meaning," *Proceedings Workshop on Meta-Level Architectures and Reflection*, Sardinia, October 1986.

Stich, S. *From Folk Psychology to Cognitive Science: The Case Against Belief*, MIT Press, 1984.

Suchman, L. "Plans and situated actions," Technical Report ISL–6, Xerox Palo Alto Research Center, February 1985.

Tarski, A. "Der Wahrheitsbegriff," in den formalisierten Sprachen, *Studia Philosophia 1*, pp. 261–405, 1936.

Thomason, R. "A note on syntactical treatments of modality," *Synthese 44*, pp 391–395, 1980.

Bare Plurals as Plural Indefinite Noun Phrases

Brendan S. Gillon

1 Introduction

An English noun phrase whose head noun is a count noun usually occurs
with a determiner. Examples of such a noun phrase are found in the subject
position of each of these sentences:

(1) a. The desk is made of wood.

  b. A friend just arrived from Montevideo.

  c. This cup is fragile.

Such noun phrases in the singular are not permitted to appear without a
determiner.

(2) a. *Desk is made of wood.

  b. *Friend just arrived from Montevideo.

  c. *Cup is fragile.

Yet the same noun phrases may appear without a determiner, if they are
also in the plural.

(3) a. Desks are made of wood.

  b. Friends just arrived from Montevideo.

  c. Cups are fragile.

These noun phrases, apparently without determiners, have been called "bare
plurals."

It has been observed that bare plurals bear a syntactic and semantic
affinity to (singular) indefinite noun phrases, that is, noun phrases whose
determiner is the indefinite article. This is borne out by the observation that
sentences which are alike in structure can tolerate one or the other type of
noun phrase without difference is syntactic acceptability.

H.E. Kyburg, Jr. et al. (eds.), Knowledge Representation and Defeasible Reasoning, 119–166.
© 1990 *Kluwer Academic Publishers. Printed in the Netherlands.*

(4) a. An elephant is a pachyderm.

b. Elephants are pachyderms.

(5) a. There is an agent behind the door.

b. There are agents behind the door.

This is further borne out by the fact that such pairs of sentences are analogous in their construals. So, for example, the following pair of sentences expresses the fact that the property of barking is characteristic of dogs.

(6) a. A dog barks.

b. Dogs bark.

And the next pair of sentences expresses the fact that the lawn is occupied, in the first case, by one dog, and in the second, by more than one.

(7) a. A dog is on the lawn.

b. Dogs are on the lawn.

These observations have inclined some to hold that the only difference between the pairs of sentences in (4) through (7) is that in the one case the noun phrase has a singular count noun and a phonetically overt indefinite article and in the second case the noun phrase has a plural count noun and a phonetically covert indefinite article. In other words, there are singular indefinite noun phrases and plural indefinite noun phrases, the only difference between them is grammatical number. The apparent additional difference with respect to the occurrence (or non-occurrence) of a determiner is explained by the claim that there is a plural form of the indefinite article but that it is phonetically null. This claim accrues plausibility from the fact that, of all the determiners which go together with count nouns to form acceptable noun phrases, only the indefinite article has no overt phonetic form.

Carlson [Carlson77a], in his pioneering treatment of the grammar of bare plurals, has rejected this analysis. He points out that if bare plurals are in fact plural indefinite noun phrases then any difference between two sentences which differ only insofar as one has a (singular) indefinite noun phrase where the other has its bare plural version is merely the difference in grammatical number [Carlson77a; pp. 415–416]. He proceeds to adduce pairs of sentences in which the difference between the construals of the sentences appears to exceed any difference ascribable to their difference in grammatical number. To show such a discrepancy, Carlson introduces two auxiliary hypotheses. First, he supposes that the grammatically available interpretation of the indefinite article is that of the existential quantifier; and second, he supposes that the semantic import of grammatical number is to determine whether a noun phrase denotes one object or more than one object [Carlson77a; p. 416]. In lieu of the analysis he rejects, Carlson proposes that bare plurals are proper names which denote kinds. It is through this denotation that sentences with bare plurals as subjects, exemplified in (6b) above, express characteristics of species denoted by the bare plurals. However, bare plurals also seem to behave as if they really are plural indefinite noun phrases, as exemplified in (7b) above. To handle this, Carlson posits the existence of a phonetically null operator associated with the tense-aspect-complex of the verb in the bare plural's clause. This operator converts a bare plural into a existentially quantified noun phrase (see [Carlson77a; §4]).

Carlson has done two things: he has criticized and rejected one analysis of bare plurals, on the one hand; and he has proposed one of his own in its stead, on the other.[1] Carlson's own analysis has spawned an extensive literature which has attempted to improve upon his basic proposal.[2] It is not my intention to contribute to this important literature. My intention, rather, is to show that the analysis of bare plurals which Carlson rejects does not suffer from the inadequacy which he ascribes to it.

As was pointed out above, Carlson introduces two auxiliary hypotheses to reject the analysis to be defended here. However, work subsequent to Carlson's has shown that, independently of any considerations of the facts pertaining to bare plurals, both of the auxiliary hypotheses he adopts are empirically inadequate: the definite article does not have simply the semantics of the existential quantifier (see [Fodor&Sag82], among others cited below); and the semantic import of grammatical number is not simply to determine whether or not a noun phrase denotes one or more than one object (see [Langendoen78] and [Higginbotham81], among others cited below). In fact, as I shall show, when adequate auxiliary hypotheses are adopted, the analysis of bare plurals which Carlson rejects does not entail the discrepancies in construal which he ascribes to it.

---

[1] His own analysis is developed and supported in [Carlson77b].
[2] For a clear overview of the developments in this literature, see [Schubert&Pelletier87].

My goal, then, is to defend the analysis of bare plurals as plural indefinite noun phrases from Carlson's criticisms. To accomplish this, I shall introduce what I shall show to be empirically more adequate versions of Carlson's auxiliary hypotheses. The first part of this paper is devoted to this task. Next, I shall show how the grammatical facts pertaining to bare plurals can be derived from the analysis of bare plurals as plural indefinite noun phrases together with the two revised auxiliary hypotheses. In doing so, I shall pay especial attention to the data Carlson believes to pose problems for the analysis I wish to vindicate. The second part of the paper is devoted to these tasks.

2   The Grammar of the Indefinite Article

It has long been recognized that the indefinite article is susceptible to construals. As early as the nineteenth century, Spalding pointed out that one of its two construals corresponds to the Latin word "*quidem*" ("a certain") and another to the Latin word "*aliquis*" ("some").[3] Following Fodor and Sag [Fodor&Sag82], I shall call these the referential and quantificational construals, respectively. The referential construal is ascribed to an indefinite noun phrase when its user is thought to have a specific person or thing in mind. This construal has an especially apt application, when a speaker has a specific person or thing in mind of whom, or of which, he wishes to assert something but is unwilling, or unable, to be specific with his audience. For example, a student may want to make it clear to his instructor that he has good reason to say that there has been cheating on an exam, but he does not want to identify the culprit to the instructor. Provided the circumstances were right, he could accomplish this by saying:

(8)   A friend of mine cheated on the exam.

It should be noted that this construal of the indefinite noun phrase can be highlighted by such adjectival modifiers as "certain" or "particular".

(9)   A certain person cheated on the exam.

Still another way to see this difference in construal is to attend to the contrast between the definite and indefinite noun phrase. Suppose two people, say Reed and Dan, are in an apartment. Neither is expecting a visitor.

---

[3]Cited by Keynes [Keynes1884; p. 61].

There is a knock at the door. Reed answers. It turns out that a door-to-door salesman is calling. Reed, having no reason to think that Dan would be able to identify the person who is at the door, could appropriately say

(10) a. A salesman is at the door,

but could only inappropriately say

(10) b. The salesman is at the door.

Now suppose that Reed and Dan have an appointment with a particular salesman. Though Reed, in answering the door, could identify the person at the door with either sentence in (10), nonetheless he would fully specify the person's identity only with the sentence in (10b). If the referential construal of the indefinite noun phrase can be got at through the contrast between it and the definite noun phrase, then the quantificational construal of the indefinite noun phrase can be observed in those cases where the contrast just made is attenuated. The quantificational construal is ascribed to an indefinite noun phrase when its user is thought to have no specific person or thing in mind. Imagine, then, a grader who cannot identify any of the writers of the exam he is grading. Yet, on the basis of the distribution of grades, he is convinced that there had been cheating. He might report it to the instructor this way:

(11) A student in the class cheated on the exam.

Is there anything more to this discrepancy in construal than mere semantic indeterminacy? Several authors have adduced evidence that there is. In particular, it has been claimed that the indefinite article is a homonym of a quantifier and a demonstrative (*e.g.*, [Fodor&Sag82]). In adopting this view here, I shall present only some of the evidence in its favor, referring the interested reader to the relevant literature.[4]

First, there is a correlation between the referential and quantificational construals of the indefinite noun phrase, on the one hand, and the pronouns for which it can serve as antecedent, on the other [Ioup77; pp. 233–234]. This is exemplified by the following pair of sentences:

(12) a. Rajan will buy [a mattress]$_i$; in fact, he will buy [it]$_i$ today.

---

[4]Besides the work [Fodor&Sag82], there are the articles [Ioup77], [Chastain75], and [Wilson82].

    b. Rajan will buy [a mattress]$_i$; in fact, he will buy [one]$_i$today.

Observe that when the indefinite noun phrase is the antecedent of the third
person singular personal pronoun, its construal is referential, as in (12a);
but that when it is the antecedent of the pronoun "one", its construal is
quantificational, as in (12b). Recall the observation made above that an
adjective such as "particular" or "certain", when a modifier in an indefinite
noun phrase, renders the referential construal the salient one of the two. This
implies that the insertion of such adjectives in the indefinite noun phrases
of the sentences in (12) should not disturb the acceptability of the first, but
should disturb the acceptability of the second.

   (13) a. Rajan will buy [a particular mattress]$_i$; in fact, he will buy [it]$_i$
       today.

      b. Rajan will buy [a particular mattress]$_i$; in fact, he will buy *one*
       today.

The view that the indefinite article is a homonym for a quantifier and a
demonstrative accounts for the otherwise anomalous fact regarding the pronouns for which the indefinite noun phrase can serve as antecedent.

    Carlson, like many others, has assumed that the indefinite article is a
quantifier. There is good reason for this assumption. After all, it seems to
be a near-synonym of "some". So, for instance, just as sentences like the
one in (14a), have pairs of construals, so do sentences like the one in (14b).

   (14) a. Every man admires some woman.

      b. Every man admires a woman.

The only difference between the sentences is that one has "some" where
the other has "a". So, the question here is not: is the indefinite article a
quantifier; rather the question is: is the indefinite article only a quantifier?

    The answer to the last question is no, so long as one wishes to retain
the otherwise attractive generalization that quantified noun phrases are assigned scope within the clauses in which they occur.[5] Thus, for example,
the following sentence has only one reading, as far as the scope-like aspect
of the construal of its quantified noun phrase is concerned.

---

[5]See [Hornstein84; Ch. 3] for discussion.

(15) Some instructor overheard the rumor that each student in the class
was expelled.

It could be used to express the situation in which one instructor overheard
one statement to the effect that each student was expelled; yet, it could
not be used to express the situation in which each student in the class was
the subject of a rumor to the effect that he had been expelled and no two
of these rumors were overheard by the same instructor. This contrasts, as
has been pointed out by Fodor and Sag [Fodor&Sag82; pp. 373–374], with
sentences just like (15) except that "each" is replaced by "a" and "some" is
replaced by "each".

(16) Each instructor overheard the rumor that a student in the class was
expelled.

This can express the situation in which there is a different student rumored
to have been expelled for each different instructor; it can also express the
situation in which there is only one. Moreover, this latter situation cannot
be dismissed as a limiting case of the former, since the indefinite noun phrase
often can be understood as though it had scope wider than other quantified
noun phrases would have in its place.

(17) a. Some instructor thinks that for each student in my class to be
expelled is preposterous.

    b. Each instructor thinks that for a (certain) student in my class to
be expelled is preposterous.

In the first sentence, the construal of the quantified noun phrase is confined
to the sentential subject of the embedded clause; in the second sentence, the
construal of the indefinite noun phrase is not so confined. These observations
pertaining to the indefinite noun phrase are anomalous with respect to the
widely accepted constraint on scope assignment for quantified noun phrases,
only if one assumes the indefinite article to be only a quantifier.

    There is a further reason why the indefinite article is not just a quantifier.
Recall that relative clauses are distinguished into two kinds: appositional
and restrictive. This distinction is reflected in the convention for punctua-
tion: the former kind of relative clause is set of by commas, while the latter
is not.

(18) a. The man next door, who has long been active in gay politics, is
getting married.

b. The man who had detonated the bomb died in the ensuing explosion.

Quantified noun phrases tolerate restrictive relative clauses, not appositional ones.

(19) a. *Each candidate, who is elected, will support the amendment.
b. Each person who attends is given a prize.

In contrast, an indefinite noun phrase can tolerate either kind of relative clause.

(20) a. A student in my class, who does not want to be identified, appealed his grade.
b. A student in my class who does not want to be identified appealed his grade.

Again, these observations pertaining to the indefinite noun phrase present an anomaly only if the indefinite article is taken to be only a quantifier.

2.1   Grammatical and Extra-Grammatical Aspects of Grammatical Number

It has long been recognized that plural noun phrases introduce ambiguity into the sentences in which they occur.[6] A plural noun phrase can accommodate a collective reading as well as a distributive one. Consider this sentence:

(21) The men wrote operas.

If "the men" denotes Mozart and Handel, then the only reading on which it is true is the distributive one: Mozart wrote operas, Handel wrote operas, but they never collaborated to write even one opera. If "the men" denotes Gilbert and Sullivan, then the only reading on which it is true is the collective one: Gilbert and Sullivan collaborated to write operas, but neither wrote even one opera on his own.

While the notion of collaboration helps to highlight the difference between collective and distributive readings of plural noun phrases, it does not characterize the difference between tham. For plural noun phrases retain this ambiguity even in cases where no sense can be made of collaboration and failure to collaborate. These examples from [Copi82; p. 125] make the point.

---

[6]That ambiguity is the relevant semantic concept is shown in [Gillon87].

(22) a. The buses in this town consume more gasoline than the cars.

b. The conventional bombs dropped in World War II did more damage than the nuclear bombs dropped.

The first sentence is true when "buses in this town" and "the cars (in this town)" are each read distributively but false when each is read collectively; conversely, the second sentence is false when "the conventional bombs dropped (in World War II)" are each read distributively, but true when each is read collectively.

It is also important to observe that the adverbs "together" and "separately", when appended to (simple) sentences with plural noun phrases for subjects, do not provide disambiguating paraphrases of the collective and distributive readings the sentences acquire through their subjects being plural noun phrases. The sentence,

(23) The men travelled to Edmonton,

does not have its collective and distributive readings isolated by this pair of sentences:

(24) a. The men travelled to Edmonton together.

b. The men travelled to Edmonton separately.

The sentence in this pair are contraries: they cannot both be true at the same time. But (23) can be true on both its collective and distributive readings at the same time. For suppose that the Montreal Canadiens get on a single plane to travel to Edmonton to play the Edmonton Oilers. It is certainly true that the team, the Montreal Canadiens, travelled to Edmonton; it is also true that each member of the team travelled to Edmonton. If "the men" in (23) denotes those of the Montreal Canadiens who actually travelled to Edmonton to play the Oilers, then (23) is true on both its collective and distributive readings.

How, then, are collective and distributive readings to be understood? In general, the collective and distributive reading of a plural noun phrase is one where the objects in the set associated with the noun phrase (*i.e.*, the denotation of the noun phrase) are treated as a unit, or collective object; the distributive is one where it is not the case that any two distinct members of the noun phrase are treated as a unit, or collective object. So, consider a (simple) sentence of this form: [s NP_{+PL} VP]. Such a sentence is true on the collective reading of the subject noun phrase just in case the verb phrase is true of the collective object made up of all the members of the denotation of the subject noun phrase; otherwise, it is false (on the collective reading). It is true on the distributive reading just in case the verb phrase is true of each member of the denotation of the subject noun phrase.

A moment's reflection shows that the collective and distributive readings are not the only readings to which a plural noun phrase is susceptible. For suppose that "the men" denotes Mozart, Handel, as well as Gilbert and Sullivan. Surely (21) is true then as well. However, it is not true on the collective reading, since the four did not collaborate on any opera; and it is not true on the distributive reading, since neither Gilbert nor Sullivan ever wrote an opera on his own. So, there must be other readings; but what are they? Consider again the denotation of "the men" and the division imparted to the denotation by the situation verifying (21).

(25) a. {Mozart, Handel, Gilbert, Sullivan}

b. {{Mozart}, {Handel}, {Gilbert, Sullivan}}

The latter is a partition of the former. Now a partition is a family of sets, each of which is a non-empty subset of a given set, distinct sets in which family are disjoint, and the union of which family is the given set. This can be put more formally as follows:

(26) X partitions Y iff $X \subseteq \mathcal{P}(Y)$ & $\emptyset \notin X$ & $UX = Y$ & $(\forall x, y) \in X \ (x \cap y \neq \emptyset \rightarrow x = y)$.

(where "$\mathcal{P}(Y)$" means "the power set of X"). Note that the collective and distributive readings of a plural noun phrase correspond to two partitions of the noun phrase's denotation, namely, the greatest and least partitions as many readings of a plural noun phrase as there are partitions of its denotation.

This conclusion is supported by the syntax and semantics of sentences with the reciprocal pronouns. There are two desiderata on such sentences: first, that these sentences be special cases of sentences which have plural noun phrases in lieu of reciprocal pronouns; and second, that the reciprocal relation be a symmetric and connected one. Now Langendoen [Langendoen78] has shown that no analysis can both respect the second desideratum and define the reciprocal relation over individual objects in the denotation of the antecedent noun phrase to the reciprocal pronoun. Higginbotham

[Higginbotham81] has shown that both can be respected, if the reciprocal relation is defined over some partition of the denotation of the reciprocal pronoun's antecedent. These points are illustrated by this sentence:

(27) [Her grandparents]$_i$ hate [each other]$_i$.

As has been pointed out by Lauri Carlson [Carlson80; Part I, §12], this sentence is true even if the reciprocal hatred is only between the maternal grandparents on the one hand and the paternal grandparents on the other. In this case, there is no symmetric, connected relation of hatred definable over the four grandparents, but there is one definable over a partition of the grandparents into the paternal ones and the maternal ones.[7]

Although the partitions of the denotation of a plural noun phrase provide many of the readings to which the plural noun phrase is susceptible, they do not provide all of them. This is shown by a variant of the sentence in (21).

(28) The men wrote musicals.

Let "the men" denote Rodgers, Hammerstein, and Hart. This sentence is true when these men are the denotation of its subject noun phrase. Yet there is no partition of the set containing these three men in which the verb phrase "wrote musicals" is true of the unit corresponding to each element of the partition. Rather, the sentence is true because Rodgers and Hammerstein collaborated to write musicals and Rodgers and Hart collaborated to write musicals. Thus the number of readings to which a plural noun phrase is liable is not the number of partitions, but the number of minimal covers, to which its denotation is liable. A cover is just like a partition except it is not restricted to disjoint sets.

(29) X covers Y iff $X \subseteq \mathcal{P}(Y)$ & $\emptyset \notin X$ & $UX = Y$.

A minimal cover of a set is a smallest family of non-empty subsets of a set which still manage to cover it.[8]

---

[7] For further discussion, see [Gillon84; Ch. 4.3.1].

[8] It is interesting to note that "minimal cover" can also be defined as:
  (i) X minimally covers Y iff X covers Y & $(\exists x \in X)(x \subseteq U(X - \{x\}))$.
The right-hand side of this definition is, in fact, a generalization of the notion of plurality cover introduced in [Gillon84]. This generalization was suggested to me by Rick Lanthrop.

(30) X minimally covers Y iff X covers Y & $(\forall Z)((Z$ covers Y & $Z \subseteq X) \rightarrow Z = X)$.

In the case just considered, the set consisting of Rodgers and Hammerstein as well as the set consisting of Rodgers and Hart together form a set which minimally covers the set consisting in Rodgers, Hammerstein, and Hart. I shall assume henceforth that the minimal covers correctly characterize the range of readings to which subject plural noun phrases are liable.[9]

In light of the foregoing remarks on the range of readings for plural noun phrases, it will prove convenient to introduce some terms to simplify discussion. Let a collective be an object constituted of one or more members from a given background set. Suppose that a, b, and c are members of some background set and that they constitute a collective. Let the collective they constitute be designated as "abc". Let a maximal collective be one constituted of all the members of the background set; and let a minimal collective be one constituted of just one member of the set. So if the background set contains only a, b, and c, then abc is the maximal collective (with respect to the set) and a, b, and c are each minimal collectives (with respect to the set). In addition, a plurality is defined to be a set of collectives in which the set formed from the set of the constituents for each collective (in the set of collectives) minimally covers the background set. If the background set contains the individuals a, b, and c, then ab, c and a, b, c are pluralities with respect to it. Below are given all the pluralities of this background set. Notice that the collective reading of a plural noun phrase whose denotation is a, b, c corresponds to the plurality abc and its distributive reading corresponds to the plurality a, b, c (see Figure 1).

Having introduced pluralities, which are formed from the denotation of a noun phrase, one may reasonably raise two questions. First, does the grammar, via the predicate, impose any restriction on the range of pluralities with respect to which it is to be evaluated? Second, what is the relationship between a predicate's being true of elements of a noun phrase's denotation and its being true of a collective which those elements together constitute?

Beginning with the first question, one may wonder whether or not, for example, the predicate "to be left-handed" imposes grammatical restriction on the plural noun phrase "the men"?

(31) a. The man is left-handed.

b. The men are left-handed.

---

[9]For a defense of the choice of minimal cover, as opposed to cover, see [Gillon87; §2].

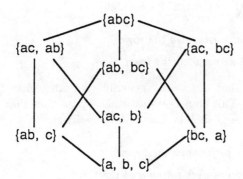

Figure 1.

Now left-handedness is a property of human bodies. This is compatible with the literal interpretation of the distributive reading of (31b). But can (31b) have a non-distributive reading? It seems odd to attribute left-handedness to a non-minimal collective. One might be tempted thereby to impute the source of the oddity to a violation of some grammatical rule. But if that were so, there could be no accounting for the unimpeachability of this sentence:

(32) The team is left-handed.

Or consider the contrast in the acceptability of the next pair of sentences, which was pointed out by [Kroch74; Ch. 5.5.0].

(33) a. *The man surrounded the town.

b. The men surrounded the town.

It might be thought that the verb "surround" subcategorizes for a plural noun phrase subject. This conjecture is bellied by the fact that the verb in question accommodates a singular noun phrase subject.

(34) a. The array surrounded the town.

b. The swarm of bees surrounded the town.

One might suppose, in response to these examples, that the restriction on the subject noun phrase is not syntactic, but semantic, requiring a selectional restriction instead, perhaps to the effect its subject noun phrase be evaluated with respect to a non-minimal collective. But even this revision runs afoul of the facts.[10]

(35) a. The river surrounded the town.

b. The amoeba surrounded the paramecium.

Indeed, is there any reason to suppose that the contrast in acceptability of the sentences in (33) really has a grammatical basis? Imagine that "the man" denotes Gulliver and "the town" denotes the capital of Lilliput. It seems, then, that (33a) is judged unacceptable, not because a grammatical principle hs been violated, but because one does not expect that a human being can surround a town. In the appropriate situation, this belief can be suspended and the oddity of (33a) evanesces. The view to be adopted here

---

[10]I owe these examples to Rick Lanthrop.

is that the grammar does not impose any restriction via the predicate on the range of pluralities associated with any noun phrase in an argument-position of the predicate; and that if oddity does occur, its source is extra-grammatical.[11]

To address the second question, let me distinguish between the upward and downward inheritability of a predicate. Roughly, a predicate which is upwardly inherited is one which, being true of each of the individuals forming a non-minimal collective, is true of the collective constituted from them; and a predicate which is downwardly inherited is one which, being true of a non-minimal collective constituted from a set of individuals, is true of at least one individual in the set. A few predicates are not upwardly inherited. For example, the predicate "to be light" may be true of each marble in a collection of marbles but need not be true of the collection itself.[12] A number of predicates are not downwardly inherited. One class of such predicates, dubbed "covert reciprocals" by [Langendoen78], include such intransitive verbs as "gather", "disperse", and "meet". These predicates may be true of a group without being true of the individuals forming the group.[13] However, most predicates are both downwardly and upwardly inherited. Certainly this is so with the predicate "to be left-handed". For, if each man on a team is left-handed, then the team is left-handed; and if the team is left-handed, than at least one of its members is left-handed.

Predicates which are upwardly and downwardly inherited were charac-terized with respect to limiting cases, that is, cases where the predicate holds either of each one or at least one of the individuals constituting a non-minimal collective. Yet, these very same predicates may be upwardly and downwardly inherited in non-limiting cases as well. In such cases, in-heritance seems to be a matter of vagueness, in a sense directly adaptable from the one which was originated by Peirce [Peirce01] and elaborated by Alston [Alston64; Ch. 5].

According to them, an expression is vague inasmuch as there are cases in which no definite answer exists as to whether or not it applies. Vagueness is well exemplified by such words as "city". Though a definite answer does exist as to whether or not it applies to Montreal or to Kingsville (Ontario);

---

[11] A similar point has been made by [Roberts87; p. 124], citing unpublished work by Dowty.

[12] These predicates have been studied in traditional logic under the rubric of the fallacy of composition.

[13] Some of these predicates have been studied in traditional logic under the rubric of the fallacy of division.

nonetheless, no definite answer exists as to whether or not it applies to Red Deer or Moose Jaw. Nor is the lack of an answer here due to ignorance (at least if one is familiar with the geography of Western Canada): no amount of knowledge of Red Deer or Moose Jaw will settle whether or not "city" applies. Any case in which further knowledge will settle whether or not the expression applies is simply not a case evincing the expression's vagueness; rather it evinces the ignorance of its user. So, for example, multiple sclerosis does not evince the vagueness of the word "curable" for it is ignorance of its aetiology which precludes a definite answer as to whether or not the word applies to multiple sclerosis. Vagueness is not alleviated by the growth of knowledge, ignorance is.

The adaptation of this characterization of vagueness to situation in which predicates are assessed with respect to collectives is straightforward. There are two cases to consider: the case where the collective is minimal and the case where it is non-minimal. The former case is simply the case as envisioned by Peirce and Alston, since a minimal collective is just the individual constituting it. The latter case is a case analogous to the one envisioned by Peirce and Alston. Consider the predicate "to be red" applied to an object with a number of sides. If each surface of the thing is entirely red, then there is no question that the predicate "to be red" applies; if no surface of the thing is red at all, the there is no question that the predicate does not apply. Things evincing the vagueness of the predicate, then, must fall between these two limits. To ascertain whether or not such things evince the predicate's vagueness, one must determine how many of a thing's surfaces, and how much of each of its surfaces, must be red for it to be said to be red. Now, consider the predicate "to be left-handed" applied to a non-minimal collective, like a team. As observe above, if each member of the team is left-handed, then there is no question that the predicate applies to the team; if no member of the team is left-handed, then there is no question that the predicate does not apply to the team. Yet, between these two extremes lie many instances where, again, there is a real question whether or not the predicate applies. Here too, one must determine, for any such instance, how many of the team's members must be left-handed for the team to be said to be left-handed.

A predicate's applicability in these non-limiting cases is, to a large extent, modulated by context. How much of a car, for example, has to be red for the car to be said to be red? A car must be said to be red even though none of the following are red: the surface of the engine, the underside of the chassis, the chrome, the tires, the interior surfaces, *etc.* How much of a book has to be red for it to be said to be red? Usually just the outside of the front and back of the cover as well as the spine — but even then, exclusive of the color of any symbol or picture which may appear on these surfaces. And how many members of a boxing team must be left-handed for the team to be left-handed? Certainly the coach and the trainer need not be left-handed, though one would expect the pugilists themselves to be each left-handed in view of the import of the left-handedness for sparring. Yet, how many members of a baseball team must be left-handed for the team to be left-handed? Perhaps, only the principal pitcher need be, in view of the import of this player, as opposed to the remainder of the players in the field, being left-handed.

The role of context in modulating the width of the range of instances which can evince the vagueness of a predicate cannot be over-emphasized. Reflect upon a variation of an example due to Lauri Carlson [Carlson80; Part 1, §4].

(36) **The soldiers found the guerrillas.**

Now consider this sentence in the light of two contrasting scenarios. In the first, the soldiers form a squad and it is out tracking a band of guerrillas fleeing over a border into a neighboring country. The squad is properly deployed and the soldier on point spots a guerrilla serving as rear guard to the band, none of the other soldiers being able to see any of the other guerrillas. In the second scenario, the soldiers of the squad are on furlough and each has gone his own way. The guerrillas have dispersed among the civilian population. Now, the same soldier as before happens to spot the same guerrilla as before. Surely, although one soldier sees one guerrilla, nonetheless it is not true that the soldiers, or the squad of soldiers, found the guerrillas, or the band of guerrillas.

In short, the separation of grammatical from extra-grammatical aspects of grammatical number comes to this. First, a predicate (paradigmatically, a verb phrase) is evaluated, not with respect to the denotation of its argument noun phrase (paradigmatically, the verb phrase's subject noun phrase), but with respect to a plurality, whose members, recall, are constituted from the noun phrase's denotation. Second, the grammar does not constrain the choice of plurality, though beliefs and expectations do. That is to say, inheritance of a property by a collective from its constituents is modulated by such extra-grammatical considerations as beliefs and expectations.

2.2   Grammatical Principles of Grammatical Number

The syntactic principles pertaining to grammatical number in English are fairly straightforward. To begin with, a count noun in any acceptable sentence has either singular or plural morphology. It is natural to see this morphological fact as a phonological reflex of a syntactic requirement that each count noun be assigned exactly one of the two features, +PL and −PL. It is not so obvious that the noun phrase node immediately containing a count noun inherits the feature assigned to the count noun it contains. However, consideration of agreement in number between a count noun and its determiner as well as between a pronoun and its antecedent suggests that this is so.

English, as morphologically impoverished as it is, still requires that determiners agree in number with the count nouns with which they occur. Consider:

this table	*this tables
*these table	these tables
that dart	*that darts
*those dart	those darts
each friend	*each friends
*all friend	all friends

In addition, the verb, in English, agrees with its subject in number.[14]

---

[14]There is an interesting class of apparent exceptions to this generalization, pointed out by [Hoeksema83; pp. 71–72], among others:

    (i)   Twenty-five cents doesn't buy a cup of coffee anymore.

Here "twenty-five cents" seems to be a plural noun phrase, while "does" seems to be a singular verb. The productivity of this pattern is limited to noun phrases where trhe head noun is the plural form of a unit of measure. Compare, for example,

    (ii)   Twenty-five cents is on the floor.

    (iii)   *Twenty-five marbles is on the floor.

It is interesting to observe that there are languages which have the same pattern, except that the noun for the unit of measure is singular. Jespersen [Jespersen25; p. 208] reports the following examples from German and Danish.

(37) a. This person is always punctual.

     b. *This person are always punctual.

These facts about agreement in number and compositionality are respected, if one assumes that the features of a count noun are assigned to its first dominating noun phrase node (*i.e.*, its maximal projection) and that the features assigned to a determiner must be consistent with the features of its first dominating noun phrase node. English also requires that pronouns agree in number with their antecedents.

(38) a. [The critic]$_i$ admires [himself]$_i$.

     b. *[The critic]$_i$ admires [themselves]$_i$.

     c. [The critics]$_i$ think that [they]$_i$ are great.

     d. *[the critics]$_i$ think that [he]$_i$ is great.

Moreover, the antecedence relation is defined over noun phrase nodes. Again, these facts and compositionality are respected if one assumes that the features of a count noun (or a pronoun) are assigned to its first dominating noun phrase node and that the features of two noun phrase nodes, one of which bears the relation of antecedence to the other, must be consistent.[15]

    Given these syntactic principles, one can inquire into the semantic import of the two features which these principles govern. For the sake of ease of exposition I shall confine my discussion to the semantic interpretation of noun phrases consisting of either a demonstrative or a quantifier and a count noun. I shall refer to these two kinds of noun phrases, henceforth, as demonstrative noun phrases and quantified noun phrases respectively.

    Presumably, a count noun is assigned a denotation from the individuals in the domain of discourse. A demonstrative, too, is assigned a denotation from the individuals in the domain of discourse, not individuals from the

---

    (iv)   drei mark (two marks)

    (v)   fem daier (five dollars)

This suggests that such nouns in English are pseudo-plurals.

[15]Conjoined noun phrases require that the feature of the conjunction are a function of the features of the conjuncts. In English, the function for grammatical number is trivial: if a singular noun phrase is conjoined with a noun phrase, the conjoined noun phrase is plural. [Hoeksema83] discusses some apparent counter-examples to this rule under the rubric of "intersective conjunction".

entire domain, but only individuals from that part of the domain for which is defined the situation of utterance, in the sense of Lyons [Lyons77; Ch. 15]. In effect, a demonstrative is an adjective whose denotation is given by the situation of utterance. The denotation of a demonstrative noun phrase is simply the intersection of the denotation of the demonstrative and the denotation of the count noun. The semantic import of the features +PL and −PL assigned to a noun phrase node is to constrain the size, or cardinality, of the denotation of the noun phrase. The feature −PL requires the size of the denotation to be one; whereas the feature +PL permits the sizer of the denotation to be greater than one. In other words, if the noun phrase node, NP, is assigned the feature −PL, then $\mid$ NP $\mid^D$; if the noun phrase node, NP, is assigned +PL, then $\mid$ NP $\mid^D \geq 1$. Next, the denotation of the noun phrase makes available to the predicate of which it is an argument pluralities any of which the predicate can be evaluated with respect to.

It might seem odd that the feature +PL permits, rather than requires, the denotation of the noun phrase to which it is assigned to be greater than or equal to one. After all, the supposition one usually makes when a plural noun phrase is used is that more than one individual in the domain of discourse is involved. This supposition, however, cannot be based in grammar, for there are just too many unimpeachable sentences where a plural noun phrase has a singleton for a denotation.

(39) a. Although it was the ancient Babylonians who first observed [The Morning Star and The Evening Star]$_i$; nonetheless, it was the ancient Greeks who first discovered [them]$_i$ to be the same planet.

b. These men, Mark Twain and Samuel Clemens, are the same man.

Rather, the supposition is based on extra-grammatical considerations, like conversational implicature.

Before turning to the semantic principles governing quantified noun phrases, one may be well served by seeing a few illustrations of the application of the semantics adduced above for demonstrative noun phrases. Suppose that the subject noun phrase of the next sentence denotes Tom, Dick, and Jerry.

(40) These men rowed.

The denotation of the subject noun phrase certainly satisfies the constraint placed on it by the +PL feature assigned to the noun phrase node.

Moreover, there are exactly eight pluralities which can be constituted from this denotation of three elements (see Figure 1 above). Now consider these situations:

(41) a. Tom, Dick, and Jerry were in one boat, each pulling an oar.
　　 b. Tom and Jerry were in one boat, at some point, each pulling an oar; and, Tom and Dick were in one boat, at some other time, each pulling an oar.
　　 c. Tom and Dick were in one boat, each pulling an oar; while Jerry was in another boat rowing.
　　 d. Tom was in one boat rowing; Dick was in another boat rowing; Jerry was in still another boat rowing.

These situations render the sentence in (40) true on the readings of its plural noun phrase subject corresponding to the following pluralities of the noun phrase's denotation.

(42) a. [Tom – Dick – Jerry]
　　 b. [Tom – Jerry, Tom – Dick]
　　 c. [Tom – Dick, Jerry]
　　 d. [Tom, Dick, Jerry]

where the first and the last pluralities correspond to the collective and the distributive readings respectively.

The principles outlined and illustrated above apply equally as well to sentences with transitive verbs and with plural demonstrative noun phrases for subject and object. In the sentence,

(43) Those men endorsed these women,

suppose "those men" denotes Rick and Randy and "these women" denotes Diane and Lillian. Certainly the sentence in (43) would be true if Rick and Randy collectively endorsed Diane and Lillian taken collectively; that is, Rick and Randy make up a committee and decide as a committee to endorse the slate made up of Diane and Lillian. The sentence would also be true if Rick endorsed the slate of Diane and Lillian and Randy endorsed the same slate. If Rick and Randy as a committee endorsed Diane and also endorsed Lillian, the sentence would still be true. And finally, if Rick endorsed Diane and Randy endorsed Lillian, or if Rick endorsed Lillian and Randy endorsed Diane, the sentence would be true. In other words, there are two choices of pluralities for each of the noun phrases.

(44) M_1: Rick – Randy W_1: Diane – Lillian

    M_2: Rick, Randy W_2: Diane, Lillian

The sentence in (43) is true on any given choice, just in case, on that choice each collective in the subject's plurality bears the relation expressed by the verb to some collective in the object's plurality and each collective of the object's plurality has the same relation borne to it by same collective in the subject's plurality. Such situations are depicted by means of directed bipartite graphs (see Figure 2).

Notice that each graph is complete. The first three choices of pluralities admit of only one complete directed bipartite graph each; the last choice admits of five of which only two, which are shown above, are minimal. The point is that non-minimal ones are superfluous.[16] If Rick's endorsing of Diane and Randy's endorsing of Lillian are together sufficient even if, in addition, either Rick endorses Lillian or Randy endorses Diane.

Supplement the previously adduced principles governing grammatical number with the following principle governing the interpretation of a noun phrase which contains only a pronoun and has an antecedent within the sentence.[17]

(45) If NP_1 is the antecedent of NP_2, then the denotation of NP_2 is the same as the denotation of NP_1 (*i.e.*, $\mid NP_1 \mid^D = \mid NP_2 \mid^D$).

So, the semantic import of the relation of antecedence is merely to guarantee identity of denotation in the interpretation of the *relata* of the relation of antecedence; it places no restriction on the pluralities with respect to which the predicates having the noun phrases related by antecedence for arguments are to be evaluated. This is exemplified by the following variant of (43).

(46) [These candidates]$_i$ endorsed [themselves]$_i$.

Suppose that "these candidates" denotes Rick and Randy. The available readings of (46) are essentially those of (43), except that Rick and Randy have replaced Diane and Lillian as the denotation of the object noun phrase (Figure 3).

---

[16]For an elaboration of this point in a simpler setting, see [Gillon87; §2].

[17]For the sake of ease of exposition, attention is confined to simple cases of sentences containing referentially dependent pronouns. For a more complete treatment of the problem, the reader is referred to [Gillon84]. The treatment there is based on [Higginbotham83].

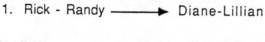

1. Rick - Randy ——————▶ Diane-Lillian

2. Rick ——————▶ Diane-Lillian
   Randy

3. Rick - Randy ——————▶ Diane
                    Lillian

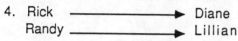

4. Rick ——————▶ Diane
   Randy ——————▶ Lillian

5. Rick   Diane
   Randy   Lillian

Figure 2

1. Rick - Randy ——————▶ Rick - Randy

2. Rick ——————▶ Rick - Randy
   Randy

3. Rick - Randy ——————▶ Rick
                    Randy

4. Rick ——————▶ Rick
   Randy ——————▶ Randy

5. Rick   Rick
   Randy   Randy

Figure 3

The reciprocal pronoun differs from the third person personal pronouns which are not used deictically and the reflexive pronouns in two ways. First, the reciprocal pronoun requires an antecedent which has plural grammatical number.

(47) a. *[Eliza]$_i$ saw [each other]$_i$.

b. [The women]$_i$ saw [each other]$_i$.

Nor should this distribution be viewed as a matter of common sense, that is an extra-grammatical matter, for collective nouns which denote collections of objects, are never acceptable antecedents of reciprocal pronouns, unless they have plural grammatical number.

(48) a. *The [array]$_i$ shot at [each other]$_i$.

b. *[The swarm of bees]$_i$ flew after [one another]$_i$.

Second, it requires that the predicate to which it and its antecedent are arguments express a symmetric, connected relation. Adapting a proposal put forth by Higginbotham [Higginbotham81], one can capture the intuition as follows:

(49) Let NP$_2$ be the first noun phrase node dominating the reciprocal pronoun. Let NP$_1$ be the antecedent of NP$_2$. Let NP$_1$ be a demonstrative noun phrase. The predicate which has NP$_1$ and NP$_2$ for arguments is to be evaluated with respect to every pair of distinct elements in a partition of the denotation of the antecedent NP$_1$.

To see how appealing this principle is,[18] consider this sentence:

(50) [Those grandparents]$_i$ hate [each other]$_i$.

---

[18][Heim *et al.*88] have criticized this approach, maintaining that it cannot properly distinguish some readings which arise in sentences such as:

(i)   [John and Mary]$_i$ told [each other]$_i$ that [they]$_i$ should leave.

I believe that this criticism cannot be sustained, though I do not have the space to show it here. In any event, the analysis of reciprocal pronouns presented by Heim *et al.*[Heim *et al.*88] cannot, by their admission, capture well known readings of reciprocal pronouns such as the one of the sentence in (53) associated with the graph in Figure 5.

Let "those grandparents" denote the maternal grandparents and the paternal grandparents of some person. Call them Mary and Marvin and Patricia and Peter respectively. Now, if the hating expressed in (50) is a symmetric, connected relation defined over these four individuals, then only one situation can render the sentence true (Figure 4).

But, as has been observed (*e.g.*, [Langendoen78]), it is also true, and more naturally true perhaps, in a situation like the one depicted in Figure 5.

But the hating in this situation is not connected, since Mary does not hate either Peter or Marvin, for example. However, if the relation is defined over collectives, and not individuals, this situation too can embody a symmetric connected relation (Figure 6).[19]

To conclude this presentation of how the principles governing plural demonstrative noun phrases are antecedents of pronouns, reflect on how these principles easily accommodate on important observation due to Lauri Carlson [Carlson80; Part 1, §9]. He observed that, in circumstances in which two window washers, who are standing on a window platform, pull on rope on opposite sides of the platform thereby raising the platform, both sentences in the pair below are true when "those men" denotes the two window washers.

(51) a. [These men]$_i$ pulled [themselves]$_i$ up.

b. [These men]$_i$ pulled [each other]$_i$ up.

The first sentence is true on the reading in which the plurality selected for the subject noun phrase and object noun phrase is the one whose sole member is the collective made up of both men. The second sentence is true on its only available reading in which the plurality selected for the subject noun phrase is the one which contained the two minimal collectives, each made up of one of the window washers.

Having stated and illustrated the principles governing plural demonstrative noun phrases, I turn to those governing plural quantified noun phrases. Again, a count noun is assigned, presumably, a denotation from the individuals in the domain of discourse. The range of the quantifier is restricted to a plurality constituted from the denotation of the count noun. If the feature assigned to the noun phrase node of the quantified noun phrase is +PL, then the choice of the plurality is unconstrained; but if it is −PL, then the choice is constrained to the minimal plurality. Notice that this is analogous to the

---

[19] Recall that collectives can inherit the properties or relations of their constituents.

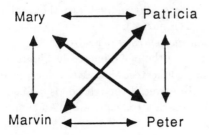

Figure 4

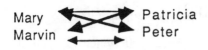

Figure 5

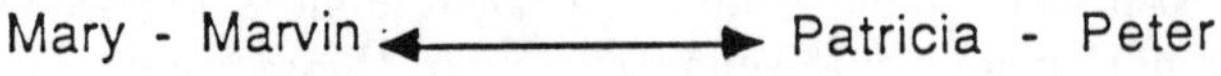

Mary - Marvin ⟷ Patricia - Peter

Figure 6

constraint imposed by these features on the denotation of demonstrative noun phrases. Next, if the quantifier is universal, then the predicate must be true of each collective in the plurality to which the quantifier is restricted; and, if it is existential, then the predicate must be true of some collective in the plurality to which the quantifier is restricted. Under this account, it is, in principle, possible for the plural universal quantifier and the plural existential quantifier to share a reading, namely where the plurality to which each is restricted is the maximal plurality, since in that case there is only one collective in the domain of the quantifier, namely the maximal collective. But "all" and "some" do not share a reading. For reasons which will be clear later, I shall assume that this is a peculiarity of the plural existential quantifier "some", which is handled in its lexical entry by a stipulation to the effect that, say, its domain of quantification is a non-maximal plurality.

To see how the principles work, consider this sentence with plural quantified noun phrases.

(52) **All men endorsed some women.**

Suppose the denotation of "men" is m_1, m_2, m_3, m_4, m_5, m_6, m_7 and the denotation of "women" is w_1, w_2, w_3, w_4, w_5. Suppose further that the men form committees of various sizes (including committees of one), say m_7, $m_1m_2m_3$, $m_1m_2m_4$, and $m_4m_5m_6$ and that the women too form committees, say, w_1w_2, w_1w_3, and w_4w_5. Finally, suppose that there is an endorsement of the female committee by the male committee, as depicted in Figure 7.

(53) [$_S$ [$_{NP}$ **All men**]$_x$ [$_S$ [$_{NP}$ **some women**]$_y$ [$_S$ [$_{VP}$ X] [$_{VP}$ **endorsed** [$_{NP}$ y]]]]]].

Next, the following two sets are pluralities constituted from the denotation of "men" and "women" respectively.

(54) a. m_7, $m_1m_2m_3$, $m_1m_2m_4$, $m_4m_5m_6$
b. w_1w_2, w_2w_3, w_4w_5

Finally, each collective in (54a) bears the relation of endorsing to some collective in (54b).

No illustration of sentences with singular quantified noun phrases is required, since the semantic principles adduced here reduce to those for restricted quantifiers ranging over the denotation of the noun of the quantified noun phrase. For the quantifier ranges over the minimal plurality, each member of which is a minimal collective, or an individual, of the denotation.

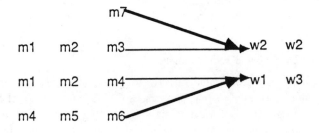

Figure 7

3 Bare Plurals as Plural Indefinite Noun Phrases

Before showing just how much bare plurals and indefinite noun phrases have in common, let me stress that bare plurals are, syntactically speaking, plural noun phrases. First, and most obviously, the head noun of a bare plural has plural morphology. Moreover, when a bare plural occurs in a position, say the subject position, requiring agreement in grammatical number from another item in its sentence, say the subject's verb, the item must have plural grammatical number in order to be acceptable.

(55) a. Unicycles are fun to ride.
b. *Unicycles is fun to ride.

Furthermore, if a bare plural is the antecedent of a pronoun, the pronoun must have plural grammatical number.

(56) a. [Canadians]$_i$ think that [they]$_i$ are tolerant.
b. *[Canadians]$_i$ think that [he]$_i$ is tolerant.

Notice also that a bare plural may be the antecedent of the reciprocal pronoun, which was seen earlier to require an antecedent of plural grammatical number.

(57) a. [Lovers]$_i$ never quarrel with [each other]$_i$.
b. [Children]$_i$ are playing with [one another]$_i$.

In addition, as was observed at the outset, sentences which are alike in structure can tolerate either an indefinite noun phrase or a bare plural without disparity in syntactic acceptability (provided, of course, that the conditions on agreement in grammatical number have been set). In fact, the only anomaly there is for the hypothesis that a bare plural is a plural indefinite noun phrase is that count nouns, which are the requisite kind of noun to serve as the head of a bare plural, usually occur with determiners. Now, coincident with this anomaly is the anomaly that, of all the determiners which go together with count nouns to form acceptable noun phrases, only the indefinite article has no phonetically overt plural form. The hypothesis adopted here eliminates a major syntactical anomaly by assuming a minor gap in the phonetic realization of a single form of a single lexical item. There can be no reason to balk at the hypothesis that bare plurals are indefinite plural noun phrases, unless the discrepancies in the construals of bare plurals and singular indefinite noun phrases exceed that permitted by their disparity in the grammatically sanctioned construal of grammatical number.

3.1   Bare Plurals and Singular Indefinite Noun Phrases

One reason adduced above for supposing that the indefinite article is not only a quantifier but also a demonstrative is that an indefinite noun phrase, unlike paradigmatic quantified noun phrases, admits both restrictive and appositive relative clauses.[20] Bare plurals do as well.

(58) a. Students, whom I shall not mention, appealed their grades.

   b. Students whom you know appealed their grades.

This fact about bare plurals is particularly significant in light of the claim by Carlson [Carlson77a; p. 442] that "the bare plural acts as the proper name of a kind"; for it has long been observed that proper names admit appositive, but not restrictive, relative clauses.

(59) a. Dave, who never attended class, appealed his grade.

   b. *Dave who never attended class appealed his grade.

Another characteristic of the indefinite noun phrase is that it is liable to both a quantificational and a referential reading. First, one observes the contrast between the referential readings of the bare plural and the plural definite noun phrase.[21]

(60) a. The salesmen are at the door.

   b. Salesmen are at the door.

Reference of the plural definite noun phrase, to be felicitous, requires both the speaker and the hearer to identify the referent of the noun phrase on the basis of its descriptive content and shared information. Reference of the bare plural, to be felicitous, requires only the speaker to identify the referent of the noun phrase in a way that is consistent with his information and its descriptive content. So, if two people are expecting salesmen, it is appropriate that the person answering the door use the sentence in (60a) to announce to the other person the identity of those at the door; if neither is expecting salesmen, then the sentence in (60a) is not appropriate, rather the sentence in (60b) is. Second, one observes that the contrast between referential and quantificational readings of bare plurals surfaces in the user

---

[20]See (20) above.
[21]See (8) – (10) above.

to be able to identify and sentences the referents of those whose bare plural one does *not* expect the user to be able to identify. So, for example, one expects an utterer of the sentence in (61a) to be able to identify the referents of its bare plural, but one does not expect an utterer of the sentence in (61b) to be able to identify the referents of its bare plural.

(61) a. Friends of mine cheated on the exam.

b. Students in the graduating class of 1984 cheated on the exam.

Notice also that the referential reading is encouraged by the use of such modifying adjectives in the bare plural as "certain" or "particular".

(62) Certain students in the graduating class of 1985 cheated on the exam.

Carlson [Carlson77a; §1.2] challenges the observation that bare plurals, like indefinite noun phrases, are susceptible of both quantificational and referential readings. He claims that bare plurals in opaque contexts are susceptible only of a quantificational reading, though indefinite noun phrases in the same contexts are susceptible of both a quantificational and a referential reading.[22] So, he maintains that the indefinite noun phrase "a communist", in the first sentence below, is susceptible of both a quantificational and a referential reading, whereas the bare plural "communists", in the second sentence below, is not, yet the two sentences are the same except where the first has an indefinite noun phrase the second has the bare plural version of the indefinite noun phrase.

(63) a. Max believes a communist to have robbed Macy's.

b. Max believes communists to have robbed Macy's.

Now in my judgment both the indefinite noun phrase "a communist" and the bare plural "communists" are susceptible of both the quantificational and referential readings. The availability of readings, however, is easily

---

[22]Carlson and I describe the data in somewhat different terms. What I call the referential reading, following Fodor and Sag [Fodor&Sag82], Carlson calls the transparent reading and analyses it as the noun phrase having scope wider than of the opacity-inducing expression, following Quine [Quine56]; and what I call the quantificational reading, still following Fodor and Sag [Fodor&Sag82], Carlson calls the opaque reading and analyses it as the noun phrase having scope narrower than the opacity-inducing expression, still following Quine [Quine56]. Reasons for rejecting Quine's analysis can be found in [Hornstein83; Ch. 3].

affected by extra-grammatical influences. In particular, beliefs that one has
can affect which readings one can detect in a sentence. Suppose that Max
knows a communist, knows that he is a communist and believes that he
robbed Macy's. Then the referential reading of the bare of the indefinite
noun phrase in (63a) is favored. Suppose that Max knows two communists,
knows that they are communists and believes that they robbed Macy's.
Then the referential reading becomes favored. The same favoring of the
referential reading can be achieved by enriching the descriptive content of
the noun phrase: for, as Fodor and Sag [Fodor&Sag82; §2.1A] have pointed
out, the richer the descriptive content of an indefinite noun phrase the more
salient its referential reading.[23]

> (64) a. Max believes a communist in the house next door to have robbed
>   Macy's.
>
>   b. Max believes communists in the house next door to have robbed
>   Macy's.

There are other facts which seem to militate against the view that bare
plurals admit both a quantificational and a referential reading. It was observed (at (12) – (13) above) that the referential and quantificational readings of an indefinite noun phrase can be distinguished by having it serve as
the antecedent of "one" respectively.

> (65) a. Rajan wants [a book on compiler design]$_i$. He will *take$_i$* out of
>   the library tonight.
>
>   b. Rajan wants *a book on compiler design*. He will take *one* out of
>   the library tonight.

Further evidence apparently supporting the claim that there is a discrepancy between the indefinite noun phrase and the bare plural with regard to

---

[23] All but one of the pairs of sentences adduced by Carlson [Carlson77a; §1.2] yield easily
to having both a referential and a quantificational reading for the relevant noun phrase,
provided one sets the stage properly. The exceptional pair of sentences is this:

> (i)   Minnie wishes to talk with a young psychiatrist.
>
> (ii) Minnie wishes to talk with young psychiatrists.

However, with an increase in its descriptive content, the referential reading of the bare
plural in (ii) becomes available.

> (iii)   Minnie wishes to talk with young psychiatrists in the house next door.

each's susceptibility to both quantificational and referential readings is presented by Carlson [Carlson77a; §1.5]. In a stretch of discourse in which an indefinite noun phrase is an antecedent, there is only one object at play when the pronoun is a third person singular personal pronoun, but there is more than one object at play, by presumption, when the pronoun is "one".

(67) a. Randy is yelling at *a bear* and Joel is yelling at *it* too.

b. Randy is yelling at *a bear* and Joel is yelling at *one* too.

In the first sentence, Randy and Joel are yelling at the same bear; in the second one, they are presumably[24] yelling at different bears. There appears to be no comparable contrast for bare plurals. And, as Carlson points out, even in the case where the bare plural is the antecedent of the plural form of the third person plural pronoun, the group assigned to the bare plural need not be the same as the group assigned to the third person plural personal pronoun.

(68) a. Randy wears *blue ties* and Joel *wears them* too.

b. Randy likes *peanut butter cookies* and Joel likes *them* too.

But why is there such a discrepancy? One plausible conjecture is that the third person plural personal pronoun does double duty, serving as the plural form both of the third person personal pronoun as well as of "one", which seems to lack a morphologically related plural form.

Another characteristic shared by bare plurals and indefinite noun phrases is that the former lend themselves to the same range of selectional interpretations as the latter. Thus, just the sentence

(69) a. Each person spotted a bear

is true, when there is just one bear which was seen by each person, and when there is a different bear which was seen by each person; so, the sentence

(69) b. Each person spotted bears.

is true, when there is just one group of bears which each person saw, and when there is a different group of bears which each person saw.[25]

But Carlson [Carlson77a; §1.2 – 1.3] thinks that for some parts of English sentences this sort of parallel does not hold up. One example he adduces is:

---

[24] I say presumably since it could turn out that they are yelling at the same bear.

[25] The same observation was made by Link [Link84; §2.1].

(70) a. A dog was everywhere.

b. Dogs were everywhere.

The first sentence, he judges, has the reading that there was a dog which was everywhere and lacks the reading that everywhere there was a dog; whereas, the second sentence, he judges, lacks the reading that there was a group of dogs which was everywhere and has the reading that everywhere had a group of dogs.

However, the supposition pertaining to scope assignment for quantified noun phrases adopted here, together with the hypothesis that bare plurals are plural indefinite noun phrases, implies that both sentences have both readings. Observe that a sentence just like the one in (70a), except that "everywhere" has been replaced by a more specific locative locution, admits of both readings: the one in which the choice of dog may depend on the choice of place as well as the one in which the choice of place may depend on the choice of dog.

(71) A dog was on every doorstep.

Also, notice that if one augments "everywhere" with a relative clause, both readings become easily available.

(72) A dog was everywhere one looked.

Indeed, the following sentence can express the ubiquity of soldiers in a country under martial law.

(73) A soldier was everywhere.

What about there being, apparently, only one reading for the sentence in (70b)? One fact to note in this regard is that it is an instance of an idiomatic form of expression: a sentence of the form of a bare plural followed by "are everywhere" or "were everywhere" means that the things denoted by the bare plural are very numerous. For example,

(74) Cockroaches are everywhere

is taken to say that cockroaches are all about. This idiomatic usage makes the second reading of the sentences in (70b) and (74) difficult to isolate.[26] But if one considers a sentence of the same syntactic structure and without the idiomatic overtones, one discovers that both readings are easily available.

(75) **Visitors from Sweden were in every photograph.**

it could be that each photograph depicted the same group of Swedes or different groups of Swedes.

In spite of these parallels, there remains a puzzling disparity between bare plurals and indefinite noun phrases: an indefinite noun phrase may never have a universal-like construal, whereas a bare plural may. So, for example, suppose "a cow" is the subject of a sentence, say

(75) **A cow is grazing in the field.**

There is only an existential construal:

(77) a. $(\exists x)(Cx \ \& \ Gx)$;

It never has an universal construal:

(77) b. $*(\forall x)(Cx \rightarrow Gx)$.

(where "C" stands for "is a cow" and "G" stands for "is grazing in the field"). In contrast, suppose "cows" is the subject of a sentence. Sometimes it seems that the predicate need be true of every cow for the sentence to be true; and sometimes it seems that the predicate need be true of just a few for the sentence to be true. I shall call these the universal-like and existential-like construals respectively. The pairs of sentences below illustrate them.

(78) a. **Cows are mammals.**

---

[26]Notice also that compounds formed with "every" are susceptible of a collective construal. This is illustrated by verbs such as "meet", which, on their covert reciprocal construal, cannot tolerate a non-collective, singular noun phrase as its subject.

    (i) *The man met at the church.

    (ii) *Each person met at the church.

However, they can tolerate compounds formed with "every".

    (iii) Everyone met at the church.

b. Cows are grazing in the field.

However, closer scrutiny of the data shows that, in the construal of bare plurals, there is not so much a choice between two alternative construals, one existential-like and the other universal-like; but rather it shows that there is a choice in the range of construals in which the existential-like and the universal-like construals are extremes.[27] Here are some examples:

(79) a. Cows are mammals.

b. Cows eat hay.

c. Cows give milk.

d. Cows are grazing in the field.

So, while (79a) and (70d) have a universal-like and an existential-like construal respectively, (79b) and (79c) seem to fall somewhere in between. For (79b) to be true, it seems that the predicate "eat hay" need be true only of most cows; yet for (79c) to be true, it seems that the predicate "give milk" need be true of many, though it need not be true of even half, of all cows. It appears, then, that the predicate need be true of each member of some non-empty subset of the subject's denotation; but the subset could be as small as any doubleton of the subject's denotation or as large as the subject's denotation itself. And, if it is true of each member of a non-empty subset, then it is true of the maximal collective constituted from that set.

If this observation is correct, then one wants to inquire after what determines the relevant subset of the bare plural's denotation. Consider this pair of sentences which differ only in that the verb in the first is in the simple present whereas the verb in the second is in the present progressive.

(80) a. Dogs bark.

b. Dogs are barking.

Now the first sentence has a universal-like construal while the second has an existential-like construal. It would be a mistake to think that this disparity is determined by the tense of the verb. The sentence

(81) a. Dogs in a kennel bark every morning

---

[27]This observation has been made independently by Schubert and Pelletier [Schubert&Pelletier87; p. 104].

has the same simple present tense verb as (80a). Yet (81a) can be used to
state a universal-like fact about dogs in each kennel, namely, that if one puts
a dog in a kennel, it will bark each morning it is there; or it can be used to
state an existential-like fact about dogs in a kennel, namely, that some dogs
in a kennel bark evbery morning. Similarly, the sentence

(81) b. Dogs in my neighborhood are barking more and more loudly

could be used to state a bizarre fact about all or some of the dogs in my
neighborhood.

Indeed, the factor determining the construal of the bare plural within the
range of the subsets of its noun's denotation seems to be extra-grammatical.
Consider these sentences:

(82) a. Smokers are responsible for the boom in tobacco-farming.

b. Smokers are responsible for the fire in the Ball Park Lounge.

Without reflection, one is inclined to construe "smokers" in (82b) as existential-
like; after all, it requires many more than a few smokers to produce a boom
in tobacco-farming while it requires only one careless smoker to cause a fire
in a bar. But matters could be different. It is possible that only a handful of
dedicated smokers might purchase cigarettes at a rate sufficient to produce
a boom in tobacco-farming. And if one believes that, then it would be easy
to get an existential-like construal of "smokers" in (82a). Conversely, it is
possible that the community of smokers conspired to set fire to the Ball Park
Lounge, the clandestine headquarters of a world-wide organization bent on
the eradication of smoking. And if one believes that, then it would not be
hard to get a universal-like construal of "smokers" in (82b). Nor is there
anything peculiar about the subject position of a sentence.

(83) a. Mohan loves puppies.

b. Mohan owns puppies.

the only difference between the two sentences, which have the bare plural
in the object position, is the choice of stative verb. Surely, the difference
in construal of "puppies" rests on the fact that one believes that, while
someone may love all puppies, no one owns, or is likely to own, all puppies.

3.2   The Grammar of Plural Indefinite Noun Phrases

The facts just presented, as well as others which have been already widely acknowledged, are all consequences of the hypothesis that a bare plural is a plural indefinite noun phrase, in which the determiner, the plural form of the indefinite article, is phonetically null. The widely acknowledged facts are three. First, bare plurals are plural noun phrases. Second, a singular indefinite noun phrase admits both. Third, on its quantificational reading, a singular indefinite noun phrase is assigned scope with respect to its clause. The construals to which a bare plural is liable, when considered in relation to another noun phrase, which is a quantified one, in its clause, suggests that it too is assigned scope within its clause.

Finally, recall that when a predicate is evaluated with respect to a noun phrase which is one of its arguments, it is evaluated with respect to a plurality constituted from the noun phrase's denotation. Usually more than one plurality can be constituted on the basis of a noun phrase's denotation. If a noun phrase is singular, that is, has the syntactic feature $-PL$, then the evaluation is constrained to be evaluated with respect to the minimal plurality; if a noun phrase is plural, that is, has the syntactic feature $+PL$, then it is not constrained to be evaluated with respect to one plurality or another, it can be evaluated with respect to any plurality. It was shown that when the argument is a singular indefinite noun phrase, the predicate is evaluated only with respect to the minimal plurality associated with the noun phrase. In particular, on the noun phrase's referential reading, the predicate is satisfied at its indefinite noun phrase argument if, and only if, it is satisfied by every member of the minimal plurality, which plurality must be the singleton set associated with the indefinite noun phrase. On the indefinite noun phrase's quantificational reading, the predicate is satisfied at its indefinite noun phrase argument if, and only if, it is satisfied by a member of the minimal plurality associated with the indefinite noun phrase.[28] In light of these facts about singular indefinite noun phrases, one assumes that the following will be facts about singular indefinite noun phrases. If a predicate's argument is a plural indefinite noun phrase, then the predicate would be evaluated at the plural indefinite noun phrase argument with respect to any plurality if, and only if, the predicate is satisfied at the argument for a

---

[28] In the case where a noun phrase is a demonstrative one, its associated denotation is the denotation of the noun phrase itself. In the case where it is a quantified noun phrase, the associated denotation is the domain over which the quantifier ranges, which is the denotation of the N node immediately dominated by the NP node of the quantified noun phrase in question.

given plurality if, and only if, the predicate is satisfied at that argument for some member of the plurality.

Now, it can be proved that (i) there is a reading on which a predicate one of whose arguments is a quantified plural indefinite noun phrase is satisfied at that argument if and only if (ii) the predicate is satisfied at that argument by the maximal collective constituted from some non-empty subset of the denotation associated with the noun phrase. Clearly, if (ii) holds, then (i) holds. Conversely, suppose that (i) holds. Let NP be the indefinite plural noun phrase and let D be its associated denotation. Suppose that c is a collective constituted from members of the denotation satisfying the predicate. Then c, taken with respect to its constituents, is the maximal collective constituted from the set of those constituents. By hypothesis, the members of c satisfy the predicate, so c satisfies the predicate. Essentially the same claim holds for predicates with referential plural noun phrases: if (i) there is a reading on which a predicate one of whose arguments is a referential plural indefinite noun phrase is satisfied at that argument, then (ii) the predicate is satisfied at that argument by the maximal collective constituted from some non-empty subset of the denotation associated with the noun phrase.[29] But a predicate whose argument is a bare plural is also satisfied under these conditions, as was shown above (at (79) and following).

Of particular interest is the fact that a plural indefinite noun phrase would be liable to a universal-like construal, unless specifically barred therefrom, as is the quantified noun phrase whose quantifier is the plural form of "some"; for one possible subset of its associated denotation is the denotation itself; and, as was observed above (§1.2.2 above), if each member of the denotation satisfies the predicate, then so does the maximal collective constituted therefrom. So as a result of the auxiliary hypotheses pertaining to grammatical number adopted here, one construal available to a plural indefinite noun phrase is a universal-like construal. But this is precisely the construal of a bare plural which rendered it apparently disanalogous to a singular indefinite noun phrase. Notice that the view here accommodates the disparity between the quantified noun phrases where the quantifier is the plural form of "some" and where it is the plural form of the quantifier which is the indefinite article. The former does not admit a universal-like construal, but the latter does. But this is not surprising, since the former quantifier is in opposition to the quantifier "all"; whereas the latter is in

---

[29] The weakening from the biconditional to the implication reflects the fact that the deixis of the noun phrase in question is not being considered.

opposition to no other quantifier.

3.3 Generic Construals of Bare Plurals

It has been observed for some time that a bare plural is, in some cases, susceptible to a so-called "generic" construal. In fact, Carlson [Carlson77a; §4] takes this construal as the foundation for the semantic analysis of bare plurals. But closer scrutiny of the data shows one must distinguish the fact that every noun phrase other than one which contains a proper name as its head can be used with a generic construal (in the sense to be defined below) from the fact that, in a sentence, characteristics of varying degrees of intrinsicness, including tendencies, dispositions, and habits, which are expressed by the verb phrase, are attributed to what is denoted by its noun phrase subject. Indeed, neither of these two sorts of phenomena are particular to bare plurals.

To see this, one needs to get an idea of what it is for a noun phrase to have a generic construal. Now there are noun phrases whose semantic interpretation seems to directly involve kinds: "this kind of bird", "every sort of dog", "which kind of car", *etc.* But these are not to the point. What is to the point is the fact, examples of which, in isolation, may not refer to a kind of way, in context, refer to a kind. So, as Carlson [Carlson1977a; (105a)] illustrates," this cigarette", taken in isolation, would be thought to refer to an individual (concrete) cigarette; but not so in the example:

(84) This cigarette is made in nine different countries.

I suggest that such examples provide the paradigmatic examples of the generic construal of noun phrases, and as a consequence, propose the following definition.[30]

(85) A noun phrase is used with a generic construal iff either

> (i) it is construed to refer to an entity which is a type one of whose tokens would be the noun phrase's reference were it taken in isolation,

<u>   or</u>

---

[30]This definition, as well as the examples given by [Carlson77a] in (105) and (106) of §2.3 of his article, contrasts with his later statement (p. 444) that "the generic seems to speak of tendencies, dispositions, characteristics, and the like".

> (ii) it is construed to range over entities which are types whose tokens would make up the noun phrase's range were it taken in isolation.

Consider, by way of illustration, the demonstrative noun phrase "this pen", the quantified noun phrase "each automobile in Reed's driveway", and the interrogative noun phrase "which mammal in the Edmonton zoo". In isolation, the reference of "this pen" would be to a particular pen, the range of "each automobile in Reed's driveway" would be the set of automobiles in Reed's driveway, and the range of "mammals in the Edmonton zoo" would be the set of mammals in the Edmonton zoo. But these are not the reference or range of these noun phrases in the sentence below.

(86) a. This pen is found in every house in Canada.

    b. Each automobile in Reed's driveway is driven by the affluent all over the world.

    c. Which mammal in the Edmonton zoo is native to every country in South America?

The reference of the demonstrative noun phrase in (86a) is the brand or make of the particular pen which would be its referent were it taken in isolation. The range of the quantified noun phrase in (86b) is the set of makes of automobiles of each of the automobiles in Reed's driveway. And the range of the interrogative noun phrase in (86c) is the set of genuses of each mammal in the Edmonton zoo.

Several observations should be made about the generic construal of a noun phrase. First, it is independent of the grammatical number of the noun phrase in question.

(87) a. These pens are found in every house in Canada.

    b. Alll automobiles in Reed's driveway are driven by the affluent all over the world.

    c. Which mammals in the Edmonton zoo are native to every country in South America?

Second, and not surprisingly, bare plurals have generic construals as well.

(88) a. Pens in this desk are found in every house in Canada.

b. Automobiles in Reed's driveway are driven by the affluent all over the world.

c. Mammals in the Edmonton zoo are native to every country in South America.

Third, a noun phrase need not occur in subject position to be liable to generic construal, as is borne out by the construal of the noun phrases italicized in the next set of sentences:

(89) a. Carter sells *this cigarette* in his tobacco shop.

b. This dealership sells *every car made by Tata.*

c. *Which birds* did Darwin discover during his voyage on the Beagle?

Fourth, the generic construal of a noun phrase is also independent of whether the head noun of the noun phrase is a count noun or a mass noun.

(90) a. This wine is found in every house in Canada.

b. All broccoli in Reed's refrigerator is grown by farmers all over the world.

c. What furniture in this store is found in every country in South America?

Finally, and of especial significance in light of Carlson's view that a bare plural names a kind, proper names do not have generic construals.

(91) a. *Reed lives in every house in Canada.

b. *Dan is native to nine different Southeast Asian countries.

Distinct from the fact that noun phrases are liable to generic construals is the fact that sentences can be used to attribute to things denoted by their subjects such things as habits, dispositions, and characteristics of varying degrees of intrinsicness. These facts are not only distinct but even completely independent of one another. This independence is borne out by sentences whose verb phrases express either habits, dispositions, or characteristics of various sorts, and whose subjects are proper names, which were just shown to be immune from generic construal. The following pairs of sentences are examples of sentences whose verb phrases express habits, dispositions, and characteristics respectively.

(92) a. Ferrell smokes cigarettes.

b. Ferrell bites his fingernails.

(93) a. Ferrell is irritable.

b. Ferrell does not like foreigners.

(94) a. Ferrell is a man.

b. Ferrell thinks about young girls a lot.

In short, there is no unified notion of generic reference which distinguishes the referential properties of bare plurals from those of other noun phrases. On the one hand, suppose that by "generic construal of a noun phrase" one understands the fact that a noun phrase can be an argument to a verb phrase which expresses a habit, disposition, or intrinsic characteristic. Then it turns out that every type of noun phrase is liable to a generic construal. On the other hand, suppose that by "generic construal of a noun phrase" one understands what is defined in (85) above. Then it turns out that every type of noun phrase whose head is a count noun or a mass noun is liable to a generic construal.

4 Conclusion

Up to this point, attention has been devoted solely to showing that the analysis of bare plurals as plural indefinite noun phrases does not suffer from the inadequacy ascribed to it by Carlson, namely, that pairs of sentences which differ only in whether or not a given noun phrase is an indefinite one or its bare plural counterpart have a difference in construal which exceeds what is permitted by their difference in grammatical number. In particular, I have shown that when the auxiliary hypotheses used by Carlson for his criticism of this analysis are replaced by empirically more adequate and independently motivated hypotheses, the discrepancy he encounters disappears. But, one might wonder, even if this discrepancy is eliminated when better auxiliary hypotheses are adopted, still why should the analysis of bare plurals as plural indefinite noun phrases be preferred to Carlson's analysis.

To begin with, recall that Carlson's analysis is based on a distinction between generic and non-generic construals of noun phrases which conflates the fact that a noun phrase may have a genuine generic construal (as defined in

(85) above) with the fact that verbs may attribute to their arguments, properties or relations of varying degrees of intrinsicness. Moreover, as pointed
out just above, any noun phrase may serve as an argument to a verb which
expresses a habit, disposition, tendency, *etc.*; and, except for proper names,
any noun phrase may, in the appropriate context, have a genuine generic construal. Yet in spite of his rather heterogeneous notion of generic construal,
Carlson cannot encompass within its ambit the existential-like construal of
bare plurals (*e.g.*, "cows" in "Cows are grazing in the field"). To account for
this construal, Carlson posits the existence of a phonetically null operator in
the verb phrase which acts on a bare plural to convert it into an existentially
quantified noun phrase. The basis for this positing is an alleged correlation
between the presence (or absence) of the progressive aspect of the verb, on
the one hand, and the presence (or absence) of the existential-like construal
of the bare plural, on the other (see [Carlson 77a; p. 445]). But it was
shown earlier (see (80) through (83) above) that this correlation is spurious;
rather, the availability (or unavailability) of the existential-like construal results from the extra-grammatical factor of background beliefs impinging on
the construal of the sentence. In contrast, the analysis advocated here does
not conflate these two notions of generic reference; and, moreover, it honors
the fact that one form of generic reference is common to all types of noun
phrases and the other to all types of noun phrases except those consisting
of just proper names.

   Second, although both analyses of bare plurals require the positing of
a phonetically null operator; the analysis argued for here posits such an
operator to exist on the basis of independent syntactic grounds, namely, the
completion of the paradigm suggested by the fact that, of all the determiners
which go together with count nouns to form acceptable noun phrases, only
the indefinite article has no overt phonetic form; and the analysis posits such
an operator in an independently motivated syntactic position, namely, the
position of determiners. Carlson's analysis, however, posits an operator with
no independent syntactic motivation and posits it to exist in a position which
is not otherwise syntactically motivated. In addition, Carlson himself points
out, an operator must be posited to exist in the tense-aspect-complex of the
verb for each argument position in the clause, if his analysis is to account
for the contrast between sentences such as these.[31]

   (95) a. Canadians give blankets to victims in emergencies.

---

[31]See (83) above, too.

b. Canadians in Mexico are giving blankets to friends injured in the earthquake.

Third, on the analysis proposed by Carlson, the plural grammatical number of bare plurals constitute a productive and systematic exception to the grammar; whereas, on the analysis he rejects, it does not. Indeed, bare plurals, even when construed generically, in either sense discussed previously, are not immune from the semantic import of their plural grammatical number.

(96) a. [Thai boxers]$_i$ are trained to kick [each other]$_i$.

b. [These two parts]$_i$ depend on [each other]$_i$ in every machine in which both are installed.[32]

The reciprocal relation, which, by anyone's account, is not definable over a singleton set, cannot be defined in cases where the denotation of the reciprocal pronoun's antecedent is an individual, even if the individual is an abstract entity, like a kind. While these facts need special provision in Carlson's analysis, they do not when bare plurals are taken to be plural indefinite noun phrases.

Acknowledgements The first version of this paper was presented in November of 1986 to the Logical Grammar Study Group of the University of Alberta, which comprised, among others, Matthew Dryer, Bernie Linsky, Jeff Pelletier, and Len Schubert. A second version was presented in June of 1988 at the annual meeting of the Society for Exact Philosophy (Rochester, New York). I am grateful to those in attendance at each occasion for their comments. I am also grateful to Yves Roberge for his helpful criticism of the current version.

---

[32]See (57) above as well.

5   Bibliography

Abbott, J. *Sets, Lattices, and Boolean Algebras*, Allyn and Bacon, 1969.

Alston, W. *Philosophy of Language*, Prentice–Hall, 1964.

Baldwin, J., ed. *Dictionary of Philosophy and Psychology*, Macmillan, 1901.

Bauerle, T., Schwarze, C., and A. von Stechow, eds. *Meaning, Use, and Interpretation of Language*, De Gruyter, 1983.

Ballmer, T., and M. Pinkal, eds. *Approaching Vagueness*, Elsevier, 1983.

Black, M. "Vagueness," *Philosophy of Science 4*, 4, pp. 427–455, 1937.

Carlson, G. "A unified analysis of the English bare plural," *Linguistics and Philosophy 1*, pp. 413–457, 1977.

Carlson, G. *References to Kinds in English*, University of Massachusetts, unpublished Ph.D. dissertation, 1977.

Carlson, L. *Plural Quantification*, MIT, unpublished manuscript, 1980.

Chastain, C. "Reference and context," *Language, Mind, and Knowledge*, Gunderson, K., ed., pp. 194–269, University of Minnesota Press, 1975.

Chomsky, N. *Lectures on Government and Binding: The Pisa Lectures*, Foris, 1982.

Copi, I. *Introduction to Logic*, Macmillan, 1982.

Fodor, J., and I. Sag. "Referential and quantificational indefinites," *Linguistics and Philosophy 5*, pp. 335–398, 1982.

Gillon, B. *The Logical Form of Plurality and Quantification in Natural Language*, MIT, unpublished Ph.D. dissertation, 1984.

Gillon, B. "The readings of plural noun phrases in English," *Linguistics and Philosophy 10*, pp. 199–200, 1987.

Gunderson, K., ed. *Language, Mind, and Knowledge*, University of Minnesota Press, 1975.

Heim, I., Lannik, H., and R. May. "Reciprocity and plurality," *Essays on Logical Form*, May, R., ed., unpublished manuscript, 1988.

Higginbotham, J. "Reciprocal interpretation," *Linguistic Research 3*, 1, pp. 97–117, 1981.

Higginbotham, J. "LF, binding, and nominals," *Linguistic Inquiry 14*, 3, pp. 395–420, 1983.

Hoeksema, J. "Plurality and conjunction," *Studies in Model Theoretic Semantics*, ter Meulen, ed., pp. 63–83, 1983.

Hornstein, N. *Logic as Grammar*, MIT Press, 1984.

Ioup, G. "Specificity and the interpretation of quantifiers," *Linguistics and Philosophy 1*, pp. 233–245, 1977.

Jesperson, O. *A Modern English Grammar on Historical Principles*, George Allen and Unwin, 1909.

Jesperson, O. *The Philosophy of Grammar*, George Allen and Unwin, 1924.

Kempson, R. *Semantic Theory*, Cambridge University Press, 1977.

Kempson, R., and A. Cormack. "Ambiguity and quantification," *Linguistics and Philosophy 4*, pp. 259–310, 1981.

Keynes, J. *Studies and Exercises in Formal Logic*, Macmillan, 1884.

Kroch, A. *The Semantics of Scope*, MIT, unpublished Ph.D. dissertation, 1974.

Langendoen, D. "The logic of reciprocity," *Linguistic Inquiry 9*, 2, pp. 177–197, 1978.

LePore, E., ed. *New Directions in Semantics*, Academic Press, 1987.

Link, G. "The logical analysis of plurals and mass terms: a lattice-theoretic approach," *Meaning, Use, and Interpretation of Language*, Bauerle, T., Schwarze, C., and A. von Stechow, eds. pp. 302–323, De Gruyter, 1983.

Link, G. "Pural," *Handbook of Semantics*, D. Wunderlich and C. Schwarze, eds., to appear.

Lyons, J. *Semantics*, Cambridge University Press, 1977.

Massey, G. "Tom, Dick, and Harry, and all the king's men," *American Philosophical Quarterly 13*, 2, pp. 89–108, 1976.

May, R. *The Grammar of Quantification*, MIT, unpublished Ph.D. dissertation, 1977.

May, R., ed. *Essays on Logical Form*, unpublished manuscript, 1988.

Peirce, C. "Vague," *Dictionary of Philosophy and Psychology volume 2*, Baldwin, J., ed., p. 748, Macmillan, 1901.

Pelletier, F., and L. Schubert. *Three Papers on the Logical Form of Mass Terms, Generics, Bare Plurals, and Habituals*, University of Alberta, Department of Computing Science: Technical Report (TR 87-3), 1987.

Quine, W. V. "Quantifiers and propositional attitudes," *The Journal of Philosophy 53*, 5, pp. 177–187, 1956.

Quine, W. V. *The Ways of Paradox*, Random House, 1966.

Roberts, C. *Modal Subordination, Anaphora, and Distributivity*, University of Massachusetts, unpublished Ph.D. dissertation, 1987.

Schubert, L., and F. Pelletier. "Problems in the representation of the logical form of generics, plurals, and mass nouns," *New Directions in Semantics*, LePore, E., ed. pp. 387–453, Academic Press, 1987.

Short, D., tr. *Problems of Semantics: A Contribution to the Analysis of the Language of Science*, Reidel, Translation from Czech of Tondl (1966) 2nd ed., 1981.

ter Meulen, A., ed. *Studies in Model Theoretic Semantics*, Foris, 1983.

Tondl, L. *Problemy Semantity*, English translation by Short, tr., 1966.

Ware, R. "Conjunction, plurality, and aggregate particulars," University of Zimbabwe, unpublished manuscript.

Wilson, G. "On definite and indefinite descriptions," *The Philosophical Review 87*, 1, pp. 48–76, 1978.

Wilson, R. *Introduction to Graph Theory*, Longman Group, 2nd ed. 1979, 1972.

Wunderlich, D. and C. Schwarze., eds. *Handbook of Semantics*, to appear 1984.

Seeing To it That: A Canonical Form for Agentives

I-PITT-Q Nuel Belnap and Michael Perloff I-PITT-Q

1 Introduction.

J. L. Austin told us that "The beginning of sense, not to say wisdom, is to realize that 'doing an action', as used in philosophy, is a highly abstract expression — it is a stand-in used in the place of any (or almost any) verb with a personal subject ..." [Austin56; p. 178].[1] In that paper he tried to throw light on the question of "doing an action" by looking at the range of cases in which excuses are offered both in everyday usage and in the law, and to arrive at a proper vocabulary for action by "induction" on the proper uses of words. Many years have passed, the lesson has been learned, and it is time for philosophy to go beyond the mere beginnings of sense and progress toward a deeper understanding of an agent doing an action. How should we proceed? Our suggestion is that the next step in the progression toward greater sense and wisdom is to have available the sort of clean and well honed linguistic resource that Austin, and other philosophers, have realized to be necessary. We think that the most promising path to a deeper understanding of an agent making a choice among alternatives that lead to action is to augment the language with a class of sentences whose fundamental syntactic and semantic structures are so well designed and easily understood that they illuminate not only their own operations but the nature and structure of the linguistic settings in which they function.

An example of a sentence that Austin might have had in mind is

Ahab sailed in search of Moby Dick.

---

[1] The legacy of J. L. Austin is a particularly rich one that is being carried on in a variety of ways. One way attempts to explain certain facts about language in terms of propositional content and illocutionary forces. That is not *our* program. Instead we are following in the wake of Austin's suggestion that when faced with the question of the meaning of a word or a term "reply by explaining its syntactics and demonstrating its semantics" [Austin70; p. 60].

H.E. Kyburg, Jr. et al. (eds.), Knowledge Representation and Defeasible Reasoning, 167–190.
Kluwer Academic Publishers. Printed in the Netherlands.

It has a personal subject, "Ahab", and an action-like verb "sailed", and seems to be describing an action in Austin's deliberately wide sense. We take the sentence not only to be true, but to be agentive for Ahab, for Ahab's sailing in search of Moby Dick was a direct result of a choice he made among alternatives available to him. On the other hand, although the perfectly ordinary sentence,

The Pequod sailed in search of Moby Dick

is surely true, and though we may be hard pressed to say exactly why, we are not hard pressed to say that it is not agentive: it does not even have a personal subject.

Consider now

Ishmael sailed in search of Moby Dick.

Ishmael signed on as a member of the ship's company in total ignorance of Ahab's vengeful purpose; are we then to say that the sentence is agentive for Ishmael, but false, on the consideration that both "Ahab" and "Ishmael" are appropriately "personal" subjects? Or is the sentence true on analogy with the example about the Pequod? English is not to be trusted in these waters.

Since English fails to serve us as an adequate pilot, what we want is a resource sensitive to the difference between those cases using an action-like verb in which agency is ascribed, and those cases in which there is merely the appearance of agency. With decent Austinian respect and regard for the structure of the language, we propose, insofar as is possible, to locate such a resource within English itself, a resource that will also allow us to become clearer about the relation between agentive sentences in their declarative uses and agentives in their imperative uses; for surely

Mr. Starbuck, hand me yon top-maul[2]

Mr. Starbuck handed Ahab the top-maul

are, in context, more than accidentally related. In fact, except for context-determined indexicals, they are the same agentive sentence in two different appearances: the former is an imperative issued to Mr. Starbuck by Ahab, while the latter is an agentive declarative whose truth or falsity is intimately connected to the satisfaction or failure of satisfaction of the imperative.

---

[2]p. 137.

2 Agentives.

Let us accordingly begin with the following convention: the agentive form that we are about to introduce shall be set off with square brackets [—...—]. It shall have two open places as indicated, the first to take an agent term, the second to take a declarative sentence (the *declarative complement* of the new form). The point about the second open place is non-trivial: having noted that declarative sentences can either ascribe agency or not, we specifically include as possible declarative complements for the second open place both those sentences that do ascribe agency and those that do not ascribe agency. The resulting square-bracket sentence is to say that the proposition expressed by the declarative complement is guaranteed true by a prior choice of the agent.

So

[the carpenter ... Ahab has a new snow white ivory leg]

is to be agentive for **the carpenter**, and is to say that he is the agent in the matter of Ahab's having a new snow white ivory leg.

With what verb or verb phrase shall we replace the ellipsis in that sentential form (it was after all only elliptical)? Among the candidates in English that history suggests are the following:[3]

1. brings it about that

---

[3] One of us has discussed these matters a little in [Belnap88] and [Belnap89], and numerous other philosophers have made or considered suggestions along similar lines, including at least Anderson, Åqvist, Bennett, Chellas, Chisholm, Danto, Davidson, Hamblin, Hilpinen, Hohfeld, Humberstone, the Kangers, Kenny, Lindahl, Makinson, Melden, Needham, Prn, Talja, Thalberg and von Wright. Bibliographic access to the literature with which we are familiar can be gained through [Thalberg67], [Åqvist84], [Bennett88], [Makinson86], and [Belnap89]. Although we cannot in this paper undertake to discuss these contributions, we do want to make the following two points. First, each of us was introduced to this family of ideas by our teacher, Alan Ross Anderson — see his [Anderson62] and [Anderson70]. Second, we observe that in an influential paper Davidson [Davidson66] has canvassed similar proposals and found them wanting. Partly he objects that these constructions do not solve his problems, for example variable polyadicity; we concur, noting only that we are concerned with different problems, for example the problem of providing a form for agentive sentences that will show how they contribute to the larger contexts — imperative, deontic, *etc.* — to which they are peculiar. Partly he offers an argument that "many sentences that do attribute agency cannot be cast in this grammatical form"; but his 1966 argument is perforce based on a pre-Kripke [Kripke72] understanding of the relation between the Morning Star and the Evening Star, and is not in any event intended to do justice to the nature of agency as we conceive it.

2. makes it the case that

3. causes it to be the case that

4. is responsible for the fact that

5. lets it be the case that

6. allows it to be the case that

7. takes steps in order that

8. behaves so that in consequence

9. sees to it that

As you can see, these are all grammatically acceptable; but items 1–3 suggest that causal processes are either at work or hovering in the background, whereas we wish to deemphasize this suggestion. Items 4–6 give the impression of moral judgment and ethical responsibility, and whereas those are important ideas (none more so), it is inappropriate to build them into the foundation of this enterprise. Items 7 and 8 are closer to the mark in their straightforward association of an agent and something made true by the agent, but even these candidates might suggest to some ears that we want you to concentrate on a second, prior *action* performed by an agent. The English verb form 9 *sees to it that*, has, to our ears at least, fewer of the obvious defects of the others, and *sees to it that* has the definite advantage of suggesting alternatives and choices. So our preferred sentence form is

$$[\alpha \text{ sees to it that } q],$$

which for logical emphasis we abbreviate as

$$[\alpha \text{ stit: } q],$$

referring to such a sentence as a *stit* sentence.

It is a consequence of what has just been said that a sentence $[\alpha \text{ stit: } q]$ with α as its subject is always agentive for α. The complement, q, may be agentive for α or not (this is the *Stit Complement Thesis*); it may, for that matter, be any sentence at all, but $[\alpha \text{ stit: } q]$.is always agentive for α — perhaps difficult to interpret, perhaps false, but always agentive for α (this is the *Agentiveness of Stit Thesis*).

So,

[Ishmael *stit:* Ishmael sailed on board the Pequod]

is agentive for Ishmael and a true sentence, while

[Ishmael *stit:* Ishmael refused to share a room at the Spouter Inn]

is equally agentive for Ishmael, but false.

The *stit* sentence

[Queequeg *stit:* the Pequod is fitted out for its voyage],

which has a non-agentive as its declarative complement, is agentive for Queequeg but false, for it is not due to Queequeg, but to Peleg, that the Pequod is fitted out for its voyage.

At this point you may fairly ask how agentive sentences differ from non-agentive ones; our answer is contained in the following

> *Stit Paraphrase Thesis: a sentence q is agentive for α if, and only if, q can be paraphrased as (or is strongly equivalent to) [α stit: q].*

We intend this strategy, clarification by paraphrase, as neither definitional nor reductive. It is rather an attempt to isolate, by way of a canonical form, a particular set of English sentences in order to study them more closely as they interact with each other and with other parts of language in different linguistic environments, just as a biologist might stain a particular organism to follow its activities as it interacts with members of its own species and with other species in various physical environments. Analogically, most of us are comfortable in saying that an English sentence is *conditional* if it can be paraphrased into the canonical form "if q_1 then q_2," and in going on to reveal that the sentence

The Prophet will tell Queequeg and Ishmael about Ahab provided they stop a minute

is in fact conditional by paraphrasing it as

If Queequeg and Ishmael stop a minute then the Prophet will tell them about Ahab.

By our thesis, then, since Ahab sailed in search of Moby Dick is correctly paraphrased as [Ahab *stit:* Ahab sailed in search of Moby Dick], both the original and its longer transform are not only true but agentive for Ahab. Notice that Ishmael sailed in search of Moby Dick is doubtless true on its non-agentive interpretation, but arguably false when construed as an agentive because arguably false when paraphrased as [Ishmael *stit:* Ishmael sailed in search of Moby Dick].

3   Stit: Simple cases.

We now use the strategy of clarification by paraphrase to demonstrate how *stit* sentences can help us better to know our way around in some areas in which agency counts. Consider for example

Ahab found the White Whale.

Certainly it is true, but is it agentive? In order to answer we have to address ourselves specifically to the question: did Ahab see to it that Ahab found the White Whale? As we have seen already, Ahab was agentive in his search for Moby Dick, but was he agentive in finding it? We think not. Although Ahab was a participant in guiding the Pequod to the ultimate outcome, and the major participant, his actually finding the White Whale was due in large part to chance, to natural forces beyond his control.[4] Thus, though Ahab found the White Whale is true, it is false when paraphrased as [Ahab *stit:* Ahab found the White Whale]. Therefore, in so far as the sentence Ahab found the White Whale is true, it is non-agentive; and in so far as it is agentive it is not true.

Consider the following pair:

(1) Queequeg struck home with his harpoon

(2) Queequeg's harpoon struck home.

Some careful speakers of English might always use (1) as an agentive and (2) as a non-agentive, whereas most of us are liable to use them interchangeably, sometimes in one way and sometimes the other. But

(3) [Queequeg *stit:* Queequeg struck home with his harpoon]

and

(4) [Queequeg *stit:* Queequeg's harpoon struck home]

come to much the same thing. Such differences between (1) and (2) as there are disappear when they are embedded into *stit* contexts; the *stit* sentences (3) and (4), regardless of the uncertainties of their complements, are transparent with respect to agency.

---

[4]"Time and tide flow wide," remarks Mr. Starbuck. "The hated fish has the round watery world to swim in ...."

3.1   Imperatives.

"Clear away the boats! Luff!" cried Ahab. Following an established tradition, we think of imperatives as having a force and a content.[5] With regard to force, Ahab's imperatives may have been orders or commands, which many think the only possibilities; but Ahab might instead have been inviting, requesting, suggesting, advising, ... the helmsman to luff. Putting force to one side, however, we are after the content:

Imperative Content Thesis: regardless of its force, the content of every imperative is agentive.

For example, Luff! can have its content represented as The helmsman luffs, which in turn, since it is agentive, can be paraphrased as The helmsman sees to it that he luffs. Thus, Luff! can be paraphrased as Helmsman, see to it that you luff!. In this case the application of our thesis is easy because The helmsman luffs, which looks to be the most plausible content for the imperative, is already agentive. Still, there is more to be learned. To luff is to see to it that the bow of the boat is heading directly into the wind. Accordingly, the content of the imperative

Luff!

can be put into the canonical form

[Helmsman *stit:* the helmsman luffs]

or equivalently,

[Helmsman *stit:* the boat is headed into the wind].

The two *stit* sentences are equivalent, but while the complement of the former is agentive, the complement of the latter doesn't mention the agent at all.[6]

Unlike Luff!, the imperative Be on deck at dawn! does not show its content so obviously; the *stit* apparatus, however, increases in value as problems

---

[5]C. L. Hamblin tells us that "imperatives are not only among the most frequent of utterances; they are also, surely, among the most important. If the human race had to choose between being barred from uttering imperatives and being barred from uttering anything else, there is no doubt which it should prefer" [Hamblin87; p. 2]. In fact it was a study of his book that set us under weigh and helped us avoid some threatening reefs.

[6]We hope no one confuses complement and content.

become more complex. Consider **Be on deck at dawn!** as addressed to the helmsman. The obviously nonagentive **the helmsman is on deck by dawn** cannot, by our thesis, represent its content; we need an agentive form, and fortunately there is already something at hand: the *stit* sentence, [**The helmsman** *stit:* **the helmsman is on deck at dawn**]. This, in turn, can be transformed back into the imperative **Helmsman, see to it that you are on deck at dawn**, which we take to be an accurate paraphrase of the original imperative **Be on deck at dawn**. This is important because you might be tempted to think that **the helmsman is on deck at dawn**, inasmuch as it displays an agent as its subject, is the content of the imperative **Be on deck at dawn**; but there are many ways in which it might be true that the helmsman is on deck at dawn, while false that he sees to it that he is. Because the content of every imperative must be agentive, an accurate paraphrase will not merely have the name of the addressee as its subject: that name will appear as subject of a sentence of the form [α *stit: q*].

We therefore have the following: since every imperative has agentive content, and since every agentive can be paraphrased as a *stit* sentence, it must be that every imperative will have a *stit* paraphrase of the form [α *stit: q*] — sometimes with q an agentive (hence a possible content of an imperative) and sometimes not.

3.2   Deontic contexts.

The traditional account (see *e.g.* [Åqvist84]) has that deontic statements have one of the forms

$\mathbf{O}q$: it is obligatory that q

$\mathbf{F}q$: it is forbidden that q, or

$\mathbf{P}q$: it is permitted that q,

where q is a declarative. Among its many virtues, this approach allows such great latitude that it can be connected to every possible action by any agent. On the other hand, agents have in this grammar no distinguished place; if invoked at all, the agent's name is only an accidental feature of the declarative complement. It is an easy mistake to think that $\mathbf{O}q$ says more than it actually does say. It does not say, for example, who, if anyone is obliged to see to it that q. Consider **It is forbidden that cooks be on the bridge.** It is tempting to read this as though it imposes a prohibition on the cook, but it doesn't, as we can see from the analogous **It is forbidden that dogs be on the bridge;** in either case the sentence form is not fit to tell us who is to see to it that no cooks (or dogs) are on the bridge. While a deontic language of declarative-sentence complements may be satisfactory for impersonal oughts, many within the tradition have seen that agents need to be treated with more care.[7]

Some deontic logicians have suggested the step of changing the grammar so that **O**, **P**, and **F** are taken to be adjectives modifying action-nominals. The fundamental forms are then taken as

$\mathbf{O}a$: a is obligatory

$\mathbf{F}a$: a is forbidden, or

$\mathbf{P}a$: a is permitted,

where a stands in place of a term designating an action. So $\mathbf{O}a$ might be instanced by **Sailing is obligatory**, or $\mathbf{F}a$ by **Bringing the boat into the wind is forbidden.** Since actions are always the actions of agents, this step is in the right direction, but it still fails appropriately to recognize the agent. Furthermore, there is a considerable loss in expressive power, since clearly understood declarative sentences, q, are so much easier to come by than are clearly understood action-nominals, a. In order to regain the headway lost in the move from sentences to action-nominals, some have tried adding negative doings such as not-sailings, or disjunctive doings such as luffing-or-flensing; but even with these additions, there remain two features missing from the overhauled model: first, the flexibility that follows from permitting an arbitrary declarative within the scope of a deontic statement, and second, the grammatical means to identify and keep track of the agent.

We propose a combination having the strengths of both the declarative complement ($\mathbf{O}q$) plan and the action-nominal complement ($\mathbf{O}a$) plan: we propose to focus on deontic statements that have only agentives for their complements and thus can always be paraphrased into one of the forms

$\mathbf{O}[\alpha \ stit: \ q]$: α is obligated to see to it that q

$\mathbf{F}[\alpha \ stit: \ q]$: α is forbidden to see to it that q

---

[7]Foremost among those who have argued that these standard alternatives are inadequate is Castaneda, *e.g.* in [Castaneda74].

P[α *stit: q*]: α is permitted to see to it that *q*

Though **P**[α *stit: q*], for example, is not agentive (in our technical sense), we intend it as *quasi-agentive* in the loose sense that it involves both an agent and an agentive, and in the stricter sense that like an agentive, it has the agent itself as a recoverable part of its intension.

Our proposal calls, then, for a deontic language enriched by the restriction that the complements of Obligation, Permission and Prohibition be limited to *stit* sentences (this is part of the *Restricted Complement Thesis*). Recall that (i) *stit* sentences always express an action, (ii) *stit* sentences never lose or misplace the agent, and (iii) *there are no grammatical or metaphysical or semantic restrictions on the declaratives that may be put in place of q*. Such a plan, we think, retains the most valuable features of both the declarative-sentence complement (**O***q*) account and of the action-nominal complement (**O***a*) account.

For example, in context the burden of the prohibition of cooks (or dogs) from the bridge might be

O[the Third Mate *stit:* no cooks (*or dogs*) are on the bridge].

Or we might have **F**[the cook *stit:* the boats are lowered]. Question: does this imply **O**[the cook *stit:* ¬(the boats are lowered])?

3.3   Could have.

> A short rushing sound leaped out of the boat; it was the darted iron of Queequeg. Then all in one welded commotion came an invisible push from astern, while forward the boat seemed striking on a ledge; the sail collapsed and exploded; a gush of scalding vapor shot up near by; something rolled and tumbled like an earthquake beneath us. The whole crew were half suffocated as they were tossed helter-skelter into the white curdling cream of the squall. Squall, whale, and harpoon had all blended together; and the whale, merely grazed by the iron, escaped.

Queequeg missed. His harpoon did not strike home. But *could* Queequeg have struck home with his harpoon? Questions of this kind have been notoriously difficult to answer, partly because of an inability to tie down the relevant sense of "could have." Consider the vexed examples of §3, and the consequent result of applying "could have" thereunto:

Queequeg struck home with his harpoon

Queequeg *could have* struck home with his harpoon

Queequeg's harpoon struck home

Queequeg's harpoon *could have* struck home.

If you are not clear whether Queequeg's striking home with his harpoon comes to the same thing as Queequeg's harpoon striking home, then you will not be clear whether Queequeg's ability to strike home with his harpoon is about Queequeg's agency or the powers of nature. The one appears more a question of an agent's ability and the other appears more a question of the squall; but paraphrase into canonical form settles the issue:

Queequeg could have *stit*: Queequeg struck home with his harpoon

and

Queequeg could have *stit*: Queequeg's harpoon struck home

are both unambiguously concerned with agentive powers. A recipe emerges: take any sentence, whether agentive, non-agentive or unclear as to agency, feed it as complement to the *stit* construction, and the result is bound to be an agentive; feed that intermediate result as the complement of a "could have" and you are bound to have a claim about agency.[8] As notation we suggest

Could-have[α *stit: q*],

which makes "could have *stit*" sentences *look* like the quasi-agentives that they *are*.

The point is that when approaching questions about "could have," first become clear about the complement of "could have", because that is essential to being clear about "could have" itself; further, to focus on the "could have" of agency, paraphrase into canonical form, that is into a *stit* sentence.

You may think that such canonical forming is too much trouble, and sometimes it is; if you are concerned, however, to give a general account of agentive "could have," then the availability of a canonical form is exactly what is required: 1) Since every *stit* sentence is an agentive, you will not have explained "could have" unless you explain "could have seen to it that *q*" for arbitrary *q*. 2) Since every agentive can be paraphrased as a *stit* sentence, if you do explain "could have seen to it that *q*" for arbitrary *q*, you will have done the whole job.

---

[8] Exercise: carry out this plan for "Queequeg missed."

4   Grammar and semantics of stit

Here we work some more at clarifying *stit* by "explaining its syntactics and demonstrating its semantics."

4.1   Grammar

Idealizing our language to be adequate for agents and their doings leads to the awareness that many English sentences are agentives, each of which can be paraphrased by means of a *stit* sentence. We saw above that a *stit* sentence takes in one of its open places an agent name and, in the other, as sentential complement, a declarative. *Stit* sentences are thus the canonical form of any and every English language agentive.

Agentives in English may occur as stand-alone sentences or as constituents of other sentences. Ahab might issue an order with the stand-alone imperative,

Hand me yon top-maul.

But also Ahab might make a request in which a constituent form of that imperative appears embedded within another imperative, as in

Mr. Flask, request *Mr. Starbuck to hand me yon top-maul.*

Here the constituent imperative is italicized. Further, it becomes clear that the sentential complement of any of a long list of English verbs such as request, order, permit, demand, *etc.*, is always an imperative — *i.e.*, an agentive, that is paraphrasable as a *stit* sentence. No matter the form of words in English, a constituent imperative such as the italicized portion of Ahab ordered *Starbuck to hand him the top maul* or of Ahab requested *that Starbuck hand him the top-maul* must be representable as a *stit* sentence — in this case as [Starbuck stit: 'Starbuck hands Ahab the top-maul"].

Similarly, English stand-alone declarative sentences may have agentive content, as in the capitalized and perioded specimen,

The top-maul was handed to Ahab by Starbuck.

Or a constituent form (no capital, no period) of that agentive declarative may appear as embedded within other declaratives, as illustrated by the italicized portion of

That *the top-maul was handed to Ahab by Starbuck* was of no concern to Mr. Flask.

In all these cases the paraphrase into canonical form allows us to see that whatever the complications of natural language, we have one and the same agentive sentence, its surface grammatical form varying from context to context.

Since "seeing to it that" sentences are always agentive, it follows that the variety of grammatical forms in which we might find exactly the same *stit* sentence is extensive, including such constructions as

α sees to it that q (indicative; with caps and a period if stand-alone, but not if constituent)

α saw to it that q (tensed indicative)

α, see to it that q (stand-alone imperative)

α see to it that q (constituent imperative — subjunctive)

α to see to it that q (constituent imperative — infinitive)

α's seeing to it that q (constituent imperative — gerund)

But these subtle alterations required by English grammar obscure rather than reveal the fact that we can locate the self-same agentive in a variety of contexts: sometimes as a stand-alone declarative, sometimes as an embedded declarative, sometimes as a stand-alone imperative, and sometimes as an embedded imperative. Our paraphrase of agentives into canonical form clarifies that situation. A *stit* sentence, [α *stit: q*], since it displays its agent and appropriate declarative complement publicly and obviously, is the appropriate picture of the underlying agentive partly because it remains recognizably the same in any and every context.

Finally, let us recall that when concerned with the modalities of agency, it is similarly helpful to use a *stit* sentence in order to keep track of the agentive. The English **Starbuck could have handed the top-maul to Ahab** is helpfully paraphrased as *Could-have*[Starbuck *stit:* **Starbuck hands the top-maul to Ahab**], while **Starbuck is obligated to hand the top-maul to Ahab** is paraphrased as **O**[Starbuck *stit:* **Starbuck hands the top-maul to Ahab**]. In all these cases it is crucial that the content of the order and the obligation, the ability and the action are all the very same, all captured by a single *stit* sentence.[9]

---

[9]You might think that because we refer to the action and the obligation, the ability and the order each with a singular term that English drives us to having actions as individuals in our ontology. You might think that unless you are clear on agents and agentives.

4.2   Semantics

Without any claim to completeness or exclusivity, we offer a semantic account of *stit* based on a combination of (1) a picture of the future as replete with possibilities as expressed in a theory of *branching time* in the sense of *e.g.* Thomason [Thomason70] or McCall [McCall76] and (2) von Neumann's theory of games as in [vonNeumann44]. We hope that the following helps in spite of its necessary brevity and severity.[10]

Moments, on the branching time theory, are ordered in a tree-like structure so that from each moment, there is a single route into the past but multiple possible future routes. A *history* is a set of moments that constitutes a single complete branch of the tree; on Thomason's semantics for tense and modality, truth is primarily relative to moment-history pairs, and secondarily relative to moments themselves by a supervaluation; *i.e.*, truth at a moment *simpliciter* is defined as truth at all pairings of that moment with a history passing through it. Some modal concepts require that we add that moments can be partitioned "horizontally," with moments that are partitioned together thought of as *alternates* to each other — that is, as alternate ways of "filling" the same instant of time. It is satisfying to suppose that if moment m_0 precedes moment m, then every history through m_0 contains exactly one alternate to m.

On this picture all the histories passing through a given moment, m, can be divided into equivalence classes, with two histories said to be *undivided at* m just in case they both pass through a moment that is later than m. Thus, histories passing through m that are not undivided at m must perforce branch off from each other at that very moment, m.

To branching time we add a concept, "absolute" in the sense of Bressan [Bressan72], of an *agent*. That the concept is absolute means that it serves not only as a principal of application but also as a principle of identity in the sense of Gupta [Gupta80], so that under that concept each agent is re-identifiable across all moments of time, with no possibility of fission or fusion, nor even of non-existence.[11]

---

[10]These semantics are not as it happens derived from those of Hilpinen, Kanger, Lindahl, Needham, and Pörn, cited in [Åqvist84], of which we learned when our thoughts were already fixed. The reader who compares will nevertheless find numerous points of overlap between those semantics in the style of "a relation R" and our suggested semantics grounded in branching time and game theory. There are also significant differences, as there are between our semantics and the tree-based semantics of Åqvist [Åqvist78], of which we also learned late.

[11]We will use a trick to deny agency to an agent at moments when intuitively we would

What now needs to be added comes from von Neumann: at each moment each agent is faced with a set of alternatives representing his or her available or possible choices.[12] A *choice set* for an agent α at a moment m is a partition of all the histories passing through m, subject to the condition that if two histories are undivided at m, then they shall belong to the same member of the partition.[13] A *possible choice* is a member of a choice set. The picture makes no sense unless the following *the-world-goes-on condition* is satisfied: for each way of selecting one possible choice for each agent from his or her choice set, the intersection of all the choices selected must not be empty.[14]

Points at which this picture diverges from that provided by von Neumann are the following. (1) It is assumed by von Neumann that every game is finite, an assumption obviously inappropriate in the present context — though our semantics will work also perfectly well in the special finite case. (2) In the "extended" form of the game, von Neumann puts a single agent or player fully in charge of each moment, so that at any one node of a von Neumann game tree, at most one player (possibly nature) is entitled to move. That convenient bit of fancy seems all right in the finite case, but appears to border on the ludicrous in the context of the full theory of branching time. In his "normal" form of the game, however, von Neumann permits simultaneous independent choices by each agent or player to determine the outcome, and that is what is required for the present construction. (3) In contrast to von Neumann, we have assigned no payoffs as structural features; when the agents make their choices at a moment m, all that happens is this: the world goes on.

Where the intension of α falls under the concept of an agent, we can now give a semantic account of [α *stit: q*] as follows: [α *stit: q*] is true at a moment, m, relative to any history h through m, if there is a prior witnessing "choice-point", w_0, satisfying two conditions. First, find the possible choice in the choice set for α at w_0 that contains h. Pick any history located in that possible choice, and locate the moment m' that is both contained in

---

want to say that he or she does not exist; see the note below.

[12]See [Perloff79] for some considerations concerning alternatives.

[13]P. Kremer pointed out the need for this requirement.

[14]The the-world-goes-on condition is relevant only for consideration of multiple agents. That the choice set for α at m is a partition evidently already implies that the union of all the possible choices for an agent α at a moment m must exhaust the histories passing through m. In line with this, we artificially deny agency to an agent at a moment, m, by stipulating that his or her choice set contains but one possible choice, a Hobson's choice, namely, the set of *all* histories passing through m.

that history and is an alternate to m. Then q must be true at m' relative to every history through m'. Second, there must be some alternate m^* to m lying on a history through w_0 such that q is not true at m^* relative to some history through m^*.[15]

The first condition says that the choice made by α at w_0 guarantees the truth of q at the point of time in question; that is, the truth of q at the moment in question is fully due to a prior choice of α because given that choice, q would have been true no matter what happened. The second condition says that α really did have a choice concerning q at w_0; that is, it was not the case that q would have been true independently of the choice of α.

Though we do not have the space here for developments, there is room to enlarge our account to include cases in which $[\alpha \; stit: \; q]$ is true on the basis of an interval of choices rather than on the basis of a single choice moment, to include cases of joint agency, to add local "payoffs," to add a probability measure, *etc.*

The foregoing account is "intensional" rather than extensional, as is surely right for $[\alpha \; stit: \; q]$. To the extent, however, that the truth of $[\alpha \; stit: \; q]$ depends on more than the intension of q, *e.g.* on its sense or on its structure or perhaps on how α grasps or takes q, our account fails to catch its full meaning. Our account is more apt for the pattern "the present fact that q is guaranteed by a prior choice of α," which we take to be a valuable approximation to $[\alpha \; stit: \; q]$.

5   Embedded *stits*

Our preferred locution $[\alpha \; stit: \; q]$ is partially a connective, and connectives invite embedding one within another; accordingly we illustrate the results of accepting this invitation.

5.1   Refraining

The trouble with refraining, as most people appreciate, is that it is often hard to do. The trouble with refraining, as most philosophers appreciate, is that it is hard to pin down because it is both acting and not acting; discussions of this topic in the recent literature show how difficult it is to avoid being confused. Consider the two imperatives:

---

[15]This paragraph says what was supposed to be said by the garbled version in [Belnap&Perloff89]; we are indebted to W. Edelberg for calling the confusion to our attention.

Turn not thy back on the compass.

Refrain from turning thy back on the compass.

These stand-alone imperatives seem to have the same content. That is, they seem to offer the same advice, or create the same obligation, or make the same demand, ..., depending on the force with which they are uttered. Maybe that will help us see what it is to refrain.

To refrain from turning thy back certainly entails not turning thy back, that is, *not acting* in a certain way. But we cannot accept that refraining from turning thy back is the same as not turning thy back, for not turning thy back does not entail refraining from turning thy back: there are plenty of things in the world out there that are neither turning their backs nor refraining from turning their backs. Further, since many things that aren't turning their backs are not even agents, it cannot be that not turning thy back is necessarily acting in a certain way.

A standard but often useless analytic technique when faced with this sort of situation is to suggest that therefore refraining from turning thy back is: not turning thy back plus "something else." But what else? One might think the something else is mental, and certainly the mind may come into it, but let us leave it out as long as we can, for surely thou canst refrain from turning thy back without paying attention, without having a plan not to turn thy back, even without intending not to turn thy back. Also one might think that the something else has something to do with obeying or refusing an order, piece of advice, demand, request, *etc.*, but to think the thought is to reject it: thou canst refrain from turning thy back to the compass without there being any such injunction anywhere about.

If, however, we look for the solution not in something external to the canonical form, but as something already contained in it, we take the first step toward the appropriate solution. As von Wright says [vonWright63; p. 45], refraining is a doing, it's a kind of action. But of course the action in question is not the action of turning thy back! So maybe, someone might think, refraining from turning thy back is the action of not turning thy back; that sounds kind of right. But it cannot be exactly or clearly right, since we just said that not turning thy back does not entail refraining from turning thy back, and is not even an action, and that sounds right, too.

So the problem is still with us: refraining seems to be not acting (not turning thy back), but also acting (not turning thy back). No wonder von

Wright posited refraining (or forbearing) as indefinable in terms of action alone.[16]

Our perplexity makes us see why it is so tempting to start trying to distinguish

> **not turning thy back to the compass** (not acting)

from

> **not turning thy back to the compass** (acting)

by beginning to make noises about external *vs.* internal negation, even when we know perfectly well that we do not know what we mean by this distinction; and why it is tempting to invent the-act-of-not-turning-thy-back-to-the-compass, thus enriching our ontology, also without having any sense that we know what we are talking about.

In the framework of *stit*, with its clear recognition that embedding is not only possible but encouraged, there is an easy solution to this puzzle about refraining. It involves a simple series of steps:

- α **is turning his back to the compass** is equivalent to [α *stit:* α **is turning** α'**s back to the compass**]. Indeed, this equivalence is (by the Stit Paraphrase Thesis) our test for a sentence agentive for α, and will clearly distinguish **Stubb is turning his back to the compass** from **Queequeg is a native of Kokovoko.**[17]

- α **is not turning his back to the compass** is equivalent to $\neg$(α **is turning** α'**s back to the compass**).

- Conclude that α **is not turning his back to the compass** is equivalent to $\neg$[α *stit:* α **is turning** α'**s back to the compass**].

- $\neg$[α *stit:* α **is turning** α'**s back to the compass**] is *not* agentive for α, that is (by a negative use of the Stit Paraphrase Thesis), it is *not* in general equivalent to [α *stit:* [$\neg$[α *stit:* α **is turning** α'**s back to the compass**]]].

- Recall that refraining is agentive, so that the content of a refraining sentence must have a canonical form [α *stit:* q], and equally keep

---

[16]He tried a definition of the "something else" in terms of "ability" (*ibid.*), an attempt that we follow Brand in rejecting [Brand70; pp. 234–235].

[17]p. 56.

in mind that the negative imperative, Turn not thy back on the compass, must have the same canonical form.

- The following are then seen to be equivalent:

    α refrains from turning his back to the compass, and

    [α *stit:* ¬[α *stit:* α is turning α's back to the compass]].

- Now you can (literally) see that refraining from turning thy back to the compass is agentive and also (literally) involves an inaction: refraining from turning thy back to the compass is (actively) seeing to it that thou dost not (actively) turn thy back to the compass.

- But let us continue more generally. We know that any agentive proposition can be expressed in the form [α *stit:* q], where q might or might not itself be agentive. We now add that any refraining proposition can be expressed in the form

    [α *stit:* ¬q],

    whether q is agentive or not.[18] The Refrain from turning thy back to the compass example above chose q as agentive, but there is also Refrain from being (or don't be) on deck at dawn, or Don't get caught by the cook. Because q is not agentive these have simpler, non-nested analyses, just [α *stit:* ¬(α is on deck at dawn)], or [α *stit:* ¬(α is caught by the cook)].

- Without postulating new "negative acts" as ontological items or strange *undefined* internal *vs.* external negations, all is clear: the agency of α refrains from seeing to it that q flows from the agency of [α *stit:* ¬q], and the negation comes from what it is that α sees to: namely, that not q. When q is itself agentive, this can of course be further filled out, as in the turning thy back to the compass example.

- Now we see the drive for the double use of α isn't turning α's back to the compass. If taken as non-agentive, it is canonically just ¬[α

---

[18]English will always demand that the subject of q is α, but it does not care whether or not q is agentive for α.

stit: α is turning α's back to the compass]; but if it is to be taken in an agentive sense, then you will *have* to read it as: [α *stit:* ¬[α *stit:* α is turning α's back to the compass]]. English does not have a short and precise way to make the distinction; but the *stit* locution does the job.

Who would have thought that refraining from acting involved an embedding of a non-acting within an acting, a non-agentive within an agentive? Only through attending to the grammar of the canonical form [α *stit: q*], which promotes such embedding by its very design, is the truth revealed.

5.2   Deontic contexts again

As a final illustration of the beneficial consequences of using the canonical form of *stit* for agentives, we produce a surprise in the course of exploring an aspect of our earlier suggestion that deontic statements be put in their own canonical form as follows:

$\quad$ **O**[α *stit: q*]: α is obligated to see to it that *q*

$\quad$ **F**[α *stit: q*]: α is forbidden to see to it that *q*

$\quad$ **P**[α *stit: q*]: α is permitted to see to it that *q*

The standard equivalences for forbidden/permitted continue to make sense, *e.g.*,

$\quad$ **F**[α *stit: q*] ↔ ¬**P**[α *stit: q*],

but it is not equally easy to find a sensible forbidden/obligation equivalence accordant with the tradition because the first line below is clearly false and the second involves bad grammar:

$\quad$ **F**[α *stit: q*] ↔ **O**[α *stit:* ¬*q*] (false — when *q* is not agentive in α)

$\quad$ **F**[α *stit: q*] ↔ **O**¬[α *stit: q*] (bad grammar).

That the first line fails is illustrated by the following example: though the cook is forbidden to see to it that the boats are lowered, he is not thereby obligated to see to it that they are not lowered. The point about the second line is that since to be obligated is always to be obligated to do something, and since not doing something is not doing something, by our restriction that the complements of deontic modalities be limited to *stit* sentences, it follows that $O\neg[\alpha \ stit: \ q]$ *makes no sense*. But the solution is obvious: to be forbidden to see to it that q is to be obligated to refrain from seeing to it that q, and we know what refraining means. Accordingly, the proper equivalence, forced on us by our commitment to good grammar, is just

$$\mathbf{F}[\alpha \ stit: \ q] \leftrightarrow \mathbf{O}[\alpha \ stit: \ \neg[\alpha \ stit: \ q]].$$

If the cook is forbidden to see to it that the Pequod is headed up into the wind, then the cook is obligated to see to it that he does not see to it that the Pequod is headed up into the wind, and conversely.

Symmetry suggests as well that to be obligated to see to it that q is to be forbidden to refrain from seeing to it that q.

$$\mathbf{O}[\alpha \ stit: \ q] \leftrightarrow \mathbf{F}[\alpha \ stit: \ \neg[\alpha \ stit: \ q]].$$

If the helmsman is obligated to see to it that the Pequod is headed up into the wind, then the helmsman is forbidden to see to it that he does not see it that the Pequod is headed up into the wind, and conversely.

And now the surprise: if both of these hold, then by substitution (of $\neg[\alpha \ stit: \ q]$ for q) and transitivity, so does

$$\mathbf{O}[\alpha \ stit: \ q] \leftrightarrow \mathbf{O}[\alpha \ stit: \ \neg[\alpha \ stit: \ \neg[\alpha \ stit: \ q]]].$$

This equivalence says that the only way to be obligated to refrain from refraining from luffing is to luff. Right or wrong? It would seem that the only way the equivalence could possibly hold or fail to hold were if as a matter of *stit* fact itself, the following held or did not hold:

$$[\alpha \ stit: \ q] \leftrightarrow [\alpha \ stit: \ \neg[\alpha \ stit: \ \neg[\alpha \ stit: \ q]]].$$

Can you think of a case in which the right side holds without the left? Does refraining from refraining imply doing? In another place we will show that this *stit* equivalence can indeed be justified on our suggested semantics, at least in certain special cases, but we take it that our general point of view commits us only to trying to get clear on the matter, not to already having accomplished that desirable end.

6   Conclusion

Although not so grand as Ishmael's, we think our story well worth the telling, and though we have not sailed far, our mainsail has been unfurled and we have caught the first breeze. What we have proposed is an augmentation of our current linguistic resources with a linguistic form, the *stit* sentence [α *stit: q*], that i) leads us carefully to attend to the agent of an action, ii) is capable of taking any English declarative as its complement, iii) is recoverable as the same *stit* sentence either as a declarative or an imperative, iv) is grammatically suitable for embedding within wider contexts. Among its other virtues, the *stit* sentence sheds light on refraining and helps to clarify some of the agentive modalities. This linguistic addition, attentive to grammatical form and semantic structure, promotes greater clarity in the way we talk and think about the phenomena of our world, and thus justifies its added complexity.[19]

---

[19] An earlier version of this piece appeared as [Belnap&Perloff89]; we are grateful to the editors of *Theoria* for the requisite permission.

7 Bibliography

Anderson, A. "Logic, norms, and roles," *Ratio 4*, pp. 36–49, 1962.

Anderson, A. "The logic of hohfeldian propositions," *Logique et Analyse 49-50*, pp. 231–242, 1970.

Åqvist, L. "An analysis of action sentences based on a 'tree' system of modal tense logic," *Papers on Tense, Aspect and Verb Classification*, C. Rohrer, ed. Tbingen (TBL Verlag Gunter Narr), pp. 111–161, 1978.

Åqvist, L. "Deontic logic," *Handbook of Philosophical Logic, volume II*, D. Gabbay and F. Guenthner, eds., Reidel, pp. 605–714, 1984.

Austin, J. "A plea for excuses," *Proceedings of the Aristotelian Society 1956-57*, reprinted in *Philosophical Papers*, Oxford University Press, 1970.

Austin, J. "The meaning of a word," *Philosophical Papers*, Oxford University Press, 1970.

Belnap, N. "Declaratives are not enough," unpublished manuscript, forthcoming in *Philosophical Studies*, 1988.

Belnap, N. "Backwards and forwards in the modal logic of agency," unpublished manuscript, 1989.

Belnap, N., and M. Perloff. "Seeing to it that: a canonical form for agentives," *Theoria 54* pp. 175–199, 1989.

Bennett, J. *Events and Their Names*, Hackett, forthcoming 1988.

Brand, M. *The Nature of Human Action*, Scott, Foresman, and Company, 1970.

Bressan, A. *A General Interpreted Modal Calculus*, Yale University Press, 1972.

Castaneda, H. N. *The Structure of Morality*, Charles C. Thomas, 1974.

Davidson, D. "The logical form of action sentences," *The Logic of Decision and Action*, N. Rescher, ed., University of Pittsburgh Press, pp. 81–95, 1966.

Gupta, A. *The Logic of Common Nouns: an Investigation in Quantified Modal Logic*, Yale University Press, 1980.

Hamblin, C. *Imperatives*, Basil Blackwell, 1987.

Kripke, S. "Naming and necessity," *Semantics of Natural Language*, D. Davidson and G. Harman, eds., Reidel, pp. 253–355, 1972.

Makinson, D. "On the formal representation of rights relations," *Journal of Philosophical Logic 15*, pp. 403–425, 1986.

McCall, S. "Objective time flow," *Philosophy of Science 43*, pp. 337–362, 1976.

Perloff, M. "A better alternative," *Analysis 39*, pp. 106–108, 1979.

Thalberg, I. *Enigmas of Agency*, George Allen & Unwin, 1972. See especially Chapter I, "Do we cause our own actions?".

Thomason, R. H. "Indeterminist time and truth-value gaps," *Theoria 36*, pp. 264–281, 1970.

von Neumann, J. and O. Morgenstern. *Theory of Games and Economic Behavior*, Princeton University Press, 1944.

von Wright, G. *Norm and Action*, Routledge and Kegan Paul, 1963.

von Wright G. "A new system of deontic logic," *Deontic Logic: Introductory and Systematic Readings*, R. Hilpinen, ed., Reidel, pp.105–120, 1970.

Speaker Plans, Linguistic Contexts, and Indirect Speech Acts

Andrew McCafferty

Some indirect speech acts are unrelated to the semantic meaning of the sentence uttered, how ever widely we construe "semantic meaning". Searle gives this example:

> A: Let's go to the movies tonight.
> B: I have to study for an exam.
> (Searle, Indirect Speech Acts [Searle75])

The sentence "I have to study for an exam" is not lexically tied to turning down proposals to go to the movies. There is no sense in which this is part of its meaning. However, in this context B uses it to do just this.

Explaining indirect speech acts of this sort is a complex task. To get some feel for the difficulties, consider the following conversations:

(1)   A: What about our plans to see a movie tonight?
       B: I'd like to see a Bogart film.
       C: *Casablanca* is showing at the Fulton.

In this conversation, C indirectly proposes the plan to see *Casablanca* at the Fulton. By stating that it is showing there, he puts this plan forward for consideration.

On the other hand, consider

(2)   A: What about our plans to see a movie tonight?
       B: I'm not particular, only I'd rather not see a Bogart film.
       C: What's showing at the Fulton?
       A: *Casablanca* is at the Fulton.

191

H.E. Kyburg, Jr. et al. (eds.), Knowledge Representation and Defeasible Reasoning, 191–220.
© 1990 *Kluwer Academic Publishers. Printed in the Netherlands.*

This exchange does not propose seeing *Casablanca*. The group would not assume that A is recommending this. He is simply answering C's question.

A more difficult example (for reasons we will see):

(3)   A: What about our plans to see a movie tonight?
       B: I'd like to see a Bogart film.
       C: Is *Casablanca* showing at the Fulton?
       A: No, *The African Queen* is at the Fulton.

Here, C wants to consider the plan of seeing *Casablanca* at the Fulton, but A's response rules this out. A's response does not, however, propose the plan to see *The African Queen* — even though this is a Bogart film. As in (2), after this exchange there is no plan under consideration.

As some evidence for these intuitions, consider the possibility of adding to each conversation:

D: That's a good suggestion.

In (1) this would be quite natural. D would be approving of C's proposal. However, since there is no plan under consideration in (2) or (3), each of the following is odd:

(2')   A: What about our plans to see a movie tonight?
        B: I'm not particular, only I'd rather not see a Bogart film.
        C: What's showing at the Fulton?
        A: *Casablanca*.
        *D: That's a good suggestion.

(3')   A: What about our plans to see a movie tonight?
        B: I'd like to see a Bogart film.
        C: Is *Casablanca* showing at the Fulton?
        A: No, *The African Queen* is at the Fulton.
        *D: That's a good suggestion.

In (2') D's remark must be interpreted as some sort of joke. In (3') it is hard to interpret at all.

There are many possible variants of these conversations. Consider:

(4)   A: What about our plans to see a movie tonight?
C: *Casablanca* is showing at the Fulton.
B: I'd rather not see a Bogart film.

(5)   A: What about our plans to see a movie tonight?
B: I'd like to see a Bogart film.
C: What's showing at the Fulton?
A: *Casablanca*.
D: That's a good suggestion.

(6)   A: What about our plans to see a movie tonight?
B: I'd like to see a Bogart film.
C: What's showing at the Fulton?
A: *Annie Hall*.
*D: That's a good suggestion.

In (4) C proposes the plan of seeing *Casablanca*, but B immediately rules it out. In (5) C wants to consider the Fulton. Upon hearing what is showing there, D states his approval. (6) is odd, because A's answer does not suggest the plan of seeing *Annie Hall*.

In many ways, these conversations are not nearly as complex as typical conversations. They don't contain a variety of naturally occurring features which affect speech acts.[1] Yet, they already raise the problem. Why do two of them suggest the plan of seeing *Casablanca*, while the others do not? More generally, how can we explain or predict the indirect speech acts of simple conversations such as these? The goal of this paper is to defend an approach to these questions. In a word, I argue that indirect speech acts derive from the speaker plan for the linguistic context.

From the philosophical/linguistic literature, I adopt a contextual change theory of meaning. According to this theory, the significance of an utterance is the change it brings about in the linguistic context. For example, in

---

[1] I have in mind here sub-dialogues, changes in topic, interruptions, syntactical problems, intonational clues, pragmatic clue words ("o.k."), standard sequences (What's up?, Not too much), subtle uses of background knowledge, accommodation (see [Lewis79]), *etc.* They also don't contain any imperatives, which are substantially more problematic than indicatives or interrogatives.

the first conversation C proposes the plan of seeing *Casablanca* because his utterance adds this plan to the context. With certain qualifications, this is what it is to propose a plan. I intend to show that this rather mundane theory is actually quite useful.[2]

From the natural language understanding literature I borrow the concept of a speaker's plan. In a series of papers, James Allen — along with Cohen, Levesque, and Perrault — argues that indirect speech acts derive from the speaker's intentions for the beliefs and intentions of hearers. Suppose someone says, "Can you reach the salt?". An informal description of the "speaker's plan" might be for the hearer to reason as follows:

> She (the speaker) wants to know if I can reach the salt. Why so? Well, she must want me to realize that this is the case. Why so? Well, since my being able to reach the salt is a precondition of my passing the salt, perhaps what she really wants me to know is that she wants me to pass the salt.

This indirectly requests that the salt be passed, because it involves the hearer recognizing that this is intended. The core of Allen's work is to show how speaker plans can be reconstructed, even at this level of complexity.[3]

In their original papers, Allen and company apply their theory to single utterances. They show how saying "I'm cold" can be interpreted as a request to close the window, why "Do you know the secret?" can function as a request to tell the secret, *etc.* They do not, however, discuss longer conversations. A secondary goal of this paper is to show how a context change theory is useful in extending their work in this direction.[4]

---

[2]See [Hamblin71], [Stalnaker72], [Lewis78], and [Gazdar81] for context change theories of meaning. It is important to be clear what the issue is. That an utterance's meaning is given by the change it makes in the context is insightful, but in one sense mundane. The hard task of any theory of indirect speech acts is to show why utterances change the context as they do. It's mundane to say that someone indirectly proposes a plan if and only if he or she (indirectly) adds it to the context. The problem is to explain why a plan is added to the context in conversations (1), (4) and (5), but not in the other three. How could these results be predicted?

[3]See [Allen83] for details.

[4]More recently, Allen and a number of his students have begun to develop his theory for conversations. See for example, [Litman&Allen87], [Hinkelman86]. See as well [Pollack87], and [Grosz&Sidner86]. I should also note that this literature is explicitly indebted to Grice's work on speaker meaning and Searle's on speech acts.

1   Domain Plans

Before considering conversations, I need to say something about domain plans (for reasons which will become clear). Consider the following directed labeled graph (Figure 1). It represents some simple knowledge about domain plans to see a movie.

The arcs are (roughly) means-end relations. For example, 'Be at cinema X' is a means to 'See movie X at cinema Y'. The labels ("precondition," "effect," "abstraction") are fairly self-explanatory, for our purposes. A path through the net can be defined in the usual way, *i.e.*, a sequence of nodes each of which is connected to its successor by a directed arc. A plan consists of a set of paths all of which end at the same node. This final node is the goal of the plan.[5]

To see the idea, consider the following sub-net (Figure 2). It represents a reasonable plan for seeing *Casablanca* at the Fulton. The plan involves going to the Fulton, buying a ticket, and seeing the movie; but remains noncommittal on whether the agents will drive or walk. There are three paths, each of which ends at the goal: 'See *Casablanca* at the Fulton'. A more adequate representation of domain actions would contain planning at different levels of abstraction, and a number of other features. But this will do for us.

2   Explaining Indirect Speech Acts: Sample Conversations

Now, consider the opening contribution to the above conversations:

A: What about our plans to see a movie tonight?

The significance of this sentence fragment can't be reconstructed without detailing some initial context. I'll assume that it reminds the group that they have tentatively agreed to see a movie, and have not decided on details.

To represent this, we include in the context a set of conversational goals. The function of A's utterance is to modify this set, adding the goal of making plans to see a movie. Following Allen, we assume that A has a set of intentions or plan. It can be represented as in Figure 3. This "speaker plan" has two events: an utterance by A and the addition of a conversational goal to the linguistic context. The arrow is a means-end relation. A's

---

[5] For discussions of this way of representing knowledge, see [Kautz87] and [Allen83].

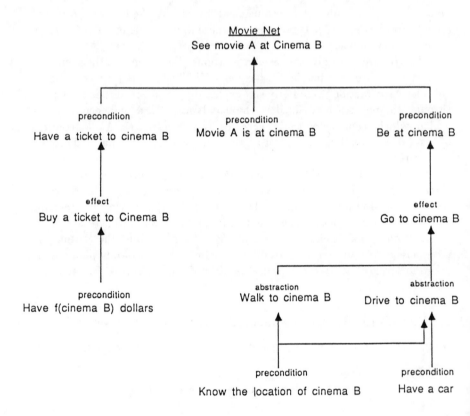

Figure 1

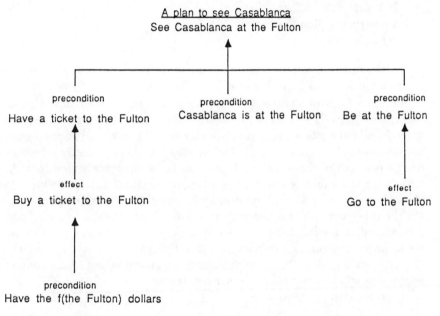

Figure 2

plan is to bring about the addition of the conversational goal by means of his utterance.

Assuming that no one objects to the plan, it yields the simple context:

Conversational goals:
    Construct a plan to see
    a movie

As the conversation proceeds, the representation of context will become more complex, containing elements other than conversational goals.

In some form or another, every theory of context must include conversational goals. These serve to constrain the interpretation of subsequent utterances. For example, suppose a speaker says, "There is no police protection at the bank in the evening". The significance of this utterance depends on the goal of the conversation. If the goal is to construct a plan to withdraw a large amount of money, the utterance cautions against doing it in the evening. The speaker is concerned with the possibility of being robbed. On the other hand, if the goal were to rob the bank, the speaker would be recommending an evening plan. An evening plan will not face the obstacle of police protection. To recognize this difference, we must include the conversational goal in the context; there must be something in the context which says what sort of plan is under construction.

Conversation (1) continues:

B: I'd like to see a Bogart film.
C: *Casablanca* is showing at the Fulton.

Intuitively, B's plan is to make it part of what is mutually believed, part of what has been called the "presumptions" of the conversation, that he wants to see a Bogart film. The reason he wants to do this is obvious. The group is constructing a plan to see a movie, and he wants that plan to be a plan to see a Bogart film. B's primary concern is to express a goal for the plan being constructed.

To account for this we include in linguistic context a set of presumptions, and a set of domain goals. The set of presumptions contains the propositions established by the conversation. For example (as we shall see), by asserting that *Casablanca* is showing at the Fulton, C adds this proposition to the

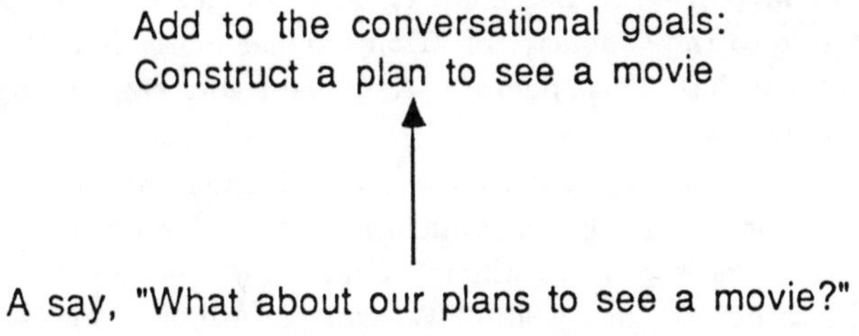

Add to the conversational goals:
Construct a plan to see a movie

↑

A say, "What about our plans to see a movie?"

Figure 3

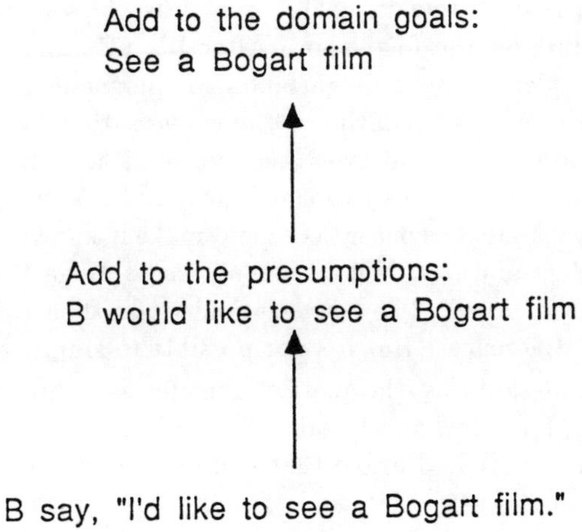

Add to the domain goals:
See a Bogart film

↑

Add to the presumptions:
B would like to see a Bogart film

↑

B say, "I'd like to see a Bogart film."

Figure 4

set of presumptions. Similarly, one effect of B's utterance is to add that B would like to see a Bogart film.

The domain goals are the goals which participants have expressed for domain plans. In our context, this set can include "See a Bogart film," "Drive to the Cinema," or "Don't spend more than three dollars on a film that you have seen before". A domain goal can be any qualification on a domain plan.[6]

On this account, B's speaker plan is as shown in Figure 4. The principle intention behind B's utterance is to make seeing a Bogart film a domain goal. This is brought about by means of making it known that he would like to do see such a film. We can picture the linguistic context after B's utterance as follows:

Conversational goals:	Domain goals:	Presumptions:
Construct a plan to see a movie	See a Bogart film	B wants to see a Bogart film

A established the conversational goal, and B added the presumption and domain goal.

The role of domain goals, or at least of some of them, is to serve as constraints on the final plan. After B's utterance, the group must either select a plan to see a Bogart film, or persuade B to give up his goal. It would be rude if C continued the conversation by saying, "Let's go to see *Chariots of Fire*," and everyone agreed without comment (except B). This suggestion violates B's expressed goal, and it's inappropriate to adopt such a plan without B's consent. C could make it known that he has a conflicting goal. He could say, "I'd rather not see a Bogart film" or "I want to see *Chariots of Fire*". The conversation would then naturally turn to working out the differences. But it's not possible to simply ignore B's goal.

Having said this, the question remains as to how we can reason about B's speaker plan. How do we realize that B is intending to add this presumption and domain goal? I argue that adding the presumption is a default consequence of B's utterance, and that there is a reasonable rule which implies the domain goal.

---

[6]Domain goals are separated from the conversational goals because they serve a different role. They aren't goals for the conversation, they are goals for the domain plan being constructed.

Sentences are correlated with default consequences for the linguistic context. A normal declarative sentence adds the proposition which the sentence expresses to the context. If a speaker utters a declarative Φ, and no one objects, the proposition expressed by Φ is added to the presumptions of the conversation. We have the following rule for reasoning about speaker plans:

1. If a speaker utters a declarative sentence Φ, and Φ expresses the proposition p in the context, than the speaker can be assumed (by default) to be intending to add p to the set of presumptions, *i.e.*, to the set of things mutually believed.

Of course, there are exceptions. If the sentence is uttered with an ironic tone of voice, then we can't apply it. Here we might want to suppose that the speaker is intending to add the negation of the proposition or whatever. But unless we have some reason to believe otherwise, we can assume that the intention is to add the proposition to the set of presumptions.

This explains the first link in B's speaker plan. He has uttered a declarative and so can be assumed to be adding the proposition it expresses to the presumptions. A reasonable rule for the second link:

2. If a speaker adds to the set of presumptions the proposition that she wants i, then she might be intending to add i to the set of domain goals.

Suppose the conversation is devoted to planning a picnic. If someone says, "I want to go to North Park," we can assume that he or she wants to limit the possible plans to ones which include North Park. Similarly, for utterances such as "I'd like to go fishing" or "I'd rather go swimming in the afternoon." By Rule 1, all of these add a presumption about the speakers wants, and so we can apply Rule 2. These utterances express domain goals.[7]

Rule 2 is not a default rule. Whether it applies must be determined from the context. Consider B's utterance. In our context it is reasonable to apply Rule 2 as well as Rule 1, because the conversational goal is to construct a plan to see a movie and "See a Bogart film" constrains such a plan. On the other hand, if the conversation were about how people feel about Bogart films, it would not be reasonable to apply Rule 2. We wouldn't assume

---

[7] "i" is a variable ranging over the objects of intentions; actions, events, states of affairs or whatever. Also, in representing the context, we should mark who added the goal and what plan this goal is intended to constrain. This would be important if there were several plans under construction. In general, for the sake of clarity I oversimplify the representation of context.

B to be registering a domain goal. His only purpose would be to add the presumption that he would like to see a Bogart film.

Turning to C's utterance, "*Casablanca* is showing at the Fulton," the default plan adds "*Casablanca* is showing at the Fulton" to the set of presumptions. This follows from our first rule of speaker plans. The default plan of a declarative utterance is to add the semantic meaning of the phrase uttered.

It is intuitively clear that adding "*Casablanca* is showing at the Fulton" is not C's complete plan. He is also (indirectly) putting the plan of seeing *Casablanca* forward for consideration. Knowing that it's showing at the Fulton is useful for constructing a plan to see it there, and constructing such a plan is the conversational goal. Given this, it is reasonable to suppose that C is suggesting this plan.

This makes explicit something that has been assumed all along. The linguistic context contains the domain plan(s) which are being constructed. This is one of its elements. As a planning conversation proceeds, various plans will be suggested, filled out, modified, *etc.* To follow the conversation, we must follow exactly what plans are in this set, details which have been decided on, details which are still under discussion, *etc.* In fact, our hypothesis that the conversational goal is to construct a plan to see a movie amounts to this: that the conversational goal is to have an executable domain plan to see a movie in the set of domain plans by the end of the conversation.

Consider the following rule:

> 3. If a speaker adds a proposition to the set of presumptions of a conversation, and knowing the proposition is useful in constructing a reasonable domain plan, then the speaker might be suggesting that plan (*i.e.*, intending that it be added to the set of domain plans).

Again, this is not a default rule. Not every proposition which is useful in constructing a plan actually suggests the plan. Knowing *Casablanca* is showing at the Fulton might be useful in constructing a plan to steal a Bogart film, but B's utterance does not suggest this. We need some positive reason to judge that the plan is actually being suggested. One such positive reason would be that having such a plan is a conversational goal. Another might be that the plan meets the domain goals which have been expressed. A negative reason for supposing the plan is being proposed is its violating a domain goal.[8]

This rule implies that C's speaker plan includes suggesting the plan to see *Casablanca*. C has added a proposition to the context which is useful in constructing this plan, and there are positive reasons in the context supporting it. Constructing such a plan is the goal of the conversation, and the plan meets B's domain goal of seeing a Bogart film.

To use the rule, however, we must (1) determine that C's utterance is useful in constructing the plan. We must also (2) be specific about exactly which plan is suggested, *i.e.*, how much detail is included, *etc.*

It's not hard to see, in a rough way, why C's utterance is useful in constructing a plan. *Casablanca* showing at the Fulton is a precondition of seeing it there.[9] And in general, before deciding on a plan, it is useful to know that its preconditions are true. A full discussion of this would take us into issues in domain plan reasoning — which I'm trying to avoid. My concern is with speaker plans, given that we can reason about domain plans. To use Rule 3, I'll simply assume that learning the truth of a precondition of a plan is useful in constructing it. Learning where a movie is showing is useful in constructing a plan to see it.

The second question is what plan C's utterance suggests. How much detail does it have? We can assume that it contains a link to the action whose precondition C established, namely (Figure 5). But, we can assume it includes more than this. For example, C is also intending to go to the Fulton and buy a ticket.

Again, to discuss this fully would take us too far into domain plan reasoning. But briefly, one feature of robust plans is that they are closed under preconditions. That is, the preconditions of the actions of a plan must either be true before the plan is put in effect, or the plan must contain some means for making them true. If you're not already at cinema a, a plan for seeing a movie at cinema a must contain some means for getting there. Similarly, if you're going to drive and you don't have access to a car, the plan must include a sub-plan for finding one. This "closure under presupposition" rule implies that the plan C suggests is shown in Figure 6. The plan is not yet complete. It does include "Go to the Fulton," but it doesn't say how this

---

[8]Intonation is also important. The intonation pattern of a request strongly supports Rule 3. On the other hand, intonation can be used to express disappointment. This would argue against Rule 3 being intended. An intonation pattern that suggested surprise or bewilderment would be hard to interpret. To see the point, read C's contribution to conversation (1) with these different intonations.

[9]This is represented in the movie net, see §A.

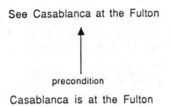

See Casablanca at the Fulton

precondition

Casablanca is at the Fulton

Figure 5

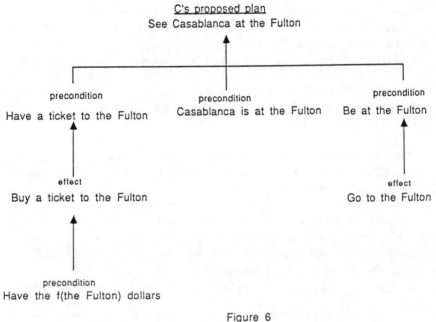

C's proposed plan
See Casablanca at the Fulton

precondition   precondition   precondition
Have a ticket to the Fulton   Casablanca is at the Fulton   Be at the Fulton

effect   effect
Buy a ticket to the Fulton   Go to the Fulton

precondition
Have the f(the Fulton) dollars

Figure 6

will be done. However, we can't add this yet, because we can't be sure if C is intending to drive or walk (see the movie net).

Returning to Rule 3, it implies — together with the intervening exposition — that C's speaker plan is (Figure 6). This, in turn, updates the context to:

Conversational goals:	Domain goals:	Domain plans:	Presumptions:
Construct a plan to see a movie	See a Bogart film	(See above domain plan)	*Casablanca* is showing at the Fulton

To illustrate a related rule, suppose C had asked, "Is *Casablanca* showing at the Fulton?," rather than stating that it was. The default plan of a question is to make knowing the answer a conversational goal. The rule:

4. If a speaker asks a question Φ, then the speaker is intending to make knowing the answer(s) a conversational goal (by default).

Of course, if the answer is already mutually known, then the question must be interpreted differently. Perhaps it's rhetorical, or perhaps the speaker wants reassurance that the supposed answer is actually right.[10]

Using this rule, we can conclude that C's plan includes the following link (Figure 7). Again it is clear, however, that this is not C's complete plan. C is also suggesting — at least tentatively — that the group go to the Fulton.

That C has this tentative plan follows from a slight modification of Rule 3. C has nearly satisfied the antecedent to this rule. C intends that the answer to his question be added to the set of presumptions, and knowing this

---

[10]This rule could be improved. Hamblin, followed by Belnap and Steel, argues that the semantic interpretation of a question is its set of answers. For example, the semantic interpretation of "How much does the Fulton cost?" includes "Movies at the Fulton cost $2.00," "Movies at the Fulton cost $3.25," *etc.* We could modify Rule 4 to explicitly include this idea.

4. If a speaker asks a question Φ and Φ's semantic interpretation is the set of answers b, then the speaker is (by default) intending to make knowing which answers in b are true a conversational goal.

The advantage to this form of rule is that it allows us to recognize when a reply to the question should be interpreted as an answer: only when it adds to the presumptions an element of b. Also, we can often glean from the question whether the speaker wants all the true answers, one of them, or some other number.

Add the domain plan:
See Casablanca at the Fulton
(i.e. the above domain plan)

rule 3
Add to the presumptions:
Casablanca is showing at the Fulton

rule 1
C say, "Casablanca is showing at the Fulton."

Figure 7

Add to the conversation goals:
Discover if Casablanca is showing at the Fulton

rule 4
C ask, "Is Casablanca showing at the Fulton?"

Figure 8

is useful in constructing a plan to see a movie (*i.e.*, the plan to see *Casablanca* at the Fulton). Therefore, by the rule (ignoring the discrepancy), C might be intending to add the plan of going to see *Casablanca* at the Fulton.

The discrepancy is that C is not intending his utterance to add the answer to his question, his goal is for the future conversation to add it. That is, C is not intending (as Rule 3 requires) "to add a proposition to the set of presumptions ...." C is intending "to add a conversational goal of adding a proposition ...."

To resolve this we add a rule, similar to Rule 3:

5. If a speaker adds a conversational goal of knowing Φ, and knowing Φ is useful in constructing a reasonable domain plan, then the speaker might be suggesting that plan (*i.e.*, intending that it be added to the set of domain plans).

(Φ is a question, such as "what is showing at the Fulton," or "if everyone can afford a $5.00 movie"). The reasons for supposing that a speaker is intending Rule 5 are similar to those for Rule 3: the plan meets a conversational goal, it fulfills all the expressed domain goals, *etc.*

From Rule 5, C's speaker plan can be judged to be as in Figure 8.

Notice that the plan to see *Casablanca* is marked as a conditional plan. It is conditional on whether *Casablanca* is showing at the Fulton. If it is discovered that *Casablanca* is showing, then this marking can be dropped. On the other hand, if it is discovered that *Casablanca* is not showing at the Fulton, then the plan is not feasible and it must be dropped.[11] That is, at this point the context would be:

---

[11] The Φ of Rule 5 is a question, and as such is interpreted as a set of propositions — the set of possible answers. For each answer, we determine if knowing it would be useful in constructing a plan to satisfy a conversational goal. We form a set of the useful answers; the domain plan is then dropped if it turns out that none of these answers are true (this assumes that there is only one relevant conversational goal and that the answers which suggest a plan suggest the same plan). Conditional plans are similar to Belnap's conditional assertion (see [Belnap71]). The group has the plan if the condition is met, otherwise there is no plan.

Conversational goals:	Domain goals:	Domain plans:	Presumptions:
Construct a plan to see a movie	See a Bogart Film	If *Casablanca* is showing at Fulton: The plan to see *Casablanca* at Fulton	
Discover if *Casablanca* is showing at Fulton			

If A were to answer, "Yes, *Casablanca* is at the Fulton," then the condition on the domain plan could be dropped. The resulting context would be:

Conversational goals:	Domain goals:	Domain plans:	Presumptions:
Construct a plan to see a movie	See a Bogart Film	The plan to see *Casablanca* at Fulton	*Casablanca* is showing at Fulton

On the other hand, if A were to answer in the negative, "No, it's not showing there." The plan would be dropped, and the context would become:

Conversational goals:	Domain goals:	Domain plans:	Presumptions:
Construct a plan to see a movie	See a Bogart Film		*Casablanca* is not showing at Fulton

The search for an acceptable domain plan would begin anew.

To consider a more difficult case, suppose A responds, "No, *The African Queen* is at the Fulton". The conversation would then be:

(3)   A: What about our plans to see a movie tonight?
        B: I'd like to see a Bogart film.
        C: Is *Casablanca* showing at the Fulton?
        A: No, *The African Queen* is at the Fulton.

In the introduction I argued that this response does not propose the plan of going to see *The African Queen*. It would be odd for D to continue, "Oh, that's a good idea."

However by the rules, A's response would add the plan to see *The African Queen*. A has answered C's question in the negative. Therefore, the plan to see *Casablanca* is dropped. However in answering the question, A has also fulfilled the antecedent of Rule 3. A has added a proposition to the context which is useful in constructing a domain plan to see a movie (*i.e.*, the plan to see *The African Queen*). Furthermore, this plan is in line with the domain goal to see a Bogart film. The rules we have developed so far yield the following plan (Figure 9).

I'd argue that the problem here is that this plan addresses two conversational goals. According to it, A is answering C's question and suggesting a domain plan. This problem can be resolved by placing a filter on speaker plans: other things being equal, assume that a speaker is only addressing one conversational goal. In interpreting A's utterance, once we determine that (by Rule 1) it answers C's question, we don't attempt to find other purposes for it. We don't apply Rule 3.

Next, suppose that C had asked, "What's showing at the Fulton?," rather than "Is *Casablanca* showing at the Fulton?" The conversation:

A: What about our plans to see a movie tonight?
B: I'd like to see a Bogart film.
C: What's showing at the Fulton?

Both Rules 4 and 5 apply to this question. C has asked a question, and discovering the answer is useful in constructing a domain plan to see a movie. So we can judge that C's plan is as shown in Figure 10.

Any answer to C's question is useful for constructing a domain plan to see a movie (except for "I don't know" , "No movie is showing at the Fulton" or something similar). "Gone with the Wind" would be useful in constructing a domain plan to see *"Gone with the Wind"*. However, only Bogart films are in line with the domain goals. C's conditional plan is shown in Figure 11. If the answer to C's question turns out to be either *"Casablanca"* or *"The African Queen,"* then the condition is fulfilled. If the answer is a non-

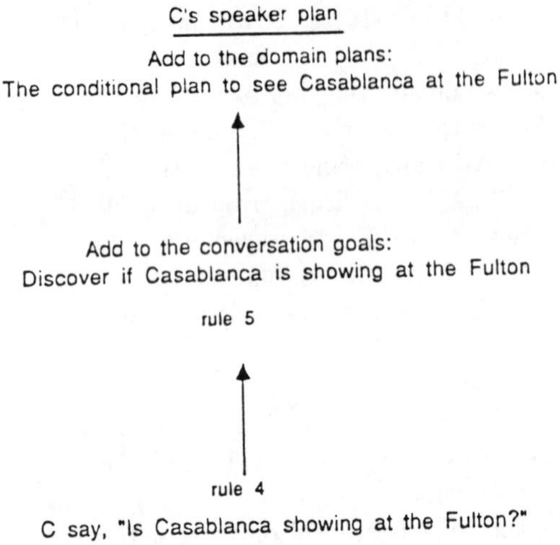

C's speaker plan
_____

Add to the domain plans:
The conditional plan to see Casablanca at the Fulton

Add to the conversation goals:
Discover if Casablanca is showing at the Fulton

rule 5

rule 4

C say, "Is Casablanca showing at the Fulton?"

Figure 9

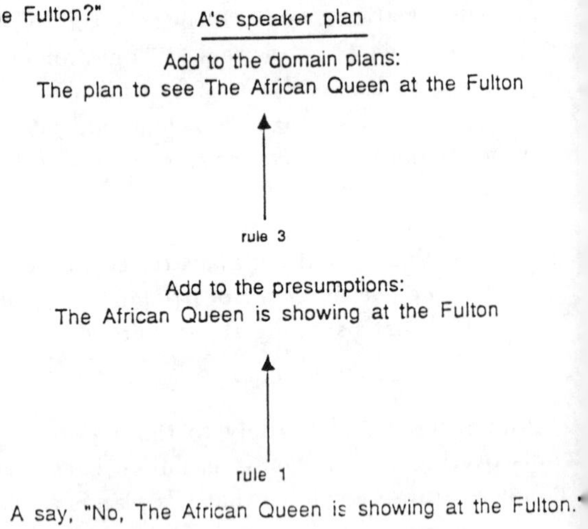

A's speaker plan

Add to the domain plans:
The plan to see The African Queen at the Fulton

rule 3

Add to the presumptions:
The African Queen is showing at the Fulton

rule 1

A say, "No, The African Queen is showing at the Fulton."

Figure 10

C's speaker plan:
_____

Add to the domain plans:
The conditional plan to see the movie which is showing at the Fulton
(See below for the exact plan.)

rule 5

Add to the conversation goals:
Discover what movie is showing at the Fulton

rule 4

C say, "What's showing at the Fulton?"

Figure 11

Bogart film (*Annie Hall*), the condition is violated and the plan is dropped.

This agrees with the following intuitions, discussed in the introduction:

(5)   A: What about our plans to see a movie tonight?
        B: I'd like to see a Bogart film.
        C: What's showing at the Fulton?
        A: *Casablanca.*
        D: That's a good suggestion.

(6)   A: What about our plans to see a movie tonight?
        B: I'd like to see a Bogart film.
        C: What's showing at the Fulton?
        A: *Annie Hall.*
        *D: That's a good suggestion.

After A's second utterance in (6), there is no longer a plan in the context, which makes D's remark odd.

Conversations in which someone expresses a goal not to see a Bogart film don't raise any special problems. Consider for example:

        A: What about our plans to see a movie tonight?
        B: I'm not particular, but I'd rather not see a Bogart film.
        C: What's showing at the Fulton?

As before, A adds a conversational goal and B adds a domain goal. The only difference is that the Goal B adds is to not see a Bogart film. As in the previous case, both Rules 4 and 5 apply to C's utterance. He has asked a question and knowing the answer is useful in constructing a domain plan to see a movie. The only difference is that the condition on C's plan has changed. Now the plans which do not violate the domain goal are those for seeing a non-Bogart film. So the condition on the plan which C adds is that the answer be a non-Bogart film. Therefore, if the answer is *Annie Hall*, the condition is dropped. If, on the other hand, the answer is *Casablanca* or *The African Queen*, the plan is dropped. The rules developed so far imply that the first of these, but not the second, suggest a plan:

A: What about our plans to see a movie tonight?
B: I'm not particular, but I'd rather not see a Bogart film.
C: What's showing at the Fulton?
A: *Annie Hall.*
D: Oh, that's a good suggestion.

(2)   A: What about our plans to see a movie tonight?
B: I'm not particular, but I'd rather not see a Bogart film.
C: What's showing at the Fulton?
A: *Casablanca.*
*D: Oh, that's a good suggestion.

Rules 1 through 5 are not exhaustive. Consider for example:

6. If a speaker adds a domain goal, and it is violated by a proposed domain plan, then the speaker might be intending to remove the domain plan from the context.

This rule, like those above, is frequently used in conversation. Consider:

(4)   A: What about our plans to see a movie tonight?
B: I'd like to see a Bogart film
C: *Casablanca* is showing at the Fulton.
A: I'd rather not go to see *Casablanca* again.

C's utterance adds the plan to see *Casablanca* to the set of domain plans. A adds a domain goal (Rule 2) and it conflicts with this plan. Rule 6 implies that A's speaker plan includes removing this domain plan.[12]

3   Conclusions

On the account I've been developing, the speech acts of a given utterance depend on the speaker's plan for the linguistic context. If this plan contains

---

[12]Some of my rules are related to Allen's "Plan inference rules".[13]. Rule 5 replaces "Know-positive," "Know-negative," and "Know-term". His "Precondition-action," "Body-action," and "Action-effect," can produce some of the inferences of my Rule 3 (Allen uses these three rules for domain plan reasoning, which I have separated from reasoning about speaker plans). One advantage of a full representation of linguistic context is that it allows for a variety of rules which Allen doesn't include, such as Rule 6.

only two nodes, the utterance and its default effect, there will be no indirect speech act. These result when the plan is more complex.

For example, suppose someone asks, "Do you have a telephone?" Consider two contexts. In the first, the speaker is taking a survey, and his only goal is to discover how many homes have telephones. In this context the complete plan is as shown in Figure 12. Since this contains only the default effect of the utterance, we have only the direct act of questioning.

On the other hand, suppose that the group is discussing plans for ordering a pizza. Given enough context, Rule 5 would apply. C would be suggesting that the group call in an order. Figure 13 shows the speaker plan. The third node indirectly suggests the conditional plan.

I've also been arguing that there are a set of rules which are used to reconstruct the speaker's plan, based on the context and the sentence which is uttered. They come in two types. Some of them give the default consequence of an utterance. For example, Rule 1 — a declarative adds to the set the presumptions the proposition which that declarative expresses. Others suggest indirect effects which the speaker may be intending. For example, Rule 6 — if a speaker adds a domain goal which is in conflict with an accepted domain plan, the speaker may be intending to remove that domain plan from the context.[14]

Each of the rules also has a set of conditions under which it applies, or doesn't apply. Rule 4 is that a question adds a conversational goal of knowing the answer. This applies unless the answer is already known, in which case the question must be interpreted differently. Consider:

A: *Casablanca* is showing at the Fulton.
B: I'd rather see *Chariots of Fire.*
C: What's showing at the Fulton?

Here C is not intending to discover the answer to his question. Rather, he is probably intending an indirect effect, *i.e.*, suggesting the plan of going to the Fulton (as an alternative to seeing *Chariots of Fire*).

---

[14]The default rules replace what [Levinson83] calls the "Literal Illocutionary Force Hypothesis," roughly that declaratives are used for stating, interrogatives for questioning, imperatives for requesting. The entire approach could be considered an "inference theory" of indirect speech acts, in some ways similar to that of Searle's. (See [Searle75], [Levinson83]). However, unlike Searle, there is no use of Grice's maxims, which — I would argue — are too general to produce detailed explanations.

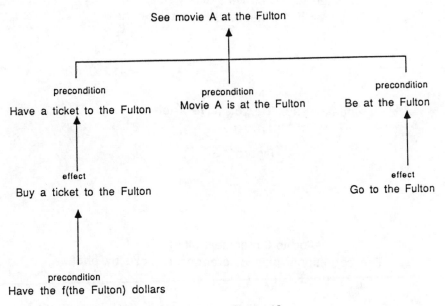

Figure 12

Add to the conversation goals:
Discover if the hearer has a telephone

rule 4

Speaker say, "Do you have a telephone?"

Figure 13

Add to the domain plan:
The conditional plan of ordering a pizza by phone

rule 5

Add to the conversation goals:
Discover if the hearer has a telephone

rule 4

Speaker say, "Do you have a telephone?"

Figure 14

There are also filters on speaker plans. We saw one example of this. I suggested that — other things being equal — we should assume that a speaker is only addressing one conversational goal. When a speaker answers a question, for example, we don't look for other reasons behind the utterance.

Finally, in a complex conversation the rules will not be deterministic. They may suggest two or more unrelated speaker plans, a set of heuristics determining which is the actual plan.[15]

Although I can't argue it here, there is reason to believe that the theory is useful in explaining more complex features of conversation, such as sub-dialogues and pragmatic clue words. Suppose that after C's question "What's at the Fulton?," A began a sub-dialogue with either:

> A: There is a newspaper in the den.
> or
> A: Does anyone have a newspaper?

Both of these suggest the domain plan of reading the movie section. Rules 1 and 3 apply to the declarative. A adds the proposition that there is a newspaper in the den, and this is useful in constructing a plan to answer C's question. The interrogative also suggests the plan to read the paper (by Rules 4 and 5). The difference is that it is conditional on someone having a paper.

Finally, consider the difference the pragmatic clue word "but" can make:

> (3")   A: What about our plans to see a movie tonight?
> B: I'd like to see a Bogart film.
> A: Is *Casablanca* showing at the Fulton?
> C: No, but *The African Queen* is.

Here, C does suggest the plan of seeing *The African Queen*. It would be quite natural for D to respond, "Oh, that's a good suggestion". The reason? Because "but" is an indicator of C's speaker plan. Now it it reasonable to suppose that C is not simply answering A's question. He is also using Rule

---

[15] These would include such things as "Assume that the speaker is addressing the more recently added goal," "Assume a speaker is modifying an existing plan rather than suggesting a new one."

3: *i.e.*, indirectly suggesting a plan by adding a presumption which is useful in constructing it.[16]

In "Pragmatic Presuppositions" Stalnaker calls for "the development and application of a theory in which detailed explanations of pragmatic phenomena ... can be given." [Stalnaker77; p. 123] As Stalnaker was aware, this is a tremendously complex problem. The methodology I've adopted is to severely limit the types of conversations under consideration. The ones I've analyzed consist of simple indicatives and interrogatives concerning movies. And even here I've only been able to outline the general approach, not giving — for example — details of the conditions under which the various rules apply. Even this much, however, gives reason to believe that reasoning about speaker plans for linguistic context is a promising approach.

---

[16]If this much is right, the hard task is to say what "but" indicates about a speaker's plan.

4 Bibliography

Allen, J. and C. Perrault. "Analysing intentions in utterances," *Artificial Intelligence 15*, 143–178, 1980.

Allen, J. "Recognizing intentions from natural language utterances," *Computational Models of Discourse*, M. Brady and R. Berwick, eds., pp. 108–166, Cambridge University Press, 1983.

Belnap, N. "Conditional assertion and restricted quantification," *Nous IV*, pp. 1–13, 1970.

Belnap, N. and T. Steel. *The Logic of Questions and Answers*, Yale Press, 1976.

Brand, M. "Intentional action and plans," *Midwest Studies in Philosophy X*, P. French, *et al.*, eds., Minnesota University Press, 1985.

Cohen, P. and C. Perrault. "Elements of a plan based theory of speech acts," *Cognitive Science 3*, pp. 177–212, 1979.

Cohen, P. and H. Levesque. "Speech acts and the recognition of shared plans," Proceedings of the Third Biennial Conference of the Canadian Society for Computational Studies of Intelligence, pp. 263–271, 1980.

Gazdar, G. "Speech act assignment," *Elements of Discourse Understanding*, A. Joshi, B. Webber, I. Sag, eds., Cambridge University Press, pp. 64–83, 1981.

Grice, H. "Meaning," *Philosophical Review 66*, pp. 377–388, 1957.

Grice, H. "Logic and conversation" *Syntax and Semantics 3: Speech Acts*, P. Cole and J. Morgan, eds., Academic Press, pp. 41–58, 1975.

Grosz, B. and C. Sidner. "Attention, intention, and the structure of discourse," *Computational Linguistics 12*, pp. 175–204, 1986.

Hamblin, C. "Mathematical models of dialogue," *Theoria 37*, 1971.

Hinkleman, E. "A plan-based approach to conversational implicature," unpublished.

Hobbs, J. "Towards an understanding of coherence in dialogue," *Strategies for Natural Language Processing*, W. Lehnert and M. Ringle, eds., Lawrence Erlbaum Associate, pp. 223–243, 1982.

Hobbs, J. "On the coherence and structure of discourse," *The Structure of Discourse*, L. Polanyi, ed., Ablex, 1987.

Kautz, H. "A Formal theory of plan recognition," Ph.D. thesis, University of Rochester, 1987.

Levinson, S. *Pragmatics*, Cambridge University Press, 1983.

Lewis, D. "Scorekeeping in a language game," *Journal of Philosophical Logic 8*, pp. 339–359, 1979.

Litman, D. "Linguistic coherence: a plan-based alternative," *Coling 86*, pp. 215–223, 1986.

Litman, D. and J. Allen. "A plan recognition model for subdialogues in conversation," *Cognitive Science 11*, pp. 163–200, 1987.

Perrault, C. and J. Allen. "A plan based analysis of indirect speech acts," *Computational Linguistics 6*, pp. 167–182, 1980.

Polanyi, L., ed., *The Structure of Discourse*, Ablex, 1987.

Searle, J. *Indirect speech acts, Syntax and Semantics 3: Speech Acts*, P. Cole and J. Morgan, Academic Press, pp. 59–82, 1975.

Stalnaker, R. "Presuppositions," *Journal of Philosophical Logic 2*, pp. 447–457, 1973.

Stalnaker, R. "Pragmatic presuppostions," *Semantics and Philosophy*, M. Munitz and P. Unger, eds., Academic Press, 1975.

Thomason, R. *Accommodation, Conversational Planning, and Implicature*, (draft), unpublished.

Part III.
Inference Rules and Belief Revision :

Belief Revision, Non-Monotonic Reasoning, and the Ramsey Test

Charles Cross /- REED-Q

In [Gärdenfors86] Peter Gärdenfors proves that two interesting principles about belief revision — the Ramsey rule and the Preservation principle — cannot both be true given certain arguably innocuous background assumptions about the logic of rational belief change. The two principles can be formulated roughly as follows: the *Ramsey rule* states that the indicative conditional propositions that an agent believes record that agent's dispositions to revise beliefs in light of new information; the *Preservation Principle* states that an agent should not give up old beliefs when revising his or her beliefs to accommodate new information unless the new information contradicts the old beliefs. Faced with a choice between these principles, Gärdenfors tentatively argues for giving up the Ramsey rule.

My aim here is to show that Gärdenfors' theorem can and should be interpreted in quite a different way, a way that is in fact consistent with the Ramsey rule. What Gärdenfors' theorem really shows, I claim, is that no rational agent who modifies his beliefs in response to new information can avoid reasoning in a *non-monotonic* way.[1] This follows from Gärdenfors' theorem, given the Ramsey rule and certain background assumptions about the logic of rational belief change. One upshot of this is that *Rational* agents reason non-monotonically, given the Ramsey rule, and so any adequate theory of belief revision must take non-monotonic reasoning into account. Existing theories of belief revision[2] do not take non-monotonic reasoning into account.

What I have to say here has several other upshots that warrant mention. For the philosophy of science there is this upshot: one crucial component of rational scientific inquiry is the formation of theories that go beyond the logical content of available evidence. Non-monotonic logic can be expected to shed some light on the problem of theory choice, since, as I show in §8,

---

[1] An inference relation is said to be non-monotonic if there exist sets of propositions Γ and Δ such that some things inferable from Γ are not inferable from Γ ∪ Δ.

[2] Here I mean, specifically, the theories proposed by Carlos Alchourrón, Peter Gärdenfors, David Makinson, Isaac Levi, and Robert Stalnaker in their various books and essays (see the references).

H.E. Kyburg, Jr. et al. (eds.), Knowledge Representation and Defeasible Reasoning, 223–244.
© 1990 *Kluwer Academic Publishers. Printed in the Netherlands.*

non-monotonic reasoning is the only kind of reasoning capable of forming consistent theories that go strictly beyond the logical content of consistent evidence. Thus even if non-monotonic logic fails to provide an adequate solution to the Frame Problem,[3] (as some AI theoreticians fear it may not[4]) there are important philosophical programs in which the study of non-monotonic reasoning must play a central role.

I will begin by looking briefly at the Preservation principle, the Ramsey rule, and the theorem that forces us to choose between them. Next I will consider Gärdenfors' own response to the dilemma and show that his argument against the Ramsey rule is inconclusive. Taking the dilemma by its other horn, I will argue that the Preservation principle is fallacious and show that counterexamples to it always involve the use of non-monotonic reasoning. I will then prove a theorem that justifies the claim that rational agents who modify their beliefs in response to new information cannot avoid reasoning non-monotonically, and in the process of proving this I will suggest a new direction for the theory of belief revision.

1   The Model

Rational inquiry — the enterprise of acquiring knowledge for such purposes as explanation and decision-making — crucially involves the modification or revision of what is initially accepted in response to new information. The rationality of any such revision is constrained by two opposing interests: (a) the agent's interest in believing as much as possible in order to maximize usable information, which is a valuable resource, and (b) the agent's interest in believing as little as possible in order to minimize error and the risk of error, which usually make a negative contribution to his cognitive goals. The *theory* of belief revision aims to show or explain how these competing interests are balanced one against the other when an agent incorporates a new belief. An account of the *logic* of belief revision can contribute to the theory of belief revision by displaying the abstract structure of the revision operation, so that it becomes clear what a belief change is and what the rationality of a belief change is a function of.

---

[3]The original Frame Problem (see [McCarthy&Hayes69]) is a problem about how to formalize information about temporal change. In particular, it is the problem of how to give an *explicit* specification of what *changes* when an event of a given type occurs that is at the same time an *implicit* specification of what does *not* change when an event of that type occurs.

[4]See, for example, [McDermott87].

One obviously crucial component of this abstract structure is an account of how states of belief are individuated: an account, in other words, of what *counts* as a change of belief. The account that I will sketch here is the one that is invoked by Robert Stalnaker, Carlos Alchourrón, David Makinson, and Peter Gärdenfors in their various writings on belief change and its logic.[5] It is also the account that Gärdenfors' theorem presupposes. According to this account, which I will call the *Belief Theory Paradigm*, states of belief are individuated by and identifiable with deductively closed sets of propositions, which will often be referred to as *belief sets*. Since belief sets are deductively closed, it follows that, according to the Belief Theory Paradigm, agents are "logically omniscient," *i.e.* they believe all logical truths and all of the logical consequences of their beliefs. This would be an untenable position to take if one regarded all of an agent's beliefs as being directly or explicitly represented in some cognitive apparatus. Accordingly, the Belief Theory Paradigm does not claim that all, or indeed *any*, of an agent's beliefs are explicitly represented in the agent's mind. Instead, an agent's beliefs are identified with whatever epistemic *commitments* can be attributed to the agent, whether explicit mental representations turn out to be involved or not. The Belief Theory Paradigm simply does not address the nature of mental representation; it provides an account of how *commitments* evolve, not an account of how mental representations evolve.[6] Given this account of belief states, the crucial question now becomes: on what does the rationality of revision of commitment depend?

According to the Belief Revision Paradigm, the rationality or reasonability of a given revision of commitment is a function of just four things: (i) the agent, (ii) the factual situation of the agent, (iii) the commitments of the agent, and (iv) the newly learned piece of information. In a simple version of this theory, where the agent and situation are fixed, the rationality of a revision of commitment is a function only of the agent's initial commitments and the new piece of information. One can express this idea by saying that a belief revision model is a pair consisting of a set of belief states and a revision function that maps a belief state K and a proposition A to a new belief state K_A, the revision of K in light of A.

---

[5]See [Alchourrón *et al.*85], [Alchourrón&Makinson82,85], [Gärdenfors78,81,82b,84,86], [Makinson86,87a].

[6]In [Stalnaker84] Stalnaker argues that what I call the Belief Theory Paradigm, with its deductive closure requirement, fits together naturally with a theory of belief that denies the existence of sentence-like mental representations.

2   The Preservation principle

Given the Belief Theory Paradigm, one would like to think of the belief revision operation as always *expanding* the set of propositions comprising belief state K to yield the set of propositions comprising belief state K_A, but obviously this cannot generally be the case. Sometimes A and K are incompatible, in which case the move from K to K_A represents the correction of a perceived mistake rather than an expansion of what is already believed. In some cases, however, it *is* possible for the revision function to work as an expansion operation, namely whenever K and A are compatible, which is to say whenever K does not commit the agent to the falsity of A. One can require that expansion should occur whenever possible in belief revision by insisting on the following principle:

> *Preservation*:   For any given belief revision model, any belief state K belonging to the model, and any proposition A, if $\neg A$ does not hold in K, then every proposition that holds in K holds in K_A, as well.

New information, it is claimed, should be accommodated in a consistency-preserving way that disturbs the initial belief set as little as possible. If the new information is already consistent with the initial belief set, then, it is argued, all initial commitments should be retained because consistency can be preserved without sacrificing any of them.

One can also argue for the Preservation principle on the basis of a slightly different but closely related account of states of belief according to which belief states are individuated by sets of possible worlds. Intuitively, such a set represents the class of situations allowed as epistemically possible by the beliefs of an agent in the belief state in question.[7] In such an account, propositions, too, are identified as sets of possible worlds, and an agent's belief set is defined as containing exactly those propositions that contain every possible situation allowed by his belief state. In this context, the Preservation principle is equivalent to the plausible idea that revision to accommodate a proposition A should *narrow down* the possible situations allowed by the agent's belief state whenever the possible situations comprising A overlap the possible situations allowed by the belief state.

The narrowing-down metaphor and the idea of minimal change both provide motivation for the Preservation principle. In §6 we will examine whether or not this motivation can be defeated by other considerations. For

---

[7]See [Stalnaker84], where this account is defended in detail.

now, let us move on to the second of the two belief revision principles that concern us here.

3 The Ramsey Test

Imagine that you are interested to know whether or not a given indicative conditional *If A then B* is among the propositions to which your beliefs commit you. It is very sensible to think, as some authors have thought,[8] that one can work this out in principle by means of the following thought experiment:

> *Ramsey Test*: First, add *A* to your *actual* stock of beliefs, making adjustments to preserve consistency where necessary. These adjustments should be as small as possible. The result is a new set of propositions, a *hypothetical* epistemic state representing what you would accept if you came to accept *A*, the antecedent of the conditional. If *B* is among the propositions accepted in this hypothetical epistemic state, then you can be said to accept *If A then B* in the *original* epistemic state; otherwise not.

We call the principle that endorses the validity of this thought experiment the *Ramsey Rule*. The Ramsey rule derives its intuitive appeal from the fact that it seems to capture perfectly the way we reason with indicative conditionals.

It is important to stress that the Ramsey rule applies only to indicative conditionals and not at all to subjunctive or counterfactual conditionals. Consider this pair of conditionals, for example:

If Tolstoy did not write *War and Peace*, then someone else did.

If Tolstoy had not written *War and Peace*, then no one else would have.

I can consistently believe both of these conditionals, and yet it would be wrong to suggest that I am or ought to be disposed to believe a contradiction upon learning that Tolstoy did not write *War and Peace*. Surely we want to say that the first (indicative) conditional, but not the second (subjunctive) conditional, correctly indicates what I should believe if I come to learn that Tolstoy did not write *War and Peace*.

Unlike The Preservation principle, the Ramsey rule does not depend for its motivation on particular formal models of belief or belief revision.

---

[8]Notably Robert Stalnaker in [Stalnaker68; p. 102].

Still, it is sensible to think that the very real intuitions behind the Ramsey rule should be easy to incorporate into any formal model of belief revision. Gärdenfors' important theorem, discussed below, shows that this is not so.

4   Gärdenfors' Theorem

Putting the Belief Theory Paradigm into a more formal context, Gärdenfors asks us to consider a formal language L with truth functional connectives $\neg$, $\wedge$, $\vee$, and $\supset$, and with a conditional connective $>$ and a propositional constant $\bot$ (which expresses the absurd proposition). Formation rules are as usual, and L is assumed to have an underlying classical logic whose consequence relation is denoted by $\vdash$. Belief states are represented (in accordance with the Belief Theory Paradigm) as deductively closed sets of formulas. $K_{\bot}$ represents the (unique) absurd belief state, which includes every statement whatsoever. A *belief revision model* is a pair $\langle \mathbf{K}, \mathbf{F} \rangle$, where $\mathbf{K}$ is a set of belief states and $\mathbf{F}$ is a function mapping a pair $\langle K, A \rangle$, where $K \in \mathbf{K}$ and A is a formula, to a belief state K_A belonging to $\mathbf{K}$. Intuitively, K_A is the result of minimally revising K in light of the acceptance of A.

In addition to *revising* a belief state with new information we can *expand* a belief state with new information, as well. Define the *expansion* K/A of K with A to be the deductive closure of $K \cup \{A\}$ under $\vdash$, for any formula A and any belief state K. The set $\mathbf{K}$ of belief states in a belief revision model is assumed to be closed under expansions as well as revisions.

A belief revision model is defined to be *nontrivial* iff it contains a belief state X which is compatible with each of three formulas A_0, B_0, and C_0 that are pairwise incompatible. That is, $\neg A_0, \neg B_0, \neg C_0 \notin X$, but $\vdash \neg(A_0 \wedge B_0) \wedge \neg(B_0 \wedge C_0) \wedge \neg(A_0 \wedge C_0)$.

Next, Gärdenfors asks us to consider the following claims about belief revision:

(1) $A \in K_A$;

(2) if $K \neq K_{\bot}$ and $K_A = K_{\bot}$, then $\vdash \neg A$.

The first principle states that accepting A produces a belief state in which A holds. The second says that the revision function always maps a consistent belief state to a consistent belief state unless the newly accepted proposition is itself absurd. These two principles, along with classical logic, form the background assumptions that Gärdenfors uses to prove the incompatibility of the Ramsey rule and the Preservation principle in nontrivial belief revision models. The two principles (the Ramsey rule and The Preservation principle) are formalized, respectively, as follows:

(**R**) $A > B \in K$ iff $B \in K_A$;

(**P**) if $\neg A \notin K$, then $K \subseteq K_A$.

It is trivial to prove that (R) implies:

(**M**) if $K \subseteq K'$, then for all A, $K_A \subseteq K'_A$.

What Gärdenfors actually proves is this:

Theorem 1 (Gärdenfors 1986) *(1), (2), (P), and (M) cannot be jointly satisfied in any nontrivial belief revision model.*[9]

Since (R) implies (M), it follows that (1), (2), (P), and (R) cannot be jointly satisfied in a nontrivial belief revision model.

5 A Misleading Example

What conclusions or morals about belief revision should we draw from the theorem presented above? Gärdenfors uses an example to argue tentatively that we should give up the Ramsey rule. In this section I want to consider

---

[9] The idea of the proof can be sketched briefly as follows, but see [Gärdenfors86], pp. 84–86 for more details.

Given X, A_0, B_0, and C_0 as described in the definition of *nontrivial belief revision model*, and given assumptions (1), (2), and (P), it follows that either (a) $\neg C \notin (X_{A_0})_{(B_0 \vee C_0)}$ or (b) $\neg B \notin (X_{A_0})_{(B_0 \vee C_0)}$. If (a) holds, then the following is a counterexample to (M):

$$K = X/(A_0 \vee B_0)$$
$$K' = X_{A_0}$$
$$A = (B_0 \vee C_0)$$

On the other hand, if (b) holds, we have this counterexample to (M):

$$K = X/(A_0 \vee C_0)$$
$$K' = X_{A_0}$$
$$A = (B_0 \vee C_0)$$

In either case we see that (M) must be false.

whether the example he presents actually provides any intuitive evidence against the Ramsey rule. I will argue that it does not.

Recall that Gärdenfors' theorem directly concerns not (R), the Ramsey rule, but (M), a principle that follows trivially from the Ramsey rule:

(M) if $K \subseteq K'$, then for all A, $K_A \subseteq K'_A$.

Gärdenfors' tentative conclusion is that counterexamples to (M) can be found having the following form: K is a belief set such that $C \in K$, $\neg A \notin K$, and $C \in K_A$. Letting $K' = K/(C \supset \neg A)$, it follows that K'_A cannot contain both $C \supset \neg A$ and C. Condition (M) would require the agent to keep C and give up $C \supset \neg A$, since $C \in K_A$, but, Gärdenfors claims, there are cases in which we want to do just the opposite. These cases, in other words, conform to the following diagram.

$$\neg A \notin \{C, \ldots\} \;=\; K \quad\subseteq\quad K/(C \supset \neg A)$$

$$\Downarrow \qquad\qquad \Downarrow$$

$$C \;\in\; K_A \qquad C \notin [K/(C \supset \neg A)]_A$$

Gärdenfors writes:

> In many cases there may be strong reasons for giving up C rather than $C \supset \neg A$. The implication may, for example, be supported by a well-established scientific law. However, in such a case, $C \in K_A$, but $C \notin K'_A$ which contradicts (M).

To give an example which illustrates this abstract argument, consider Miss Julie and her alleged father Johan. Let us assume that Miss Julie, in her present state of belief K, believes that her own blood group is O and that Johan is her father, but she does not know anything about Johan's blood group. Let A be the proposition that Johan's blood group is AB and C the proposition that Johan is Miss Julie's father. If she were to revise her beliefs by adding the proposition A, she would still believe that C, that is $C \in K_A$. But, in fact, she now learns that a person with blood group AB can never have a child with blood group O. This information, which entails $C \supset \neg A$, is consistent with her present state of belief K, and thus her new state of belief, call it K', is an expansion of K. If she then revises K' by adding the information that Johan's blood group is AB, she will no longer believe that Johan is her father, that is $C \notin K'_A$. Thus (M) is violated.[10]

Is this a counterexample to (M)? In order to decide we need an answer to this question: What intuitive grounds are there for denying that, since C belongs to K_A and not to K'_A, $A > C$ belongs to K but not to K'? Here is Gärdenfors' answer:

> In fact, if we assume (R) and not only (M), then Miss Julie would have believed $A > C$ in K. But then the information that a person with blood group AB can never have a child with blood group O, would *contradict* her beliefs in K, which violates our intuitions that this information is indeed consistent with her beliefs in K.[11]

Is this right? Suppose that Miss Julie *does* accept that (even) if Johan's blood group is AB, (still) Johan is her father and her own blood group is O. Is this incompatible with the principle that no father with type AB blood can possibly have a child with type O blood? Gärdenfors reasons as follows: suppose that Miss Julie believes in K that even if Johan's blood is type AB, her own blood is nevertheless type O and Johan is nevertheless her father. If we regard conditionals as being about hypothetical situations in which their antecedents hold, then the hypothetical situation that Miss Julie envisions in which Johan's blood is type AB seems, in this case, to witness the possibility of a type AB father having a type O daughter. And so, it is argued, Miss Julie is committed in K to this possibility. But this is wrong, or misleading. What she is committed to in K is the *epistemic* possibility that some type AB father has a type O daughter, in the sense that for all she knows, this is so. Regarding the *physical* or *biological* or *nomological* possibility of this, she may remain agnostic, and it is this nomological possibility that Miss Julie is *supposed* to be agnostic about!

Consider an analogous case: You show me a match being struck inside an airtight tank. The match lights, and you say to me, "That match lit, didn't it?" "Yes, it did," I reply, "I saw it light up." "Do you suppose that the tank was filled with ozone?" "I don't know," I reply, "But that match lit up, even if the tank was in fact filled with ozone." Now, even as I write this, I do not know what a match struck inside a tank of ozone will do: light up, fail to light up, or detonate the ozone — I simply do not know. But I believe that the match lit even if the tank was in fact filled with ozone. *I*

---

[10][Gärdenfors86], pp. 86–87.
[11][Gärdenfors86], p. 87.

saw it. And though I believe *this*, I neither believe nor disbelieve that it is physically possible for a match to light up when struck in a tank of ozone.

The general point here is that if an agent believes *if A, then B*, where *if* is the indicative conditional, and if this agent neither believes nor disbelieves *A*, then for all this agent knows *A and B* might be true, *i.e.*, from this agent's point of view, *A and B* is possible in a certain epistemic sense. This does not in and of itself, however, commit the agent to the possibility of *A and B* in any other sense. And so, just as our intuitions suggest, the information that a person with blood group AB can never have a child with blood group O does *not* in fact contradict Miss Julie's initial beliefs, not even if we assume that Miss Julie believes that Johan is her father even if he has blood group AB. Accordingly, we may conclude that Gärdenfors' example does not provide intuitive evidence against the Ramsey rule after all.

6   Preservation Fails

Our rejection of Gärdenfors' argument against the Ramsey rule lands us back in the dilemma posed by his theorem. My view is that we should resolve this dilemma by rejecting not the Ramsey rule but the Preservation principle. As it happens, the latter seems to fail, on intuitive grounds, in a whole class of straightforward cases, such as the following:

> You are in the restaurant of a hotel that is hosting a conference of Catholic priests. You are not a Catholic priest, but every other customer in the restaurant is. It is Friday, and you have ordered a steak. As you look around you see that one of the food bringers, call him Moe, is bringing out a steak. There are two other food bringers, Manny and Jack, but you have not seen them yet, and you have no views about what they are doing. In particular, you neither believe nor disbelieve that Moe is the only person bringing out a steak. But since it is Friday and you are the only customer who is not a Catholic priest, you conclude that Moe is bringing *your* steak. This is your initial belief state.
>
> As you continue looking around you notice the two other food bringers, Manny and Jack, and see that each of them is bringing out a steak, too. On the basis of this new information you suspend your belief that Moe is bringing out your steak.

In this example, the agent begins with three pieces of evidence: the fact that it is Friday, the fact that he is the only person in the room who isn't a Catholic priest, and the fact that Moe is bringing out a steak. Given this, the agent reasons that Moe is bringing out *his* steak. So far our agent has no opinion about whether anyone else is bringing out a steak, and so he learns something compatible with his prior opinions when he sees the other food bringers Manny and Jack also carrying out steaks. This new information defeats the original conclusion that Moe is bringing the agent his dinner, and thus the example shows that a piece of new information can undermine and defeat some of an agent's initial beliefs without actually contradicting *any* of them. The example shows, in other words, that the Preservation principle is false.

Examples of this sort abound in our common sense understanding of belief change, and they seem to refute the Preservation principle. It is especially important, however, to be clear about what else these examples show. Consider this passage, in which Gilbert Harman presents a case like the one given above in order to argue that in such cases agents are forced to revise their implicit beliefs regarding the reliability of evidence:

> William looks out the window and, on the basis of what he sees, forms the belief that the girl his daughter is playing with is the girl he met yesterday, named Connie. Later he learns Connie has an identical twin Laura, whom he cannot distinguish from Connie. This leads him to realize that his reasons for his belief about the identity of the girl he saw playing with his daughter in the backyard are "no good." ... It may seem ... that William does not have to suppose that his original justification relied on any false beliefs. In particular, he needn't have explicitly considered whether Connie might have an identical twin.
>
> But in such a case William at least implicitly relied on the belief that the perceptual appearances were an objectively reliable indicator of the identity of the girl he saw with his daughter. On learning that Connie has an identical twin, he now thinks appearances were not an objectively reliable indicator, so he thinks he was (subjectively) justified only because he relied on a false belief.[12]

Is it true that William must have relied implicitly on the belief that certain visual evidence was an objectively reliable indicator of Connie's identity? Is it true that William must have changed his mind (at least insofar as

---

[12][Harman86], p. 44.

his commitments are concerned) about the reliability of the visual evidence when he learned of Connie's identical twin? We need not draw either of these conclusions. There is a better way to reconstruct the implicit reasoning in this example and in the restaurant example, too.

If all that I know about someone is that he is a Quaker, I am entitled to presume that he is a pacifist. In fact, I can know a great deal about someone and still be entitled to presume that he is a pacifist if I also know him to be a Quaker. If, however, I know that the person is not only a Quaker but also a Republican, like Nixon, and if I know nothing else about the person, then I am *not* entitled to presume that the person is a pacifist. So suppose that I know that Dick is a Quaker, and then I *learn* that he is a Republican. When I learn that Dick is a Republican, I become unwilling to maintain the belief that he is a pacifist, but have I changed my mind about the reliability of the evidence I used to have? *No, I have not!* If it turns out that Dick is not a Republican after all, I will once again presume that he is a pacifist, unless other new information overdetermines my skepticism or convinces me that he is not a pacifist. And whether I continue believing that Dick is a Republican or not, I will conclude of the *next* Quaker I meet that he is a pacifist, unless there is evidence to the contrary.

What normally goes on in examples like this one, as well as in Harman's twins example and my restaurant example, is *not* a change of opinion about the reliability of the evidence for a defeated conclusion. What we have instead is the consistent application of a *non-monotonic reasoning policy*. Given what I know at first, I am willing to conclude that Dick is a pacifist, that Connie is in the backyard playing with my daughter, and that Moe is bringing out my steak; in each case, knowing more leads me to withdraw my conclusion. And yet, in each case, the evidence I started with was perfectly adequate at the time for the conclusions I drew at the time, given what I knew *at the time*. And the evidence continues to have been adequate, even in retrospect.

I do not say all of this just in order to quibble with Harman about an arcane epistemological point. The real point is to illustrate what I will show formally in the next section, namely that *every case in which the Preservation principle fails is an example in which an agent has reasoned non-monotonically*.

7 Non-Monotonic Reasoning, Preservation, and The Levi Identity

In order to show that any counterexample to the Preservation principle involves the use of non-monotonic reasoning, we will need to introduce the notion of a *generalized belief revision model*. This notion relaxes many of the assumptions that define the belief revision models of §4 while at the same time adding certain assumptions about belief revision that Gärdenfors does not make. One important difference between generalized belief revision models and Gärdenfors' belief revision models is that in a generalized model an agent's state of belief is not identified with the set of his belief commitments. As I will show, rejecting the Preservation principle requires us to individuate states of belief more finely than they are individuated in the Belief Theory Paradigm, for it turns out to matter not only what the agent's commitments are but also which of his commitments are the product of inference and which are not. This suggests that a belief state might be identified as a set of commitments having a distinguished subset, the set of uninferred beliefs. Since an agent's commitments are determined by his uninferred beliefs together with his inference policy, we can capture this structuring of the agent's commitments very simply by identifying an agent's belief state with the set of his uninferred beliefs. And so, in a generalized belief revision model, an agent's state of belief is identified with a set of propositions representing those of his commitments that are *not* the product of inference. Accordingly, belief sets in generalized belief revision models are not assumed to be deductively closed.

Let the formal language be as defined in §4. A *generalized belief revision model* is defined to be a triple $\langle \mathbf{K}, \div, \vdash \rangle$, where $\mathbf{K}$ is a set of sets of formulas, where $\vdash$ is a consequence relation, and where $\div$ is a *belief retraction* operation that maps a member of $\mathbf{K}$ and a formula to another member of $\mathbf{K}$. $K \div A$ is the result of suspending or deleting from K any commitment to A. For the reasons presented in the preceding paragraph, members of $\mathbf{K}$ are *not* assumed to be closed under $\vdash$. Generalized belief revision models are, however, assumed to satisfy postulates (C-1) and (C-2), described below. Before looking at (C-1) and (C-2), however, let us consider how belief *revision* enters into generalized belief revision models.

We will define belief revision by means of a version of the *Levi Identity*,[13] which asserts that the operation of revising a belief set to accommodate new information can be decomposed into two operations: *contraction* and

---

[13]See [Levi77].

expansion. As we noted above, contraction (or retraction) involves only the removal or suspension of beliefs. Expansion involves only the addition of beliefs.[14] Levi's proposal is that the revision K_A of K in light of A can be constructed by first contracting K so as to suspend belief in $\neg A$. This yields the set $K \doteq \neg A$, the retraction of $\neg A$ from K. We obtain K_A, according to Levi, by expanding $K \doteq \neg A$ with A. This characterization of belief revision seems intuitively right, but since we do not here assume that belief sets are closed under $\vdash$, we substitute set theoretic union for expansion:

(L) $K_A =_{df} (K \doteq \neg A) \cup \{A\}$

To see that this yields the right result, let us, for a given set X of propositions, define $\overline{X}$ to be the closure of X under $\vdash$ (that is, if we let $\overline{X} = \{A : X \vdash A\}$). We then obtain what Levi originally had in mind if we notice that (L) implies:

$$\overline{K_A} = \overline{(K \doteq \neg A) \cup \{A\}}$$
$$= (K \doteq \neg A)/A$$

That is, an agent's *commitments* when he revises his beliefs in light of A are the result of first retracting $\neg A$ from his initial beliefs and secondly expanding the resulting set with A. This is exactly Levi's original proposal.

What properties can the contraction operation be assumed to have? One property that is relevant to our concerns here is this one, where K is a belief set in a generalized belief revision model.

(C-1) If $K \not\vdash A$, then $K \doteq A = K$.

In other words, if a proposition is not included among an agent's commitments, then suspending belief in that proposition is the same as doing nothing at all. We will assume that the retraction operation in any generalized belief revision models satisfies this postulate.

We will not assume that the consequence relation $\vdash$ of a generalized belief revision model is an extension of classical logic, but we will assume that $\vdash$ satisfies the following simple requirement, where X is any set of propositions:

(C-2) If $A \in X$, then $X \vdash A$.

---

[14] As in §4 we define here the *expansion* of K with A to be the closure of $K \cup \{A\}$ under the consequence relation $\vdash$ of the model. See [Alchourrón *et al.*85], [Alchourrón&Makinson82,85], [Makinson87a] for a detailed account of the relation between expansion, contraction, and revision.

Finally, let us note that the Preservation principle for generalized belief revision models is formulated as follows:

(P') if $\neg A \notin \overline{K}$, then $\overline{K} \subseteq \overline{K_A}$.

Note that we do not define (P') as holding of generalized belief revision models.

We can now prove the following fact. Notice that in the proof of Proposition 1, the example of $\vdash$'s non-monotonicity comes from the very belief change that witnesses the failure of (P').

Proposition 1 *If (P') fails for a generalized belief revision model $\langle \mathbf{K}, \dot{-}, \vdash \rangle$, then $\vdash$ is non-monotonic in $\langle \mathbf{K}, \dot{-}, \vdash \rangle$.*

Proof: It suffices to show that if there is a $K \in \mathbf{K}$ and a proposition A such that $\neg A \notin \overline{K}$ and $\overline{K} \not\subseteq \overline{K_A}$, then $\vdash$ is non-monotonic. Let K belong to a generalized belief revision model, and suppose that $\neg A \notin \overline{K}$ and $\overline{K} \not\subseteq \overline{K_A}$. Let B be a proposition such that $B \in \overline{K}$ but $B \notin \overline{K_A}$. By the definition of closure we know that $K \vdash B$, and by (L) and (C-1) we know that

$$\overline{K_A} = \overline{(K \dot{-} \neg A) \cup \{A\}}$$
$$= \overline{K \cup \{A\}}.$$

Thus $B \notin \overline{K \cup \{A\}}$, and so by the definition of closure $K \cup \{A\} \nvdash B$. But $K \vdash B$, so $\vdash$ is non-monotonic, as required.□

Given this much, it is easy to see why we are forced to distinguish states of belief more finely once we reject the Preservation principle. Consider a generalized belief revision model and suppose that $\neg A \notin \overline{K}$ and $K = \overline{K}$. Then

$$\overline{K} = K$$
$$\subseteq K \cup \{A\}$$
$$\subseteq \overline{K \cup \{A\}}$$
$$= \overline{K_A}.$$

So if belief sets are assumed to be closed under $\vdash$, it follows that there are no counterexamples to the Preservation principle. That is, we have

Proposition 2 *(P') holds of any generalized belief revision model $\langle \mathbf{K}, \dot{-}, \vdash \rangle$ of which it is true that each $K \in \mathbf{K}$ is closed under $\vdash$.*

Hence the need to distinguish an agent's uninferred beliefs K from the set $\overline{K}$ of propositions to which these uninferred beliefs commit him.

In a model of belief revision that incorporates non-monotonic reasoning, an agent's belief set K represents the set of propositions that serve as the subjective foundation of his epistemic state. These propositions are foundational in that they, unlike other of the agent's commitments, do not rest on the application of defeasible, and therefore especially "risky," non-monotonic reasoning policies. This does *not*, however, mean that these uninferred basic beliefs are indubitable, nor does it mean that they have an objectively privileged justification status or pedigree of any sort. An agent's uninferred basic beliefs are not, in other words, a foundation in the sense required by Epistemological Foundationalism. They are, instead, the *natural* foundation — the actual basis, good or bad — of the agent's commitments. What Proposition 2 shows is that if an agent is not disposed to revise beliefs in conformity with the Preservation principle, then this agent's beliefs must have a subjective foundation of this kind.

One is tempted to attach psychological significance to the distinction between uninferred beliefs and commitments. The distinction is, in fact, purely epistemological. Whether it happened to correspond to a psychological distinction, such as the distinction between explicit and implicit beliefs, would depend, in any particular case, on how the cognitive apparatus of the agent in question happened to work. An agent with a limited amount of room to store information in its own cognitive machinery might explicitly store some of its basic beliefs in an external location, such as a reference book, a filing cabinet, or a database. An agent with plenty of memory to spare might explicitly store all of its uninferred beliefs and some of its *other* commitments, too, within its own cognitive machinery. Each of these possibilities illustrates how basic beliefs might differ from explicitly represented beliefs for an agent whose cognitive apparatus stores information in sentence-like representations. Some agents, by contrast, might store even their uninferred beliefs in an entirely implicit nonlinguistic way, perhaps in the way described by Stalnaker's version of the Belief Theory Paradigm.[15] Since a Stalnaker-agent has no explicit beliefs but only implicit ones, the basic-beliefs/commitments distinction and the explicit/implicit distinction obviously would not coincide for such an agent.

At the end of the previous section I claimed that (i) every case in which the Preservation principle fails involves non-monotonic reasoning, and I

---

[15]See [Stalnaker84], especially Chapters 1 and 4.

claimed that this allows us to use Gärdenfors' theorem to argue that (ii) rational agents who revise their beliefs in response to new information cannot avoid reasoning in a non-monotonic way. The proof of Proposition 1 establishes (i), but we cannot simply conjoin Proposition 1 with Gärdenfors' theorem and deduce (ii). We might wish to say that we can establish (ii) by showing that *any non-trivial belief revision model satisfying (1), (2), and the Ramsey rule must contain examples of non-monotonic reasoning.* This might seem to follow straightforwardly from Proposition 1 and Gärdenfors' theorem, but notice that Proposition 1 and Gärdenfors' theorem make different and, in part, incompatible assumptions about belief revision. For example, Proposition 1 assumes that belief revision is defined in terms of a contraction operation whereas Gärdenfors' theorem makes no such assumption, and Proposition 1 assumes that belief sets are not deductively closed, whereas Gärdenfors' theorem assumes that they are. Moreover, Gärdenfors' theorem assumes that ⊢ is an extension of classical logic, which is monotonic, whereas Proposition 1 does not. In order to prove something that could serve as an justification for (ii), we need a common framework, a model of belief revision that is neither a Gärdenfors belief revision model nor a generalized belief revision model, in which both facts can be formalized. Finding this framework will illustrate how to formulate a theory of belief revision that takes non-monotonic reasoning into account, and we turn to this in the next section.

8   A New Model of Belief Revision

Let the formal language be as described in §4, and let an *enriched belief revision model* be defined as a quadruple $\langle K, \dot{-}, \Vdash, cl \rangle$, where $\Vdash$ is a consequence relation that extends classical logic, and **K** is a set of sets of formulas each of which is closed under $\Vdash$. cl is a function that maps an element K of **K** to a $\Vdash$-theory that is a superset of K. Fixed points are allowed, and the cl-image of an element of **K** must itself belong to **K**. $\dot{-}$ maps a formula and an element of **K** to another element of **K**. Intuitively, elements of **K** are sets of basic beliefs, and instead of the undifferentiated consequence relation $\vdash$ of the previous section, we now have two reasoning formalisms: $\Vdash$ and cl. $\Vdash$ formalizes the classical fragment of the agent's reasoning dispositions, *e.g.*, his disposition to conclude A from $A \wedge B$. The image $cl(K)$ of an element K of **K** under cl represents the result of applying whatever *additional* reasoning principles the agent might be disposed to reason with, be they monotonic or non-monotonic. I will call the collection of these principles the agent's *extra-logical reasoning policy*. Our models specify this policy holistically as a function from a classical theory to an expansion thereof. We will not specify anything that might be called a *system* of extra-logical reasoning because we do not need to go into that much detail in order to express the notion that the agent reasons non-monotonically. We simply note that the agent's extra-logical reasoning policy is monotonic provided that for any K, $K' \in \mathbf{K}$, if $K \subseteq K'$, then $cl(K) \subseteq cl(K')$. That is, an agent's extra-logical reasoning policy is monotonic provided that additional information always preserves or enlarges the class of conclusions that are allowed by the policy.[16]

Next we make some definitions: for any set X of propositions, define $\overline{X}$ to be the closure of X under $\Vdash$, and define the expansion K/A of a belief set K under A to be $\overline{K \cup \{A\}}$. We assume that $\mathbf{K}$ is closed under $\dot{-}$ and under expansion, and we assume that for any $K \in \mathbf{K}$, $cl(K)$ is closed under $\Vdash$. We let $K_\perp$ stand for the absurd belief state, containing every proposition. Let an enriched belief revision model be called *nontrivial* iff it contains a belief state X such that there exist three formulas A_0, B_0, and C_0 such that $\neg A_0, \neg B_0, \neg C_0 \notin cl(X)$, but $\Vdash \neg(A_0 \wedge B_0) \wedge \neg(B_0 \wedge C_0) \wedge \neg(A_0 \wedge C_0)$.

In addition to what is given above, we stipulate that all enriched belief revision models satisfy the following postulates:

(C-1′) if $A \notin cl(K)$, then $K \dot{-} A = K$;

(S) if $A \in cl(K \dot{-} A)$, then $\Vdash A$;

(CST) If $cl(K) = K_\perp$, then $K = K_\perp$;

(L′) $K_A =_{df} (K \dot{-} \neg A)/A$.

As (C-1) did in the previous section, postulate (C-1′) here expresses the idea that if a proposition is not included among an agent's commitments, then suspending commitment to that proposition involves no change in basic beliefs. Postulate (S) expresses the same idea as David Makinson's Postulate of Success, namely that a commitment persists after it has been suspended

---

[16]Note that in an enriched belief revision model, an agent's belief set is closed under $\Vdash$ though not under cl. Thus a basic belief set in an enriched belief revision model does not represent an agent's uninferred beliefs *simpliciter*. Instead it represents those of an agent's *commitments* that were not inferred by means of the agent's extra-logical reasoning policy. Closure under $\Vdash$ is an appropriate assumption if one accepts that the set of conclusions yielded by a rational agent's extra-logical reasoning policy should depend only on what the premises say and not on how they are formulated.

only if that commitment is a logical truth. Postulate (CST) states the sensible requirement that extra-logical inference policies cannot lead one from consistent basic beliefs to inconsistent commitments. Postulate (L') defines revision of commitment in terms of contraction and expansion, according to the Levi Identity.

Consider now the following postulates for contraction, revision, and extra-logical reasoning, which are not themselves part of the definition of *enriched belief revision model*:

(R') $A > B \in cl(K)$ iff $B \in cl(K_A)$;

(P") if $\neg A \notin cl(K)$, then $cl(K) \subseteq cl(K_A)$;

(I) For all $K \in \mathbf{K}$, $K = cl(K)$;

Postulates (R') and (P") express the Ramsey rule and Preservation principle, respectively, for enriched belief revision models. Postulate (I) holds when an agent has no extra-logical inference policies, *i.e.* his commitments extend only as far as his basic beliefs. Postulate (I) is interesting because any enriched belief revision model that satisfies (I) reduces to a Gärdenfors belief revision model, *i.e.* a belief revision model as defined in §4. In fact, we have:

Lemma 1 *If* $\langle \mathbf{K}, \doteq, \Vdash, cl \rangle$ *is a nontrivial enriched belief revision model satisfying (I) and (R'), then* $\langle \mathbf{K}, \mathbf{F} \rangle$ *is a nontrivial Gärdenfors belief revision model having consequence relation* $\Vdash$ *and satisfying Gärdenfors' postulates (1), (2), (R), and (P), where* $\mathbf{F}(K, A) = K_A$.

Proof: Since **K** is closed under contraction and expansion, it follows that **K** is closed under revision and expansion, so $\langle \mathbf{K}, \mathbf{F} \rangle$ is a Gärdenfors revision model. The nontriviality of $\langle \mathbf{K}, \mathbf{F} \rangle$ as a Gärdenfors model follows from (I) and the nontriviality of $\langle \mathbf{K}, \doteq, \Vdash, cl \rangle$ as an enriched belief revision model. Postulate (1) follows from postulate (L'), the definition of revision in enriched models. Gärdenfors' postulate (2) follows from (I) and postulates (C-1'), (S), and (L'). Gärdenfors' (R) follows from (I) and our (R'), and Gärdenfors' (P) follows from (I) and our postulates (C-1') and (L'). $\square$

Using this fact, together with Gärdenfors' theorem, we can immediately deduce:

Lemma 2 *There is no nontrivial enriched belief revision model satisfying both (I) and (R').*

Surely there is nothing surprising about Lemmas 1 and 2. What *is* surprising is that the only way to have a monotone extra-logical reasoning policy is to have no extra-logical reasoning policy at all, or, to put it another way, a consistent extra-logical reasoning policy can take one beyond the purely logical content of one's evidence *only if* that reasoning policy is non-monotonic. This is demonstrated by the following lemma:

Lemma 3 *For any enriched belief revision model, if* cl *is monotonic, then (I) holds.*

Proof: By contraposition — suppose that (I) fails; since K has to be a subset of $cl(K)$, there must be a proposition A such that $A \in cl(K)$ but $A \notin K$. This implies that $K/\neg A \neq K_\perp$, and so by (CST) we know that $A \notin cl(K/\neg A)$. Clearly, $K \subseteq K/\neg A$, and yet $A \in cl(K)$. Hence, cl is non-monotonic, as required.□

One straightforward consequence of Lemma 3 is the following analogue of Proposition 1 in the context of enriched belief revision models:

Corollary 1 *For any enriched belief revision model, if (P'') fails, then* cl *is non-monotonic.*

Returning to our main line of argument, notice that Lemmas 2 and 3 imply:

Theorem 2 *There is no non-trivial enriched belief revision model satisfying (R') for which* cl *is monotonic.*

This theorem conveys in a precise way the interpretation that I want to attach to Gärdenfors' theorem. Given the Ramsey rule and the background assumptions about belief change that define the notion of an enriched belief revision model, Theorem 1 implies that no rational agent who revises his beliefs in response to new information can avoid reasoning non-monotonically. To the extent that Theorem 1 shows this, it also shows that an adequate *theory* of belief revision, one that would describe the behavior of such agents, must take non-monotonic reasoning into account.

We have gone some of the way in this section toward developing an account of the logic of belief revision in the context of non-monotonic reasoning. It would be interesting to develop the logic of belief revision as thoroughly in this context as it has been developed in the context of the Belief Theory Paradigm, but I must leave that for another occasion.

9 Bibliography

Alchourrón, C., Gärdenfors, P., and D. Makinson. "On the logic of the-ory change: partial meet contraction and revision functions," *Journal of Symbolic Logic 50*, pp. 510–530, 1985.

Alchourrón, C. and D. Makinson. "On the logic of theory change: contraction functions and their associated revision functions," *Theoria 48*, pp. 14–37, 1982.

Alchourrón, C. and D. Makinson. "On the logic of theory change: safe contraction," *Studia Logica 44*, pp. 405–422, 1985.

Doyle, J. "A truth maintenance system," *Artificial Intelligence 12*, pp. 231–272, 1979.

Gärdenfors, P. "Conditionals and changes of belief," *The Logic and Epistemology of Scientific Belief*, I. Niiniluoto and R. Tuomela, eds., *(Acta Philosophica Fennica 30*, issues 2–4, Elsevier, 1978).

Gärdenfors, P. "An epistemic approach to conditionals," *American Philosophical Quarterly 18*, pp. 203–211, 1981.

Gärdenfors, P. "Imaging and conditionalization," *Journal of Philosophy 79*, pp. 747–760, 1982.

Gärdenfors, P. "Rules for rational changes of belief," *320211: Philosophical Essays Dedicated to Lennart Åqvist on His Fiftieth Birthday*, T. Pauli, ed., Department of Philosophy, University of Uppsala, pp. 88–101, 1982.

Gärdenfors, P. "Epistemic importance and minimal changes of belief," *Australasian Journal of Philosophy 62*, pp. 136–157, 1984.

Gärdenfors, P. "Belief revisions and the Ramsey test for conditionals," *Philosophical Review 95*, pp. 81–93, 1986.

Gärdenfors, P. "Variations on the Ramsey test: more triviality results," *Studia Logica 46*, pp. 321–327, 1987.

Gärdenfors, P. *Knowledge in Flux*, MIT Press, 1988.

Gibbard, A. "Two recent theories of conditionals," *Ifs: Conditionals, Beliefs, Decision, Chance, and Time*, R. Stalnaker and G. Pearce, eds., Reidel, 1981.

Harman, G. *Change in View*, MIT Press, 1986.

Harper, William L. *Ifs: Conditionals, Beliefs, Decision, Chance, and Time*, R. Stalnaker and G. Pearce, eds., Reidel, 1981.

Lewis, D. "Probabilities of conditionals and conditional probabilities," *Philosophical Review 85*, pp. 297–315, reprinted in *Ifs: Conditionals, Beliefs, Decision, Chance, and Time*, R. Stalnaker and G. Pearce, eds., Reidel, 1981.

Levi, Isaac. "Subjunctives, dispositions, and chances," *Synthese 34*, pp. 423–455, 1977. Reprinted in *Decisions and Revisions: Philosophical Essays on Knowledge and Value*, Cambridge University Press, 1984.

Levi, Isaac. "Serious possibility," *Decisions and Revisions: Philosophical Essays on Knowledge and Value*, Cambridge University Press, 1984.

Levi, Isaac. *The Enterprise of Knowledge*, MIT Press, 1980.

Levi, Isaac. *Decisions and Revisions: Philosophical Essays on Knowledge and Value*, Cambridge University Press, 1984.

Levi, Isaac. Review of Harman in *Journal of Philosophy 84*, pp. 376–384, 1987.

Makinson, D. "How to give it up: a survey of some formal aspects of the logic of theory change," *Synthese 62*, pp. 185–186, 1986.

Makinson, D. "On the status of the postulate of recovery in the logic of theory change," *Journal of Philosophical Logic 16*, pp. 383–394, 1987.

Makinson, D. Review of Harman, *History and Philosophy of Logic 8*, pp. 113–115, 1987.

McCarthy, J. and P. Hayes. "Some philosophical problems from the standpoint of artificial intelligence," *Machine Intelligence 4*, B. Meltzer and D. Michie eds., Edinburgh University Press, 1969, pp. 463–502. Reprinted in *Readings in Artificial Intelligence*, B. Webber and N. Nilsson, eds., Morgan–Kaufmann, 1981.

McDermott, D. "A critique of pure reason," *Computational Intelligence 3*, pp. 151–160, 1987.

Pendlebury, M. "Stalnaker on inquiry," *Journal of Philosophical Logic 16*, pp. 229–272, 1987.

Reiter, R. "A logic for default reasoning," *Artificial Intelligence 13*, pp. 81–132, 1980.

Stalnaker, R. "A theory of conditionals," *Studies in Logical Theory*, N. Rescher, ed., Blackwell, APQ Monograph No. 2, 1968.

Stalnaker, R. *Inquiry*, MIT Press, 1984.

1131298

Jeffrey's Rule, Passage of Experience, and *Neo*-Bayesianism

Judea Pearl

1 Introduction

A technically convenient assumption underlying most of probabilistic epistemology is that the state of beliefs of a rational agent can be represented by a coherent probability function P, defined over the sentences in some appropriate language. Curiously, aside from the algebraic requirement of coherence (*i.e.*, that P be an additive function on a sigma-algebra of sets) very few structural properties were attributed to P. For example, in the algebraic description all propositional formulas are treated on an equal basis and conditional probabilities are defined as ratios of joint probabilities. Thus, the algebraic description of P does not permit us to distinguish the input information $P(A \mid B) = 0$ from its logical equivalent $P(A, B) = 0$, even though the two have different meanings in human discourse. Likewise, judgements about dependencies must be extracted from judgments about probabilities; there is no way to ascertain the independence of A and B unless P also contains the information necessary for computing $P(A)$, $A(B)$ and $P(A, B)$.

The main objective of this paper is to demonstrate, using familiar issues in probability kinematics, that to give an adequate account of belief revision we must postulate that belief states contain structural information which cannot be captured by purely algebraic descriptions of coherent probability functions. The movement which I call *Neo-Bayesianism* acknowledges the insufficiency of coherence, explores concrete methods of representing and utilizing the structural information needed, and attempts to establish a theoretical characterization of this information.

2 Traditional Bayesianism and Virtual Conditionalization

The defining attributes of the traditional school of Bayesianism can be summarized by the following three maxims:

245

H.E. Kyburg, Jr. et al. (eds.), *Knowledge Representation and Defeasible Reasoning*, 245–265.
© 1990 *Kluwer Academic Publishers. Printed in the Netherlands.*

willingness to accept subjective belief as an expedient substitute for raw
data

reliance on complete (*i.e.*, coherent) probabilistic models of beliefs and

adherence to Bayes' conditionalization as the primary mechanism for updating belief in light of new information.

Bayes' conditionalization rule is defined as follows: Given a subjective
probability distribution P, the revised distribution Q that should prevail
after observing event E, must satisfy:

$$(1) \qquad Q(A) \; = \; P(A|E) \; = \; P(A, \; E)/P(E)$$

for every proposition A. In theory, this rule seems to require that both $P(E)$
and $P(A, \; E)$ be quantified prior to the observation, and when this is not
the case, alternatives to Bayes' rule are to be sought. Diaconis and Zabell
[Diaconis&Zabell86] cite three situations where Bayes' rule is not directly
applicable.

Probable knowledge — New information does not arrive in the form "event
E occurred" but, instead, E is assigned a probability measure
(*e.g.*, "the fingerprints are *likely* to be those of the suspect").

Unanticipated knowledge — We may have not thought about event E be-
forehand. Thus $P(E)$ and $P(A, \; E)$ could not have been quantified so as to permit the application of Bayes' rule.

Introspective knowledge — Our probabilities can change in the light of
calculations or of pure thought, without any change in the empirical data [Good77].

In practice, however, Bayesian practitioners have devised effective means
of circumventing these difficulties, using a method which I call *virtual conditionalization* in [Pearl88]. The idea is that the calculation of $Q(A)$ does
not in fact require the absolute values of $P(A, \; E)$ and $P(E)$, but can be
accomplished using more accessible quantities, such as the likelihood ratio

$$(2) \qquad L(A) \; = \; P(E|A)/P(E|\neg A),$$

yielding

$$(3) \qquad Q(A)/Q(\neg A) \; = \; L(A)P(A)/P(\neg A),$$

or

$$(4) \qquad Q(A) = L(A)/(1 - P(A) + L(A)P(A))$$

Good [Good84] has shown that any reasonable explication of the notion of *strength of evidence* must be a function of the likelihood ratio (see also [Heckerman86]). Accordingly, Bayesian practitioners have regarded the likelihood ratio as an intrinsic property of the experience E, and as a sufficient encoding of the process by which E should cause belief state P to change into Q.

We cannot of course expect to be given $L(A)$ for every proposition A of interest. To fully specify Q, it is sufficient to identify just one partition $\{B_i\}$, called a *basis* or a *relevant partition* for E, and assess the effect of E on $\{B_i\}$ by the likelihood-ratio vector

$$(5) \qquad L_i = \beta P(E \mid B_i)$$

where β is any convenient constant. Judgmentally, the identification of $\{B_i\}$ is done by asking the human interpreter to name the variables upon which the *evidence E bears most directly*. Formally, a relevant partition $\{B_i\}$ for E is defined by the conditional independence assertion

$$(6) \qquad \forall A, \forall i \quad P(A \mid E, B_i) = P(A \mid B_i),$$

namely, the partition $\{B_i\}$ summarizes E relative to any proposition A. It is easy to see that condition (6) leads to

$$(7) \qquad Q(A) = P(A \mid E) = \Sigma_i P(A \mid B_i) Q(B_i)$$

or

$$(8) \qquad Q(A) = P(A \mid E) = \alpha \Sigma_i P(A \mid B_i) P(B_i) L_i$$

where α is a normalization constant. In particular, substituting for A any element of $\{B_i\}$ yields

$$(9) \qquad L_i = (1/\alpha)Q(B_i)/P(B_i) .$$

Thus, if L_i can be assessed directly as a measure of impact of E, or computed as an aftermath from the ratio $Q(B_i)/P(B_i)$, then the entire belief state Q is determined from information contained entirely within P.

The method of virtual conditionalization has been practiced routinely by Bayesian decision analysts (*e.g.*, [Kelly&Barclay73], [Schum87]) and has been implemented in several expert systems (*e.g.*, [Duda *et al.*76]). The advantage of the method is that L does not require the assessment of absolute probabilities, hence, it is easier to assess under conditions of unanticipated or probable evidence. In the philosophical literature, Eq. 7 came to be known as Jeffrey's Rule of conditioning [Jeffrey65], and Eq. 8 as the likelihood ratio form of Jeffrey's Rule [Diaconis&Zabell82].

The philosophical underpinnings of this method are of course questionable, because it is not clear how assertions of relevance and independence, such as (6), can be made about a hypothetical experience E which is not quantified in P. The objective of theoretical *Neo*-Bayesianism is to explore mechanisms that generate rational judgements of dependencies, relevance, directness and sufficiency without resorting to probability distributions. The theory of graphoids, to be described briefly in §6, provides an axiomatic characterization of such notions, and defines conditions under which they can be represented and processed by graphical means.

Our plan in the next sections is, first, to trace the development and interpretations of Jeffrey's Rule from its original inception and to analyze its empirical content (§3). Second, we shall argue that virtual conditionalization provides useful means of accessing the structural knowledge required to ascertain the validity of Jeffrey's Rule (§4). Later, we criticize the minimum-divergence criterion as a justification of Jeffrey's Rule (§5) and finally, we provide a brief survey of graphoid theory (§6) to illustrate the kind of structural knowledge that should supplement the algebraic description of belief states.

3   Observation by Candlelight and The Testimony of The Senses

An extreme case of probable knowledge occurs when the process of gathering information is delegated to autonomous agents, each using private procedures which for various reasons cannot be explicated in full detail. The autonomous agents used in Jeffrey's original example are our sensory organs, as described in the following passage [Jeffrey65]:

> The agent inspects a piece of cloth by candlelight and gets the impression that it is green, although he concedes that it might be blue or, even (but very improbably), violet. If G, B and V are the propositions that the cloth is green, blue and violet, respectively, then the outcome of the observation might be that,

whereas originally his degrees of belief in G, B and V were 0.30, 0.30 and 0.40, his degrees of belief in those same propositions after the observation are 0.70, 0.25 and 0.05. If there were a proposition E in his preference ranking (*i.e.*, knowledge base) which described the precise quality of his visual experience in looking at the cloth, one would say that what the agent learned from the observation was that E is true. If his original subjective probability assignment was *prob*, his new assignment should then be $prob_E$, and we would have

$$prob\ G\ =\ .30 \quad prob\ B\ =\ .30 \quad prob\ V\ =\ .40$$

representing his opinions about the color of the cloth before the observation, but would have

$$prob(G\,|\,E)\ =\ .70 \quad prob(B\,|\,E)\ =\ .25$$
$$prob(V\,|\,E)\ =\ .05$$

representing his opinions about the color of the cloth after the observation .... When the agent looks at the piece of cloth by candlelight there is a particular complex pattern of physical stimulation of his retina, on the basis of which his beliefs about the possible colors of the cloth change in the indicated ways. However, the pattern of stimulation need not be describable in the language he speaks; and even if it is, there is every reason to suppose that the agent is quite unaware of what that pattern is, and is quite incapable of uttering or identifying a correct description of it. Thus, a complete description of the pattern of stimulation includes a record of the firing times of all the rods and cones in the outer layer of retinal neurons during the period of the observation. Even if the agent is an expert physiologist, he will be unable to produce or recognize a correct record of this sort on the basis of his experience during the observation.

With this story in mind, Jeffrey wonders how the new information should be used to influence other propositions that depend on the color of the cloth:

Then the problem is this: Given that a passage of experience has led the agent to change his degrees of belief in certain propositions B_1, B_2,..., B_n from their original values,

$$prob\ B_1, \quad prob\ B_2, \quad ..., \quad prob\ B_n$$

to new values,

$$\text{PROB}B_1, \text{PROB}B_2, \ldots, \text{PROB}B_n,$$

how should these changes be propagated over the rest of the structure of his beliefs? If the original probability measure was *prob*, and the new one is PROB, and if A is a proposition in the agent's preference ranking (*i.e.*, knowledge base) but is not one of the n propositions whose probabilities were directly affected by the passage of experience, how shall PROB A be determined?

Jeffrey's solution is based on the assumption that the propositions B selected to summarize the experience possess a special property: "...while the observation changed the agent's degree of belief in B and in certain other propositions, it did not change the *conditional degree of belief* in any propositions on the evidence B or on the evidence $\neg B$" (italics added). Thus, if $B_1, B_2, \ldots, B_n$ form a partition (like *Green, Blue,* and *Violet* in the candlelight example), Jeffrey maintains that, for every proposition A not "directly affected by the passage of experience," we should write

$$(10) \qquad \text{PROB}(A \,|\, B_i) \;=\; prob\,(A \,|\, B_i) \quad i = 1, 2, \ldots, n,$$

an equality known as *J-condition*. This, together with the additivity of PROB, leads directly to *Jeffrey's Rule* of updating

$$(11) \qquad \text{PROB}(A) = \Sigma_i \; prob\,(A \,|\, B_i)\, \text{PROB}(B_i),$$

(see Eq. 7, with *prob* replacing P and PROB replacing Q).

The convenience of the rule is enticing in a way that is reminiscent of the logical rules of deduction; we need not know anything about how $prob(B_i)$ was updated to $\text{PROB}(B_i)$ *only* the net result matters. We simply take $\text{PROB}(B_i)$ as a new set of priors and apply the textbook formula of total probability. Unfortunately, the rule is applicable only in situations where the J-condition of Eq. 10 holds, and these situations, as we shall soon see, are not easy to identify.

In §2 we showed that virtual conditionalization gives a more familiar criterion to decide when Eqs. 10 and 11 are applicable. If we denote by e the evidence actually observed and equate $\text{PROB}(A)$ with $prob(A \,|\, e)$, we get

$$(12) \qquad prob(A \,|\, e) \;=\; \Sigma_i \; prob(A \,|\, B_i,\, e)\, prob(B_i \,|\, e),$$

which coincides with Eq. 11 when A and e are conditionally independent given B_i, *i.e.*, when

(13) $prob(A \mid B_i, \; e) \; = \; prob(A \mid B_i).$

However, philosophers argue that it makes no sense to equate PROB(A) with $prob(A \mid e)$ or even to talk about $prob(A \mid e)$, e being an elusive, nonpropositional experience. Indeed, the textbook definition of conditional probability, $P(A \mid e) \; = \; P(A, \; e) \; / \; P(e)$, suggests that before $P(A \mid e)$ can be computed one must have the joint probability $P(A, \; e)$, so e must already be integrated in one's knowledge base as a proposition that might later be an object of attention. This condition clearly is not met in the candlelight story; the precise sensory experience responsible for the color judgment cannot have been anticipated in anyone's belief state. In such cases, so the argument goes, Bayes' conditionalization is not applicable and should give way to the more general Jeffrey's Rule. Likewise, the conditional independence criterion of Eq. 13 is a quality ascertainable only by Bayes' conditionalization and therefore is clearly inadequate for delineating the class of propositions A to which Jeffrey's Rule applies.

While no alternate criterion for testing the J-condition (Eq. 10) is formulated in Jeffrey's original analysis, some hint is provided by the requirement that A "is not one of the n propositions whose probabilities were directly affected by the passage of experience." Jeffrey apparently believed that the question of whether a proposition A is affected directly or indirectly can be decided on qualitative grounds, by information external to *prob*. This amounts to admitting that qualitative dependence relationships, supplemental to algebraic descriptions of probability functions, are essential to the process of belief revision.

In a subsequent publication [Jeffrey68], Jeffrey replaced the intuitive notion of directness with that of a *basis*, where a basis B for an observation is defined as the set of propositions $B_1, \; B_2, \; \ldots, \; B_n$ that satisfy Eq. 10 for every A not in B. Unfortunately, even this "formal" definition still requires the support of one's intuition, because it does not define how an agent ascertains that a given partition is a basis, prior to actually computing PROB.

Thus we face the paradoxical situation that if we regard Jeffrey's Rule as a plausible prescription for constructing a new belief state PROB from the transition $prob(B_i) \; \to \; \text{PROB}(B_i)$, we must first test which proposition A satisfies the J-condition and this, in turn, requires that we inspect in advance the very state PROB that we wish constructed. If, on the other hand, we regard Jeffrey's Rule merely as a criterion for certifying candidate belief states PROB, then the rule will certify every coherent state imaginable. Given any coherent probability function PROB, we can always find a partition $\{B_i\}$ that satisfies Eqs. 10 and 11 for every A not in $\{B_i\}$ [Diaconis&Zabell82]. In the next section we shall argue that the J-condition can actually be verified within belief state *prob*, if only we supplement this state with some rudimentary structural information.

4   The Structural Information Needed

To demonstrate the type of information required for determining the applicability of Jeffrey's Rule, let us return to the candlelight example and contrast two cases in which we would be willing and also unwilling to accept the J-condition.

Case 1 e — B — A: Assume that the proposition A stands for the statement "The cloth will be sold the next day," and we know the chances of selling the cloth depend solely on its color:

(14)
$$P(A|Green) = 0.40,$$

$$P(A|Blue) = 0.40,$$

and

$$P(A|Violet) = 0.80.$$

The legitimacy of the J-condition, in this case, rests on interpreting the phrase "depend solely on its color" to mean that the probabilities given in Eq. 14 will remain the same in both belief states, *prob* and PROB. In other words, our beliefs regarding the effect of cloth colors on the behavior of potential buyers will not change by the act of observing the cloth (see Figure 1). Once the J-condition is affirmed, Jeffrey's Rule (Eq. 11) allows us to calculate the updated belief in the salability of the cloth, based only on the color inspection. Prior to the test, our belief in selling the cloth measured

$$prob(A) = (0.4)(0.3) + (0.4)(0.3) + (0.8)(0.4) = 0.56,$$

and once the test results become known, our belief should change to

$$PROB(A) = (0.4)(0.7) + (0.4)(0.25) + (0.8)(0.05) = 0.42.$$

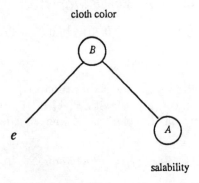

Figure 1. A network representing the conditional
independence of A and e, given B.

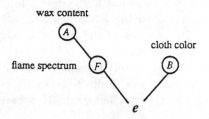

Figure 2. A network representing an evidence
(e) mediating between A and B.

Virtual conditionalization yields, of course, the same results, taking as a likelihood vector

(15)

$$L_i \triangleq \beta \ P(e \,|\, B_i) \ = \ \beta' \ \text{PROB}(B_i) \,/\, prob(B_i)$$

$$= \ \beta' \ (\{0.70 \,/\, 0.30\}, \ \{0.25 \,/\, 0.30\}, \ \{0.05 \,/\, 0.40\})$$

$$= \ \beta' \ (2.330, \ 0.833, \ 0.125)$$

(see Eqs. 5 through 9). However, the justification of the J-condition is now based on identifying PROB $(A \,|\, B_i)$ with $P(A \,|\, B_i, \ e)$ and interpreting the phrase "depends solely on its color" as A and e being conditionally independent:

(16) $P(A \,|\, Color, \ e) \ = \ P(A \,|\, Color).$

This is equivalent to our previous justification, phrased as "the effect of cloth colors on the behavior of potential buyers will not change by the act of observing the cloth," except that now the act of observing the cloth (or the outcome of that act) is given an explicit notation, e, to facilitate reasoning about the relationship of e to other propositions. This is especially important when multiple pieces of evidence are available. In contrast, the original representation of the J-condition, PROB$(A \,|\, color) \ = \ prob(A \,|\, color)$, leaves the cause of the transition from $prob$ to PROB unnamed. In other words, modern Bayesians take the liberty of writing equations such as Eq. 16, even though $P(A \,|\, Color, \ e)$ is available nowhere and cannot be computed numerically. The equation does convey the qualitative information expressed in the story – that color is the only factor relevant to salability – and it thus draws legitimacy not from numerical probability values but from another, more reliable knowledge source: people's qualitative reasoning about dependencies.

Note that since the likelihood vector requires no absolute probability assessments, it avoids the difficulties associated with non-propositional evidence (*e.g.*, the visual stimulus in the candlelight story) and, moreover, it is often a more reliable quantity to assess than the final product PROB(B_i). Thus, an alternate way of characterizing the impact of sensory experience on one's knowledge is by a likelihood vector impinging on the basis B.[1]

Next, examine a case where the J-condition is obviously violated.

---

[1] A similar idea was advanced by Field [Field78].

Case 2 A — e — B: Imagine that the main interest of our candlelight observer lies not in the color of the cloth but rather in the chemical composition of the candle wax. The agent inspects the color of the cloth, adjusts his belief from $prob(B_i)$ to $\text{PROB}(B_i)$, and then wonders how to update $prob(A)$, where A is now the proposition that the wax is a notoriously cheap brand known to produce flames deficient in violet content.

Are we justified in using Jeffrey's Rule? Since the color of the cloth $\{B_i\}$ is of no relevance to A (the wax content) prior to the observation, we have $prob(A \mid B_i) = prob\ A$. If we blindly apply Eq. 11, we obtain a paradoxical result

$$(17) \qquad \text{PROB}\ (A) = \Sigma_i\ prob(A)\ \text{PROB}\ (B_i) = prob\ (A),$$

which states that no matter how violet or greenish the cloth looks under the candlelight, the observer's belief regarding the makeup of the wax ought to remain unaltered.[2]

Is there any information in the story that could warn us against applying Jeffrey's Rule here? Modern Bayesians claim that even though we lack the knowledge required for a precise description of the measurement process, our qualitative understanding of the process of color perception is sufficient to alert us to the falsity of $P(A \mid B_i,\ e) = P(A \mid B_i)$ and thus protect us from drawing a false conclusion like Eq. 17. Much of this qualitative understanding is cast in causal schemata, which provide convenient codes for intricate patterns of conditional independence relationships. Colloquially, we say that in Case 1, the color of the cloth (B) was the sole *cause* influencing its salability (A), while in Case 2, it was A (the wax content) and B (the color) which influenced the experience e. Cast in graphical metaphors, we say that in Case 1, the color of the cloth *stood between* the evidence and A (the salability of the cloth), while in Case 2 it was the evidence that mediated between the color and A (the brand of wax), as shown in Figure 2. The process by which we convert causal or graphical relationships into qualitative assertions about conditional dependency (*e.g.*, that $P(A \mid B_i, e) \neq P(A \mid B_i)$) will be discussed in §6.

One might argue that Jeffrey's original criterion of "directness" also draws upon such causal information and, in Case 2, proposition A presumably should qualify as "one of the n propositions whose probabilities were directly affected by the passage of experience." However, this does not match our intuitive understanding of directness as an unmediated bond

---

[2]Similar objections to the J-condition were discussed by Levi [Levi67,69].

between two entities. In other words, it is hard to see how the visual experience bears directly on the nature of the wax (A), when it is the flame that mediates between the two (see Figure 2). If anything, B seems more directly affected by e than A is; the agent's judgment about the color was reported first, and color bears a closer semantic relation to visual experience than wax chemistry does.

The criterion of a "basis," too, cannot provide the desired distinction between Case 1 and Case 2. Whereas $\{B_i\}$ was clearly accepted as a basis of e relative to selling the cloth, we are no longer willing to accept $\{B_i\}$ as a basis (of the same observation e) relative to the wax content. Apparently, the notion of a basis must be a three-place, not a two-place relationship.

If the road map outlining one's passage of experience is so crucial for understanding the structure of stories (*i.e.*, which propositions should be affected by the evidence and how), it is unfortunate that the literature on probability kinematics does not provide a more complete analysis of this crucial source of information. Evidently, some believed that this road map is so deeply entrenched in human intuition that no further explication is required or possible.

Neo-Bayesian philosophers go one step beyond this point. They say any assertions one wishes to make about "passage of experience" ought to be explicated formally, using the familiar syntax of probability calculus, and treated as assertions of conditional independence. For example, one's intuition that A is not directly affected by the passage of experience ought to be written in the format of Eq. 13, treating e as a genuine propositional entity. On the surface, this requirement seems vacuous. If one interprets Eq. 13 merely as a notation for expressing intuitions about the "passage of experience," then Bayes' conditionalization $P(A \mid e)$ ceases to be a statement about the numeric magnitudes of $P(A)$ and $P(A \mid e)$ and becomes no more informative than the verbal, intuitive sentences it purports to replace. However, there is a profound significance to the use of the $P(* \mid *)$ syntax instead of some other notation.

First, it embodies the claim that passages of experience have traffic laws of their own and that these laws are similar, if not identical, to those governing Bayes' conditionalization. For example, one traffic law states that it is inconsistent for an agent to assert, "B stands between e and a pair of propositions $\{A_1, A_2\}$" without also asserting, "B and A_1 together stand between e and A_2." This consistency requirement holds both in Bayes' conditionalization and in the road map metaphor [Pearl&Verma87]. Thus, even if one insists that sentences such as Eq. 13 represent intuitive assertions about the passage of experience, not conditional probabilities, by agreeing to manipulate these sentences by the rules of Bayes conditionalization one is guaranteed never to violate any of the traffic laws that govern the road maps of experience. The question of whether graphical representation of dependencies can provide similar guarantees is discussed in §6.

Second, the use of the $P(*|*)$ syntax to define criteria such as Eq. 13 suggests useful procedures a person should use to test mentally the validity of the criterion in any given situation. Eq. 13 instructs a person to imagine first that the cloth has a definite color, say $B_i = Green$, then test whether any visual experience e could significantly sway the belief in A one way or the other. In Case 1 the answer is clearly no, because the salability was proclaimed to be a function only of the cloth color. In Case 2, however, this mental exercise would evoke some vivid scenarios that could sway our belief. For example, a green cloth that appears totally violet under the candlelight would induce a different opinion about the candle's wax than a green cloth that appears totally yellow under candlelight. Although the actual observation e is non-propositional, it is crucial in these mental exercises to denote symbolically the type of evidence one is dealing with (visual appearance, in our case), because this denotation identifies and delineates the set of scenarios one is permitted to simulate. Thus, Bayes conditionalization has syntactic and psychological merits beyond the numerical definition

$$(18) \qquad P(A|B) = P(A, B) / P(B)$$

that appears in probability textbooks.

5   The Minimum Divergence Principle

Our discussion so far aimed at demonstrating that the justification of Jeffrey's Rule (as well as any other adequate rule of belief revision) must rely on structural information not available in P. The subjective and hitherto informal nature of this information has motivated several authors to seek a more objective justification, based on the principle of least change [Williams80], [vanFraassen80], which renders structural information unnecessary. Given a prior P, a partition $\{B_i\}$, and a new measure Q on $\{B_i\}$, find the *closest* measure to P that agrees with Q on the partition and take this as defining Q on the whole space [Diaconis&Zabell82]. Since this way of proceeding does not rely on introspection (to test whether $\{B_i\}$ meets the J-condition), Diaconis and Zabell called this approach "mechanical updating." They showed that if "close" is defined in any of several common ways, for example, by the Kulbach-Leibler *divergence* (or cross entropy) measure

$$(19) \qquad I(Q, P) = \Sigma_w \, Q(w) \, log(Q(w)/P(w)),$$

then the closest measure Q is that given by Jeffrey's Rule. We shall argue that any such principle is bound to clash with human intuition, especially with our conception of causality.

That the minimum divergence principle leads to occasional clashes with commonsense is clear from the example described in Case 2. There, the principle translates to an unacceptable conclusion that observations can only destroy dependencies, never create new ones – if B and A are independent in P they will remain independent in Q. Indeed, ignoring structural information external to P, there is nothing to alert us to the fact that the observation e is causally influenced by both A and B and, therefore, once their consequence is observed, a new dependency is created between the two causes. Since the creation of new intercausal dependencies is a prevailing pattern of causal reasoning, we conclude that such paradoxical consequences are not isolated incidents, but reflect a characteristic weakness of the method; the minimum divergence updating is oblivious to common understanding of causality.

The inadequacy of the minimum divergence approach is especially pronounced when the new information arrives in the form of conditional sentences. Consider the following story: a party is about to take place and, normally, each of your friends arrives at such parties independently, with probability p. Before the party you meet your friend Tom and he tells you that if Mary goes, he will definitely not go. Oddly, if we revise our state of belief P using a minimum divergence approach, namely, adopt the closest Q that satisfies

$$Q(Tom \ goes \,|\, Mary \ goes) = 0,$$

we end up with the paradoxical situation that in the new state of belief, Q, the probability that Mary goes to the party suddenly becomes greater than p ($= p/(1 - p^2)$), as if Tom's determination to avoid meeting Mary would encourage her to go. The reason is that the minimum divergence approach cannot distinguish information in the form of a conditional sentence, "If Mary goes, Tom does not go," from an observational sentence, "Mary and Tom were not both at the party." The latter is evidential information that should be assimilated by Bayes' conditionalization, while the former conveys an instruction to change the conditional probability $P(Tom \ goes \,|\, Mary \ goes)$, without altering $P(Mary\ goes)$, a change that yields a higher divergence $I(P,\ Q)$. Evidently, the purpose of the English word *if* is to convey a distinction between these two modes of assimilating information. It instructs the listener to refrain from straight conditionalization and, instead, to perform permanent adjustment of the parameters of P. In other words, borrowing logical terminology, conditional sentences are to be treated as rules of inference, not as object-level sentences (see [Geffner&Pearl88] for a similar distinction in the context of default reasoning).

This example demonstrates that epistemic states are best understood as having multiple levels of organization, where transitory beliefs about the current world are distinguished from knowledge that remains invariant in all possible worlds. At the object level, we have Boolean sentences which reflect possible happenings in our current world, *e.g.*, that Tom goes to this party. Higher up in the hierarchy we have a probabilistic model M_P which reflects generic and permanent knowledge about all possible worlds, *e.g.*, that your friends' decisions to come to the party are independent events, each occurring with probability p. This model admits as input factual sentences about the particular world we are in (*e.g.*, that Mary went to the party), and produces new beliefs about this world (*e.g.*, that Tom goes to the party) by straight Bayes' conditionalization. Once the factual information is removed, all beliefs revert back to their original state P which is reproduced from the information stored permanently in M_P (see [Skyrms83] for alternative ways of describing "deconditionalization").

But beliefs can be revised by means other than factual information; both the parameters and the structure of M_P can also undergo changes, for example, when new statistical data arrives, or when a reliable source of information instructs us to do so (*e.g.*, Tom's proclamation that if Mary goes he will not). Information about model revision is processed in totally different ways than information about specific observables. For example, if the model M_P is governed by a set of numerical parameters $\alpha_1,\ \alpha_2, \ldots, \alpha_n$, and the agent receives information that α_k should take on the value v_k, the revision then is straightforward – simply replace the current value of α_k by v_k. If, on the other hand, the information comes as a constraint on a group of parameters (*e.g.*, $\alpha_1 + \alpha_2 = v$), the revision process is not straightforward and may involve intricate statistical considerations. Fortunately, because humans tend to organize probabilistic knowledge around conditional probabilities and in causal schemata, the revision required by conditional sentences such as "If Mary goes, Tom will not" involves the revision of a single parameter. It calls for the addition of a causal link between two propositions, ensuring

$P(Tom\ goes\,|\,Mary\ goes) = 0$, but leaves $P(Mary\ goes)$ unaltered.[3]

Our analysis does not mean that revision principles based on minimum change should be completely abandoned. However, these principles should be made to reflect the organizational features of human knowledge and to respond to any structural information that is conveyed by the messages received. Unfortunately, this structural information is often provided in a very subtle way, such as via the use of the English word "if," and is not captured by the Kulbach-Leibler divergence or any other distance measure which unconditionally sanctions Jeffrey's Rule.

6   Graphs, Graphoids and The Passage of Experience

So far, we have used the diagrams in Figures 1 and 2 primarily as mnemonic devices to distinguish among the cases discussed and to make an occasional association with Jeffrey's "passage of experience" notion. However, the preceding discussion also demonstrates a rather useful pattern produced by graphical representations (Figures 1 and 2): Jeffrey's Rule is applicable if and only if *B separates A* from *e*. This may be what Jeffrey meant by requiring that *A* not be "one of the *n* propositions whose probabilities were directly affected by the passage of experience." The graphical notion of *separation* and its relation to the informational notion of *relevance* is given formal treatment by the theory of *graphoids*. [Pearl&Paz85], [Pearl88].

The central aim of the theory of graphoids is to articulate the conditions under which one item of information is considered relevant to another, given what we already know, and to encode knowledge in structures that vividly display these conditions as the knowledge undergoes changes. Of course, different formalisms give rise to different definitions of relevance. For example, in probability theory relevance is identified with dependence; in relational databases relevance is associated with induced constraints – two variables are said to be relevant to each other if we can restrict the range of values permitted for one by constraining the other [Fagin77]. However, it is not really necessary to consult numerical probability distributions (or database tables) before relevance relations can be encoded, verified and manipulated. For example, a person might be hesitant to assess the likelihood of two events but feel confident about judging whether or not the events are relevant to each other. People provide such judgments swiftly and consistently

---

[3]With this interpretation in mind, it is not to be wondered that conditional sentences become assertible by criteria different than those of factual sentences [Lewis76], and nested conditionals are very rarely used in ordinary discourse.

because – we speculate – relevance relationships are stored and processed qualitatively before making any numerical assessment. It is precisely this qualitative representation of relevance that permits us to determine, in the candlelight story, whether the J-condition (Eq. 10) is valid, despite the fact that e is not quantified probabilistically.

It turns out that the essence of relevance can be identified with a structure common to both the probabilistic and the database definitions of conditional dependence and, in fact, to every sensible explication of the intuitive relation "knowing Z renders X and Y independent," denoted $I(X, Z, Y)$. The structure consists of four axioms:

(20a)   *Symmetry* $I(X, Z, Y) \leftrightarrow I(Y, Z, X)$

(20b)   *Decomposition* $I(X, Z, YW) \rightarrow I(X, Z, Y)$

(20c)   *Weak union* $I(X, Z, YW) \rightarrow I(X, ZY, W)$

(20d)   *Contraction*
$$I(X, ZY, W) \& I(X, Z, Y) \rightarrow I(X, Z, YW)$$

where X, Y and Z represent three disjoint subsets of objects (*e.g.*, variables, attributes or partitions). These axioms were first proposed by Dawid [Dawid79], and independently by Spohn [Spohn80], as the basic properties of conditional probabilistic independence.

Axioms (20c) and (20d) convey the simple idea that when we learn an irrelevant fact, the relevance relationships of all other propositions remain unaltered; any information that was irrelevant remains irrelevant and that which was relevant remains relevant. Structures that conform to these four axioms are called *semi-graphoids*, while if a fifth axiom holds

(20e)   *Intersection*
$$I(X, ZY, W) \& I(X, ZW, Y) \rightarrow I(X, Z, YW),$$

the structure is called a *graphoid*. Interestingly, both undirected graphs and directed acyclic graphs conform to the graphoid axioms (hence the name) if we associate the sentence "variable X is irrelevant to variable Y once we know Z" with the graphical condition "every path from X to Y is intercepted by the set of nodes corresponding to Z."[4]

---

[4] A special definition of *intercept* is required for directed graphs [Pearl88].

With this perspective in mind, graphs, networks, and diagrams can be viewed as inference engines devised for efficiently representing and manipulating relevance relationships: The topology of the network is assembled from a list of local relevance statements (*e.g.*, direct dependencies); this list entails (using the graphoid axioms) a host of additional statements, and the function of the graph is to ensure that a substantial portion of the latter can be read off by simple graphical criteria. Such a mapping enables one to determine, purely by qualitative means, which information items are relevant to each other, in any state of knowledge Z.

An important result from the theory of graphoids states that Bayesian networks [Pearl88] constitute a sound and complete inference mechanism relative to probabilistic dependencies, *i.e.*, it enables us to identify, in polynomial time, each and every conditional-independence relationship that logically follows from those used in the construction of the network [Pearl&Verma87] [Geiger&Pearl88]. Similar results hold for other types of relevance relationships, *e.g.*, partial correlations and database dependencies. However, the essential requirement for soundness and completeness is that the network be constructed *causally*, *i.e.*, that we specify, recursively, the relationship of each variable to its predecessors in some total order.[5]

One can speculate whether it is this soundness-completeness feature that renders causal schemata so important in knowledge organization. However, there is hardly any dispute that causal relationships are processed by qualitative, non-probabilistic methods. We conclude by proposing that it is this qualitative representation of causal relationships which should supplement the algebraic description of epistemic states.

7 Conclusions

Jeffrey's Rule of belief updating was devised to replace Bayes' conditioning in cases where the evidence cannot be articulated propositionally. Our analysis shows that to determine whether the rule is valid in any specific case, qualitative structural information must be available, discerning which beliefs are directly related and which are only indirectly related. If such knowledge is available, it can be faithfully represented by the syntax of conditional independence sentences, and virtual conditionalization can be used to update beliefs.

---

[5]Once the network is constructed, the original order can be forgotten; only the partial order displayed in the network matters.

The formal identity between Jeffrey's Rule and virtual conditionalization renders the two semantically equivalent, *i.e.*, beliefs updated by Jeffrey's Rule cannot be distinguished from those updated by Bayes' conditionalization on some virtual evidence. Virtual conditionalization sidesteps the requirement that all evidence be quantified *apriori* in one's epistemic state. This option expands the repertoire of Bayes' analysis by permitting us to assimilate evidence by means other than straight conditioning, and it simultaneously facilitates the manipulation of belief updates within the traditional syntax of probability calculus.

Our analysis also shows that simple criteria based on graphical considerations lead to conclusions that match our intuition. This suggests that the structural information which supplements the algebraic description of epistemic states can be represented by networks of relations, and perhaps intuitive judgments are really mental tracings of those networks. The theory of graphoids supports these suggestions.

There are, of course, items of information that cannot and should not be handled as evidential data for conditionalization neither real nor virtual, but must be treated as permanent parametric adjustments to the probabilistic model we currently possess. Conditional sentences are typical examples of such information. Hence, it is tempting to suggest that the main purpose of the English word *if* is to convey a distinction between these two modes of belief revision.

Acknowledgments. I thank R. Jeffrey for clarifying the historical origins of probability kinematics and to I. Levi for pointing out how close my current analysis is to his first reactions to Jeffrey's ideas.

This paper is an expanded version of §2.3.3 in Pearl, J., *Probabilistic Reasoning in Intelligent Systems: Networks of Plausible Inference,* Morgan-Kaufmann, 1988.

This work was supported in part by National Science Foundation Grant #IRI–86–10155 and Naval Research Laboratory Grant #N00014–89–2007.

8 Bibliography

Dawid, A. "Conditional independence in statistical theory," *Journal of The Royal Statistical Society Series A 41*, 1, pp. 1–31, 1979.

Diaconis, P., and S. Zabell. "Updating subjective probabilities," *Journal of the American Statistical Association 77*, pp. 822–830, 1982.

Diaconis, P., and S. Zabell. "Some alternatives to Bayes's Rule," in *Information Processing and Group Decision Making*, B. Grofman and O. Guillermo, eds., JAI Press, pp. 25–38, 1986.

Duda, R., Hart, P., and N. Nilsson. "Subjective Bayesian methods for rule-based inference systems," *Proceedings of the National Computer Conference (AFIPS) Vol. 45*, pp. 1075–1082, 1976.

Fagin, R. "Multivalued dependencies and a new form for relational databases," *ACM Transactions on Database Systems 2*, 3, pp. 262–278, 1977.

Field, H. "A note on Jeffrey conditionalization," *Philosophy of Science 45*, pp. 361–367, 1978.

Geffner, H., and J. Pearl. "A framework for reasoning with defaults," 1988. This volume.

Geiger, D., and J. Pearl. "On the logic of causal models," *Proceedings Fourth Workshop on Uncertainty in AI*, pp. 136–147, Philadelphia 1988.

Good, I. "Dynamic probability, computer chess, and the measurement of knowledge," *Machine Intelligence 8*, E. Elcock and D. Mitchie, eds., Ellis Horwood Ltd. and John Wylie, pp. 139–150, 1977.

Good, I. "The best explication for weight of evidence," *Journal of Statistics, Computers, & Simulation 19*, 4, pp. 294–299, 1984.

Heckerman, D. "A rational measure of confirmation," *Uncertainty in Artificial Intelligence 2*, L. Kanal and J. Lemmer, eds., Elsevier, pp. 11–12, 1986.

Jeffrey, R. *The Logic of Decisions*, McGraw-Hill, 1965, (2nd Ed., 1983, University of Chicago Press), 1985.

Jeffrey, R. "Probable knowledge," *The Problem of Inductive Logic*, I. Lakatos, ed., Elsevier, 1968.

Kelly, C. III, and S. Barkley. "A general Bayesian model for hierarchical inference," *Organizational Behavior and Human Performance 10*, pp. 388–403, 1973.

Levi, I. "Probability kinematics," *British Journal for The Philosophy of Science 18*, pp. 197–209, 1967.

Levi, I. "If Jones only knew more!" *British Journal for The Philosophy of Science 20*, pp. 153–159, 1969.

Lewis, D. "Probabilities of conditionals and conditional probabilities," *Philosophical Review 85*, 3, pp. 297–315, 1976.

Pearl, J. *Probabilistic Reasoning in Intelligent Systems: Networks of Plausible Inference*, Morgan–Kaufmann, 1988.

Pearl, J., and A. Paz. "GRAPHOIDS: A graph-based logic for reasoning about relevance relations," Technical Report 850038 (R-53-L), Cognitive Systems Laboratory, Los Angeles, University of California, 1985. Short version in *Advances in Artificial Intelligence 2*, B. Du Boulay, D. Hogg, and L. Steels, eds., Elsevier, 1987.

Pearl, J., and T. Verma. "The logic of representing dependencies by directed graphs," *Proceedings of Sixth National Conference on AI (AAAI-87)*, Seattle, pp. 374–379, 1987.

Schum, D. *Evidence and Inference for The Intelligence Analyst*, University Press of America, 1987.

Skyrms, B. "Three ways to give a probability assignment a memory," *Minnesota Studies in the Philosophy of Science 10*, J. Earman, ed., University of Minnesota Press, pp. 157–161, 1983.

Spohn, W. "Stochastic independence, causal independence, and shieldability," *Journal of Philosophical Logic 9*, pp. 73–99, 1980.

van Fraassen, B. "Rational belief and probability kinematics," *Philosophy of Science 47*, pp. 165–187, 1980.

Williams, P. "Bayesian conditionalization and the principle of minimum information," *British Journal for the Philosophy of Science 31*, pp. 131–144, 1980.

1131299

Two Perspectives on Consensus for (Bayesian) Inference and Decisions

Teddy Seidenfeld

Based on collaborations with M. Schervish and J. Kadane, [89] and [89a]

0   Introduction and Overview

In this paper I discuss questions of consensus among Bayesian investigators, from two perspectives:

> §1. Regarding inference: What are the agreements in (posterior) probabilities that result from increasing shared data? When do these agreements converge on practical certainties?

and

> §2. Regarding decisions: What are the shared, strict preferences of Bayesian decision makers? When do these shared preferences support "coherent" compromises?

Section 1 deals, first, with Savage's [Savage54] well known result, which applies both to questions of certainty and consensus of posterior opinions. That finding establishes:

> (a) the (almost sure) approach to certainty of the posterior probability for the true hypothesis, given an increasing set of evidence.

and

> (b) the (almost sure) consensus between two investigators, as measured by the (maximum) difference between their posterior probabilities for hypotheses, when they share the common evidence.

267

H.E. Kyburg, Jr. et al. (eds.), Knowledge Representation and Defeasible Reasoning, 267–286.
© 1990 *Kluwer Academic Publishers. Printed in the Netherlands.*

Savage's finding depends upon restrictions involving both the statistical model for the data and the set of competing statistical hypotheses. For (a), the data are assumed to be identically, independently distributed [i.i.d.] given each one of a finite (yet exhaustive) set of hypotheses; where each hypothesis has positive, "prior" probability. For (b), in addition, Savage assumes the two agents agree on these (conditional) i.i.d. probabilities and on the finite (yet, exhaustive) set of hypotheses. Thus, the two agents agree completely on which events carry 0 probability.[1]

I discuss generalizations of these certainty and consensus results without the need of either "i," without the assumption that there are only finitely many hypotheses, and without the assumption that the data have positive (initial) probability.

(a) Concerning asymptotic certainty — that the posterior probability goes to a 0–1 distribution — the result is known and can be shown in at least two ways: using the theory of martingales [Doob53], or from some basic measure theory [Halmos50].

(b) Concerning asymptotic consensus among different investigators (whose opinions lie within a "closed" set of m.a.c. opinions) we have shown that the result obtains, but is sensitive to the topology used to define "closure" of the community of rival opinions. That is, the consensus depends upon how "extreme" views are defined. In particular, we get different kinds of consensus depending upon whether the set of extreme points in a (convex) set of (m.a.c.) opinions is compact: in the discrete topology; or in the uniform-distance topology; or in the weak-star topology.

§2 of this paper investigates the extent to which coherent agents hold common preferences over acts.[2] The important case is one where the agents differ both in their degrees of beliefs for states and in their values for outcomes — when they hold different personal probabilities and different utilities. The question asked is this. When two such agents face a common (group) decision, what are the possibilities for a coherent (weak) Pareto compromise, a compromise that preserves the (strict) preferences which they share?

Based on our recent work [89a], the answer is that all coherent (weak) Pareto solutions to the group decision problem are *autocratic*. There are

---

[1] Their initial opinions are mutually, absolutely continuous [m.a.c.].

[2] "Coherence" is explicated using Anscombe & Aumann's [63] "horse-lottery" theory.

no Bayesian compromises. Only the agents' own two probability and utility pairs support preferences that agree with the (weak) Pareto condition. Moreover, there are *no* coherent solutions that respect the strong Pareto condition.

Thus, the questions about consensus are very different when asked about agreements in probabilities and about agreements in decisions. Nonetheless, we may resolve the conflicting senses of "agreement" by relaxing one of the axioms for coherent preferences. When preference is a partial order, rather than a weak order, Pareto compromises exist and are represented by sets of probability/utility pairs. These sets of probabilities support the (positive) results on inferential consensus and certainty, summarized in Part 1.

1 *Inferential* Consensus and Certainty

1.1 Some Conceptual Preliminaries

Assume that a rational agent has (unconditional) degrees of belief represented by a probability $P_K(Y)$ – the probability of Y with background knowledge K.[3] K, the agent's background knowledge, fixes the space of possibilities. An important *idealization* about K: Assume K is closed under mathematical and logical consequences. Hence, this investigation into changing beliefs has little to say about learning arithmetic or about belief in the occurrent sense, which involves the growing recognition of, *e.g.*, deductive consequences of what you already believe.

Next, it is useful to distinguish two schools of Bayesian thought regarding the extent to which K determines P_K.

The *subjectivists* allow that two agents with the same background knowledge may, nonetheless, have different degrees of belief. For example, the positions advocated by [deFinetti37], [Ramsey31], and [Savage54] are *subjective* in this sense. The *objectivists* or (as they are sometimes called) *necessitarians* argue that K determines $P_K(Y)$. For example, based on their (respective) treatment of states of "ignorance," H. Jeffreys [Jeffreys67], and E. T. Jaynes [Jaynes83], defend a Bayesian position that is *necessitarian* in this sense. Also, early Carnap [Carnap45] tried this view out, but came to reject it [Carnap62].

Of course, by objectivist standards, a consensus among posterior probabilities is automatic once the agents share the same total evidence, K.

---

[3] The condition that the agent's degrees of belief are represented by a single distribution is relaxed, below, where I discuss consensus and convergence for *sets* of probabilities.

Therefore, to avoid trivializing the investigation into consensus and certainty, I adopt the subjectivist Bayesian perspective.

1.2   Two Models of Bayesian Learning (Where K Changes)

First, distinguish learning by *deliberation* from learning by *routine* [Levi80].

In a *deliberated expansion* of K, new knowledge arises by deciding what proposition is worthy of (full) belief. Such epistemic decisions occur when the acts are cognitive and the utilities reflect cognitive goals. Some examples from the literature include Levi's [Levi67] treatment of *acceptance*, and Savage's [Savage54, §15] treatment of statistical *point estimation*, where the epistemic utility of an act is defined through a "loss" function.

Routine expansion of K combined with *Bayes' rule* for updating, — temporal conditionalization, as Levi [Levi74] calls it — is the more familiar Bayesian model of learning. Here, observation reports are admitted as evidence. For example, an agent sees that E, "The coin lands heads." and adds E to the evidence K.[4]

$$K \quad \longrightarrow observe\ E \longrightarrow \quad K' = closure\{K + E\}.$$

So, given K', $\neg E = \bot$. That is, "$\neg E$" is no longer a possible event with respect to the new background assumptions K'. Bayes' rule for updating,

$$P_K{'}(Y) = P_K(Y \mid E),$$

makes the new probability of Y to be just the old conditional probability of Y, given E. Note: temporal conditionalization does not preclude contracting K' in a subsequent revision of the evidence, *e.g.*, moving "back" to K in order to make learning *corrigible*.[5]

---

[4] I. Levi [Levi80] generalizes this mode of learning with his "routine expansions": $K \longrightarrow stimulus\ X \longrightarrow K' = closure\{K + Y\}$, where Y is some, perhaps general, proposition. The routine makes Y a function of X, $r(X) = Y$. Learning by direct observation is the identity function with "observation reports" the stimuli. An interesting application of generalized routines is Levi's [Levi80, §17.6] Bayesian model for some orthodox, (Neyman-Pearsonian) statistical inferences.

[5] R. C. Jeffrey [Jeffrey65, §11; 68] offers a rival approach to observation with his kinematics: the output of the routine is to shift from $P_K(\ .\ )$ to $P'_K(\ .\ )$ without changing K. Instead, "observing E" just makes E more probable, not certain, while preserving the conditional probabilities:

$$P_K(\ *\ \mid E) = P'_K(\ *\ \mid E) \text{ and } P_K(\ *\ \mid \neg E) = P'_K(\ *\ \mid \neg E).$$

Diaconis and Zabell [Diaconis&Zabell82] give an interesting presentation of Jeffrey's rule, as it relates to some *necessarian* proposals to minimize the change in *information* that

1.3 How Do Routine Expansions Affect Consensus and Certainty?

Savage [Savage54, §3.6] notes a particularly interesting phenomenon that occurs when temporal conditionalization is iterated with i.i.d. data.

Theorem 1.1:

(i) Suppose Jane is a Bayesian whose background knowledge fixes $\Theta = \{\theta_1, \ldots, \theta_t\}$, a partition into t disjoint, mutually exhaustive states, each with positive probability, $P_K(\theta_j) > 0$ $(j = 1, \ldots, t)$. Imagine an experiment with m possible outcomes $\Omega = \{e_1, \ldots, e_m\}$, whose conditional probabilities, given θ_j, are denoted $P_K(e_i \mid \theta_j) = p_{i,j}$ (for $i = 1, \ldots, m$ and $j = 1, \ldots, t$).

(ii) Suppose that for each distinct pair of states $\theta_i \neq \theta_j$, there is an outcome $e \in \Omega$ with distinct likelihoods, *i.e.*, $P_K(e \mid \theta_i) \neq P_K(e \mid \theta_j)$.

(iii) Suppose that the experiment can be repeated indefinitely and that repetitions of the experiment have independent outcomes, given θ. That is, $\forall(j,n)$, $P_K(<e_{i1}, e_{i2}, \ldots, e_{in}> \mid \theta_j) = \Pi_k(p_{ik,j})$ $(k = 1, \ldots, n)$. Given θ_j, the $<E_i>$ form an i.i.d. sequence.

Denote by $P_K^n(\Theta)$, Jane's probability over Θ given the evidence from n-repetitions of the experiment. In other words, given a history of n-trials, let $P_K^n(\Theta)$ be obtained by Bayes' rule from $P_K(\, . \,)$ and routine expansions.

Then, regardless which θ_j obtains, with the exception of a set of complete histories of P_K-probability 0, $lim_{n \to \infty} P_K^n(\Theta) = \chi(\theta_j)$.

In words, $P_K^n(\Theta)$ approaches a two-valued probability which assigns θ_j probability 1.

---

results from a change in probabilities. This is a view advocated, for example, by Jaynes — who indexes the information in a distribution according to its entropy. In general, however, minimum information shifts do not admit Bayesian models, and have only a limited value as an approximation to Bayesian updating. For discussion, see [Seidenfeld86] and [Skyrms85], and references therein.

Though it reneges on the epistemological promise to avoid *acceptance*, Jeffrey's theory can be absorbed into the familiar *subjectivist*'s account of observation by enlarging the algebra of possibilities, so that, *e.g.*, one only "seems to see E" and then learns this qualified report in the usual way: accepting it and conditionalizing.

Thus, Jane becomes convinced (almost surely) of the certainty of the true, unknown state θ_j in light of the sequence of observations $<E_1,\ldots>$.[6]

Let Dick be another Bayesian agent. Similar reasoning applies to his beliefs. All it takes to ensure that the two investigators come to agree about Θ with increasing evidence is the added condition that, initially, they share the same set of theoretical possibilities: that $\Theta = \{\theta\colon P(\theta) > 0\}$ is the same set for Dick and Jane.[7] Savage [Savage54, §4.6] expresses the resulting consensus between Dick and Jane, which I formulate as:

Theorem 1.2:

Under the same conditions as Theorem 1, if Dick agrees with Jane about which θ's have positive probability then, with probability 1 [a.s.], their posterior probabilities converge uniformly.

$$lim_{n\to\infty}\ sup_\Theta\ |\ P^n_{Dick}(\theta_j)\ -\ P^n_{Jane}(\theta_j)\ |\ =\ 0. \qquad [\text{a.s.}]^8$$

1.4   Consensus in A Larger Community

We can treat Dick and Jane as extreme members in a (convex) community **C** of opinions:

$$\mathbf{C} = \{P_\alpha(\Theta) = \alpha P_{Dick}(\Theta) + (1-\alpha)P_{Jane}(\Theta)\colon 0 \le \alpha \le 1\}.$$

Then, under the conditions of the previous results:

Theorem 1.3:

$$lim_{n\to\infty}\ sup_C\ sup_\Theta\ |\ P^n_\alpha(\theta_j)\ -\ P^n_\beta(\theta_j)\ |\ =\ 0.$$

That is, then the entire community **C** achieves consensus, uniformly.

We may use this to relax an assumption of the previous results. Instead of requiring that agents use Bayes' rule for updating, it suffices for asymptotic certainty and consensus that each agent updates his/her probability with some element of the set $C^n = \{P_\alpha^n(\Theta)\}$, the set of conditionalized probabilities. We report this as a

---

[6]Savage offers a simple proof based on the strong law of large numbers.

[7]This guarantees that their probabilities are mutually absolutely continuous.

[8]These results are internal to Dick and Jane's initial agreements. That is, they are relativized to common (m.a.c.) judgments about events of zero probability.

Corollary: Within **C**, mere static coherence suffices for asymptotic certainty and consensus. Temporal conditionalization is not required.[9]

Question: For how large a community **C** do these limiting results obtain?

The next example provides a partial answer. To wit: the merging of posterior opinions (but not the certainty) involves the *closure* of **C**. To see that is so, here is a simple example where consensus fails.

Example 1. Consider a binomial (coin-flipping) inference problem, with a coin of unknown bias $\Theta = \{ 0 < \theta < 1 \}$. A class **C** of (m.a.c.) prior probabilities over Θ is given by the *beta-distributions*:

$$p_{\alpha,\beta}(\theta) \propto \theta^{(\alpha-1)}(1 - \theta)^{(\beta-1)} \quad (0 < \alpha, \beta).[10]$$

Using a beta prior, we find that the conditional probability for θ, given n-flips of which m land heads and $(n-m)$ land tails, is

$$p^n_{\alpha,\beta}(\theta) \propto \theta(\alpha - 1 + m)(1 - \theta)(\beta - 1 + (n - m)).$$

Though, asymptotically, each element of this class achieves certainty for the true θ^*, there is no limiting consensus since, for each data set $<E_1,\ldots,E_n>$ and for each θ, there is some $p^n_{\alpha,\beta}(\theta)$ which is concentrated near that θ.

Next, I discuss several generalizations of these findings.

1.5 Structural Assumptions For The Measure Space $(X, \mathcal{B}, P)$ of Hypotheses and Possible Observations

Consider a denumerable sequence of sets X_i $(i = 1, \ldots)$ with associated σ-fields $\mathcal{B}_i$. Form the infinite Cartesian product $X = X_1 \otimes \ldots$ of sequences $(x_1, x_2, \ldots) = x \in X$, where $x_i \in X_i$; that is, each x_i is an atom of its algebra $\mathcal{B}_i$. [11] Let the measurable sets in X (the events) be the elements of of the σ-algebra $\mathcal{B}$ generated by the set of measurable rectangles. (A measurable rectangle $A = A_1 \otimes \ldots$ is one where $A_i \in \mathcal{B}_i$ and $A_i = X_i$ for all but finitely many i).

Define the spaces of histories $(H_n, \mathcal{H}_n)$ and futures $(F_n, \mathcal{F}_n)$ where $H_n = X_1 \otimes \ldots \otimes X_n$, $\mathcal{H}_n = \mathcal{B}_1 \otimes \ldots \otimes \mathcal{B}_n$, $F_n = X_{n+1} \otimes \ldots$ and where $\mathcal{F}_n = \mathcal{B}_{n+1} \otimes \ldots$.

---

[9] For additional discussion of static versus dynamical standards of coherence, see: [Kyburg80], [Levi80, §4.3–4.4], and [Skyrms87].

[10] $\alpha = \beta = 1$ is the uniform prior, Carnap's c^*.

[11] This is a mild condition as the $\mathcal{B}_i$ may be unrelated.

Let P be a (countably additive) probability over the measure space $(X, \mathcal{B})$. Assume P is *predictive* [Blackwell&Dubins62], so that there exist conditional probability distributions of events given past events, $P^n(\ .\ |\ \mathcal{H}_n)$. In particular, given a history h_n, there is a conditional probability distribution for the future, $P^n(\ .\ |\ h_n)$ on $\mathcal{F}_n$.[12]

Denote the characteristic function of a set E by $\chi_E(x) = 1$ (or $= 0$) if $x \in$ (or $\notin$) E, for x a complete history.

1.6   Asymptotic Certainty and Consensus

The almost certain approach to certainty for events measurable with respect to $(X, \mathcal{B})$ is given by the next result.

Theorem:

$$\forall(E \in \mathcal{B})\ lim_{n \to \infty}\ P^n(E\ |\ h_n) = \chi_E(x).\qquad [\text{a.e. } P]$$

The theorem asserts that, for each event E and for all but a set of complete histories of P-measure 0 (depending upon E), the sequence of conditional probabilities, $P^n(E\ |\ h_n)$, converges to 1 or to 0 as E occurs or not.

Proof(s). In our [89] essay, we indicate two ways this theorem has been shown: (1) using martingale theory [Doob53]; and (2) by approximating events with rectangles [Halmos50, T.13.D and T.49.B].[13]

Next, I address the question of consensus. Consider any probability Q which is in agreement with P about events of measure 0 in $\mathcal{B}$, i.e., $\forall E \in \mathcal{B}$, $P(E) = 0$ iff $Q(E) = 0$, so that P and Q are mutually absolutely continuous. Then Q, too, is predictive if P is, with conditional probability distributions: $Q^n(\mathcal{F}_n\ |\ h_n)$.

---

[12]These conditional probabilities are defined without the assumption that $P(h_n) > 0$.

[13]Halmos' T.49.B applies without supposing P is predictive. For asymptotic certainty, the relevant features of conditional probabilities for an event E, $P(E\ |\ .\ )$ $(n = 1, \dots)$, are supplied by the Radon-Nikodym derivatives of $P(E)$ with respect to $P(E \cap\ .\ )$.

Also, this approach applies directly to the measure completion of P. Thus we have the Lebesgue Density Theorem as a corollary.

Definition: Let m be Lebesgue measure. For each measurable set E on the real line $\mathcal{R}$, define the density at the point x by, $lim_{h \to 0}$

$m(E \cap [x-h, x+h])/2h$, and denote by $f(x)$ the set of points of density 1.

Corollary: For each measurable set $E \subset \mathcal{R}$, $m(E \bigtriangleup f(E)) = 0$.

In their important paper of 1962, Blackwell and Dubins establish (almost sure) asymptotic consensus between the conditional probabilities P^n and Q^n. In particular, they show:

Theorem:

For each P^n there is a (version of) Q^n so that, almost surely, the distance between them vanishes with increasing histories:

$$lim_{n \to \infty} \, \rho(P^n, Q^n) = 0 \quad \text{[a.e. } P \text{ or } Q\text{]},$$

where ρ is the uniform distance metric between distributions (That is, with μ and ν defined on the same measure space $(M, \mathcal{M})$, $\rho(\mu,\nu)$ is the l.u.b., over events $E \in \mathcal{M}$, of $|\, \mu(E) - \nu(E)\,|$).

What can be said about the merging of opinions when considering a set **C** of mutually absolutely continuous probabilities? Based on Example 1, unless **C** is closed there may be no agreement among the conditional probabilities in **C**. In this vein, we note a simple corollary to the "consensus" Theorem (above).

Corollary 1.1:

Let **C** be a closed, convex set of probabilities, all mutually absolutely continuous, and generated by finitely many of its extreme points. Then, asymptotically the conditional probabilities in **C** achieve consensus uniformly. That is, for almost all $x \in X$,

$$\forall \epsilon > 0, \quad \exists m, \quad n > m, \quad \forall P, Q \in \mathbf{C} \;\; \rho(P^n, Q^n) < \epsilon.$$

Note, also, Corollary 1.1 ensures consensus and certainty when agents are merely statically coherent but take updated probabilities from **C**. The following illustrates this point.

Example 2. Let x_i be i.i.d. Normal(μ, σ^2), where the conjugate priors for these parameters have hyperparameters which lie in a compact set. Given the observed history, h_n, let two agents choose probabilities P^n, Q^n (given h_n) in any manner (even as a function of h_n) from this set. Then, consensus and certainty obtains, almost surely, with observation of the x_i's.

The next result, which has a weaker conclusion, helps to identify the role played by the topology in fixing closure of **C**.

Corollary 1.2:

Let **C** be a compact set (under the topology induced by ρ) of mutually absolutely continuous, predictive probabilities on the space $(X, \mathcal{B})$. Let $\{P_n, Q_n\}$ be any sequence of pairs from **C**. Then, $\forall R \in \mathbf{C}$

$$\rho(P_n^n, Q_n^n) \xrightarrow{R} 0 \quad \text{as } n \longrightarrow \infty.$$

That is, $\forall(\epsilon > 0) \quad lim_{n \to \infty} R(\{h_n: \rho(P_n^n, Q_n^n) > \epsilon\}) = 0.$

Corollary 2 shows that sequences of (arbitrary) pairs of agents in **C** achieve consensus "in probability," provided **C** is closed under uniform limits.

We show this conclusion is false for the "a.e." version, [89].

Hence, ρ-compactness of **C** does *not* suffice for the "almost everywhere" convergence, which obtains, according to the first corollary, when **C** is generated by finitely many extreme points.

Nor is Corollary 2 true when compactness of **C** is by the weak-star topology. Even when **C** is closed under pointwise limits, pairwise ρ-consensus may fail. That is, in this case, there may be an event E and a sequence of pairs (P_n, Q_n) from **C** where the (paired) conditional probabilities of E differ by a fixed amount: $|P_n^n(E) - Q_n^n(E)| > \delta > 0$ (we provide an illustration in [89]). So, weakening the standard for consensus, to match the sense of compactness from the weak-star topology, does not help. Thus, the extent to which consensus occurs depends upon how **C** is closed.

1.7   A Summary of Results Presented in §1

Without exception, increasing evidence pushes conditional probabilities for a (*measurable*) event E to certainty, almost surely.

Against the background of this certainty, I report conditions which guarantee asymptotic consensus (under the uniform distance metric) for conditional probabilities taken from a set **C** of unconditional distributions.

Not surprising, depending upon how **C** is closed, different conclusions obtain. When **C** is (contained within or) generated by finitely many (mutually absolutely continuous) elements, *i.e.*, when **C** is convex and its extreme points form a compact set in the discrete topology, consensus of conditional probabilities occurs, almost surely. Here, *static* coherence suffices for all the results.

When the extreme points of **C** form a compact set in the uniform topology, there is *in-probability* (but not *almost sure*) consensus for sequences of pairs of conditional probabilities.

When **C** is compact in the weak-star topology, there may be no limiting consensus. In this case, there can be an event E and a sequence of pairs (P_n, Q_n) from **C** where the (paired) conditional probabilities of E differ by a fixed amount, $|P_n^n(E) - Q_n^n(E)| > \delta > 0$.

All these results apply, directly, to theories of *indeterminate probability*, where opinions are represented by a (convex) set of probabilities (for example see [Levi74]). Also, these results about consensus can be interpreted as a variety of *Bayesian robustness* (see [Berger85], §4.7). However, these large sample results fail to provide bounds on the rates with which consensus and certainty occur.

What they do show is the surprising fact that these asymptotic properties of conditional probabilities do not depend upon exchangeability or other kinds of symmetries of the (unconditional) probabilities in **C**, the community of opinions. No appeal to i.i.d. processes is necessary for these findings. Rather agreement on events of zero probability and a suitable *closure* suffice for consensus, while the approach to certainty is automatic — almost surely.

2 *Decision-Theoretic* Agreement among Different Agents

Thematic Question: Subject to a unanimity (Pareto) condition, can coherence be extended from individual preferences to group decisions?

In other words, what are the Bayesian compromises open to coherent agents facing common, group decisions? Throughout, I bypass problems of elicitation, *e.g.*, due to *strategic* voting. In the discussion of group decisions, I assume the agents can act cooperatively (joint decisions are binding), and the agents know each other's beliefs and desires.

Specific Question: What are the Bayesian models for the shared preferences of two coherent agents?

Let us investigate a group of two Bayesians in a setting where acts, A_i, are [Anscombe&Aumann63] *horse lotteries*. Coherence is characterized in their theory by (four) axioms on the preference relation, denoted by $\preceq$ (the reader is referred to the Appendix for an explanation of the Anscombe-

Aumann theory).[14] My purpose here is to summarize the findings of our [89a] essay in answer to the specific question, above.

Let $\preceq_k$ [and $\prec_k$] $(k = 1,2)$ denote, respectively, the agents' [strict] preferences and, similarly, let $\preceq_G$ [and $\prec_G$] be the group's [strict] preference relation. Define two versions of the Pareto condition.[15]

The *Weak Pareto* condition: Group preference respects unanimous, individual strict preference. If $A_1 \prec_k A_2$ $(k = 1, 2, \dots)$, then $A_1 \prec_G A_2$.

The *Strong Pareto* condition: Group preference for A_2 over A_1 is strict whenever someone's is, and when no one strictly prefers A_1. If $A_1 \preceq_k A_2$ $(k = 1, 2, \dots)$, with at least one preference strict, then $A_1 \prec_G A_2$.

Since preferences are coherent, we can use an expected utility representation to depict it. Each $\preceq_k$ $(k = 1, 2)$ is given by a (unique) probability/utility pair (P_k, U_k); where, $A_1 \preceq_k A_2$ if and only if the E_{P_k, U_k}-expected utilities satisfy $E_{P_k, U_k}(A_1) \leq E_{P_k, U_k}(A_2)$. Likewise, indicate $\preceq_G$ by the probability/utility pair (P_G, U_G).

Theorem 2.1.   ([Harsanyi77], among many):

If $U_k = U$ $(k = 1, 2)$ then the Weak Pareto Bayesian compromises satisfy

$$U_G = U \text{ and } P_G \in \{\alpha P_1 + (1-\alpha)P_2\}$$

or, if $P_k = P$, then $P_G = P$ and $U_G \in \{\alpha U_1 + (1-\alpha)U_2\}$, with $0 \leq \alpha \leq 1$.

The Strong Pareto Bayesian compromises have the same form, but $0 < \alpha < 1$.[16]

Theorem 2.2.   [89a]:

However, if both $P_1 \neq P_2$ and $U_1 \neq U_2$ then, subject to a minor assumption on the utilities, U_k:

(1) The *sole* Weak Pareto Bayesian solutions are the two agent themselves, $\preceq_G = \preceq_1$ or $\preceq_G = \preceq_2$. (We call such solutions *autocratic*).

---

[14] For those familiar with Savage's [54] theory, an important difference with Anscombe-Aumann's [63] theory is that horse-lottery acts are defined using an extraneous, "objective," probability.

[15] Only the first is judged to be necessary in a compromise, for reasons given in T.2.2.

[16] Note, the result extends to larger groups.

(2) There are *no* Strong Pareto Bayesian models of $\preceq_G$, at all.

This result applies to *each* pair of Bayesian agents with different beliefs and values. Thus, (a) it depends in *no* way on how close the two agents are in their preferences. Any difference is too much! Also, (b) it depends in no way on assumptions about *interpersonal* utility comparisons. Third, (c) it does not require that group probability and utility are amalgamated separately.

Therefore, it is a strengthening of Arrow's [Arrow51] famous impossibility result, in that:

corresponding to *a*, there is no assumption that a social welfare rule has an unrestricted domain;

and

corresponding to *b*, the Arrovian principle of "independence of irrelevant alternatives" (that only rank order matters) is not needed. Unlike the case with Arrow's theorem, interpersonal utilities do not offer a way out of the negative findings of T.2.2. Last [as we explain in 89a], because of (c), T.2.2 is a strengthening of results by [Hylland&Zeckhauser79] and [Hammond81].

It appears there is a dilemma. Either use different norms for rational preference in individual versus group decisions: coherence applies only to individuals. Or else, modify the Bayesian norms to permit a unified theory for individual and group decisions.

Savage [Savage54, §13.5] adopts the former approach. We are developing the latter proposal [87 and 89c]. In particular, suppose that (strict) preference is a strict partial order rather than a weak order. Our efforts are directed at a representation of preference by expected utility in terms of *sets* of probability and utility pairs. Modifications of Anscombe-Aumann axioms are required, and the proofs follow rather different lines.

Summary of §2:

For two coherent agents who differ both in their beliefs and values, when facing common decisions there are no Bayesian compromises which preserve their unanimous, strict preferences — only *autocratic* solutions exist. And there are no Bayes models (at all) that satisfy the Strong Pareto condition. Thus, the shared preferences of coherent agents do not provide the basis for a decision-theoretic compromise which is coherent and captures all that they agree on.

3   Conclusions

The results of Part 1 suggest that a Bayesian consensus of posterior probabilities is almost certain within suitably circumscribed communities of agents whose opinions agree on events of probability 0. However, the results of Part 2 indicate that, despite the convergence of posterior opinions, a Bayesian consensus on decisions is not forthcoming. No matter how near the posterior probabilities of two decision makers, if their values are not in perfect agreement there are no Bayesian, Pareto compromises open to them.

In order to avoid this dilemma, we are investigating a relaxation of Bayesian decision theory which is obtained by *not* requiring a comparison, in terms of preference, between all act pairs. Then, preference is represented by sets of probability/utility pairs. That yields a model which can be applied both in individual decision-making and to cooperative groups. Also, it is a model to which the positive results of Part 1 apply.

4 Appendix — A Summary of The Anscombe-Aumann Theory

Acts are functions from states to outcomes. The canonical decision matrix is shown in the table below.

acts $\otimes$ states

	s_1	s_2			s_j			s_n
A_1	O_{11}	O_{12}			O_{1j}			O_{1n}
A_2	O_{21}	O_{22}			O_{2j}			O_{2n}
A_m	O_{m1}	O_{m2}			O_{mj}			O_{mn}

$$A_i(s_j) = \text{outcome } o_{ij}.$$

What are *outcomes*? That depends upon which version of expected utility you consider. In the Anscombe-Aumann theory, they are von Neumann-Morgenstern lotteries, as explained below.

The central idea is axiomatize preference $\preceq$ so that

$$A_1 \preceq A_2 \quad \text{iff} \quad \Sigma_j\, P(s_j)U(o_{1j}) \leq \Sigma_j\, P(s_j)U(o_{2j}),$$

for one personal probability $P(\,\cdot\,)$ and utility $U(\,\cdot\,)$. Then:

(1) Acts and states are probabilistically independent, $P(s_j) = P(s_j|A_i)$.

(2) Utility is state-independent, $U_j(o_{ij}) = U_h(o_{gh})$, if $o_{ij} = o_{gh}$ (where $U_j(o._j)$ is the conditional utility for outcomes, given state s_j).[17]

First, review the von Neumann-Morgenstern utility theory.

---

[17] As in Savage's theory, and as in deFinetti's, Anscombe and Aumann use state-independent utilities to ensure a unique representation of preference. See our [89b] for discussion of this point.

von Neumann-Morgenstern utility theory

Let $\mathfrak{R}$ be a finite set of rewards (or prizes).

Acts are lotteries:

a lottery L_i is a probability distribution $p_i(\, . \,)$ over $\mathfrak{R}$.

The convex combination of two acts, denoted by "+",

$$x L_1 + (1-x)L_2 = L_3 \quad (0 \le x \le 1)$$

is the convolution of their distributions: $p_3(\, . \,) = x p_1 + (1-x)p_2$.[18]

The von Neumann-Morgenstern preference axioms

Axiom-1. Preference is a weak order (*i.e.*, $\preceq$ is reflexive and transitive, with full comparability).

Axiom-2. (Independence) $\forall(L_1, L_2, L_3)$, $\forall \, 0 < x \le 1$,

$$L_1 \preceq L_2 \quad \text{iff} \quad x L_1 + (1-x)L_3 \preceq x L_2 + (1-x)L_3.$$

Axiom-3. (Archimedes) If $L_1 \prec L_2 \prec L_3$, then $\exists \, 0 < x, y < 1$,

$$x L_1 + (1-x)L_3 \prec L_2 \prec y L_1 + (1-y)L_3.$$

(von N-M) Theorem:

Axioms 1–3 are necessary and sufficient for existence of a (real-valued) utility $U(\, . \,)$ where:

(i) $L_1 \preceq L_2 \quad \text{iff} \quad U(L_1) \le U(L_2)$,

(ii) $U(x L_1 + (1-x)L_2) = x U(L_1) + (1-x)U(L_2)$,

and

(iii) U is unique up a positive linear transformation.

---

[18]This is sometimes referred to as the "0-th" axiom — the "reduction" postulate.

Anscombe-Aumann "horse lotteries"

An act (a "horse lottery") is function from states to von Neumann-Morgenstern lotteries. That is, *outcomes are lotteries*. The matrix is shown in the table below.

	s_1	s_2			s_j			s_n
H_1	L_{11}	L_{12}			L_{1j}			L_{1n}
H_2	L_{21}	L_{22}			L_{2j}			L_{2n}
H_m	L_{m1}	L_{m2}			L_{mj}			L_{mn}

The convex combination of two acts, denoted by "+,"

$$xH_1 + (1-x)H_2 = H_3 \quad (0 \le x \le 1)$$

is the convolution of their distributions, $p_{3j}(\ . \ ) = xp_{1j} + (1-x)p_{2j}$ ($j= 1, \ldots, n$).

Anscombe-Aumann preference axioms:

Axiom-H1. Preference is a weak order.

Axiom-H2. Independence is satisfied.

Axiom-H3. The Archimedean condition obtains.

The fourth axiom leads to state-independent utilities. Let H_{L_i} denote the "constant" horse lottery that awards the outcome L_i in every state.

Axiom H-4.

Given lotteries L_1 and L_2, let H and H' be two horse lotteries which differ only in that, for some state s_j, $o_{ij} = L_1$ and $o'_{ij} = L_2$ ($o_{ik} = o'_{ik}$ for $k \ne j$). Then, $H_{L_1} \preceq H_{L_2}$ iff $H \preceq H'$.

(Anscombe-Aumann) **Theorem:**

Axioms H-1, ..., H-4 are necessary and sufficient for the existence of a unique state-independent utility U and personal probability P where:

$$H_1 \preceq H_2 \quad \text{iff} \quad \Sigma_j P(s_j) U(o_{1j}) \leq \Sigma_j P(s_j) U(o_{2j}).$$

5 Bibliography

Anscombe, F. and R. Aumann. "A definition of subjective probability," *Annals of Mathematical Statistics 34*, pp. 199–205, 1963.

Arrow, K. *Social Choice and Individual Values*, Wiley, 1951.

Berger, J. *Statistical Decision Theory and Bayesian Analysis*, (2nd edition), Springer, 1985.

Blackwell, D. and L. Dubins. "Merging of opinions with increasing information," Annals of Mathematical Statistics 33, pp. 882–887, 1962.

Carnap, R. "On inductive logic," *Philosophy of Science 12*, pp. 72–97, 1945.

Carnap, R. "The aim of inductive logic," *Logic, Methodology and Philosophy of Science*, E. Nagel, P. Suppes, and A. Tarski, eds., Stanford University Press, 1962.

deFinetti, B. "La prévision: ses lois logiques, ses sources subjectives," 1937, translated in *Studies in Subjective Probabilities*, H. Kyburg and H. Smokler, eds., Wiley, 1964.

Doob, J. *Stochastic Processes*, Wiley, 1953.

Halmos, P. *Measure Theory*, Van Nostrand, 1950.

Harsanyi, J. *Rational Behavior and Bargaining Equilibrium in Games and Social Situations*, Cambridge University Press, 1977.

Hammond, P. "Ex-ante and ex-post welfare optimality under uncertainty," *Economica 48*, pp. 235–250, 1981.

Hylland, A. and R. Zeckhauser. "The impossibility of Bayesian group decisions with separate aggregation of beliefs and values," *Econometrica 47*, pp. 1321–1336, 1979.

Jaynes, E. *Papers on Probability, Statistics and Statistical Physics*, R. Rosenkrantz, ed., Reidel, 1983.

Jeffrey, R. *The Logic of Decision*, McGraw Hill, 1985.

Jeffrey, R. "Probable knowledge," *The Problem of Inductive Logic*, I. Lakatos, ed., Elsevier, 1968.

Kyburg, H. "Conditionalization," *Journal of Philosophy 77*, pp. 98–114, 1980.

Levi, I. *Gambling With Truth*, A. A. Knopf, 1967.

Levi, I. "On indeterminate probabilities," *Journal of Philosophy 71*, pp. 391–418, 1974.

Levi, I. *The Enterprise of Knowledge*, MIT Press, 1980.

Ramsey, F. *The Foundations of Mathematics and Other Essays*, Harcourt Brace, 1931.

Savage, L. *The Foundations of Statistics*, Wiley, 1954.

Schervish, M. and T. Seidenfeld. "An approach to consensus and certainty with increasing evidence," *Journal of Statistical Planning and Inference*, forthcoming. Also available as Technical Report #389, Department of Statistics, Carnegie Mellon University, 1989.

Schervish, M., Seidenfeld, T., and J. Kadane. "State dependent utilities," Technical Report #445, Department of Statistics, Carnegie Mellon University, 1989b.

Seidenfeld, T. "Entropy and uncertainty," *Philosophy of Science 53*, pp. 467–491, 1986.

Seidenfeld, T., Schervish, M., and J. Kadane. "Decisions without ordering," *Acting and Reflecting*, W. Sieg, ed., Reidel, in press. Also available as Technical Report #391, Department of Statistics, Carnegie Mellon University, 1987.

Seidenfeld, T., Kadane, J., and M. Schervish. "On the shared preferences of two Bayesian decision makers," *Journal of Philosophy 86*, pp. 225–244, 1989a.

Seidenfeld, T., Kadane, J., and M. Schervish. "A representation for preference as a strict partial order in terms of sets of probabilities and utilities," Technical Report #453, Department of Statistics, Carnegie Mellon University, 1989c.

Skyrms, B. "Maximum entropy inference as a special case of conditionalization," *Synthese 63*, pp. 55–74, 1985.

Skyrms, B. "Coherence," in N. Rescher, ed., *Scientific Inquiry in Philosophical Perspective*, University of Pittsburgh Press, 1987.

Conditionals and Conditional Probabilities: Three Triviality Theorems

I- TMPL-Q Hugues Leblanc and Peter Roeper *S- ANU-Q*

> We might then define a sense of 'if' by saying that the degree of confirmation of a hypothetical on evidence e is the degree to which e, conjoined with the antecedent, confirms the consequent.
> — Richard C. Jeffrey[1]

1

Talk of conditionals rather than hypotheticals, and of conditional probabilities rather than degrees of confirmation. Also, write '$A \rightarrow B$' for 'If A, then B', '$P(A, B)$' for 'The conditional probability of A on (or given) B', and 'T' for '$\neg(A \,\&\, \neg A)$', A here some fixed but arbitrary statement. The conditionals Jeffrey advocates then are those which issue from, and hence for which P meets, this constraint

$$(1) \qquad P(A \rightarrow B, C) = P(B, A \,\&\, C),$$

hence this one

$$(2) \qquad P(A \rightarrow B, T) = P(B, A).$$

We show in §2 that when $A \rightarrow B$ is $A \supset B$, the Popper conditional probability functions that meet (1) have but two distinct values (*Triviality Theorem One*). The material conditional, to be sure, is hardly what Jeffrey had in mind. But, generalizing, we go on to show in §3 that when $A \rightarrow B$ is *any* of the conditionals that conjoin with other statements, *and Jeffrey's is one of them*,[2] (i) the Popper conditional probability functions that meet (1) have but two distinct values as well (*Triviality Theorem Two*), (ii) the equality

---

[1] "If," *Journal of Philosophy 61*, pp. 702–703, 1964.
[2] As appears from the unpublished paper [Jeffrey64] of which "If" is an abstract. Copy of the paper was graciously passed on to us by Professor Jeffrey.

H.E. Kyburg, Jr. et al. (eds.), Knowledge Representation and Defeasible Reasoning, 287–306.
© 1990 *Kluwer Academic Publishers. Printed in the Netherlands.*

$$P(A \rightarrow B, C) = P(A \supset B, C)$$

holds true (*Triviality Theorem Three*), and (iii) $A \rightarrow B$, as a result, is but a material conditional.

Equation (2) is tantamount to

> *For some absolute probability function P',*
> $$P(A, B) = P'(B \rightarrow A).^3$$

This, called by van Fraassen *Stalnaker's Thesis* and often read

Conditional probabilities are the (absolute) probabilities of conditionals,[4]

has been espoused by many. Since (2) follows from (1), the conditional probability functions in §3 accord with Stalnaker's Thesis. But (1) does not generally follow from (2).[5]

So conditional probability functions that only meet (2) and thus more strictly accord with Stalnaker's Thesis, have proved of interest. How many distinct values they have is one of two questions we take up in §4.[6]

2

L, the first of two languages considered in this paper, has as its *statements* those that can be compounded by means of '$\neg$' and '$\&$' from given atomic

---

[3] The absolute probability function in question is what we call later the T-restriction of P. Since P proves to be what we call a *Kolmogorov* conditional probability function, P' proves to be as well the absolute probability function that generates P.

[4] See [vanFraassen76; p. 273].

[5] These two equalities hold true by (2):
$$P(C \rightarrow (A \rightarrow B), T) = P(A \rightarrow B, C)$$
and
$$P((A \ \& \ C) \rightarrow B, T) = P(B, A \ \& \ C).$$
But they yield (1) only if $P(C \rightarrow (A \rightarrow B), T) = P((A \ \& \ C) \rightarrow B, T)$ also holds true, which it does with Jeffrey but not with Stalnaker. See [Stalnaker70] for an early account of Stalnaker's conditionals; see [Nute84] for a detailed study of conditionals in general and Stalnaker's conditionals in particular. Of course,
$$P(C \supset (A \supset B), T) = P((A \ \& \ C) \supset B, T)$$
holds true. So, with $A \supset B$ as $A \rightarrow B$, (1) and (2) are equivalent.

[6] The literature on conditionals and conditional probabilities is quite extensive. Some of the key papers appear in [Harper&Hooker76] and [Harper *et al.*81]. In Note 3 of [Lewis76; p. 146], Lewis named Jeffrey, Ellis, and Stalnaker as authors who professed that conditional probabilities are the probabilities of conditionals. Jeffrey and Stalnaker no longer hold that view, nor presumably does Ellis.

statements. Statements of the kind $A \supset B$ are short of course for statements of the kind $\neg(A \ \& \ \neg B)$, and 'T' is as in the opening paragraph of §1. The *conditional probability functions* for L are Popper's *i.e.*, the binary real-valued functions on the statements of L that meet these seven constraints (distinct in six cases from Popper's own constraints but equivalent to them):

C1. For some two statements A and B of L, $P(A, B) \neq 1$

C2. $0 \leq P(A, B)$

C3. $P(A, A) = 1$

C4. If $P(C, B) \neq 1$ for some statement C of L, then $P(\neg A, B) = 1 - P(A, B)$

C5. $P(A \ \& \ B, C) = P(A, B \ \& \ C) \times P(B, C)$

C6. $P(A \ \& \ B, C) \leq P(B \ \& \ A, C)$

C7. $P(A, B \ \& \ C) \leq P(A, C \ \& \ B).$[7]

A statement B of L is sometimes said to be *P-normal* if $P(A, B) \neq 1$ for at least one statement A of L, otherwise to be *P-abnormal*. *C1* is thus to the effect that *at least one statement of L is P-normal* (the statement proves of course to be T), and C4 to the effect that *if B is P-normal, then* $P(\neg A, B) = 1 - P(A, B)$.

Most writers assent to C1–C7. One dissenter is von Wright in [von-Wright57]. He lifts the restriction on B in C4 and preserves consistency by requiring instead that A in C3 not be truth-functionally false, but few have followed him in this. And other writers, Carnap among them, use this constraint

C4^X. If B is not truth-functionally false, then $P(\neg A, B) = 1 - P(A, B)$

in place of C4, but the autonomous C4 — which we prefer to C4^X — follows from it.

The *Kolmogorov conditional probability functions* for L are those among the conditional probability functions for L that meet this extra constraint (with 'K' in 'CK' short of course for 'Kolmogorov')

---

[7] See [Popper59] and [Leblanc&Roeper] as regards these constraints.

CK. If $P(A, T) = 0$, then A is P-abnormal;

and the X *conditional probability functions for L* (X whoever first professed that conditional probability functions are the probabilities of *material conditionals*)[8] are those that meet this extra constraint

$C_\supset$. $P(A \supset B, C) = P(B, A \& C)$,

i.e., (1) in §1 with $A \supset B$ as $A \to B$.[9] Equivalently, we may take $C_\supset$ to be

$P(A \supset B, T) = P(B, A)$,

i.e., (2) in §1 with $A \supset B$ as $A \to B$. For, on the one hand,

$P(A \supset B, T) = P(B, A)$

is a special case of

$P(A \supset B, C) = P(B, A \& C)$;

on the other, if

$P(A \supset B, T) = P(B, A)$,

then

$P((A \& C) \supset B, T) = P(B, A \& C)$

and

$P(C \supset (A \supset B), T) = P(A \supset B, C)$.

So, since

$P((A \& C) \supset B, T) = P(C \supset (A \supset B), T)$

by C1–C7,

$P(A \supset B, C) = P(B, A \& C)$.

A Kolmogorov conditional probability function for L is in effect a binary real-valued function P on the statements of L that corresponds thusly to (and, hence, is *generated* thusly by) an absolute probability function P' for L:

---

[8]We know of some who wrote of conditional probabilities in that vein, but all of them too recently to qualify as X.

[9]$C_\supset$, incidentally, is one of the constraints that the intuitionistic probability functions in [Morgan&Leblanc83] have to meet. But the functions in question do not meet constraint C4. So *Theorem 1* below does not affect [Morgan&Leblanc83].

$$P(A, B) = \begin{cases} 1 \; if \; P'(B) = 0 \\ P'(A \; \& \; B)/P'(B) \; otherwise; \end{cases}$$

and a *partial* one is a Kolmogorov conditional probability function for L defined only when $P'(B) \neq 0$. Partial functions of this sort are often associated with Kolmogorov. Hence the appellation used here,[10] and made for convenience's sake to cover as well the total ones gotten by setting $P(A, B)$ at 1 when $P'(B) = 0$. Jeffrey and Stalnaker limit themselves to partial Kolmogorov functions, which they obtain from absolute probability functions in the manner just displayed. This is quite appropriate given their intent. We consider a much broader class of functions, Popper's, but under the extra constraint $C_\supset$ in this section and the extra one $C_\to$ in the next they prove to be Kolmogorov functions after all, as *Theorem 1* and *Theorem 4* attest. So our perspective is different from Jeffrey's and Stalnaker's, but not distortingly so. And our very first lemma, invoked thrice in the rest of the section, does deal with Kolmogorov functions.

In parenthesis, the *absolute probability functions* for L are the unary real-valued functions on the statements of L that meet these six conditions (distinct in three cases from Popper's own constraints but equivalent to them):

C1'. $0 \leq P'(A)$

C2'. $P'(T) = 1$

C3'. $P'(A) = P'(A \; \& \; B) + P'(A \; \& \; \neg B)$

C4'. $P'(A \; \& \; B) \leq P'(B \; \& \; A)$

C5'. $P'(A \; \& \; (B \; \& C)) \leq P'((A \; \& \; B) \; \& \; C)$

C6'. $P'(A) \leq P'(A \; \& \; A)$.[11]

---

[10] and in [Leblanc&Roeper], where we introduced it. Note that in [Leblanc&Roeper] we talk of *relative* rather than *conditional* probability functions. We follow here the practice of most writers on the probabilities of conditionals, but with Popper far prefer the epithet 'relative' to the epithet 'conditional'. The latter may have misled all too many into assenting to what van Fraassen calls Stalnaker's Thesis.

[11] See [Popper59] and [Leblanc82] as regards these constraints.

There corresponds to each conditional probability function P for L a certain absolute one. Known as the *T-restriction of P*, it is the function P' such that, no matter the statement A of L,

$$P'(A) = P(A, T).$$

Since $P'(T) \neq 0$ and $P'(A \& T) = P'(A)$, the T-restriction of a Kolmogorov conditional probability function for L and the absolute probability function for L that generates it are one and the same. We refer to the T-restriction of a function P by means of 'P_T'; putting 'P_T' to a second but obviously related use, we also abridge

$$P(A, T)$$

as

$$P_T(A),$$

for any statement A of L. For example, in clause (a) of *Lemma 1*, '$P_T(B)$' and '$P_T(A \& B)$' are short for '$P(B, T)$' and '$P(A \& B, T)$', respectively; in clause (b), on the other hand, P_T is the T-restriction of the Kolmogorov function P under consideration.

These special cases of C1'–C6', featuring 'P_T' in place of 'P',

$$0 < P_T(A),$$

$$P_T(T) = 1,$$

$$P_T(A) = P_T(A \& B) + P_T(A \& \neg B),$$

etc.,

all follow of course from C1–C7. So, to simplify references, we invoke only C1–C7 in the next few proofs.

Lemma 1.   *Let P be a Kolmogorov conditional probability function for L. Then:*

(a) $P(A, B) = \begin{cases} 1 \text{ if } P_T(B) = 0 \\ P_T(A \& B)/P_T(B) \text{ otherwise;} \end{cases}$

(b) *If P_T is 2-valued, then so is P.*

Proof:

(a) By C1–C7, $P(A, B) = P_T(A \ \& \ B)/P_T(B)$ if $P_T(B) \neq 0$. Hence (a) by CK.

(b) Since by C1'–C6', P_T must have 0 and 1 among its values, these are its only values when P_T is 2-valued. Hence, by (a), P is 2-valued as well. □

Lemma 2. *Any X conditional probability function for L is a Kolmogorov one.*

Proof:

Suppose P is an X conditional probability function for L. Then

$$P_T(B \supset A) = P(A, B)$$

by $C_\supset$. But, if $P_T(B) = 0$, then

$$P_T(B \supset A) = 1$$

by C1–C7. Hence, if $P_T(B) = 0$, then

$$P(A, B) = 1.$$

Hence P, meeting CK, is a Kolmogorov function. □

Lemma 3. *If P is an X conditional probability function for L, then P_T is 2-valued.*

Proof:

Suppose P is an X conditional probability function for L. Then

$$P_T(A \ \& \ \neg A) = P(A, \neg A) \times P_T(\neg A)$$

by C5. But

$$P_T(A \ \& \neg A) = 0$$

by C1–C7;

$$P(A, \neg A) = P_T(\neg A \supset A) = P_T(A)$$

by $C_\supset$ and C1–C7; and

$$P_T(\neg A) = 1 - P_T(A)$$

by C1–C7. Hence

$$0 = P_T(A) \times (1 - P_T(A)).$$

So, $P_T(A)$ equals 0 or 1, for any statement A of L. So, P_T is 2-valued.   □

Hence:

Theorem 1. (*Triviality Theorem One*) *Any X conditional probability function for L is a 2-valued Kolmogorov one.*[12]

As the reader may verify, the result also holds true of any X function P for L that is defined only when $P_T \neq 0$.

To appreciate the full force of *Theorem 1* think of a *truth-value function* for L as a function from the statements of L to $(0, 1)$ (0 here the truth-value F and 1 the truth-value T) that meets these two constraints:

$$f(\neg A) = 1 - f(A)$$

$$f(A \, \& \, B) = min(f(A), f(B)).$$

Lemma 4. *Let P be a 2-valued conditional probability function for L. Then P_T constitutes a truth-value function for L.*[13]

---

[12] Jeffrey already knew in 1964, he writes in a letter dated March 16, 1988, that "$P(C, A)$ can't generally be identified with $P(A \supset C)$ because the latter is a weighted average of the former and 1:

$$P(A \supset C) = P(A) \times P(C, A) + P(\neg A) \times 1$$

so that if $P(A) \neq 0$ then $P(A \supset C) = P(C, A)$ iff $P(A) = 1$ or $P(C, A) = 1$." On p. 130 of [Lewis76] Lewis remarks that this special case of $C_\supset$,

$$P(A, B) = P_T(B \supset A),$$

holds "only in certain special cases", but passes on.

[13] The converse of *Lemma 4* also holds true, as shown in [Leblanc82]. Unbeknownst to Leblanc a like result (with proof to be published separately) had been announced on p. 52 of [Ellis69].

Proof:

Since P_T cannot have more values than P and by C1–C7 already has 0 and 1 among its values, P_T here is sure to have only these reals as its values. Now

$$P_T(\neg A) = 1 - P_T(A)$$

by C1–C7. As for $P_T(A \;\&\; B)$, if both $P_T(A)$ and $P_T(B)$ equal 1, then so does $P_T(A \;\&\; B)$ by C1–C7. If on the other hand at least one of $P_T(A)$ and $P_T(B)$ does not equal 1, then by the above considerations at least one of them equals 0, and hence so does $P_T(A \;\&\; B)$ by C1–C7. So

$$P_T(A \;\&\; B) = min(P_T(A),\, P_T(B)).$$

So P_T constitutes a truth-value function for L. $\square$

Suppose now that P is an X conditional probability function for L. Because of C⊃ the conditional probability $P(A, B)$ is the probability $P_T(B \supset A)$ of the conditional $B \supset A$. But if so, then by *Theorem 1* and *Lemma 4* the conditional probability $P(A, B)$ is but the truth-value of the conditional $B \supset A$, an unwelcome result indeed.

The converse of *Theorem 1* also holds true, a result we shall exploit in the next section. One lemma delivers it.

Lemma 5. *Let P be a 2-valued Kolmogorov conditional probability function for L. Then $P(A, B) = P_T(B \supset A)$.*

Proof:

Case 1: $P_T(B) = 0$. Then

$$P_T(B \supset A) = 1$$

by C1–C7, and

$$P(A, B) = 1$$

by CK. Hence

$$P(A, B) = P_T(B \supset A).$$

Case 2: $P_T(B) \neq 0$. Since by C1–C7 P already has 0 and 1 among its values and since P is presumed here to be 2-valued,

$$(1) \qquad P_T(B) = 1,$$

and hence

$$(2) \qquad P_T(A \ \& \ B) = P_T(A)$$

by C1–C7. But

$$\text{If } P_T(B \supset A) = 1, \text{ then } P_T(A) = 1$$

by C1–C7 and (1), and

$$\text{If } P_T(A) = 1, \text{ then } P_T(B \supset A) = 1$$

by C1–C7 alone. Hence, P being 2-valued,

$$P_T(B \supset A) = P_T(A).$$

Hence by (1) – (2)

$$P_T(A \ \& \ B)/P_T(B) = P_T(B \supset A).$$

Hence by *Lemma 1(a)*

$$P(A, B) = P_T(B \supset A). \qquad \square$$

Hence:

Theorem 2. *Any 2-valued Kolmogorov conditional probability function for L meets constraint $C_\supset$ and hence is an X function.*

Proof:

By *Lemma 5.* $\quad \square$

Hence:

Theorem 3. *Any X conditional probability function for L is a 2-valued Kolmogorov function, and vice-versa.*

3

$L_{\rightarrow}$, our second language, is exactly like L except for having (i) the *conditional sign* '$\rightarrow$' as an extra connective and (ii) *conditionals* of the kind $A \rightarrow B$ as extra compounds. Conditionals of the kind $A \supset B$ are again shorthand for statements of the kind $\neg(A \& \neg B)$. Conjoining conditionals of the kind $A \rightarrow B$ with other statements of $L_{\rightarrow}$ must be allowed if the proof of *Lemma 6* is to go through. Nesting of conditionals of the kind $A \rightarrow B$ is allowed but nowhere required. No semantic account of $A \rightarrow B$ is presupposed, hence no mention anywhere made of possible worlds or impossible ones for that matter. The *conditional probability functions* for $L_{\rightarrow}$ are the binary real-valued functions on the statements of $L_{\rightarrow}$ that meet the counterparts for $L_{\rightarrow}$ of constraints C1–C7 plus this extra constraint

$C_{\rightarrow}$. $P(A \rightarrow B, C) = P(B, A \& C)$,

i.e., (1) in §1, and the *Kolmogorov* ones are those among the conditional probability functions for $L_{\rightarrow}$ that meet the counterpart for $L_{\rightarrow}$ of constraint CK. The *T-restriction* of a conditional probability function P for $L_{\rightarrow}$ is of course the unary function P' on the statements of $L_{\rightarrow}$ such that $P'(A) = P(A, T)$ for any statement A of $L_{\rightarrow}$. As in §2 we refer to the T-restriction of a function P by means of 'P_T'; we also abridge '$P(A, T)$' as '$P_T(A)$', this for any statement A of $L_{\rightarrow}$. The absolute probability functions for $L_{\rightarrow}$ must of course meet besides C1'– C6' one or more constraints relating to $A \rightarrow B$. We return to this at the close of the section.

This lemma delivers our last two triviality theorems.

Lemma 6. *Let P be a conditional probability function for $L_{\rightarrow}$, and A be any statement of $L_{\rightarrow}$. Then:*

$$P_T(A) = 1 \text{ or } P(\neg A, A) = 1.$$

Proof:

By $C_{\rightarrow}$ at lines (3) and (6), and C1–C7 throughout,

$$(1) \quad P_T((A \rightarrow \neg A) \& A) = P_T(A \rightarrow \neg A) - P_T((A \rightarrow \neg A) \& \neg A)$$

$$(2) \quad = P_T(A \rightarrow \neg A) - P(A \rightarrow \neg A, \neg A) \times P_T(\neg A)$$

$$(3) \qquad = P(\neg A, A) - P(\neg A, A \;\&\; \neg A) \times P_T(\neg A)$$

$$(4) \qquad = P(\neg A, A) - (1 - P_T(A))$$

$$(5) \quad P_T((A \to \neg A) \;\&\; A) = P(A \to \neg A, A) \times P_T(A)$$

$$(6) \qquad = P(\neg A, A) \times P_T(A).$$

Hence, simplifying,

$$(1 - P_T(A)) \times (P(\neg A, A) - 1) = 0,$$

and, consequently,

$$P_T(A) = 1 \text{ or } P(\neg A, A) = 1.^{14}$$

□

Importantly, lines (1), (2) and (5) in the foregoing proof are the only occasions in this paper on which we conjoin a conditional of the sort $A \to B$ with another statement. On the first of these occasions we take it that P meets this special case of the *Complementation Law*

$$P(B \to C, T) = P((B \to C) \;\&\; A, T) + P((B \to C) \;\&\; \neg A, T),$$

and on the last two this special case of the Multiplication Law

$$P((B \to C) \;\&\; A, T) = P(B \to C, A \;\&\; T) \times P(A, T).$$

Note further that all steps taken by C4 could be taken as well by *C4'*.

Hence:

Theorem 4. (*Triviality Theorem Two*) *Any conditional probability function for* $L_\to$ *is a 2-valued Kolmogorov one.*

---

[14] A suggestion by Professor David Miller made this simplification of our original proof possible.

Proof:

Let P be a conditional probability function for $L_\to$.

(1) Let P be a conditional probability function for $L_\to$. If $P(\neg A, A) = 1$, then $P_T(A) = 0$ by C1–C7. Hence $P_T(A) = 1$ or $P_T(A) = 0$ by *Lemma 6*. So, P is a 2-valued conditional probability function for $L_\to$.

(2) Let A again be an arbitrary statement of $L_\to$. If $P_T(A) = 0$, then $P(\neg A, A) = 1$ by *Lemma 6*. But by C1–C7, if $P(\neg A, A) = 1$, then $P(B, A) = 1$ for every statement B of $L_\to$. So P, meeting CK, is a Kolmogorov function.   □

But, if so, then a conditional probability function P for $L_\to$ meets this constraint

$$P(A \to B, C) = P(B, A \,\&\, C) \qquad (=C_\to)$$

by definition and this one

$$P(A \supset B, C) = P(B, A \,\&\, C) \qquad (=C_\supset)$$

by the counterpart for $L_\to$ of *Theorem 2*. Hence this, our *Third Triviality Theorem*:

Theorem 5. *For any conditional probability function P for $L_\to$,*

$$P(A \to B, C) = P(A \supset B, C),$$

and hence

$$P_T(A \to B) = P_T(A \supset B).$$

So suppose you allow $A \to B$ to be conjoined with other statements and require of your conditional probability functions that they meet constraint $C_\to$. Then $A \to B$ and $A \supset B$ behave alike, the result under (iii) on the second page of this paper. More precisely, when A and B in a conditional $A \to B$ are statements of L, then by virtue of *Theorem 5* $A \to B$ behaves exactly like the material conditional $A \supset B$ of L. In the contrary case let P^L be the restriction of the function P in *Theorem 5* to the statements of L, and let A^L and B^L be the results of replacing '$\to$' everywhere in A and B by '$\supset$'. Then

$$P_T(A \to B),$$

for instance, is demonstrably the same as

$$P_T^L(A^L \supset B^L).$$

So, in this case too, $A \to B$ behaves exactly like a material conditional, the material conditional $A^L \supset B^L$. In the abstract of "If" Jeffrey remarks of his conditionals that "Deductively, they simulate material conditionals, but inductively they have various novel properties." The latter is not true of the present conditionals: inductively, *i.e.*, probabilistically, as well as deductively, they are material conditionals.

To more fully appreciate the force of *Theorem 5*, the function P^L is of course 2-valued when P is, and as just noted

$$P_T(A \to B) = P_T^L(A^L \supset B^L).$$

So, by virtue of *Lemma 4* and *Theorem 5*, $P_T(A \to B)$ is but the *truth-value* of a material conditional of L, the conditional $A \supset B$ when A and B are both statements of L, otherwise the conditional $A^L \supset B^L$, an unwelcome result in either case.

Which extra constraint besides C1'–C6' an absolute probability function P' for L$_\to$ must meet is clear in light of *Theorem 5*:

$$\text{C}_\to. \quad P'(A \to B) = P'(A \supset B),$$

trivially.

4

The conditional probability functions in §3 are *total* ones, *i.e.*, functions defined for *any* pair of statements of L$_\to$. So, in particular, is the function P in *Lemma 6*:

$$P(A, A \,\&\, \neg A)$$

and

$$P(\neg A, A \,\&\, \neg A),$$

in the proof of the lemma, each have a value (that value, 1, of course) even though

$$P_T(A \,\&\, \neg A) = 0.$$

Jeffrey's own conditional probability functions in [Jeffrey64] were *partial* ones, more specifically, Kolmogorov conditional probability functions for $L_\rightarrow$ with $P(A, B)$ defined only when $P(B, T) \neq 0$. We construct one.

Given a fixed but arbitrary real r such that

$$0 < r < 1/2,$$

let P' be the absolute probability function for $L_\rightarrow$ defined thusly:[15]

$P'(A)$	$P'(\neg A)$
0	1
r	$1 - r$
$1 - r$	r
1	0

	$P'(A\&B)$	$P'(B)$			
		0	r	$1 - r$	1
$P'(A)$	0	0	0	0	0
	r	0	r	0	r
	$1 - r$	0	0	$1 - r$	$1 - r$
	1	0	r	$1 - r$	1

	$P'(A \rightarrow B)$	$P'(B)$			
		0	r	$1 - r$	1
$P'(A)$	0	1	1	1	1
	r	0	1	0	1
	$1 - r$	0	0	1	1
	1	0	r	$1 - r$	1

This done, let P be this partial conditional probability function of Kolmogorov for $L_\rightarrow$:

$$P(A, B) = \begin{cases} P'(A \ \& \ B)/P'(B) \ \textit{if } P'(B) \neq 0 \\ \textit{undefined otherwise}, \end{cases}$$

the values of which can be tabulated as follows:

---

[15]The table for $P'(\neg A)$ is of course the only one in accord with C1'–C3', the one for $P'(A \ \& \ B)$ one of the many in accord with C1'–C6'.

	$P(B, A)$	$P'(B)$ 0	r	$1 - r$	1
	0	undefined			
$P'(A)$	r	0	1	0	1
	$1 - r$	0	0	1	1
	1	0	r	$1 - r$	1

It is easily verified by means of a 64-row table that

$$P(A \to B, C) = P(B, A \,\&\, C)$$

whenever $P(A \to B, C)$ and $P(B, A \,\&\, C)$ are both defined.

So, whereas the conditional probability functions in §3 — total Jeffrey functions if you will — are 2-valued, *Jeffrey's own (partial) functions may have as many as four distinct values.* It was Lewis's Triviality Theorem in [Lewis76] that the latter have at most four distinct values, and because of the foregoing construction on that result cannot be improved upon.

Since they may have more than two distinct values, Jeffrey's conditional probability functions are not truth-value functions, and his conditionals *do* have various novel properties, inductively. But, since the conditional probability functions in question cannot have more than four distinct values, they and the conditionals they deliver are "trivial".

Turning next to Stalnaker's conditional probability functions for L$_\to$ in [Stalnaker70], suppose we extend the partial 4-valued function P above to a total one by setting $P(A, B)$ at 1 when $P'(B) = 0$. Constraint C$_\to$ will now fail: for $P'(A)$ equal to r but $P'(B)$ and $P'(C)$ equal to $1 - r$, $P(A \to B, C) = 0$ but $P(A, B \,\&\, C) = 1$. However,

$$P'(A \to B) = P(B, A)$$

and hence,

$$P_T(A \to B) = P(B, A)$$

do hold true. But the second of these is (2) in §1, and the first is *Stalnaker's Thesis.* So the conditional probability functions for L$_\to$ exactly like those in §3 except for meeting this constraint

$$\text{SC}_\to.\ P_T(A \to B) = P(B, A)$$

(*i.e.*, (2) in §1), rather than C$_\to$ may have as many as four distinct values. In point of fact there is no maximal number of values that these functions or the partial Kolmogorov functions for $L_\rightarrow$ that meet $SC_\rightarrow$, rather than $C_\rightarrow$, may have, as we go on to show.[16] The latter functions are *basically* Stalnaker's functions in [Stalnaker70], but for convenience's sake we refer to them as *partial Stalnaker functions* and to the former as *Stalnaker functions tout court*.

In what follows the reader is to think of the statements of $L_\rightarrow$ as arranged in a certain order, one ensuring that a compound statement of $L_\rightarrow$ always occurs later in the order than any of its proper components. And, given a statement S of $L_\rightarrow$, he is to understand by A^* the statement A itself when it is not a conjunction, otherwise

$$(\ldots(B_1 \ \& \ B_2) \ \& \ldots) \ \& \ B_n,$$

where B_1, B_2, ... and B_n are in the aforementioned order the various conjuncts of A.[17]

We first establish that to any (total) Kolmogorov conditional probability function P for L there corresponds a Stalnaker one P_S for $L_\rightarrow$ such that

$$P_S(A, B) = P(A, B)$$

whenever A and B are statements of L. For proof, P_T being the T-restriction of P, let P' be the unary function on the statements of $L_\rightarrow$ defined thusly:

(i) if A is a statement of L, then $P'(A) = P_T(A)$,

(ii) if A is not a statement of L and $A \neq A^*$, then $P'(A) = P'(A^*)$,

(iii) if A is not a statement of L and $A = ((\ldots(B_1 \ \& \ B_2) \ \& \ldots) \ \& \ B_{n-1}) \ \& \ \neg C$, then $P'(A) = P'((\ldots(B_1 \ \& \ B_2) \ \& \ldots) \ \& \ B_{n-1}) - P'(((\ldots(B_1 \ \& \ B_2 \ \& \ldots) \ \& \ B_{n-1}) \ \& \ C)$,

(iv) if A is not a statement of L and $A = \neg C$, then $P'(A) = 1 - P'(C)$,

(v) if A is not a statement of L and
$A = ((\ldots(B_1 \ \& \ B_2) \ \& \ldots) \ \& \ B_{n-1}) \ \& \ (C \rightarrow D)$, then

$$P'(A) = \begin{cases} P'((\ldots(B_1 \ \& \ B_2) \ \& \ \ldots) \ \& \ B_{n-1}) \\ \qquad \textit{if } P'(C) = 0 \\ P'((\ldots(B_1 \ \& \ B_2) \ \& \ \ldots) \ \& \ B_{n-1}) \\ \qquad \times \ P'(D \ \& \ C)/P'(C) \ \textit{otherwise}, \end{cases}$$

---

[16] More meticulously, there is no maximal number of values other than $2^{\aleph_0}$, *the number of reals in the interval* $[0,1]$, that the functions may have.

[17] Clearly, A^*, when different from A, differs from it only so far as the order, bracketing, and repetitions of the conjuncts of A are concerned.

and

(vi) if A is not a statement of L and $A = C \rightarrow D$, then

$$P'(A) = \begin{cases} 1 \; if \; P'(C) \; = \; 0 \\ P'(D \; \& \; C)/P'(C) \; otherwise. \end{cases}$$

P' meets the counterparts for $L_{\rightarrow}$ of constraints C1'–C6' in §2 and hence constitutes an absolute probability function for $L_{\rightarrow}$. Let then P_S be the conditional probability function for $L_{\rightarrow}$generated by P', *i.e.*, let P_S be this conditional probability function for $L_{\rightarrow}$:

$$P_S(A, \; B) = \begin{cases} 1 \; if \; P'(B) \; = \; 0 \\ P'(A \; \& \; B)/P'(B) \; otherwise. \end{cases}$$

P_S meets constraint SC$_{\rightarrow}$ and hence constitutes a Stalnaker conditional probability function for $L_{\rightarrow}$. But P' agrees with P_T on the statements of L. Hence so do P and P_S.

Since P and P_S agree on the statements of L, P_S has no fewer distinct values than P does, a point that clearly remains true if $P_S(A, B)$ is left undefined rather than set at 1 when $P'(B) = 0$. But there is no maximal number of values that a Kolmogorov conditional probability function for L, be it partial or total, may have. So *there is no maximal number of values less than the cardinality of the continuum that a Stalnaker conditional probability function for $L_{\rightarrow}$, whether partial or total, may have.*[18]

The result may seem at variance with one of Lewis's on p. 140 of (7), according to which Stalnaker's conditional probability functions in [Stalnaker70] — like Jeffrey's in [Jeffrey64] — have at most four distinct values. But, closer reading of the text reveals, Lewis requires there that Stalnaker's functions be closed under conditionalization. Briefly, where P is a conditional probability function for a language like $L_{\rightarrow}$ and A a statement of it such that $P_T(A) \neq 0$, the function P_A defined thusly:

---

[18]The functions defined in the text are but some of Stalnaker's conditional probability functions for $L_{\rightarrow}$, but they obviously suffice to prove our point. Van Fraassen has others in [vanFraassen76], and Vann McGee has yet others in a recent letter to us. McGee's functions differ from ours in several ways, particularly, in that they deliver

$P_S((A \; \& \; B) \supset (A \rightarrow B), \; T) = 1.$

The reader may wonder why a construction like that in the previous paragraph is not at hand to generate, for arbitrary P, a conditional probability function for $L_{\rightarrow}$ that meets C$_{\rightarrow}$. Answer: the unary function recursively defined with P' there would not constitute an absolute probability function for $L_{\rightarrow}$.

$$P_A(B, C) = P(B, A \& C),$$

is said *to be gotten from P by conditionalizing on A*. Lewis requires in effect that if P is a *partial* Stalnaker function for $L_\rightarrow$, then so is P_A for any statement A of $L_\rightarrow$. It follows from this that P must meet $SC_\rightarrow$ as well as $C_\rightarrow$, hence constitutes a Jeffrey function for $L_\rightarrow$, hence cannot have more than four distinct values.[19] Stalnaker, who explicitly disallows $SC_\rightarrow$ on p. 75 of [Stalnaker70], would disallow Lewis's requirement. But many have followed Lewis in this, concluding that *Stalnaker's Thesis* as a result is "untenable on pain of triviality".[20]

In any event, Jeffrey's stronger version $C_\rightarrow$, *Jeffrey's Thesis*, if you will, is untenable on pain of utter triviality, the partial conditional probability functions for $L_\rightarrow$ that accord with it having at most four distinct values, Lewis showed in 1972, and the total ones having but 0 and 1 as theirs, we just did.[21]

---

[19] Hence by vertue of *Theorem 4* cannot have more than two distinct values if $P(A, B)$ is set at 1 when $P_T(B) = 0$, P thereby becoming a conditional probability function for $L_\rightarrow$ in the sense of 3.

[20] The phrasing of the verdict is van Fraassen's in [vanFraassen76]. Stalnaker meant to capture a certain conditional by means of $SC_\rightarrow$, the way Jeffrey meant to by means of $C_\rightarrow$. Despite his, Harper's, and van Fraassen's labors, exactly what he captured remains unclear. Wanted in our opinion, but still wanting, is an axiomatization of the *Stalnaker tautologies* of $L_\rightarrow$. As the reader may know, the statements of L that evaluate to 1 under every absolute probability function for L are axiomatizable. They are the statements of L that follow by means of *Modus Ponens* from these three axiom schemata: $A \supset (A \& A)$, $(A \& B) \supset A$, and $(A \supset B) \supset (\neg(B \& C) \supset \neg(C \& A))$; and, *being that*, they are of course the familiar tautologies of L in '$\neg$' and '$\&$'. Axiomatizing the statements of $L_\rightarrow$ that evaluate to 1 under every absolute probability function for $L_\rightarrow$ meeting this constraint
$$P(A \rightarrow B) = P(A \& B)/P(B), \text{ where } P(B) \neq 0,$$
would likewise deliver the Stalnaker tautologies of $L_\rightarrow$ in '$\sim$', '$\&$', and '$\rightarrow$', thereby disclosing at long last what kind of a conditional $A \rightarrow B$ in *Stalnaker's Thesis* is.

[21] We thank Professor Jeffrey for his remarks on an early abstract of the paper and Professors Vann McGee and David Miller for their comments on an earlier version of it.

5   Bibliography

Ellis, B. "An epistemological concept of truth," *Contemporary Philosophy in Australia*, R. Brown and C. Rollins, eds., George Allen and Unwin, 1969.

Harper, W. and Hooker, C., eds. *Foundations of Probability Theory, Statistical Inference, and Statistical Theories of Science vol. I*, Reidel, 1976.

Harper, W., Stalnaker, R., and Pearce, G., eds. *Ifs*, Reidel, 1981.

Jeffrey, R. "If," unpublished paper; abstract appears in *The Journal of Philosophy 61*, 1964.

Leblanc, H. "Popper's 1955 axiomatization of absolute probability theory," *Pacific Philosophical Quarterly 63*, 1982.

Leblanc, H. and Roeper, P. "On relativizing Kolmogorov's absolute probability functions," *Notre Dame Journal of Formal Logic*, 1989.

Lewis, D. "Probabilities of conditionals and conditional probabilities," *The Philosophical Review 85*, 1976.

Morgan, C. and Leblanc, H. "Probabilistic semantics for intuitionistic logic," *Notre Dame Journal of Formal Logic 24*, 1983.

Nute, D. "Conditional logic," *Handbook of Philosophical Logic vol. II*, D. Gabbay and F. Günthner, eds., Reidel, 1984.

Popper, K. *The Logic of Scientific Discovery*, Basic Books, 1959.

Stalnaker, R. "Probabilities and conditionals," *Philosophy of Science 37*, 1970.

van Fraassen, B. "Probabilities of conditionals," *Foundations of Probability Theory, Statistical Inference, and Statistical Theories of Science vol. I*, Harper, W. and Hooker, C., eds., Reidel, 1976.

von Wright, G. *The Logical Problem of Induction*, 1957.

Part IV.
Logical Problems in Representing Knowledge

1131301

Inheritance Theory and Path-Based Reasoning: An Introduction

Bob Carpenter and Richmond Thomason

1 Introduction

The term "semantic networks" points to a variety of graph-based formalisms that are widely used for the representation of knowledge in computational systems. These network formalisms were introduced in this computational context by Quillian (see [Quillian67]), who used them to model human associative memory and hierarchical or taxonomic reasoning.

Semantic networks have many uses and associations, including the cognitive ones that first suggested them. Here, however, we are mainly interested in their use in relatively small "frame-based" knowledge representation systems for applications in artificial intelligence, primarily in expert systems; we will use the less pretentious term "network" to indicate this focus of what we have to say.

The simplest sort of network consists of a set of nodes corresponding to properties and individuals. These nodes are linked by directed edges that represent specific or general taxonomic relationships ("IS-A" relationships, as they are often called). For instance, a network might contain nodes corresponding to the property of being a whale and to the property of being a mammal, along with an explicit link stating that whales are mammals. And if we included a node for the individual Moby, we could also have a link stating that Moby is a whale. This simple situation can be depicted as the net Γ_1 in Figure 1.

From the net Γ_1, we could infer that Moby is a whale, because this information is explicit in the net. But we can also infer that Moby is a mammal, since the class of whales is included in the class of mammals and Moby is included in the class of whales. Even this simple net delivers information that is inferred, rather than entered directly.

These networks are conceptually straightforward, but in practice they will generally involve many sorts of links, and inferences may be given no

H.E. Kyburg, Jr. et al. (eds.), Knowledge Representation and Defeasible Reasoning, 309–343.

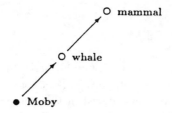

Figure 1: Positive Net

interpretation other than the code associated with the net. There may even be links to procedures (or "daemons"), and it may be difficult to separate the network from the underlying general purpose programming language in which it is formulated. In many applications, networks may only be interpreted by informal motivation that is often partial or obscure, and by the implementations themselves in which the networks are imbedded. Thus, in practice the formal properties of networks are often ignored in the context of applications, where the focus is on producing practical and tractable systems. An influential early paper by William Woods ([Woods75]) is entirely devoted to examining the various ways in which the nodes and links in network formalisms have been interpreted in practice and how they should be interpreted in theory.

The net Γ_1 corresponds in an obvious way to the first-order theory consisting of the following two axioms.

$$\forall x (whale(x) \supset mammal(x))$$

$$whale(Moby)$$

Exploiting this analogy, the AI community that is interested in more formal interpretations of networks has tended to think at least of the more tractable *monotonic* networks as fragments of first-order logic. But the assumptions on which this belief rest have, until recently, largely remained unexamined. To clarify them, it is necessary to first provide a direct theory of networks and the inferences they allow and a translation of a network Γ into a first-order theory $T(\Gamma)$. A network Γ that is interpreted in this way will correspond faithfully to a fragment of the logic if a conclusion A formulable in the language of Γ is a consequence of Γ if and only if it translates into a theorem of $T(\Gamma)$.

In this paper, we will show that this "folk theorem" in AI is not in fact correct, even for very simple monotonic networks with only positive and negative IS-A links. We will provide a general introduction to the theoretical techniques we have developed for dealing directly with semantic nets in the LINKUP project.[1] Throughout this paper, we will stress the theme that networks and their relation to logic are more complex than people have

---

[1] One of the main aims of the LINKUP project, which supported much of the work reported in this paper, is to model network inheritance and study its relation to logical formalisms. Progress has been made along a number of fronts, and reference materials can be found in [Thomason *etal.*86], [Horty *etal.*87], [Touretzky *etal.*87], [Cross&Thomason87], [Horty88], [Horty89], [Thomason&Touretzky], and [Thomason&Aronis88].

generally supposed. The results of this program are valuable, we believe, not only in clarifying the theoretical situation regarding AI formalisms, but as a new contribution to logic. When properly understood, networks are formalisms for understanding natural patterns of tractable reasoning that are as intelligible and theoretically respectable in their own right as familiar logical formalisms. The calculi of symbolic logic were designed to account for mathematical reasoning, and as a result are expressively powerful, intractable, and rather distant from commonsense language and thought patterns. Networks are expressively weak, tractable, and tend to be closer to commonsense language and thought patterns.

2   Why Inheritance?

In this section we will review some of the motivations for employing inheritance networks in knowledge representation and inference.

2.1   Computational Efficiency

The primary reason for employing inheritance mechanisms is that it is usually more computationally tractable, in terms of speed and efficiency, to perform reasoning using inheritance algorithms than to directly implement some logical theory expressed in terms of axioms and rules of inference. The reason for this is that efficient graph-theoretic algorithms can be defined for inheritance. This is in sharp contrast with the case of first-order logic, which is not even decidable.

But why is inheritance more tractable than first-order theorem proving? The answer is that the statements that can be represented in inheritance networks only form a restricted subset of the sorts of statements expressible in first-order logic. The path-based algorithms that are associated with network-based inferences can certainly be thought of as theorem proving procedures, but since, for instance, they involve little or no matching of variables, they are much simpler than the algorithms of full resolution-based theorem proving (see [Wos84]). The query retrieval algorithms for networks are not only decidable, but in the best cases have a very low order of computational complexity.

In this paper, we will restrict ourselves to the case of *monadic* inheritance theories, theories involving only unary relations or properties. In such systems we can't encode binary relationships like kissings and touchings. We should point out that the monadic case of first-order logic, unlike the general case, is decidable. But, unlike inheritance, even the weaker system of standard propositional logic is considered to be intractable because the satisfaction problem for a propositional sentence (and hence the logical consequence relation) is NP-complete.[2]

The best algorithms for computing NP-complete problems on standard deterministic machines can be shown to run in a time that is proportional in the worst case to an exponential function of the size of the problem instance. Algorithms with this exponential behavior are generally considered to be intractable because of the rate at which they slow down as they are given bigger problems. While in fact all known NP-complete algorithms are exponential, this does not preclude the possibility of a sub-exponential algorithm being discovered. But, at this point, this seems very unlikely (see [Garey&Johnson79]). It seems much more likely that there are no such sub-exponential algorithms to compute an NP-complete problem.

2.2 Modularity

A network localizes the information it encodes in a way that first-order theories do not. That is, a distance metric can be defined between nodes in a network by the number of links in the paths connecting them. The idea is then that a network will be straightforward to modify, since revisions "about" a concept will only require the modification of links close to it and not links which are arbitrarily distant. Networks not only store explicit knowledge as patterns of connected nodes, but store it in the expectation that reasoning procedures will be local. Logic, on the other hand, doesn't lend itself to such modularity. In general, it makes no sense to ask "where" a natural consequence of an axiomatized theory is stored in the axioms.

2.3 Buildability

For a knowledge representaion scheme to be technologically useful, rather than, say, a research tool, it should be possible for more or less ordinary people without a large amount of specialized training to maintain it. Networks have a kind of intuitive simplicity that makes them perform well in this respect. And the iconic nature of nets allows many of the important properties to be easily gleaned by visual inspection, thus allowing relatively untrained people to work with them, though they might not be able to

---

[2]See, for instance [Garey&Johnson79] for a definition of NP-completeness, and of other fundamental notions of the theory of computational complexity.

work directly with the LISP or C programming language that underlies the network as it is implemented in practice. It is easy for a logician who is unaccustomed to a user community to forget about usability. But it is a major concern in knowledge engineering, where the difficult task of getting the domain expert's knowledge into the system needs all the help it can get.

Maintenance is as important as buildability. No knowledge based system is ever complete. As more information is gained about a particular domain, or errors are discovered in the original data, it is necessary to modify the original knowledge base. It is important to develop knowledge representation systems that can readily be updated; among other things, this means that changes that seem intuitively to be local can be made by local modifications of the knowledge system. Without this feature, the system is especially liable to lose its integrity as it becomes larger.

It would be desirable as well to have a system that could be maintained as well as built primarily by users or domain experts, rather than requiring a computer scientist or knowledge engineer.

Networks do not provide perfect solutions to these problems, but do deliver techniques that work acceptably in many practical situations, as is witnessed by their widespread application in commercial expert systems.

2.4   Applicability to Current Technology

As things stand today, most of the knowledge representation systems available on the mass market are built using networks. We can at least hope that theoretical results in the study of inheritance will be applicable to the design of expert systems packages that would be usable in knowledge representation technology. Understanding the reasoning involved in these systems may help us to design algorithms that are sound and efficient.

We have tried to state this point cautiously, because we do not expect significant applied results to be easy or instantaneous. Applied network formalisms may contain many special-purpose forms of reasoning (*e.g.*, temporal, causal, and even numerical reasoning) that a general theory of inheritance will not address. At best, we can expect an initial *narrow* applicability of theories to the IS-A hierarchy and to general relational reasoning, with the coverage broadening as the theories are extended and developed. We believe that even a theory with relatively narrow coverage could lead to significant improvement in knowledge representation tools. But this belief has yet to be tested in practice.

2.5 Expressive Power

Of course, we want a representation scheme that will allow us to encode all of the relevant knowledge for our application domain. But as usual in computational implementations, there is a tradeoff between expressive power and computational efficiency. Adding expressive power will usually result in a less computationally tractable theory. That is, the power is inversely related to the speed of the procedures that may be designed to manipulate it. This issue is treated in some detail in relation to knowledge representation by Levesque and Brachman (see [Levesque&Brachman85]).

In our approach to inheritance theory, expressive power is given lower priority than efficiency. We ensure a computationally tractable knowledge representation system by relentlessly maintaining efficiency, while gradually enlarging the system to achieve more expressive power. We expect that there will be limits to this process; but we have not reached them yet and do not expect to reach them soon.

A more popular research strategy in knowledge representation, common to approaches as different as that of McCarthy and Sowa (see [McCarthy89] and [Sowa84]), gives expressive power priority over efficiency. This strategy begins with powerful, intractable representation systems, and then looks for tractable fragments of these systems. In view of the difficulty of the research problems in knowledge representation, it is probably just as well to have groups pursuing both strategies; one hopes that they will learn from each other, and eventually meet in the middle.

Though we are interested in logical interpretations of networks, we think of these as specifications of the networks that prove them correct; these specifications do not necessarily correspond one-to-one with representations that are associated with algorithms. But these interpretations do suggest architectures for *hybrid* reasoning systems, in which inheritance and more traditional theorem proving techniques are combined in a single system capable of both sorts of reasoning (see [Thomason&Aronis88]).

In hybrid systems, knowledge is factored into components that can be represented by inheritance and those which require more general representations.[3] Hybrid systems like KRYPTON (see [Brachman *et al.*83]) can sometimes achieve the best of both worlds, but many basic research issues need to be solved before we can feel confident about these systems. For instance, the *control problem* which concerns heuristic strategies for deciding which reasoning

---

[3] For instance, class subsumption is naturally represented by inheritance networks, while disjunctive information requires more general logical techniques.

strategy to use for a given task raises challenging design issues.

3   Describing Networks

Our earlier example, Γ_1 from Figure 1, contained only *positive* links. That
is, all of the links stand for class inclusion. In the more general case, we will
also allow *negative* links, both specific and general. A negative link between
two properties indicates disjointness. For instance, consider the network Γ_2
in Figure 2 in which we have indicated negative links by drawing slashes
through them. The negative links in Γ_2 represent the facts that beagles are
not cats and lions are not dogs.

We assume that the nodes N of a net are partitioned into disjoint sets
I of individuals and K of kinds or properties. We will use the variables
$a, b, c, \ldots$ for individuals in I, the variables $p, q, r, \ldots$ for kinds in K and the
variables $x, y, z, \ldots$ for arbitrary nodes in N. We let Γ be a set of (positive
and negative) links; for most purposes, we identify this set (the set of basic
data supplied to the network) with the network itself. We write a positive
link from x to p as $x \longrightarrow p$ and a negative link from x to p as $x \not\longrightarrow p$,
where x is an individual or kind and p is a kind. We will use the variables
$A, B, C, \ldots$ to range over links. Formally and officially, then, a net is a triple
$\Gamma = <I, K, \Gamma>$, consisting of individual and kind nodes and positive and
negative links. With these definitions, the net Γ_2 would be defined by the
sets in Figure 3.

We will be interested in arbitrary *paths* of links over a set of individuals
I and kinds K. We will use the variables $\sigma, \tau, \ldots$ to range over paths. In the
nets we will study here, our paths come in two types, *positive* and *negative*.
A positive path has the form

$$x_0 \longrightarrow x_1 \longrightarrow \ldots \longrightarrow x_n$$

and is said to enable the conclusion $x_0 \longrightarrow x_n$, where the x_i are property
nodes — with the possible exceptions of x_0 and y_0, which may be individual
nodes. A negative path has the form

$$x_0 \longrightarrow x_1 \longrightarrow \ldots \longrightarrow x_n \not\longrightarrow y_m \longleftarrow \ldots \longleftarrow y_0.$$

and is said to enable the conclusion $x_0 \not\longrightarrow y_0$, where the x_i and y_j are
property nodes — again, with the possible exception of x_0, which may be
an individual node.[4]

---

[4]Note that the links in the second half of the path are reversed. This corresponds to

Each link in a path is taken to represent a reasoning step. Thus a whole path determines a chain of reasoning and is said to *enable* a conclusion. We will write $\sigma \leadsto A$ if the path σ enables the link A. Proofs in logic, of course, also enable their conclusions, but in logic the enablement relation between a proof and its conclusion is obscured by its simplicity; the conclusion of a proof is just its last step. The relation between a path and its conclusion will in general depend on the head and tail of the path, and on global properties determining the path's logical type.

The *permission* relation which holds betweens nets and paths is a fundamental notion of inheritance theory; one of the chief purposes of the theory, in fact, is to provide implementation-independent definitions of this relation, and to establish its basic properties. The permissible paths in a network correspond roughly to the valid lines of reasoning that are licensed by the network. Similarly, the links which are enabled correspond to the set of conclusions which can be drawn from a net.

We will write $\Gamma \mathrel{|\!\!\succ} \sigma$ to say that the path σ is permitted by the network Γ. We will say that a network Γ *supports* a link A, which we write $\Gamma \mathrel{|\!\!>} A$, meaning that $\Gamma \mathrel{|\!\!\succ} \sigma$ for some path σ such that $\sigma \leadsto A$. Although similar to both, the support relation $\mathrel{|\!\!>}$ is not quite a deduction or modeling relation, since networks are not quite models or theories, but somewhere in between.

4 Monotonic Inheritance

In this section we will present the theory of monotonic inheritance. We start by defining monotonicity and go on to define the monotonic case of the permission relation. We then show how the resulting nets can be used for the classification of individuals along a number of different dimensions. Next, we discuss a folk theorem which claims that monotonic inheritance is just first-order implication and show why it is false. We then present a simple deductive system that captures our notion of monotonic inheritance.

4.1 Monotonicity

The property of monotonicity is a fundamental part of logic, not only in the case of classical logics but in virtually all the nonclassical systems that have been studied. Suppose we are working with a logic L, for which we

---

the intuitive way in which we read the class inclusion relationships. The conclusion is enabled since we can think of x_n and y_m as being disjoint, which entails the disjointness of any of their subclasses.

have the deduction relation $\vdash_L$. We will write $\Delta \vdash_L \phi$ if the sentence ϕ, called the *conclusion,* can be derived from the set of sentences Δ, called the *hypotheses* in L. A logic L is said to be *monotonic* if whenever $\Delta \vdash_L \phi$ and $\Delta \subseteq \Delta'$ we have $\Delta' \vdash_L \phi$. Monotonicity means that adding more hypotheses will always yield more conclusions. Conclusions are not cancelled when additional hypotheses are assumed. It is obvious that first-order logic is monotonic, since a conclusion follows from a set of hypotheses if and only if there is a proof of it from these hypotheses, and a proof from a given set of hypotheses is also a perfectly good proof from any larger set of hypotheses.

Proofs themselves consist of a sequence of statements satisfying certain local correctness conditions. For a sequence of statements to qualify as a proof, each statement in the sequence must be derived from previous statements and hypotheses by inference rules of the logic. Since mathematical reasoning depends heavily on this locality principle, it is hard to see how to relax locality and retain any sensible notion of proof. In nonmonotonic reasoning, however, arguments depend not only on the *presence* of certain previously established premises, but on the *absence* of other premises, which are simply assumed to be false if they have not been proven.

4.2   Permission in Monotonic Networks

Monotonic inheritance is characterized by a monotonic support relation; if $\Gamma \mathrel{\triangleright} A$ and $\Gamma \subseteq \Gamma'$ then $\Gamma' \mathrel{\triangleright} A$.

We will begin by characterizing a quite simple case of monotonic inheritance. We define our permission relation $\mathrel{\vdash\!\!\!\triangleright}$ separately for positive and negative paths. In the positive case, we take

$$\Gamma \mathrel{\vdash\!\!\!\triangleright} x_0 \longrightarrow x_1 \longrightarrow \ldots x_n$$

if and only if $x_i \longrightarrow x_{i+1}$ is a positive link in Γ for each $i < n$. Thus, a positive link is enabled by a network just in case it is in the transitive closure of the existing links. In the case of negative paths, we suppose

$$\Gamma \mathrel{\vdash\!\!\!\triangleright} x_0 \longrightarrow x_1 \longrightarrow \ldots x_n \not\longrightarrow y_m \longleftarrow \ldots \longleftarrow y_0$$

if and only if

$x_i \longrightarrow x_{i+1} \in \Gamma$ for $i < n$,

$y_i \longrightarrow y_{i+1} \in \Gamma$ for $i < m$, and

either $x_n \not\longrightarrow y_m \in \Gamma$ or $y_m \not\longrightarrow x_n \in \Gamma$.

between the two paths to go in either direction. The reason for this is that negative links contrapose, and so are symmetric. That is, we take $p \not\rightarrow q$ to be saying that no p's are q's, which implies that no q's are p's.

Now consider the paths which are permitted by the network Γ_2 from Figure 2. Of course, every basic link will be a permissible path. The complex paths allowed by Γ_2 and the links that they enable include those given in Figure 4.

It should be apparent that the permission relation as we have defined it is monotonic. This is because all of the conditions in the definition only require the existence of certain forms of links. Adding more links to a net cannot cause the failure of such existential conditions.

4.3 Multiple Inheritance

Both the definition of inheritance given here and in the next sections are cases of *multiple inheritance*. What this means is that there may be links from one node to more than one other node. For instance, we might want to say that whales are mammals and that whales are ocean dwellers. Note that nothing in the definitions prohibits such uses of multiple classification. One use of such multiple inheritance is to simultaneously classify objects along a number of different dimensions. For instance, consider the simple classification of animals in terms of their biological class and habitat in the net Γ_5 illustrated in Figure 5.

In the monotonic case just defined, a node will simply inherit all of the properties which can be obtained from any of the classes to which it belongs. For instance, anything which is a subclass of tiger will also be considered a subclass of both mammals and jungle dwellers, thus inheriting properties from each class.

4.4 A Mistaken Folk Theorem

It is often assumed that it is possible to translate a network into a first-order theory by means of the link by link mapping provided in Figure 6. But consider the somewhat artificial network Γ_7 in Figure 7. In terms of inheritance, we have both $a \longrightarrow p$ and $a \not\rightarrow p$ supported by Γ_7. This situation would correspond to the one in which we could prove the first-order sentences $p(a)$ and $\neg p(a)$. In first-order logic, if we can prove any sentence and its negation we can prove anything. That is, we have the following property:

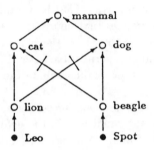

Figure 2: Net with Negation

I: Leo, Spot

K: beagle, lion, cat, dog, mammal

Γ: Leo → lion, Spot → dog,
     lion → cat, beagle → dog, cat → mammal, dog → mammal ,
     lion ↛ dog, beagle ↛ cat

Figure 3: Explicit Definition of Simple Negative Net

Permitted	*Enables*
Leo → lion ↛ dog	Leo ↛ dog
Leo → lion → cat	Leo → cat
Leo → lion → cat → mammal	Leo → mammal
lion → mammal	lion → mammal

Figure 4: Permission and Enablement in Negative Net

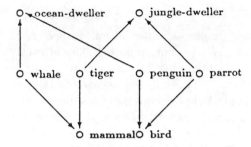

Figure 5: Multiple Inheritance Net

Link	First-Order Statement
$a \rightarrow p$	$p(a)$
$p \rightarrow q$	$(\forall x)(p(x) \supset q(x))$
$a \not\rightarrow p$	$\neg p(a)$
$p \not\rightarrow q$	$(\forall x)(p(x) \supset \neg q(x))$

Figure 6: Folk Translation of Nets

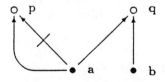

Figure 7: Folk Theorem Counterexample

If $\Gamma \vdash \phi$ and $\Gamma \vdash \neg\phi$ then $\Gamma \vdash \psi$ for every sentence ψ.

This is not the case for our definition of inheritance. For instance, in the network Γ_7, the link $a \nrightarrow q$ is not supported. This primarily stems from the modular nature of semantic networks. The monotonic permission relation is sufficient to ensure that we are only led to conclude things that are in some sense relevant to the links in the network. Local inconsistencies in semantic nets do not lead to global inconsistencies as in the case of first-order logic.

4.5   Deductive System for Monotonic Inheritance

We can give a more traditional deductive system for the case of monotonic network inheritance. The axioms and rules of inference in Figure 8 are sound and complete with respect to the given definition of monotonic inheritance. That is, a link is supported by a net just in case it has a proof in this logic from the set of links in the net. For relations to more standard proof-theoretic formulations, see [Thomason *et al.*86].

5   Nonmonotonic Inheritance

In this section, we will consider possible definitions of inheritance that produce nonmonotonic relations of permission and support. First we will consider why such nonmonotonic inheritance procedures might be useful. We will then discuss the difference between reasoning mechanisms which are *credulous* and those which are *skeptical* in the face of the conflicting evidence. We will then discuss the notion of specificity in networks and the importance of allowing more specific reasons for drawing a conclusion to override more general ones. Finally, we will present our formal definition of nonmonotonic inheritance and consider some examples.

5.1   Generic Reasoning and Counterexamples

Monotonic inheritance is designed to capture reasoning about strict class inclusion of the sort expressed by English universal sentences such as:

> **Every bird flies.**

> **Every Republican is not a pacifist.**

Nonmonotonic inheritance, on the other hand, is used to represent information about prototypical or generic members of classes. These kinds of relationships can be expressed in English with the parallel generic sentences:

Birds fly.

Republicans are not pacifists.

These sentences may be maintained even in the face of exceptions. That is, the statement that birds fly expressed above has all the earmarks of truth, and remains useful for reasoning, when *ad hoc* exceptions are known — particular birds that don't fly — and even when general exceptions are admitted — atypical birds, such as ostriches and penguins, that are naturally flightless. For an introduction to some problems in the linguistic semantics of generic sentences, see [Carlson82].[5] For more advanced and recent material, see [Pelletier&Schubert87], [Krifka87], and [Krifka88].

Consider the net Γ_9 in Figure 9, which has come to be known as the *Tweety triangle*. This net provides a reason for concluding that penguins fly; the path on the right, through the node *bird*. But the negative link from *penguin* to *flier* provides an overriding reason — since the path from *penguin* to *bird* shows that penguins are a specific kind of bird — that preempts any reason we may have had for concluding that pengiuns fly. The net contains the information that birds fly, but penguins don't.

Thus, if we add to this net the fact that Tweety is a bird, the net should support the conclusion that Tweety flies. But, if we then learn that Tweety is not only a bird but a penguin, the conclusion will be retracted — the resulting net will not support the conclusion Tweety doesn't fly. A system of inheritance that treats this example properly must be nonmonotonic.

The elements involved in our discussion of the Tweety triangle involved reasoned belief states that are updated in the face of new information. We can think of nonmonotonic nets as representing the knowledge or belief states of a rational agent capable of forming beliefs that are based on prototypical or generic expectations. The conclusions that follow from the net are then enabled by lines of reasoning compatible with what is currently known. The changes that result in conclusions when links are added can then be viewed as a representation of the way in which people reason in the light of updated information.

Pushing this idea, the LINKUP group has pursued the consequences of looking at nonmonotonic networks as *qualitative models of belief revision* (in contrast with the *quantitative* model that is associated with Bayesian probabilistic approaches). We have shown, at least in a preliminary way,

---

[5]This article is particularly helpful at demolishing the idea that generics can somehow be defined using quantifiers, such as "most."

that there are strong connections between update in nonmonotonic semantic nets and conditional logics, such as the one described in [Stalnaker68]. And we have established results that illuminate recent arguments in the literature about knowledge update, such as those in [Gärdenfors86] and [McGee85]. For specifics, see [Cross&Thomason87].

Though the techniques we have used in analyzing and interpreting networks resemble familiar logical methods, it is best to think of nets as modeling not the way the world actually is, but the way that people represent and reason about it. In this respect, inheritance theory fits well with the epistemic tradition in the interpretation of logics (see, for instance, [Ellis79]).

5.2   Credulous vs Skeptical Inheritance.

Nonmonotonic reasoning systems can be classified along many dimensions; one of the most important of these distinguishes reasoning patterns which we will call *skeptical* from those we label *credulous*. In general, we say that an inheritance algorithm is skeptical if it tends not to draw conclusions in the face of conflicting evidence. A credulous inheritance mechanism, on the other hand, will try to draw as many conclusions as possible, attempting to maintain some kind of consistency in the conclusions that are drawn. The idea behind credulous reasoning is that it is better to have many beliefs (perhaps, for instance, because we can't act without beliefs, and we need to act), and a credulous reasoner is even willing to create these beliefs, if necessary, by making arbitrary decisions.

A simple example may help to illustrate the difference between skeptical and credulous approaches. Consider the net Γ_{10} in Figure 10. This net is known as the *Nixon diamond*; using facts about Nixon, it produces a reason for his being a pacifist, and a reason for his not being a pacifist.

Under the monotonic definition of inheritance, *both* the conclusion that Nixon is a pacifist and the conclusion Nixon is not a pacifist would be supported by this net. This might be an appropriate inference if the links in the net were strict or indefeasible; but in this case, they clearly should not be interpreted that way. It is only a generic rule with exceptions that states that Quakers are pacifists and Republicans are not.

On this interpretation, it would certainly not be sensible to draw the contradictory conclusion; the premises are consistent (and in some sense true), but the contradiction is not. A credulous reasoning strategy will permit one path or the other from *Nixon* to *pacifist* by simply choosing it (perhaps randomly).

i. $x \rightarrow x$ ii. $\dfrac{p \not\rightarrow q}{q \not\rightarrow p}$

iii. $\dfrac{x \rightarrow y,\ y \rightarrow z}{x \rightarrow z}$ iv. $\dfrac{x \rightarrow y,\ y \not\rightarrow z}{x \not\rightarrow z}$ v. $\dfrac{x \rightarrow y,\ z \not\rightarrow y}{z \not\rightarrow x}$

Figure 8: Logic of Nonmonotonic Inheritance

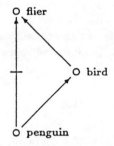

Figure 9: Tweety Triangle

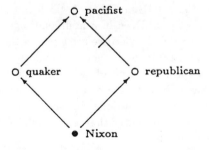

Figure 10: Nixon Diamond

Credulous reasoning strategies force us to multiply the relation of permission; given a net, we have to envisage many ways in which sets of paths through the network can come to be endorsed as sets of reasons that can yield conclusions.[6]

Thus, credulous strategies will associate with a network a number of *extensions,* or maximal coherent sets of reasons. The definition of inheritance, as in [Touretzky86], will associate a number of different credulous extensions with such a net. The Nixon diamond Γ_{10} has just two extensions on the theory of [Touretzky86]; these correspond to the belief that Nixon is a Quaker Republican who is a pacifist, and to the belief that he is a Quaker Republican who is not.

Credulous strategies are in general more complicated than skeptical ones, and in this paper we will discuss a skeptical inheritance definition, which associates a unique extension with each network. This uniqueness property is not only conceptually simple but computationally useful, since it avoids the complications of trying to compute and represent a number of possible extensions to a given network.

5.3   Specificity and Preemption

The point illustrated by the Tweety triangle is crucial and needs to be captured by any adequate theory of nonmonotonic reasoning. To do this, we need to provide a mechanism for certain paths in a network to neutralize or preempt other paths. In terms of reasoning, this amounts to an argument being overcome by a better counterargument.

In general, we will only allow compound paths to be neutralized. If we allowed links that are already in a net to be neutralized, we would violate the principle that a reasoning system should accept the information it is given directly; that if $A \in \Gamma$, then $\Gamma \mathrel{\triangleright} A$.

Consider again, the net Γ_7 in Figure 7 which contains the contradictory links $a \longrightarrow p$ and $a \not\longrightarrow p$. Even in a nonmonotonic setting, we will infer an inconsistency, since that is what we are given in this network. But, as in the monotonic case, we are in no danger of having these local inconsistencies infect the entire network. Their effects will remain strictly local.

On the other hand, in the case of the Nixon diamond Γ_{10}, we do not want to draw inconsistent conclusions. In fact, it is a desirable property of an inheritance strategy (a property that is provable of the skeptical strategy

---

[6]We have to talk of sets of paths here because the reasons that can be chosen will in general depend on what other reasons have been chosen.

we will define here) that if a network yields an inconsistent conclusion, it must already contain that conclusion directly.

But when is a compound path preempted? Here is a good guideline: a path can preempt another if contains immediately conflicting information which is more specific than the information used in the preempted path. Consider again the Tweety triangle Γ_9, and suppose we were to add an individual node *Tweety* and the link *Tweety* $\longrightarrow$ *penguin* to Γ_9. A naïve application of skepticism would lead us to avoid concluding that Tweety flies or that Tweety does not fly. This is because we have both of the paths

(i) $\qquad$ *Tweety* $\longrightarrow$ *penguin* $\not\longrightarrow$ *flier*

(ii) $\qquad$ *Tweety* $\longrightarrow$ *penguin* $\longrightarrow$ *bird* $\longrightarrow$ *flier*

But preemption applies in this case. Since (in view of the link from *penguin* to *bird*) the information that Tweety is a penguin is more specific than the information that Tweety is a bird, we allow the path in (i) above to preempt the path in (ii).

More precisely, we will say that a path of the form

(1) $\qquad x \longrightarrow \ldots \longrightarrow v \longrightarrow y$

is preempted in a net if either $x \not\longrightarrow y$ is a link in the net or there is a *permitted* path of the form

(2) $\qquad x \longrightarrow \ldots \longrightarrow z \longrightarrow \ldots \longrightarrow v$

and an explicit link $z \not\longrightarrow y$ in the net. That is, if we can take a detour through z on the way to v along a permissible path, then z gives us more specific information than v. Furthermore, if we have an explicit link telling us that z's are not y's, then we should allow this more specific information to preempt the more general conclusion reached from v.

This definition of preemption gives us a graphical characterization of specificity determined by the place of a node with respect to another in the hierarchy determined by the arcs.[7] Preemption can be pictured schematically as in Figure 11. It is important to keep in mind when viewing this diagram that the entire path from x to v along z must be permitted and not just the individual paths from x to v and from v to z. For a discussion of this difference and a number of other subtle issues, see [Horty89].

---

[7] Notice, though, that this characterization depends in general on permission, and in fact we will have to provide a simultaneous definition of permission and specificity.

To decide whether or not a path is permissible, it will be necessary to consider all of the possible conflicting paths that might preempt it, and then all of the possible paths that might preempt the parts of that path, and so on down to the individual links. This is where the recursive nature of the permission definition arises.

An exactly analogous definition holds for negative paths. In the case of nonmonotonic inheritance, though, we will only be concerned with negative paths that end in negative links. That is, the only negative paths we will consider will be of the form

$$x \longrightarrow \ldots \longrightarrow v \not\longrightarrow y.$$

Such a path will be preempted if there is a direct link $x \longrightarrow y$ in the net or if there is a path $x \longrightarrow \ldots \longrightarrow z \longrightarrow \ldots \longrightarrow v$, which is itself permitted, such that $z \longrightarrow y$ is in the net.

Note that nothing in this definition requires the paths from x to v to be the same in (1) and (2). For instance, in the case of the net Γ_{12} in Figure 12, the path $a \longrightarrow b \dashrightarrow d \longrightarrow e$ is preempted by the path $a \longrightarrow c \not\longrightarrow e$. In this case, our definition takes the node c to be more specific than the node d, and since the only place that a inherits the property e is through d, we allow the path $a \longrightarrow c \not\longrightarrow e$ to disable it. This sort of preemption is called *off-path*, since we do not require a disabling path to share the exact same initial path as the path that is disabled. Such off-path preemption is recommended in [Sandewall86] and adopted in [Horty *et al.*87], whereas [Touretzky86] treats Γ_{12} as ambiguous, allowing both an extension where a is an e and the incompatible extension where a is not an e.

To ensure that our notion of specificity is well defined, we require our nets to be acyclic. That is, we only consider nets in which there is no sequence of nodes $x_0 \ldots x_n$ with $x_0 = x_n$ and where $x_i \longrightarrow x_{i+1}$ or $x_i \not\longrightarrow x_{i+1}$ is in the net for each $i < n$. Graphically, this corresponds to not allowing ourselves to follow links out of a node and eventually return to the node.

To see that we would get into trouble without such a restriction, consider the net Γ_{13} in Figure 13. It is not clear in this net whether to allow the paths $a \longrightarrow r \longrightarrow p$ or $a \dashrightarrow t \longrightarrow q$. The reason for this is that we have potentially disabling paths for both of these cases in $a \dashrightarrow t \longrightarrow q \longrightarrow s \not\longrightarrow p$ and $a \longrightarrow r \dashrightarrow p \longrightarrow u \not\longrightarrow q$. But, since we require the initial segment of a disabling path to be permissible, we are left begging the question without a method for determining whether the original paths are permissible. Trying to reduce the problem to simpler cases recursively just leads around in circles. Such cases of circularity will never arise in the case of acyclic nets, as we note in the discussion of degree after the definition of permission.

5.4 Nonmonotonic Permission

We can define the nonmonotonic version of inheritance directly by cases. The first case simply handles links which are in the network, which as we said, are always permissible. We have two subcases, depending on whether or not the link in question is positive or negative. That is, we suppose

$$\Gamma \mathrel{|\!\!\!\succ} x \longrightarrow p \quad \text{iff} \quad x \longrightarrow p \in \Gamma.$$

$$\Gamma \mathrel{|\!\!\!\succ} x \not\longrightarrow p \quad \text{iff} \quad x \not\longrightarrow p \in \Gamma.$$

In the more complicated case of compound paths, we will simply formalize our notion of preemption. Again, we have dual subcases based on whether or not the path is positive or negative.

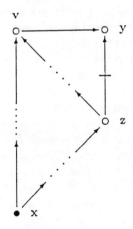

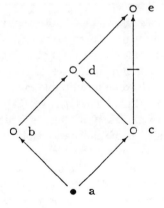

Figure 11:
Disablement Scheme

Figure 12:
Off-path Preemption Net

(3)

$$\Gamma \mathrel{\vert\!\!\!\sim} x \longrightarrow \ldots \longrightarrow u \longrightarrow y \text{ iff}$$

1. $\Gamma \mathrel{\vert\!\!\!\sim} x \longrightarrow \ldots \longrightarrow u$,

2. $u \longrightarrow y \in \Gamma$,

3. $x \not\longrightarrow y \notin \Gamma$, and

4. if $\Gamma \mathrel{\vert\!\!\!\sim} x \longrightarrow \ldots \longrightarrow v$ and $v \not\longrightarrow y \in \Gamma$ then either $x \longrightarrow y \in \Gamma$ or there is a z such that $\Gamma \mathrel{\vert\!\!\!\sim} x \longrightarrow \ldots \longrightarrow z \longrightarrow \ldots \longrightarrow v$ and $z \longrightarrow y \in \Gamma$

$$\Gamma \mathrel{\vert\!\!\!\sim} x \longrightarrow \ldots \longrightarrow u \not\longrightarrow y \text{ iff}$$

1. $\Gamma \mathrel{\vert\!\!\!\sim} x \longrightarrow \ldots \longrightarrow u$,

2. $u \not\longrightarrow y \in \Gamma$,

3. $x \longrightarrow y \notin \Gamma$, and

4. if $\Gamma \mathrel{\vert\!\!\!\sim} x \longrightarrow \ldots \longrightarrow v$ and $v \longrightarrow y \in \Gamma$ then either $x \not\longrightarrow y \in \Gamma$ or there is a z such that $\Gamma \mathrel{\vert\!\!\!\sim} x \longrightarrow \ldots \longrightarrow z \longrightarrow \ldots \longrightarrow v$ and $z \not\longrightarrow y \in \Gamma$

This definition requires some explanation before it becomes clear that we have, in fact, adequately formalized our intuitive idea of preemption and inheritance.

The first thing to note about the definition is that it employs a bottom-up, forward chaining strategy. A forward chaining inheritance mechanism builds paths from the beginning to the end, left to right. This is reflected in the first two clauses of each case. The first requires the path's initial subpath to be permissible in the network and then allows it to be extended by one link. That is, we take a permissible path $x \longrightarrow \ldots \longrightarrow p$ and try to extend it by finding a link $p \longrightarrow q$ or $p \not\longrightarrow q$ in Γ. Some other definitions of inheritance (following the metaphor of the term "inheritance" itself, according to which properties flow downwards to instances) use a top-down, backward chaining strategy, such as those discussed in [Fahlman79] or [Touretzky86]. In a backwards strategy, we might be given a permissible path $p \longrightarrow \ldots \longrightarrow q$ or $p \longrightarrow \ldots \not\longrightarrow q$ and try to extend it by finding a link $x \longrightarrow p$ in the network. As we have said, backward chaining strategies correspond well to the inheritance metaphor. Forward chaining strategies look more like argument or proof construction in a deductive system, since they tend to move in a direction flowing from assumptions to conclusions.

It would be natural to expect forward and backward chaining strategies to somehow be equivalent. However, there are subtle differences that emerge on closer analysis. And recent work suggest that these may have important effects. Bart Selman, of the University of Toronto, has recently produced NP-complete problems in connection with the calculation of multiple extensions; these proofs seem to depend on the use of a downward reasoning strategy.

Since permission in (3) is recursively defined, as should be evident by the fourth clauses, it remains to be proved that the definition is not circular. A simple inductive argument shows that the definition is well founded. First, we define the *degree* of a path to be the length of the longest sequence of nodes between its endpoints connected by (positive or negative) links. It should then be obvious that the permissibility of a path of a given degree is only dependent on the permissiblity of other paths of strictly smaller degree. For a detailed argument, the reader is referred to [Horty *et al.*87]. Note again that our definition of permission depends crucially on the acyclicity of the underlying nets. In fact, this creates rather unwelcome restrictions on the expressive power of our networks; we cannot allow networks, for instance, that say that birds have feathers and that things that have feathers are birds. An important research problem generated by this work is how to relax acyclicity while maintaining intelligibility and sound inheritance definitions. We have done some thinking along these lines, but can claim no major results.

5.5 Examples

The purpose of this section is to explain our definition of permission more fully by presenting a number of illustrative examples.

Consider one last time the Tweety triangle Γ_9 in Figure 9. This is the limiting case of our definitions. The path *penguin* $\longrightarrow$ *bird* $\longrightarrow$ *fly* is preempted by the link *penguin* $\not\longrightarrow$ *fly*. This is because the path from *penguin* to *fly* goes through the *penguin* node. The explicit link stating that penguins do not fly then matches the first disjunct in the fourth clause of our definition. Of course, in this case, there is no path that preempts the path from *penguin* to *bird*, so we are still able to conclude that penguins are birds.

In the case of the Nixon diamond, Γ_{10} in Figure 10, we can not conclude that Nixon is a pacifist or that he is not a pacifist. Both of the paths *Nixon* $\longrightarrow$ *republican* $\not\longrightarrow$ *pacifist* and *Nixon* $\longrightarrow$ *quaker* $\longrightarrow$ *pacifist* are disabled by each other. This highlights the fact that a disabling path does not have to itself be permissible in its entirety — only the path establishing specificity needs to be permitted.

The definition of permission does not depend on the length of paths involved. Consider the nets Γ_{14a} and Γ_{14b} in Figure 14. In the case of Γ_{14a}, we will not be able to conclude that $x \longrightarrow s$ or that $x \not\longrightarrow s$. The reason for this is that the paths that would enable both of these links are disabled.

We will now work through the clauses of the definition (3i) to see how they apply to the question of whether or not we have $\Gamma_{14a} \mathrel{\rhd} x \longrightarrow u \longrightarrow s$. For the first clause, we have $\Gamma_{14a} \mathrel{\rhd} x \longrightarrow u$ and for the second clause we have $u \longrightarrow s \in \Gamma$. The third clause is satisfied because we do not have a directly conflicting link $x \not\longrightarrow s$ in the net. Finally, since $\Gamma_{14a} \mathrel{\rhd} x \longrightarrow v \longrightarrow t$ and $t \not\longrightarrow s$ we must have a link $x \longrightarrow s$ in the net, which we do not, or have a path $x \longrightarrow \ldots \longrightarrow z \ldots \longrightarrow v$ permitted by Γ_{14a} such that $z \longrightarrow y$ is a link in the net. Again, this condition is not satisfied, so the path in question is not permitted. A similar line of reasoning shows that the longer path is not permitted either. Here we see the fundamental skeptical nature of the inheritance mechanism. If there is a conflict, we remain skeptical unless one of the conflicting paths is preempted.

Now consider the case of Γ_{14b}. In this net, we have a permissible path $x \longrightarrow z \longrightarrow y \longrightarrow w$ and a link $w \not\longrightarrow t \in \Gamma$ that conflicts with the path $x \longrightarrow v \longrightarrow t$. As a consequence of this disablement, the path $x \longrightarrow u \longrightarrow s$ is permitted, since the path that disabled it in Γ_{14a} is itself no longer permitted.

Finally, we will consider a case where the forward chaining nature of our inheritance mechanism allows individuals to be *decoupled* from their immediate superclasses. Consider the net Γ_{15} in Figure 15. In this case, just as in the Nixon diamond, neither $p \longrightarrow r \longrightarrow s$ or $p \longrightarrow q \not\longrightarrow s$ is a permissible path, since they conflict and neither one is preempted by another path. Of course, the single links $p \longrightarrow q$ and $p \longrightarrow r$ are permitted. But now consider the individual node a. Since $a \not\longrightarrow q$ is a direct link in the net, it is permitted. Of course, a could not inherit this property from its only immediate superclass p, since we have $p \longrightarrow q$ in the net. Γ_{15} will also permit the path $a \longrightarrow p \longrightarrow r \longrightarrow s$, since the potential conflict $a \longrightarrow q \not\longrightarrow s$ is itself preempted by the more specific information $a \not\longrightarrow q$. Again, $p \not\longrightarrow s$ is not permitted, so a does not inherit its s-ness from p. This example illustrates the situation in which a permissible path has a tail which is not permissible.

It might be thought that we could generate the skeptical extension of a network by intersecting all of its credulous extensions. But, consider the

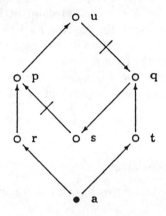

Figure 13: Acyclicity

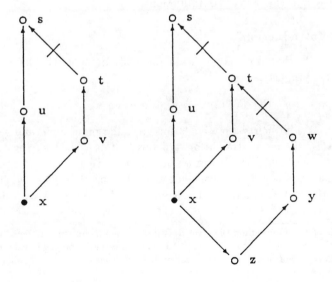

Figure 14: Path Length Examples

case of Γ_{16} in Figure 16. Γ_{16} looks like one Nixon diamond nested inside of another. This nested Nixon diamond permits the path $a \longrightarrow p \not\longrightarrow q$, since the path $a \longrightarrow s \longrightarrow t \longrightarrow q$ cannot preempt it, because its initial segment $a \longrightarrow s \longrightarrow t$ conflicts with the unpreempted path $a \longrightarrow r \not\longrightarrow t$. But, if we consider the credulous extensions of this net, one contains the link $a \longrightarrow q$ obtained by following the path $a \longrightarrow s \longrightarrow t$ and does not contain the link $a \not\longrightarrow q$. Therefore, $a \not\longrightarrow q$ is not in every credulous extension. So the skeptical approach is not merely equivalent to intersecting credulous extensions.

5.6   Logical Properties

5.6.1   Soundness and Skepticism

It has been proved that the definition we have given of nonmonotonic inheritance is sound, in that

$$\Gamma \models x \longrightarrow y \text{ and } \Gamma \models x \not\longrightarrow y \text{ iff } x \longrightarrow y \in \Gamma \text{ and } x \not\longrightarrow y \in \Gamma.$$

A proof can be found in [Touretzky *et al.*87]. Soundness thus establishes the claim that contradictions in the nonmonotonic case of inheritance are very local in nature. They can only arise from directly conflicting atomic links in the network. This also establishes the degree to which we remain skeptical about conclusions in the face of contradictions.

5.6.2   "UQ Introduction"

Consider a net Γ^a that does not contain the node a. Then we have the following logical property.

$$\Gamma^a \models p \longrightarrow q \quad iff \quad \Gamma^a \cup \{a \longrightarrow p\} \models a \longrightarrow q$$

Note that this is a property that holds for both the monotonic and non-monotonic cases. In more straightforward terms, this is just saying that a net supports the fact that p's are q's just in case if it learns of a new object only that it is a p, it will conclude that the object is also a q. The classical rule of UQ Introduction, then, continues to make good sense in a nonmonotonic context.[8]

---

[8]It is the rule of *UQ Elimination* that fails drastically in nonmonotonic settings. This corresponds to the problem of when we are entitled to infer anything from a general truth, of when it can have exceptions. It is solving this problem that makes nonmonotonic logic problematic and complex.

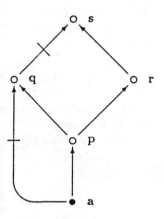

Figure 15: Decoupling

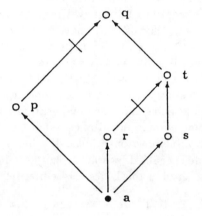

Figure 16: Nested Nixon Diamond

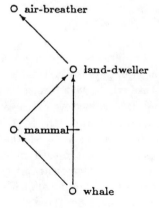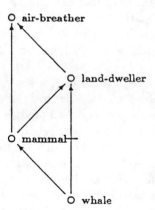

Figure 17: Generic Stability Failure

5.6.3   Stability

Even in nonmonotonic networks, an important condition called *stability*, which can be regarded as a relaxation of the monotonicity property, is desirable. In traditional logical theories, adding a consequence of a set of statements to the set will not change the set of conclusions that can be proved. That is, if we have $\Gamma \models \phi$ and $\Gamma \models \psi$ then we will also have $\Gamma \cup \{\phi\} \models \psi$. It should be obvious that our definition of monotonic inheritance is stable in this way. Adding a link which is monotonically enabled to a net does not change the set of links which are monotonically enabled.

Things are not quite so simple in the nonmonotonic case of inheritance. Before going into the complications, we note that the skeptical version of nonmonotonic inheritance defined in this paper is stable with respect to individual or atomic links. If a link from an individual node to a property node is enabled by a network, then adding it to the network will not change the set of enabled arcs. More precisely, we have

$$\text{If } \Gamma \rhd a \longrightarrow p \text{ and } \Gamma \rhd x \longrightarrow q \text{ then } \Gamma \cup \{a \longrightarrow p\} \rhd x \longrightarrow q.$$

where Γ is a set of links, a an individual node, p and q property nodes and x is an arbitrary node.

But, nonmonotonic inheritance is not stable when it comes to generic links. Consider the nets Γ_{17a} and Γ_{17b} in Figure 17, based on an example of [Sandewall86].

In Γ_{17a}, the path *mammal* $\longrightarrow$ *land-dweller* $\longrightarrow$ *air-breather* is permitted, but the path *whale* $\longrightarrow$ *mammal* $\longrightarrow$ *land-dweller* $\longrightarrow$ *air-breather* is preempted by the link *whale* $\not\longrightarrow$ *land-dweller*, thus preventing the conclusion that whales are air breathers. But, if we add the link *mammal* $\longrightarrow$ *air-breather* to Γ_{17a}, as in Γ_{17b}, then we have the permissible path *whale* $\longrightarrow$ *mammal* $\longrightarrow$ *air-breather*, which does not need to pass through the explictly forbidden *land-dweller* node. Here is a case where we added a link which was enabled by a net to produce a new net from which we can draw more conclusions than in the original. Hence, generic stability fails for the nonmonotonic case of inheritance. But, the question remains as to whether this behavior is desirable. It certainly seems necessary for the case under consideration. We take the failure of generic stability to demonstrate the sensitivity of inheritance mechanisms to the structure of arguments. Not all arguments to the same conclusion are considered equal from the point of view of our specificity based reasoner. More specific arguments, where specificity is determined by the topology of the network, are given precedence;

and this mechanism can be useful in cases such as Γ_{17a} when we wish to override a particular conclusion by positing direct exceptions to generalities represented by paths of reasoning.

6 Further Topics

In this paper we have only been able to touch upon a few of the more basic issues in inheritance theory. In this section, we will briefly introduce some further topics in the theory of inheritance networks and provide some pointers to the quickly growing literature.

6.1 Mixed Networks

Links in the nonmonotonic networks we have considered in this paper come in only one flavor — defeasible. Arguments corresponding to compound paths constructed from these links can always be defeated by more specific arguments. But, as Brachman has pointed out, it is very unintuitive to treat definitions as defeasible (see [Brachman85]); he challenges the ability of nonmonotonic inheritance to accommodate definitions. This issue is addressed in [Horty88], where an alternative characterization of inheritance is developed that combines both the strict behavior of definitional links and defeasible behavior of generic links; it is proved that this version of mixed inheritance extends the systems of monotonic and nonmonotonic inheritance that were presented above. Though this provides a framework for recognizing distinctions that must be made in the presence of definitions, it does not show how to add the capacity to make and process definitions to inheritance nets. This is an open research topic.

6.2 *n*-ary Relations

We have already mentioned the fundamental restriction of our inheritance theories to the nonrelational case. In general, of course, any approach to reasoning that is usable for practical purposes must be capable of reasoning about relations. We may want to lay it down as a general rule, for instance, that Model 4869 disk drives fit Model 70 PC's and to infer from this, and from the information that a is a Model 4869 disk drive and b is a Model 70 PC, that a fits b.

Most research in inheritance theory has ignored relations altogether, and published works that do consider relations, such as [Touretzky86], only consider the binary case. This contrasts with logics in general and in particular with nonmonotonic logics, which at the outset consider relations taking arbitrary numbers of arguments. Our own work on relations (much of it unpublished) suggests that relational reasoning leads to computational complexity, and that it is not trivial to find good compromises in the relational case between tractability and expressive power. We are looking for systems that require more computational complexity than in the simple nonrelational cases, but that are still in the low polynomial time-complexity range.

6.3   Functional Roles

Implementations of relational reasoning in inheritance networks often invoke *roles*, or secondary objects that are invoked by primary ones and that stand in given relations to the primary object and one another. For instance, we may want to lay it down as a default that a cat has a tail (which is a part of the cat). We could use this rule to infer, on learning about a new cat, Sylvester, that Sylvester has a tail, which is a part of Sylvester. We may want to invoke general exceptions to such defaults; a Manx cat does not have a tail.

Inheritance networks with these roles or functional links are common in Artificial Intelligence applications. They are discussed in [Fahlman79], but the theory of such inheritance systems has not been fully worked out in any published work that we have seen. The problems of maintaining computational tractability when roles are present seem to require even more finesse than the ones we have mentioned involving relations without roles. Unlike relations, for instance, roles can lead to the creation of new *virtual objects*, like Sylvester's tail. In even very simple cases this process can generate virtual networks that are infinite. See [Thomason&Touretzky] for details.

6.4   Composite Descriptions and Logical Operators

Network representation formalisms share with logic programming systems the inability to naturally encode disjunctive conclusions. For instance, we might know that something is a pen or a pencil, without knowing which. In particular application domains, such problems can sometimes be remedied by adding additional nodes on an *ad hoc* basis. In our example, we could add IS-A links from the pen and pencil nodes to a new writing instrument node. This would not enable us to conclude that something is a pen if it is a writing instrument and is not a pencil; if we want this conclusion, we again will have to add it in an *ad hoc* manner.

Of course, such a solution places the burden on the designer of the net, for all such disjunctive possibilities need to be considered in advance and given appropriate inclusion relationships. One possible approach is to provide an embedding of an inheritance hierarchy in some more general lattice or boolean algebra that would provide additional properties corresponding to the disjunctions, conjunctions and even negations of existing properties. The reasoning associated with these more general structures, though, might well be too complex to be qualify as inheritance reasoning.[9]

6.5 Relation to Nonmonotonic Logics

Since the tradition of nonmonotonic logics in artificial intelligence is almost as old as that of inheritance networks, it is only natural that there has been some cross-fertilization of ideas. Unfortunately, the project of translating inheritance algorithms into the framework of a well known nonmonotonic logic is unexpectedly complex, and there are many open research problems in this area.[10]

7 Conclusion

We have tried in this paper to present enough information about inheritance theory to convince the reader that it is an interesting subject in its own right, like logic but different in some important respects. Nets themselves provide a model of associative reasoning that can represent a surprisingly diverse array of generalization-based reasoning. At the moment, theoretical work on them is lagging behind the applications, but the applications are pervasive enough to make this work very desirable. It is too soon to see to what extent the ideas being developed in inheritance theory may yield important contributions to logic. But the modularity of nets, and the localized nature of inconsistencies and patterns of reasoning, may offer one promising line of development.

Nonmonotonic reasoning is already becoming an important area of research in logic. Here inheritance theory provides a rich source of intuitions that can be visually presented and related to inheritance diagrams, and serves as a testbed for the more powerful logical theories that are being developed on many fronts. For instance, since most logical theories of non-

---

[9]See [Thomason&Horty89] for an approach to nonmonotonic logic based on inheritance theory that incorporates composite descriptions.

[10]See [Thomason *et al.*86] for discussion.

monotonic reasoning favor credulity, the skeptical version of inheritance that we presented in this paper poses a challenge to these theories.

We have stressed all along the weak expressive power of networks, and that this power is sacrificed to obtain computational tractability. But computational tractability and expressive weakness should not be conflated with theoretical triviality. Even though networks can be thought of as impoverished logics, the definition of inheritance and the proofs of basic theorems are often complex. This was illustrated in this paper by the skeptical version of nonmonotonic inheritance. The theorems we discussed concerning this inheritance definition were not proved here; but the proofs of results like Stability require an inductive argument that is sensitive to the details of the inheritance definition, and that is by no means obvious. In general, the structure that is provided by nets requires a level of detail in the analysis of inheritance-based "proofs" that is not common even in most work in proof theory. And of course, even more detail is required in analyses of computational complexity. Theoretical problems are often compounded by nonmonotonicity, but are not due to nonmonotonicity alone. Even in the monotonic case, we have encountered subtle research problems in developing the theory of relations.

Inheritance theory seems to have emerged as a subject that combines the breadth, the intuitions, and the range of difficulty of associated theoretical problems, to offer a long-term theoretical challenge. In view of the potential usefulness of the applications, we expect to see it continue to develop for some time to come.

Acknowledgments In writing this paper, we received helpful comments and advice from John F. Horty. We should also point out that many of the ideas presented here — and in particular the definition of permission in the case of skeptical inheritance — are due to him. This material is based on work supported by the National Science Foundation under Grant #IST-8700705 (Logical Foundations for Inheritance and Knowledge Update).

8 Bibliography

Brachman, R., R. Fikes, and H. Levesque. Krypton: a functional approach to knowledge representation. FLAIR Technical Report #16, Fairchild Laboratory for Artificial Intelligence Research 1983.

Brachman, R. "I lied about the trees," *The AI Magazine 6*, 1985.

Brachman, R. and H. Levesque, eds. *Readings in Knowledge Representation*, Morgan Kaufmann, 1985.

Carlson, G. "Generic terms and generic sentences," *Journal of Philosophical Logic 11*, 1982.

Cross, C. and R. Thomason. "Update and conditionals," *Methodologies for Intelligent Systems*, (Proceedings of The Second International Symposium on Methodologies for Intelligent Systems), Z. Ras and M. Zemankova, eds., Elsevier, 1987.

Ellis, B. *Rational Belief Systems*, Rowman and Littlefield, 1979.

Fahlman, S. *NETL: A System for Representing and Using Real-world Knowledge*, MIT Press, 1979.

Gärdenfors, P. "Belief revision and the Ramsey test for conditionals," *Philosophical Review 95*, 1986.

Garey, M. and D. Johnson. *Computers and Intractability*, Freeman, 1979.

Horty, J. "Some Direct Theories of Nonmonotonic Inheritance," Technical Report, School of Computer Science, Carnegie Mellon University, forthcoming.

Horty, J. and R. Thomason. "Mixing Strict and Defeasible Inference," *Proceedings of AAAI-88*, Morgan Kaufman, 1988.

Horty, J. "A Defeasible Logic Based on Inheritance Theory," Technical Report, School of Computer Science, Carnegie Mellon University, forthcoming.

Horty, J., R. Thomason, and D. Touretzky. "A Skeptical Theory of Inheritance in Nonmonotonic Semantic Networks. Technical Report CMU–CS–87–175, Computer Science Department, Carnegie Mellon University 1987. An abbreviated version appears in *Proceedings of AAAI-87*, Morgan Kaufmann, 1987.

Krifka, M. "An outline of genericity," Technical Report. Seminar für Natürlich-sprachliche Systeme, Biesingerstr. 10, 7400 Tübingen, W. Germany, 1987.

Krifka, M., ed. "Genericity in natural language: Proceedings of The 1988 Tübingen conference," Seminar für Natürlich-sprachliche Systeme, 7400 Tübingen, W. Germany, 1988.

Levesque, H. and R. Brachman. "A fundamental tradeoff in knowledge representation and reasoning," *Readings in Knowledge Representation*, R. Brachman and H. Levesque, eds., Morgan Kaufmann, 1985.

McCarthy, J. "Artificial intelligence, logic and formalizing common sense," *Logic and Artificial Intelligence*, R. Thomason, ed., Kluwer, 1989.

McGee, V. "A counterexample to *modus ponens*," *Journal of Philosophy 82*, 1985.

Minsky, M. "A framework for representing knowledge," MIT Artificial Intelligence Laboratory Memo #306 1974. Reprinted without appendix in *The Psychology of Computer Vision*, P. Winston ed., McGraw-Hill, 1975.

Pelletier, J. and L. Schubert. "Problems in the representation of the logical form of generics, bare plurals, and mass terms," *New Directions in Semantics*, E. LePore, ed., Academic Press, 1987.

Quillian, M. "Word concepts: a theory and simulation of some basic semantic capabilities," *Behavioral Science 12*, 1967.

Sandewall, E. "Non-monotonic inference rules for multiple inheritance with exceptions," *Proceedings of The IEEE 74*, 1986.

Sowa, J. *Conceptual Structures: Information Processing in Mind and Machine*, Addison-Wesley, 1984.

Stalnaker, R. "A theory of conditionals," *Studies in Logical Theory*, N. Rescher, ed., Blackwell, 1968.

Thomason, R., and J. Horty. "Logics for nonmonotonic inheritance," *Non-Monotonic Reasoning* (Proceedings of the Second INternational Workshop on Non-Monotonic Reasoning), M. Reinfrank, J. de Kleer, M. Ginsberg, and E. Sandewall, eds., Springer Verlag, 1989

Thomason, R., J. Horty, and D. Touretzky. "A calculus for inheritance in monotonic semantic nets," Technical Report CMU-CS-86-138, Computer Science Department, Carnegie Mellon University 1986.

Thomason, R. and D. Touretzky. "An Inheritance Path Formulation of Roles and Relations," *Proceedings of The Catalina Conference on Formal Aspects of Semantic Networks*, J. Sowa, ed., forthcoming.

Thomason, R. and J. Aronis. "Hybridizing nonmonotonic inheritance with theorem proving," Unpublished manuscript, 1988. To appear as a Carnegie Mellon University Technical Report.

Touretzky, D. *The Mathematics of Inheritance Systems*, Morgan Kaufmann, 1986.

Touretzky, D., J. Horty, and R. Thomason. "A clash of intuitions: the current state of nonmonotonic multiple inheritance systems," *Proceedings of IJCAI-87*, Morgan Kaufmann, 1987.

Woods, W. "What's in a link: foundations for semantic networks," *Representation and Understanding: Studies in Cognitive Science*, D. Bobrow and A. Collins, Academic Press, 1975.

Wos, L., R. Overbeck, E. Lusk, and J. Boyle. *Automated Reasoning*, Prentice-Hall, 1984.

Defeasible Specification of Utilities

Ronald Loui /- WASN

> Presumably, in the long run decision theory will be integrated
> with ... planners. Before that happens, how probability and util-
> ity estimates are arrived at in realistic circumstances will have
> to be solved.
>
> — Charniak and McDermott, *Introduction to AI*
> [Charniak&McDermott84]

1 Background

1.1 Utility in Decision Theory and Goals in Planning

Decision analysis is the leading candidate for deciding among competing actions and conflicting goals in uncertain worlds. It is normally thought to
require probabilities, utilities, and a set of alternative courses of action. Presumably, work on evidential reasoning will deliver probabilities suitable for
AI's use, and planning has already discovered various ways of representing
and composing sequences of primitive actions. This leaves the specification
of utilities of outcome states.

Operations research devotees can tell us how to assess utilities, when
agents are unable to specify them directly and explicitly, but I claim that
there is more to be said about the representation of utilities even when
extraction of the information is easy, *i.e.*, even when assessment is trivial.
So I claim there is more to be said than "$u(recovery) = 15$", whether we
have to arrive at the value, 15, through extensive interviewing using certainty
equivalents and standard lotteries, or whether our agent is simply willing to
assert that *recovery* would seem to be worth 15 utils.

I will be concerned with the descriptions of the states of the world, such
as *recovery*: such descriptions are inherently incomplete, and we should
examine whether utilities can be usefully assigned to incompletely described
states of the world. But some preliminary remarks contrasting decision
theory and planning are in order.

AI's paradigmatic work on planning concerns deterministic worlds and
incompletely described states or situations. A state is terminal and has value

H.E. Kyburg, Jr. et al. (eds.), Knowledge Representation and Defeasible Reasoning, 345–359.
© 1990 *Kluwer Academic Publishers. Printed in the Netherlands.*

whenever it satisfies the sententially described goals which it is the object of the plan to guarantee. Computation consists of search through the tree of action sequences for a single path from initial to goal state: the fewer the paths considered, the better.

Decision theory concerns indeterministic worlds. There is an important distinction between a completely described terminal state, and a lottery among such states. The probability of each state is known. All states have some value, and are ordered by relative desirability, represented in the reals. Action rarely guarantees specific desiderata, and every action has some probability of achieving the desiderata. Computation consists of evaluating the value of all nodes but the root, in the entire tree of action and event sequences. The value of a node is determined by the values of all of its children. The more paths in the decision tree, the more valid the analysis.

In the worst scenario, all past work on deterministic planning will be inapplicable to decision-theoretic planning because of the differences in representation and procedure. This paper is a first step toward avoiding that worst-case scenario. Presumably, existing goal-achieving planning methods will be useful in heuristic evaluation of large decision trees, especially if there were some way of bounding risk in low-probability sub-trees (*i.e.*, restoring some determinism), and some way of identifying properties of states that contribute significantly to utility valuation (*i.e.*, identifying properties that can function as goals). My proposed representation of utility of states should make these heuristics possible.

1.2   Savage's Problem of Small Worlds and Abstraction

AI planning wants to describe states of the world by asserting sentences known to be true of the state. It sometimes leaves undetermined the truth value of sentences that are relevant to the valuation of a state.

Assigning utility to a possible world described by a maximally strong sentence in a first-order language is no special problem; this is what Richard Jeffrey's theory of decision does [Jeffrey65]. Assigning utility to a set of possible worlds, W, described by a sentence, p, is also no problem, so long as we understand it as the weighted average of the utilities of each possible world, $u(w_i)$, for w_i in W, where the weight of $u(w_i)$ is $prob(w_i)$. States are usually taken to be sets of possible worlds.

However, decision theory can make no sense of the claim that the utility of a state, s, is some value x, *pending consideration of whether I know p to be true in s or not.*

Suppose you know p is true in s, *e.g.*, that $(pitcher\text{-}tiring)$ is true in the state allegedly described by $(leading\text{-}in\text{-}7th\text{-}inning)$. And suppose p is relevant to the valuation of s, *i.e.*, it matters whether $(pitcher\text{-}tiring)$.

Then on the standard view, you should describe the state by $(and\ (pitcher\text{-}tiring)\ (leading\text{-}in\text{-}7th\text{-}inning))$ and use the utility of this state, x_p, instead of x, the utility of $(leading\text{-}in\text{-}7th\text{-}inning)$.

Meanwhile, on the standard view, if you don't know whether p or $\neg p$ is true in s, you should assess the probabilities of p and $\neg p$ respectively, *e.g.*, of $(pitcher\text{-}tiring)$ and $(not\ (pitcher\text{-}tiring))$, and use these probabilities to weigh x_p and $x_{\neg p}$, where $x_{\neg p}$ is the utility of the state described by $(and\ (not\ (pitcher\text{-}tiring))\ (leading\text{-}in\text{-}7th\text{-}inning))$ (and similarly for x_p). You should definitely not use x unless x is this weighted average.

In short, you cannot ignore relevant knowledge.

Sometimes, however, we want to ignore relevant knowledge at various levels of abstraction. It should be possible to make utility claims under various abstractions. Above, we claim the utility of s is x at a granularity that ignores p's truth. This claim is defeasible; we will revise it at a finer granularity in which we consider the truth or falsity of p. It would be nice if x, above, indeed were the appropriately weighted average,

$$prob(\ p\mid s\ )\ x_p + prob(\ \neg p\mid s\ )\ x_{\neg p}.$$

But I claim that it need not be, in order for a formalism to be useful. To insist that it be is to confuse incompleteness due to ignorance or indeterminacy (an epistemic matter) with incompleteness due to abstraction (a computational matter).

Moreover, what often prevents us from assigning an x to be the utility of an s is the fear that x will not equal the appropriate weighted average, once we consider all of the uncertainties about s, and their ramifications. So we are forced to deepen our decision trees even for the most casual decisions. We are forced to reach for leaves that are quiescent states, wherein most of the relevant possibilities have been decided one way or the other. The problem is that we cannot use x for the utility of s unless we are prepared to equate it with the expectation, which requires further analysis. My finesse of this problem will be to allow use of x defeasibly.

Leonard Savage, the foundational decision-theorist, spoke of the problem of small worlds, which is the same abstraction problem here. Savage starts with the *world*, "the object about which the person is concerned," and a *state* (of the world), "a description of the world, *leaving no relevant aspect undescribed*" (emphasis added). He writes [Savage54]

> In application of the theory, the question will arise as to which world to use .... If the person is interested in the only brown egg in a dozen, should that egg or the whole dozen be taken as the world? It will be seen ... that in principle no harm is done by taking the larger of two worlds as a model of the situation.

But computational harm is done by taking worlds too large. It can be painful to specify utilities for 2^{12} states of eggs in a dozen, instead of 2^2 states of a brown egg, and also costly to manipulate decision trees over such states. In the problems that AI planning addresses, every set of possible worlds is a state, and the combinatorics are enormously worse.

2   Defeasible Calculation

2.1   Defeasible Specification of Utility

The shrewd will give a terse specification of utilities: if a state of the dozen eggs entails that the brown egg is broken, then its utility is 0; otherwise, its utility is 1. Those who have access to a non-monotonic representational language will say:

$$defeasibly\ u(x) = 0;$$

$$\text{if } x \mathrel{\big|\!\!\!-} \neg broken\text{-}brown\text{-}egg \text{ then } u(x) = 1.$$

The latter specifies implicit exceptions to the first rule. This defeasible version is desirable for the same reasons we write

$$bird(x) \quad {>\!\!-} \quad flies(x)$$

(*i.e.*, if x is a bird then defeasibly, x flies); and

$$\neg flies(Tweety)$$

instead of

$$(bird(x)\ \&\ (x \neq Tweety)) \supset flies(x)$$

$$\neg flies(Tweety).$$

In general, we can try to discover structure among our utility assessments. Defeasibility allows the economical use of structural principles that are only approximate, *i.e.*, that admit of exceptions.

One possibility is additive structure. The multi-attribute model of utility supposes that valuation can be split among attributes whose individual contributions are additive:

$$u(<w_i>) = \Sigma_i\{k(i)u(w_i)\}$$

where $<w_i>$ is an n-vector measuring the state in each of n relevant attributes, and $k(i) / k(j)$ reflects the relative importance of the ith to the jth attribute.

Likewise, we can suppose that the contributions to a state's utility of properties holding in that state will be the sum of their individual contributions. For some conjunctions of properties, the utility contributed is not equal to the sum of each individual contribution, but these will be exceptions handled by the defeasible reasoning. There will be a payoff for using the additive model if the exceptions are few. Each of

> (*flat tennis-balls*), (*busy tennis-courts*), (*cold day*),
> (*grouchy partner*), and (*poor string-tension*)

may decrease by 10 utils the valuation of a state in which they hold, so that the utility of a state in which

> (*and* (*busy courts*) (*flat tennis-balls*))

holds is apparently -20. But in conjunction,

> (*and* (*flat tennis-balls*) (*poor string-tension*))

may be only as detrimental as a loss of 15 utils, so that a state satisfying

> (*and* (*busy courts*) (*flat tennis-balls*) (*poor string-tension*))

is apparently valued at -25 utils.

We can continue to express exception upon exception, with the right representational language. It might be that if all of the five properties above hold, the attempt to play tennis is so absurd it's enjoyable, and worth 10 utils, instead of the -45 that we might defeasibly calculate.

A non-monotonic logic with specificity defeaters allows this to be expressed economically. I will use my own defeasible reasoning system [Loui87], though others could also be used. The required mechanism is that if

$$a \; \succ\!\!- \; c$$

$$a \,\&\, b \; \succ\!\!- \; \neg c$$

then $\neg c$ can be inferred on $a \,\&\, b$ (assuming $a \,\&\, b$ entails a but not *vice versa*).

Let there be a stock of properties $P_1, \ldots, P_n$, relevant to the valuation of a state, and let a utility scale be determined (*i.e.*, it is meaningful to talk of 5 utils). Any individual contributions and conjunctive contributions may be asserted, *e.g.*

$$uconst(P_1) = 12;$$

$$uconst(P_2) = 20;$$

$$uconst(P_1 \,\&\, P_2) = 3;$$

$$uconst(P_5) = 14.$$

We use two defeasible rule schemata:

(1) $\ulcorner uconst(P) = x \,\&\, uconst(Q) = y \urcorner \; \succ\!\!- \; \ulcorner uconst(P \,\&\, Q) = x + y \urcorner$

(2) $\ulcorner holds(P, s) \,\&\, uconst(P) = x \urcorner \; \succ\!\!- \; \ulcorner u(s) = x \urcorner.$

The first says that the utility of a state in which P and Q are true is the sum of the respective utilities in which just P and just Q hold, all things being equal. The second says that if $P \,\&\, Q$ holds in s, then the utility of s is defeasibly the utility of a state in which just $P \,\&\, Q$ contribute to the utility valuation. It is defeated if

(i) $P \,\&\, Q \,\&\, R$ are known to hold in s,

(ii) we can compute $uconst(P \,\&\, Q \,\&\, R)$, and

(iii) $uconst(P \,\&\, Q \,\&\, R)$ differs from $uconst(P \,\&\, Q)$.

Example. Suppose $holds(P_1 \ \& \ P_2 \ \& \ P_5, s_0)$. What is the utility of s_0? There are several competing arguments, three of which are (see also Figure 1):

A_1:

1. $uconst(P_1 \ \& \ P_2) = 3$

2. $\ulcorner holds(P_1 \ \& \ P_2, s) \ \& \ uconst(P_1 \ \& \ P_2) = 3 \urcorner \ >\!\!- \ \ulcorner u(s) = 3 \urcorner$

3. $holds(P_1 \ \& \ P_2, s_0)$

4. therefore, $u(s_0) = 3$.

A_2:

1. $uconst(P_1) = 12 \ \& \ uconst(P_2) = 20$

2. $\ulcorner uconst(P_1) = x \ \& \ uconst(P_2) = y \urcorner \ >\!\!- \ \ulcorner uconst(P_1 \ \& \ P_2) = x + y \urcorner$

3. therefore, $uconst(P_1 \ \& \ P_2) = 32$

4. $uconst(P_5) = 14$

5. $\ulcorner uconst(P_1 \ \& \ P_2) = x \ \& \ uconst(P_5) = y \urcorner \ >\!\!- \ \ulcorner uconst(P_1 \ \& \ P_2 \ \& \ P_5) = x + y \urcorner$

6. therefore $uconst(P_1 \ \& \ P_2 \ \& \ P_5) = 46$

7. $\ulcorner holds(P_1 \ \& \ P_2 \ \& \ P_5, s) \ \& \ uconst(P_1 \ \& \ P_2 \ \& \ P_5) = 46 \urcorner \ >\!\!- \ \ulcorner u(s) = 46 \urcorner$

8. $holds(P_1 \ \& \ P_2 \ \& \ P_5, s_0)$

9. therefore $u(s_0) = 46$.

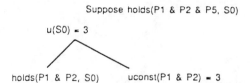

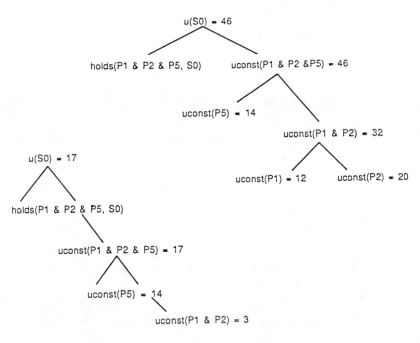

Figure 1

A_3:

1. $uconst(P_1 \ \& \ P_2) = 3 \ \& \ uconst(P_5) = 14$

2. $\ulcorner uconst(P_1 \ \& \ P_2) = x \ \& \ uconst(P_5) = y \urcorner \succ\!\!-\ \ulcorner uconst(P_1 \ \& \ P_2 \ \& \ P_5) = x + y \urcorner$

3. therefore $uconst(P_1 \ \& \ P_2 \ \& \ P_5) = 17$

4. $\ulcorner holds(P_1 \ \& \ P_2 \ \& \ P_5, s) \ \& \ uconst(P_1 \ \& \ P_2 \ \& \ P_5) = 17 \urcorner \succ\!\!-\ \ulcorner u(s) = 17 \urcorner$

5. $holds(P_1 \ \& \ P_2 \ \& \ P_5, s_0)$

6. therefore $u(s_0) = 17$.

Argument A_3 defeats both A_1 and A_2. A_3 defeats A_1 because its rule $A_3{<}4{>}$ is more specific than the rule $A_1{<}2{>}$. A_3 also uses more evidence than A_1. A_3 defeats A_2 because its conclusion $A_3{<}1{>}$ is more directly related to evidence than the conflicting conclusion $A_2{<}3{>}$. More simply, $A_1{<}1{>}$ is indefeasible while $A_2{<}3{>}$ is defeasible, so the former prevails.

Thus, on my account of how conflicting defeasible arguments interact, A_3 dominates A_1 and A_2; A_3's conclusion is apparently justified, and apparently $u(s_0) = 17$.

The beauty of this approach, which I will elaborate below, is that I have not said what other relevant properties might hold of s_0. If P_3 is considered next, and found to hold of s_0, a different calculation might be in order. Nevertheless, until that calculation is performed, found to conflict with and thus supercede the current calculation, decision analysis can identify the optimal act under the provisional value of $u(s_0) = 17$. The beauty is that we can always do a quick calculation with the best information at hand.

2.2 Normative and Conventional Rules

So far I have not touched on the idea of expected utility for the valuation of lotteries. Expected utility calculations have been presumed so far. The utility of a state, s_0, which has an undetermined event E, has utility

$$prob(E \mid s_0) \, u(s_0 \ \& \ E) + prob(\neg E \mid s_0) \, u(s_0 \ \& \ \neg E),$$

when the respective probabilities and utilities of E in s_0 and $\neg E$ in s are known. As calculations of $u(s_0 \& E)$ and $u(s_0 \& \neg E)$ are defeated by better reasoning, based on more specific evidence as above, so too is the calculation of s_0's expected utility improved.

There are also deep reasons why expected utility calculations need not be preserved.

The structural regularities expressed by defeasible additivity of attributes is not supposed to be a norm or obligation imposed by rationality. It is supposed to have descriptive validity. Or it is supposed to be an arbitrary convention adopted by the specifier of utilities for the sake of convenience, as a shorthand. In contrast, expected utility is supposed to be a norm. However, there are philosophical reasons why the distinction between norm and linguistic convention is untenable (consider, *e.g.*, [Quine53]).

So we might take the expected utility rule for utilities of lotteries to be defeasible:

$$\ulcorner u(s(E)) = x \;\&\; u(s(\neg E)) = y \;\&$$

$$s = \{\, s(E) \,/\, prob(E); \; s(\neg E) \,/\, prob(\neg E) \,\}\urcorner \;\succ\!\!- \; \ulcorner u(s) = prob(E)$$
$$x + prob(\neg E)\, y \urcorner.$$

This introduces some ambiguity, however. Sometimes $u(s_0)$ will be calculated by summing contributions of its attributes; sometimes it will be calculated by taking an expectation. There will have to be some way of indicating when one calculation defeats the other.

3   Advantages

3.1   Tractable Specification

The representation presumes that there is structure to utility assignments. I exhibited an additive model; it could as easily have been multiplicative. Defeasibility contributes to easy specification only inasmuch as it allows nearly universal structure to be used in the specification of utility, with exceptions, and exceptions to exceptions, stated inexpensively.

Both classical decision theory and the present view allow the energetic knowledge engineer to specify the utility of each and every state. Of course, that never happens. For state spaces as large as we want planners to consider, assuming structure is the only practical course. Increasing the ability to do utility calculation decreases the need for explicit specification.

Taking the expected utility rule to be defeasible also permits recovery from incoherence, *i.e.*, from violations of the classical axioms for preference. If we assert that

$$u(s(E)) = 10, u(s(\neg E)) = 0, prob(E) = .5, \text{ and}$$

$$u(\{ s(E) \ / \ .5; s(\neg E) \ / \ .5 \}) = 6,$$

this is a violation of the expected utility rule, since $.5(10) + 0 = 5$ is not 6. We can simply claim that we do not accept the classical axioms for this particular calculation and take the value to be 6. This is more of philosophical than practical interest: we will generally want our systems to conform to the classical axioms; we will want to add structure to our existing conception of preference, not delete from it. Moreover, if we want to deviate from the classical axioms, there are better ways of doing so (*e.g.*, using alternative axioms, or formalizing the effects noted by psychologists).

3.2 Flexible Procedure

The major advantage of the representation is that it permits flexibility in the formulation of decision problems.

Refinement on Demand. The logic of defeasible reasoning permits problem refinements to supercede original formulations. We may start with a very small world, in Savage's sense, in our evaluation of outcome states in our decision tree. For example, of relevant properties $P_1, \ldots, P_n$, we might evaluate each state using just the contribution of P_1.

If time permits a more detailed analysis, the world can be enlarged so that both P_1 and P_2 are relevant to the description of states, *i.e.*, are used in the valuation of states. Figure 2 shows the valuation of states based first on P_1, then on P_1, P_2, for $uconst(P_1) = 5$ and $uconst(P_2) = 3$.

Refinement need not be done uniformly. In Figure 2, $u(s(1, E))$ can be evaluated on P_1, P_2 while $u(s(2, \neg E))$ continues to be evaluated on P_1. This leads to unorderability of some competing utility calculations. Let $prob(E) = .5$. Then

$$u(a_1 \mid s_0) = .5(8) + .5(0) = 4;$$

$$u(a_2 \mid s_0) = .5(5) + .5(0) = 2.5.$$

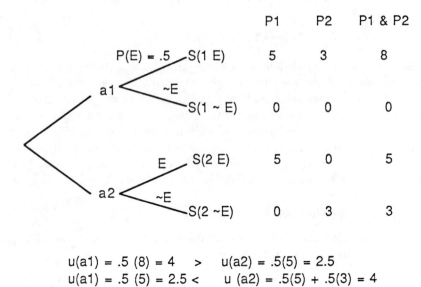

$$u(a1) = .5 \ (8) = 4 \quad > \quad u(a2) = .5(5) = 2.5$$
$$u(a1) = .5 \ (5) = 2.5 \ < \quad u \ (a2) = .5(5) + .5(3) = 4$$

Figure 2

So apparently $a_1 \succ a_2$. On a different non-uniform refinement, evaluate $u(s(1, E))$ on P_1 and $u(s(2, \neg E))$ on P_1, P_2. Then

$$u(a_1 \mid s_0) = .5(5) + .5(0) = 2.5;$$

$$u(a_2 \mid s_0) = .5(5) + .5(3) = 4.$$

So apparently $a_2 \succ a_1$. This conflict is settled by moving to a calculation more refined than each of the previous two. Of course, we try not to evaluate decisions on insufficiently fine granularities, but we acknowledge that we cannot always commit resources to the analysis at maximally fine granularity; instead, we iteratively improve our reasoning about utilities of states and actions.

A different non-comparability arises when one reasons uniformly with the world P_1, P_2, first, then uniformly with the world P_1, P_3. Any disagreement could be resolved with the common refinement, P_1, P_2, P_3.

Bounding on Demand. The ability to calculate *prima facie* utilities of non-terminal states allows decision trees to be bounded at any leaf, to be defoliated. In the decision tree above, I took $s(1, E)$ to be an outcome state, though perhaps some event F was undecided in $s(1, E)$, and F is relevant to valuation of states, *i.e.*,

$$\neg \left(u(s(1, E \,\&\, F)) = u(s(1, E \,\&\, \neg F)) \right).$$

If this is true, technically $s(1, E)$ is not a *state*, but is instead a *lottery*,

$$\{ s(1, E \,\&\, F) \mathbin{/} prob(E \,\&\, F); s(1, E \,\&\, \neg F) \mathbin{/} prob(E \,\&\, \neg F) \}$$

whose utility is given by the appropriate expectation. However, we often want to calculate $u(s(1, E))$ as if it were a terminal state, purposefully ignoring for the moment the ramifications of F versus $\neg F$. We do this defeasibly, too; expected utility calculations that explore the ramifications of F supercede the defeasible attribute-adding calculation that was done while pretending $s(1, E)$ was a terminal state. This shortcut is especially convenient when $prob(E \,\&\, F)$ is unavailable for some reason, *e.g.*, expense of calculation. It is especially plausible when attributes used in the non-probabilistic evaluation of $u(s(1, E))$ include the fact that "significant-chance-of-F" holds in $s(1, E)$.

This allows us to bound a decision tree wherever desired.

As with abstraction, bounding can be done non-uniformly and arbitrarily; there is no reason for all paths from root to leaf to have the same length.
Again, there can be non-comparability: when trees bound in different places
mandate different decisions, it cannot in general be said which provides the
better mandate. Disagreement is resolved by taking a common more extensive tree.

4   Future Directions

I have proposed a computationally attractive methodology for representing
and manipulating decision trees on spaces large enough to support non-
trivial planning. It can be based on any of a number of non-monotonic
reasoners that have specificity defeaters, and it requires only two axiom
schemata. The explored advantages were

1. practical specification of utilities;

2. abstraction on demand; and

3. bounding on demand.

With a little imagination, it should be possible to formalize heuristics in this
representation for bounding low-risk paths and guessing which attributes are
most significant in determining utility.

   This proposal is not related to the satisficing idea of Simon [Simon69], or
the keep-things-simple idea of Harman [Harman86]. Ideas from each should
lead to improvements of this proposal. It should also be possible to give a
qualitative version of defeasible calculation of preference. And it should be
possible to reason defeasibly about probabilities and utilities simultaneously.

   This proposal does avoid the meta-decision regress of deciding how much
resource should optimally be committed to the formulation and analysis of
a decison problem. Reasoning is simply completed at any level, then iteratively improved with superior reasoning — based on superior refinement and
decision tree exfoliation. If the agent starts with an unreasoned inclination
toward some act, then if *no* reasoning, however shallow, is completed by
decision time, to defeat this inclination, there is at least an answer to the
question of what to do.

Acknowledgement.   This work was completed while on a postdoctoral
fellowship in cognitive science at Stanford University. Thanks are due the

Center for The Study of Language and Information and SRI International, for sharing their resources, and the Department of Computer Science for hosting me; I especially thank David Israel, Paul Rosenbloom and the cognitive science committee, Matt Ginsberg, and Yoav Shoham.

5   Bibliography

Charniak, E. and McDermott, D. *Introduction to AI*, Addison-Wesley, 1984.

Harman, G. *Change in View*, MIT Press, 1986.

Jeffrey, R. *The Logic of Decision*, Chicago University Press, 1965.

Loui, R. "A system of defeasible inference," *Computational Intelligence 3*, 3, 1987.

Quine, W. V. O. *From a Logical Point of View*, Harvard, 1953.

Savage, L. *The Foundations of Statistics*, Dover, 1954.

Simon, H. *The Sciences of the Artificial*, MIT Press, 1969.

1131303
Introduction to A Logic of Assertions

Robin Giles 3-QEN   CR

1 Two Limitations of Classical Logic

In respect of its application to statements describing beliefs about the real world the value of classical logic is limited in two respects.

First, classical logic can deal only with statements which are "sentences" in a particularly narrow sense: not only must a sentence have, under any given conditions, a *truth value*, TRUE or FALSE, but its whole meaning must be given by prescribing the conditions, *i.e.*, the "states of the world" under which it is true. Thus a classical sentence, *i.e.*, a sentence in the sense of classical logic, is in principle completely described by giving its *truth function*, a function on the set Ω of all *states of the world*, taking values in the 2-element set $\{0, 1\}$, or equivalently $\{$FALSE, TRUE$\}$, of truth values.

Now, it is clear that a typical natural language statement is not of this type. Take, for instance, the standard example, *John is tall*. If this were a sentence of classical logic, then it would have a truth function, f say, presumably a function of the height h of John,[1] of the form shown in Figure 1. There is some particular height, say 5'11", at which the truth value changes instantly from 0 to 1. But this means there is a dramatic difference between an agent's assertions of this sentence when John is very slightly shorter than 5'11" and when he is very slightly taller. It is obvious that in real life this is not the case: in fact, there is no point at which a very small change in height would produce a large change in the acceptability of the assertion. This shows that if the statement *John is tall* has a "truth function" f at all it must be a continuous function of the height h of John. So, since all heights are possible and heights form a continuum, the set of truth values cannot be $\{0, 1\}$ but must be a connected set. It could, for instance, be the interval $[0, 1]$ with the truth function given by a graph such as in Figure 2. The ordinate $f(h)$ corresponding to a height h is a number

---

[1] We assume for simplicity that John belongs to a homogeneous population of adult humans. If this is not so — if John may be a horse or a child or a it pygmy, for instance — then the truth function still exists but the truth value is no longer a function of the height of John alone.

H.E. Kyburg, Jr. et al. (eds.), *Knowledge Representation and Defeasible Reasoning*, 361–385.
© 1990 *Kluwer Academic Publishers. Printed in the Netherlands.*

in the interval [0, 1] which may be referred to as the *degree of truth* of the statement. A statement like this, which cannot be accepted as a classical sentence but whose meaning can perhaps be represented in this way, is called a *fuzzy sentence*. In contrast, a sentence in the sense of classical logic is referred to as a *crisp sentence*.

On reflection, one sees that the sentence "*John is tall*" is not exceptional: almost all statements occuring in natural language are unacceptable as classical sentences but could be admitted as fuzzy sentences in the above sense; some examples are: "*That was a good dinner*", "*The toast is burnt*", "*Mary is careless*". Even statements such as "*John is a Welshman*" or "*Mary was born in 1948*", that appear to be classical sentences at first sight, can be seen on closer inspection to admit "borderline cases" in which the truth value is moot.

The above argument shows clearly the inadequacy of classical logic as a tool for coping with natural language statements, and it forms the basis for the currently popular "fuzzy set theory" approach to reasoning under uncertainty. However, although the argument suggests the introduction of a continuum of truth values and in particular the use of the interval [0, 1], it provides no justification for this procedure. More important, because it assigns no *meaning* to the concept of *degree of truth* it is not possible to determine how *reasoning* should proceed in such a system. So the argument is not sufficient: it shows the need for a logic that in some way can represent a "continuum of truth values" but it falls short of providing a foundation for such a logic.

The second, and quite distinct, way in which classical logic is inadequate as a tool for handling natural language statements is that it lacks any built-in procedure for expressing *degrees of belief.* It is true that Bayesian methods (expressing beliefs by giving subjective probabilities) can be used for the expression of degrees of belief which are exact in this sense, but they cannot be used in the case of uncertainty — in situations where an agent is not willing to assign any exact probability to the sentence in question. Moreover, the Bayesian approach is simply not applicable when the beliefs in question relate to fuzzy sentences, since there is then no "event" to which the notion of probability can be applied.

The problem, then, is to construct a formal logic, and of course a corresponding formal language, that will overcome these two deficiencies of classical logic. Now, we already have an informal language in which the deficiencies are overcome — namely, natural language itself. In spite of its ambiguities and lack of clarity natural language certainly provides facilities

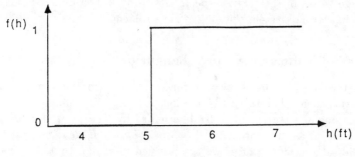

Figure 1

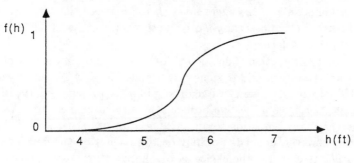

Figure 2

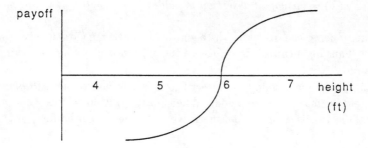

Figure 3

for formulating fuzzy sentences and expressing degrees of belief. In attacking the problem, then, it is natural that we should first try to see how natural language works in these two respects. By using it as a guide we may hope to reach a formal system that solves our problem.

2 Payoff Values in Natural Language

Let us try to find a precise way to represent the *meaning* of a natural language statement. Following the method of pragmatism [James07], we take the meaning of a statement to be determined by *the way it is used*. For example, insofar as the sentences "*It is raining*" and "*Il pleut*" are used under just the same circumstances we are justified in saying that they have the same meaning.

Now, a use of a sentence is an assertion, so we are faced with the question, How does an agent decide whether or not to assert a given sentence? Well, an assertion is an act; the agent must choose between the acts of *asserting the sentence* and *not asserting the sentence*. So the question falls within the scope of *decision theory*.

The best formulation of decision theory, particularly in the case of vagueness or uncertainty, is still to some extent under debate. The most generally accepted treatment — which we shall adopt for the present — is the Bayesian approach, based on subjective probability and expected utility. According to this view[2] any act leads to an outcome that has a certain *utility*. The outcome, however, depends not only on the act but on the current *state of the world*. As a result, the choice as to whether to make an assertion a or not is determined by the *payoff function* $a(\omega)$ of the agent where, for any world state ω,

$$a(\omega) = (payoff\ if\ assertion\ is\ made) \ - \ (payoff\ if\ it\ is\ not\ made),$$

the *payoff* being the utility to the agent of the outcome (for the given world state). Thus $a(\omega)$ can be described as the gain in utility due to making the assertion.

The payoff may usefully be described as a measure of the *willingness* of the agent to make the assertion. When positive, it constitutes his *motive* for making the assertion; when negative, it is the reason he does not make it.

---

[2]See, for instance, [Luce&Raiffa57].

According to this analysis it is the payoff function that determines when an assertion is made. So the payoff function can be taken as representative of the meaning of the assertion.

As an example, consider the statement *"John is tall"*. To identify the payoff we ask, what is the motive that causes an agent to assert this sentence? In a few cases, for instance if the agent is John's father and John is a candidate for a basketball team, the motive may be the desire to convince the listener of the truth of the statement — if the listener is convinced then the agent profits. But usually the agent has no personal stake in the statement and the motive is simply the satisfaction arising from the approval that, in normal society, is accorded to him who makes an assertion that later proves to be justified; similarly the normal reason for *not* making a statement is the hope of avoiding the disappointment that for a normal person accompanies the loss in prestige which eventually results from the making of a misleading assertion. Thus it is not simply the form of words used but the reaction of society to the assertion that in the end is responsible for the form of the payoff function and so for the meaning of the assertion.

From this it follows that the payoff function for a given assertion depends, for normal people, only on the assertion and not on the individual asserting it. In other words, we may assume that all (normal) agents agree as regards the payoff function associated with any given assertion. This is an exact analogue of the presumption in the case of classical logic that all agents are agreed on the truth function corresponding to any (classical) sentence. In both cases the assumption represents the supposition that all agents "speak the same language", in that they all attach the same meaning to any given sentence.

Of course, to arrive at the representation of meaning by a payoff function we must assume that any agent we consider is "normal" in that he gets pleasure from society's approval and disappointment from its disapproval. Clearly, some agents are not "normal" in this sense: idiots, liars, and pranksters are examples. They get their satisfaction from other sources than the approval of society, and the payoff function for an assertion in the case of such an agent may be quite different from the norm. In the following we assume that every agent is "normal" in the sense explained.

In the case of the statement *"John is tall"* the general nature of the payoff function is easy to see: if John is definitely tall, say he measures 6'6", then the payoff is positive and large; if he is far from tall, say 4'6", then it will be large negative; and in general it is an increasing function of the height of John, see Figure 3.

We see that the graph of the payoff function is qualitatively similar to that of a "continuous truth function", assuming we interpret large-negative and large-positive as equivalent to false and true respectively.

For clarity, an explanatory remark should be made in connection with Figure 3. As was noted above, the payoff is really a function of the whole world state. The graph shown in the figure applies only if we take it for granted that John is a normal male adult. If it is possible that John is something else, say a child or a horse, then the payoff will no longer be simply a function of John's height but rather of his height relative to the norm for beings of his type.

Notice that if the assertion "*John is tall*" is made *emphatically* then both the satisfaction if it turns out that he is tall and the disappointment if he isn't will be increased. Thus the payoff function for the assertion made with emphasis is like the original payoff function but "scaled up": *i.e.*, with all ordinates multiplied by some factor greater than 1. Thus the representation of meaning by a payoff function is able to take account of emphasis. Insofar as a change in emphasis may be regarded as producing a different assertion of the same sentence, this means that what we are developing here is really a logic of assertions rather than of sentences.

As we have seen, for any given assertion the payoff function is the same for every agent and represents the meaning (determined by society) of the assertion. In this respect the payoff function behaves like the truth function of a sentence in classical logic. To see that this is more than an analogy let us define a *crisp assertion* to be an assertion a whose payoff function takes at most two values; and call it (λ, μ)-*normalized* if these values are λ and μ ($\lambda < \mu$). Then to every (λ, μ)-normalized crisp assertion a there corresponds a unique classical sentence $\theta(a)$ which is true in the world states ω where $a(\omega) = \mu$ and false in those where $a(\omega) = \lambda$. Moreover, for each pair $\{\lambda, \mu\}$ with $\lambda < \mu$ the mapping θ defines a one to one correspondence from the (λ, μ)-normalized crisp assertions onto the sentences of classical logic.

The above considerations suggest that we can pass from classical logic to a *logic of assertions* by making the replacements:

$$sentence \longrightarrow assertion \text{ (an act)}$$

$$truth\ value \longrightarrow payoff\ value \text{ (a utility)}$$

In the following we'll develop a logic based on these replacements. Let's first consider the effect on *connectives*.

3 Connectives in The Logic of Assertions

In propositional classical logic we have the familiar conectives ¬ (not), ∧ (and), ∨ (or), → (implies), ↔ (is equivalent to). The first is a *unary* connective, a mapping from S into S, where S is the set of all sentences; the others are *binary*, mappings from $S^{\in}$ to S. In addition, the constant sentences T (always true) and F (always false) may be reckoned as 0-ary connectives. Each n-ary connective $\star$ is associated with an n-ary function $\tilde{\star}$ in the set of truth values $\{0, 1\}$, *i.e.*, a function on $\{0, 1\}^n$ to $\{0, 1\}$, the truth value of a composite sentence formed with this connective being obtained from those of its components by applying the function $\tilde{\star}$ to the truth values of the components. In other words, the truth *function* of the composite sentence is obtained from the truth functions of its components by applying the function $\tilde{\star}$ "pointwise on Ω". For example, for any sentences a and b,

$$(\neg a)(\omega) = \tilde{\neg}(a(\omega)),$$

$$(a \wedge b)(\omega) = (a(\omega)) \tilde{\wedge} (b(\omega)),$$

for every world state ω. The functions $\tilde{\neg}$, $\tilde{\wedge}$, ... are given, usually via "truth tables", by the equations,

$$\tilde{\neg}(v) = 1 - v,$$

$$v \tilde{\wedge} w = \begin{cases} 1 & \textit{if } v = w = 1 \\ 0 & \textit{otherwise} \end{cases}$$

and so on, where v and w denote arbitrary truth values in $\{0, 1\}$.

Mathematically, each connective $\tilde{\star}$ is defined by giving the corresponding function $\tilde{\star}$. So there are four unary connectives, sixteen binary connectives, 256 ternary connectives, and so on; but they can all be expressed in terms of a chosen few "basic connectives". The choice of basic connectives can be made in many ways. Usually, some of the connectives, ¬ (NOT), ∧ (AND), ∨ (OR), → (IMPLIES), ↔ (IS EQUIVALENT TO), are chosen, not for any special mathematical reasons but just because simple sentences formed with these connectives correspond approximately to certain common natural language statements. This correspondence — which is rather poor and should never be regarded as *defining* the connectives — is indicated by the familiar association of the connectives with the words, "not", "and", "or", *etc.*

Now let us consider the possibilities for connectives in the logic of assertions. Since the analogue of a truth value in the logic of assertions is a utility value, *i.e.*, a real number, one might imagine at first sight that there would be an *n*-ary connective corresponding to every function on $\Re^n$ to $\Re^3$ However, like length or mass, measurements of utility gain are arbitrary up to a scale factor (choice of unit of utility) and this restricts the functions that can be admitted. Suppose, for example, that $\star$ is a binary connective arising from a binary function $\tilde{\star}$ in $\Re$. For any assertions *a* and *b* the assertion *a⋆b* should, of course, be completely determined by the assertions *a* and *b*. Certainly it should not be altered by a change in the unit of utility. Now, if (for some world state ω) the payoffs for *a* and *b* are *u* and *v* then *a⋆b* has the payoff $w = u\tilde{\star}v$. But if we carried out the calculation using a different utility scale in which all utilities are multiplied by λ ($\lambda > 0$) then we would compute *for a⋆b* the utility $(\lambda u)\tilde{\star}(\lambda v)$. Since this must be equal to λw, the function $\tilde{\star}$ must satisfy:

$$(1) \quad (\lambda u)\tilde{\star}(\lambda v) = \lambda(u\tilde{\star}v),$$

for all numbers *u* and *v* and all $\lambda > 0$. Similarly, we can show that if $\star$ is any unary connective arising from a unary function $\tilde{\star}$ in $\Re$ then

$$(2) \quad \tilde{\star}(\lambda u) = \lambda\tilde{\star}(u),$$

for all *u* and all $\lambda > 0$. Similarly for 0-ary connectives, *i.e.*, constant-valued assertions: in classical logic there are two, *T* and *F*; in the logic of assertions any admissible constant must be invariant under change of utility scale, so there is only one: the function **0** given by $\mathbf{0}(\omega) = 0$ for every state ω.

We shall call a function $\tilde{\star}$ with the properties (1) or (2) *admissible*.[4] Some functions in $\Re$ are clearly inadmissible: for instance, the unary function *square*, given by $\tilde{\star}(u) = u^2$, and the binary function, *product*, given by $u\tilde{\star}v = uv$. But many simple unary and binary functions in $\Re$ are admissible. Some examples are:

Scaling:	$\tilde{\star}(u) = ku$ $(k > 0)$,
Negative:	$\tilde{\star}(u) = -u$,
Plus:	$u\tilde{\star}v = u+v$,
Minus:	$u\tilde{\star}v = u-v$,
Maximum:	$u\tilde{\star}v = u \vee v = max(u, v)$,
Minimum:	$u\tilde{\star}v = u \wedge v = min(u, v)$.

---

[3]$\Re$ denotes the set of all real numbers.

[4]In elementary algebra such a function is said to be "positive homogeneous of degree 1".

We shall call these six[5] functions, together with the "0-ary function" $\mathcal{O}$, *basic functions*, and the connectives to which they give rise *basic connectives*. Of the basic connectives the first five are the *linear connectives* and the last two, maximum and minimum, the *lattice connectives*. Of course, the basic functions are not all independent. For instance, *minus* and *minimum* can be expressed in terms of the other four basic functions: $u-v = u+(-v)$, $u \wedge v = -(-u \vee -v)$.

What other admissible functions are there? Well, any function that can be expressed (by means of composition) in terms of basic functions is also admissible. For instance *modulus*, $|u| = u \vee (-u)$, is admissible, and so is any linear combination $ku + k'v$ (where k and k' are any real numbers). This raises the question, Can every admissible function be expressed in terms of basic functions? This is essentially the question of the *truth-functional completeness* of the logic.

In the case of classical logic every function on $\{0, 1\}^n$ to $\{0, 1\}$ determines a connective. Thus all these functions (for every n) are admissible, and, as was noted above (see, for instance, [Rescher69; pp. 62–66]), every connective can be expressed in terms of (suitably chosen) basic connectives. So the answer to the question in the classical case is "yes".

It turns out that in the logic of assertions the answer is again essentially "yes". To express this precisely take the case $n = 2$. One can show, by an application of the Stone-Weierstrass theorem [Dunford&Schwartz58], that if $\tilde{\star}\colon \Re^2 \to \Re$ is any binary admissible function then, given any positive number ϵ, no matter how small, and any number N no matter how large, there is a function $\tilde{o}\colon \Re \to \Re$, built by composition from basic functions, that agrees with $\tilde{\star}$ to within ϵ at all points distant no more than N from the origin in $\Re^2$: *i.e.*, $|u\tilde{\star}v - u\tilde{o}v| < \epsilon$ whenever $\sqrt{u^2 + v^2} < N$. Since the number of admissible functions is uncountable but only a countable number of functions can be built from the basic functions, and since the discrepancy $|u\tilde{\star}v - u\tilde{o}v|$ is positive homogeneous as a function of u and v, it is clear that this is the strongest result that could be hoped for.

4   Classification of States of Belief

As we have seen, there are an infinite number of connectives in the logic of assertions, each being represented by some, generally unary or binary, real-valued function. Among them the ones we have distinguished as "basic"

---

[5] For simplicity, we shall regard the function, *scaling*, as a single function, although it is really a different function for each value of k.

are singled out only by the simplicity of their functional representation. Although this appears at first to be a purely mathematical property, the fact that the truth values of assertions are utility values, and so play a vital role in determining the conditions under which the assertions would be made, indicates that mathematical simplicity is likely to correspond to simplicity of meaning. This suggests that one should examine the interpretation of simple formal assertions in order to understand the meanings they carry.

Before we can proceed with this task, however, we must consider how an agent, given a payoff function, decides whether to make the corresponding assertion. We assume, of course, that the agent is "rational" in some sense. In particular, his decision whether to make an assertion or not is determined by the interpretation of the values of the payoff function as utilities.

One extreme case (case of perfect information) is easily dealt with: suppose the agent thinks he is omniscient in that he (thinks he) knows, the exact value ω of the present world state. Then, since utility is a measure of preference, he will certainly make the assertion a if $a(\omega) > 0$, and he will certainly not make it if $a(\omega) < 0$. We shall refer to such an agent as a *confident classical agent*, and to ω as *the corresponding world state*. The term "confident" is necessary since we shall introduce *uncertain* classical agents below; and the term "classical" is used since in the domain of crisp assertions, the beliefs of this type of agent can be directly represented by means of classical logic. Indeed, classical logic operates under the presumption that every sentence is either true or false, which corresponds in this domain with the beliefs of a confident classical agent.

It is clear that in real life no agent is, or even thinks he is, omniscient. Consider, then, an agent who recognizes that he has only an imperfect idea of what the world state is. To him, provided he is rational, but regardless of his beliefs, an assertion a will certainly be *acceptable*, in the sense that he is willing to make the assertion, if it happens that $a(\omega) > 0$ for all ω; and it will certainly not be acceptable if $a(\omega) < 0$ for all ω. Whether it is acceptable or not in other cases depends on the agent's *state of belief*: *i.e.*, on exactly what information he (thinks he) has concerning the actual state of the world.

At this point we have to take some position regarding the kinds of "uncertain belief" we are prepared to consider as rational. Two kinds are already relatively familiar: the first, and most well known, is met in the Bayesian approach to decision theory. There the state of belief of any rational agent is represented by an exactly specified (subjective) probability distribution μ over the set Ω of all world states. According to the accepted theory, the agent's choice between available acts is determined by their expected payoffs with respect to this probability distribution. In particular, he will make an assertion a iff (= if and only if) the expected payoff $\int_\Omega a d\mu$, which we shall with a slight abuse of notation denote $\mu(a)$, is ≥ 0. We will refer to an agent whose behaviour can be explained in this way as a confident Bayesian agent. The term "confident" is in contrast to "uncertain", introduced below; the term "Bayesian" reflects the representation of belief in terms of subjective probability.

The second kind of uncertain belief is unrelated to probability. Consider an agent who believes that the actual world state is a member of a certain subset Δ of the set Ω of all world states, but has no idea which state in Δ it is. Then if (as we will assume) the agent takes a conservative view, he will consider an assertion a acceptable iff $a(\omega) \geq 0$ for all ω in Δ, for only in this case will he be sure of not losing in making the assertion. We shall see below that — at least in the case of crisp assertions — a belief of this sort can still be handled by means of classical logic. For this reason we shall refer to an agent with this kind of belief as an *uncertain classical agent*. Such an agent behaves as though he has a team of advisors who are classical agents, one corresponding to each point in Δ, and he makes an assertion if and only if it is approved by every one of his advisors.

A confident classical agent is a particular case of a confident Bayesian agent, the case where the probability is a *point probability distribution*: *i.e.*, one which is concentrated on a single point. A confident classical agent is also a special case of an uncertain classical agent, that in which the set Δ is a singleton. Thus confident Bayesian agents and uncertain classical agents are generalizations in different directions of confident classical agents. It is natural to seek a common generalization of which these are particular cases. This is given by the concept of an uncertain Bayesian agent: By an *uncertain Bayesian agent* we mean an agent who conforms to the Bayesian philosophy, but is unable to decide exactly what probability distribution over Ω he should use to represent his beliefs. Any such agent A may be represented by a set of "possible probability distributions", *i.e.*, by a subset K_A of the set Σ of all probability distributions over Ω. As in the classical case, we shall assume that an uncertain Bayesian agent A behaves conservatively: he will make an assertion a only if the expected payoff is nonnegative for every probability distribution in K_A. An uncertain Bayesian agent thus behaves as though he had a team of confident Bayesian advisors: he makes an assertion if and only if all his advisors recommend it. This picture is very convenient as a way of establishing the properties of an arbitrary uncertain

Bayesian agent. Of course, a confident Bayesian agent is a special case of an uncertain Bayesian agent, that in which the set K is a singleton. Similarly, an uncertain classical agent is a special case of a uncertain Bayesian agent, that in which K is composed entirely of point probability distributions.

We shall not consider any states of belief more general than that exhibited by an uncertain Bayesian agent. This restriction may seem at present to be somewhat *ad hoc*. However, as we shall see in §6, there are good reasons for it. In fact, it can be shown to follow from rather weak *axioms of rationality*, quite independent of the notion of probability, that every rational agent is an uncertain Bayesian agent. In the generalized utility theory developed in [Giles] still weaker axioms of rationality are imposed, with the result that richer states of belief can be discussed without their being considered irrational. These generalizations lead to a more powerful language of assertions. However, for the present we will for simplicity employ only the standard theory.

In establishing results in the following, we therefore assume an arbitrary agent to be an uncertain Bayesian, and we normally make use of the picture of such an agent as reacting to the opinions of a team of confident Bayesian advisors. In this way our conclusions can be deduced from the relatively familiar behaviour of a confident Bayesian agent.

5   Interpreting The Connectives

We are now in a position to discuss the meaning of the connectives, *i.e.*, the way in which the conditions of assertability of a compound assertion are related to those of its components. Note that it is not a question of *assigning* meanings to these assertions: the meanings are already there, determined operationally via decision theory by the interpretation of the payoff values as utilities. This interpretation determines how an assertion employing the connectives is used (by a rational agent) in any given circumstances. The meaning in natural language terms of the assertion is then revealed if we can discover a natural language statement which would be used in the same way.

For the discussion, let Ω be an arbitrary set of *world states*, and let L be a language of assertions on Ω, by which we mean a set of real-valued functions on Ω, closed under the action of the basic connectives. The elements of L are *assertions*, or the *payoff functions* of assertions — for the purposes of this section it is convenient to identify an assertion with its payoff function. In the mathematical theory it is assumed for simplicity that each element of L is a *bounded* function on Ω (but it is not assumed, of course, that every bounded function belongs to L). A topology is assigned to Ω and certain "ideal points" are adjoined, to give a compact space $\tilde{\Omega}$ on which the elements of L are represented as continuous functions. The "probability measures on Ω" referred to in the present account are really probability measures on the Baire sets of $\tilde{\Omega}$. To improve the readability of the present account these and other mathematical details have been suppressed.

Let us first consider the unary connective $-$ (negative). Clearly for a confident Bayesian agent the expected payoff for $-a$, where a is any assertion, is given by $\mu(-a) = -\mu(a)$. Consequently the agent will always be willing to assert either a or $-a$, but never both except in the special case when $\mu(a) = \mu(-a) = 0$ meaning that both a and $-a$ are marginally assertable. This suggests that the connective, negative, corresponds roughly to the negation of classical logic and common language. This impression is supported by the fact that $-(-a) = a$ This equation simply means that the two sides have the same payoff function. We will see more evidence supporting the correspondence between negative and negation below. But see [Giles88] for an example showing that common language negation does not always correspond to the connective, $-$. Of course, in the case of an uncertain Bayesian agent it may happen that, for an assertion a, neither a nor $-a$ is acceptable. This is nothing new: indeed, the same applies in the case of an uncertain agent in classical logic (see §6).

Next consider the unary connective k, where k is an arbitrary positive number. We have already seen that multiplication by k changes only the *emphasis* associated with an assertion. Now, if a is any assertion then ka is acceptable to a confident Bayesian agent if and only if a is acceptable, for $\mu(ka) = k\mu(a)$ for every probability measure μ. But it should not be inferred that ka and a are equivalent insofar as their interpretation is concerned. Indeed, the payoff for ka is k times the payoff for a, so that (if $k > 1$) ka is in a sense "more acceptable" than a. To give this statement more substance let us call $\mu(a)$ the (degree of) *acceptability* to the agent of the assertion a, and denote it also $\alpha(a)$. Unlike the situation in classical logic, where a sentence is simply true or false, in the logic of assertions an assertion has, to a confident Bayesian agent, a definite *degree* of acceptability; it is *acceptable* if this degree is ≥ 0 and *unacceptable* otherwise.

Although this notion of acceptability is introduced at first only for confident Bayesian agents, it can be extended also to an uncertain Bayesian agent A by defining the acceptability to A of an assertion to be the minimum (more strictly the *infimum*) of the acceptabilities assigned to it by his confident Bayesian advisors. An assertion is then acceptable to A precisely iff its acceptability is ≥ 0. Note that this accords with our understanding that an assertion is acceptable to A if and only if it is acceptable to all his advisors.

The meaning of the concept of acceptability is made clearer by considering the case of a crisp assertion a that takes payoff values 0 and 1 (see the end of §2). For a confident Bayesian agent the acceptability of a is just the probability (for him) that the corresponding classical sentence $\tilde{a} = \theta(a)$ is true. For an uncertain Bayesian agent there are two probabilities associated with $\tilde{a}$: an *upper probability* p^+ and a *lower probability* p^-. These are given in terms of acceptabilities by $p^- = \alpha(a)$, $p^+ = -\alpha(-a)$.

Since a (confident or uncertain) classical agent is a particular case of an uncertain Bayesian agent we have now defined the notion of acceptability for all types of agent. Note that the acceptability of an assertion a to a confident classical agent is just the payoff $a(\omega)$, where ω is the corresponding world state. In the case of a crisp assertion that takes payoff values 0 and 1, it coincides with the classical truth value of the corresponding sentence.

Let us next discuss the binary linear connectives, $+$ (plus) and $-$ (minus). Since for a confident Bayesian agent the acceptability $\alpha(a)$ of an assertion a is given by a probability distribution μ, $\alpha(a) = \mu(a)$, acceptability is a linear function on the set L of all assertions: *i.e.*,

$$(3) \quad \alpha(a{+}b) = \alpha(a){+}\alpha(b) \text{ and } \alpha(ka) = k\alpha(a),$$

for any assertions a and b and for every real number k. For an uncertain Bayesian we can then deduce, using the fact that the acceptability is the infimum of the acceptabilities assigned by his confident Bayesian advisors, that

$$(4) \quad \alpha(a{+}b) \geq \alpha(a){+}\alpha(b) \text{ and } \alpha(ka) = k\alpha(a),$$

for any assertions a and b and for any *nonnegative* number k. That the statements in (4) cannot be strengthened to the forms given in (3) is shown by a simple example. Suppose A is an uncertain Bayesian agent with two confident Bayesian advisors, and suppose there is an assertion a such that one advisor finds a unacceptable while the other finds $-a$ unacceptable. Then, for A, both $\alpha(a)$ and $\alpha(-a)$ are negative, while, of course, $\alpha(a{+}(-a)) = \alpha(0) = 0$.

We can apply this result to the interpretation of the connective, $-$ (minus). Replacing b by $b-a$ in (4) we obtain

(5) $\alpha(b - a) \leq \alpha(b) - \alpha(a)$.

It follows that, for an arbitrary agent for whom $b - a$ is acceptable, b will be acceptable if a is acceptable. So if an agent makes the assertion $b - a$ then we can conclude that if he finds a acceptable then he would find b acceptable too. Thus $b - a$ may be described in the language of classical logic as an assertion that "a implies b". But it is more than this. First, if $b - a$ is acceptable then, by (5), $\alpha(b) \geq \alpha(a)$: *i.e.*, b is *at least as acceptable as a*. Thus if $b - a$ is acceptable then the stronger the acceptability of the premise a the stronger is that of the conclusion b. It is clear that this result (which naturally cannot be represented in classical logic) represents the usual situation in practical life. Observe that here we cannot conclude that the acceptability of the conclusion is *equal* to that of the premise. This is natural, since its acceptability might be increased by other evidence not mentioned in the premise.

It may sometimes be the case that the acceptability of a conclusion b is increased only slightly by an increase in acceptability of the premise a. This type of implication is easily represented in the present formalism by the assertion $b - ka$, where $0 < k < 1$. For we have $\alpha(b - ka) \leq \alpha(b) - ka(a)$ which shows that if $b - ka$ is acceptable then we can only conclude that the acceptability of b is at least k times the acceptability of a.

To illustrate further the properties of the new implication suppose that $b - a$ is unacceptable, but only *slightly* unacceptable — say $\alpha(b - a) = -\epsilon$, where ϵ is small and positive. In this case we can conclude that $\alpha(b) \geq \alpha(a) - \epsilon$: *i.e.*, the acceptability of the conclusion can only be slightly less than that of the premise. Again, there is no way in which this natural conclusion can arise as a property of implication in classical logic.

As a further illustration of the logic and to introduce the connective, + (plus), consider the natural language assertion $\mathcal{A} = $ "*If Joan has good grades and good references then she will get the job*". Let a, b, c be respectively the assertions "*Joan has good grades*", "*Joan has good references*", and "*Joan will get the job*", and consider the assertion $f = c - a - b$. Observe that it doesn't matter whether we write f as $(c - a) - b$ or $c - (a+b)$ (or several other algebraically equivalent forms); since the connectives operate on the payoff functions pointwise in Ω, algebraically equivalent expressions are logically equivalent. Taking the second of these forms, we see that f may be read briefly as "$a+b$ implies c". Note that, by (5) and (4),

(6) $\alpha(f) \leq \alpha(c) - \alpha(a+b) \leq \alpha(c) - \alpha(a) - \alpha(b)$.

It follows that if f is acceptable then

$$(7) \quad \alpha(c) \geq \alpha(a+b) \geq \alpha(a)+\alpha(b):$$

i.e., the acceptability of c is at least as great as the sum of the acceptabilities of a and b. As an immediate result this means that if a and b are both acceptable then so is c, which indicates that f may be taken as a statement of the form "(a and b) implies c". This shows first that f may tentatively be considered as a formal representative of the natural language assertion $\mathcal{A}$, and secondly, that — in this context at least — $a+b$ serves as a kind of conjunction. As in the case of the connective, minus, this "conjunction" has a number of properties distinguishing it from the conjunction of classical logic. One of these is evident already from (6): insofar as the acceptability of c is concerned a decrease in acceptability of a can be compensated by an increase in acceptability of b: *i.e.*, Joan can compensate for inferior grades by superior references. Now, something of this nature is implicit in most common language statements that have the form of $\mathcal{A}$. Insofar as this is the case, the use of plus may be justified as a way of representing natural language conjunction in the premise of an implication. A second property suggesting that the connective, plus, is a form of conjunction is also evident from (6): if a and b are both acceptable then so is $a+b$. On the other hand, unlike the situation with classical conjunction, it is not the case that if $a+b$ is acceptable then so are both a and b: it is even possible (see the example following (4)) that neither a nor b is acceptable.

Lastly, let us consider the lattice connectives $\vee$ (maximum) and $\wedge$ (minimum). In $\wedge$ we have a much stronger form of conjunction. Since, for any assertions a and b, $a \wedge b \leq a$ and $a \wedge b \leq b$, it follows that for *any* agent if $a \wedge b$ is acceptable then so are a and b. Conversely, in the case of a confident classical agent we clearly have $\alpha(a \wedge b) = min(\alpha(a), \alpha(b))$ which shows that if a and b are both acceptable then so is $a \wedge b$, and it is easy to deduce that the latter holds also in the case of an uncertain classical agent. On the other hand, for a probability measure μ we only have the inequality $\mu(a \wedge b) \leq min(\mu(a), \mu(b))$. As a result, in the case of a confident Bayesian agent a and b may both be acceptable while $a \wedge b$ is not. As an example, suppose a gives payoffs of 2 and –1 respectively according to whether it is raining or not, while the corresponding payoffs for b are –1 and 2 respectively. Then $a \wedge b$ is certain to give a payoff of –1, and so to be unacceptable, but a Bayesian agent who believes the probability of rain to be near 1/2 will find both a and b acceptable. Similar results apply to $\vee$, which acts as a strong form of disjunction.

As one might expect, the lattice connectives $\vee$ (maximum) and $\wedge$ (minimum) are related to the familiar classical connectives denoted by the same symbols, ∨ (OR) and ∧ (AND). In fact, it is clear that, given any pair of numbers $\{\lambda, \mu\}$ with $\lambda < \mu$, the mapping θ of the subset $C_{\lambda,\mu}$ of L consisting of all (λ, μ)-normalized crisp assertions onto the set of all sentences of classical logic (see the end of §2) preserves the connectives ∨ and ∧: $\theta(a \vee b) = \theta(a) \vee \theta(b)$ and $\theta(a \wedge b) = \theta(a) \wedge \theta(b)$.

Using the mapping θ we can show that the logic of assertions (LOA) is a true extension of classical logic (CL), in that LOA contains CL as a "sublogic". There are many ways of doing this, each starting by fixing a particular scale of utility. Probably the simplest is to take $\lambda = 0$, $\mu = 1$. The set $C_{0,1}$ consists of (the payoff functions of) all the $\{0, 1\}$-valued crisp assertions in L. Each such function can be interpreted as the truth function of a sentence of CL. Now, in $C_{0,1}$ there is a greatest element, the function $\mathbf{1}$ given by $\mathbf{1}(\omega) = 1$ for every world state ω. Let us define in L a connective $\neg$ by the rule: $\neg a$ *is an abbreviation* for $\mathbf{1} - a$, (for every assertion a). It is easy to see that $C_{0,1}$ is closed under the action of the connectives ∧, ∨, and $\neg$; and that $C_{0,1}$, equipped with these connectives only, is isomorphic to CL (*i.e.*, to a form of CL in which ∧, ∨, $\neg$ are taken as basic connectives). An alternative, which is in some ways nicer, is to take $C_{-1,1}$ instead of $C_{0,1}$ and simply define $\neg$ to coincide with the unary connective, negative. If we associate the payoff values 1 and -1 with the truth values TRUE and FALSE we again get a realization of the same form of CL. In these or many other ways we can see that the logic CL can be obtained by taking part of the set L of all assertions of LOA and a subset of the set of all connectives of LOA.

It may be worth noting at this time that *fuzzy logic*, in its most usual form, infinite-valued Lukasiewicz logic, can also be obtained in a natural way as a sublogic of LOA. Let $F_{0,1}$ denote the subset of L consisting of all assertions whose payoff functions take only values in the closed interval [0, 1]. Define $\neg$ as before ($\neg a$ means $\mathbf{1} - a$) and define a new binary connective $\rightarrow$ by: $a \rightarrow b$ is an abbreviation for $\mathbf{1} \wedge (1 - a + b)$. Then $F_{0,1}$ is closed under the action of the connectives ∧, ∨, $\neg$, and $\rightarrow$; and $F_{0,1}$ equipped with these connectives is a realization of the fuzzy logic of all fuzzy sentences (about the world). This shows that, technically at least, LOA is a generalization of fuzzy logic, in that it contains, in a fairly natural way, a realization of fuzzy logic. Whether the interpretation of the family of assertions $F_{0,1}$ agrees with that of the corresponding fuzzy sentences can hardly be decided, since no clear interpretation of the sentences of fuzzy logic has yet been accorded general approval.

In the logic of assertions, the lattice connectives, ∨ (maximum) and ∧

(minimum), are more difficult to handle than the linear connectives for the following reason. In the case of a (certain) classical agent the acceptability of any assertion a is the value of $a(\omega)$ for the corresponding world state ω. Since the connectives act pointwise in Ω we have as an immediate consequence:

(8)   *The acceptability of any compound assertion is determined by the acceptabilities of the components.*

In the case of a confident Bayesian agent, the acceptability of an assertion a is the expected payoff $\mu(a)$, where μ is the corresponding probability distribution on Ω. Because μ is a linear function, (8) still holds for the linear connectives, as we saw above. However, it does not hold for the lattice connectives. Suppose, for instance, that a and b are crisp assertions, taking for each world state either the value 1 (TRUE) or 0 (FALSE), and let $\tilde{a}$ and $\tilde{b}$ be the corresponding classical sentences. Then $\mu(a)$ is just the probability that $\tilde{a}$ is true, $\mu(b)$ is the probability that $\tilde{b}$ is true, and $\mu(a \wedge b)$ is the probability that the classical conjunction $\tilde{a}$ AND $\tilde{b}$ is true. But of course this is not determined by the probabilities of $\tilde{a}$ and $\tilde{b}$; it depends also on the correlation between these events. For instance, if $\mu(a) = \mu(b) = 1/2$ then we have $\mu(a \wedge b) = 1/2$ in the case of *maximum correlation* (when $\tilde{a}$ is true when and only when $\tilde{b}$ is true) but $\mu(a \wedge b) = 0$ in the case of minimum correlation (when $\tilde{a}$ is true if and only if $\tilde{b}$ is false) and any intermediate value in other cases. $\mu(a \wedge b) = 1/4$ corresponds to the case of independence of $\tilde{a}$ and $\tilde{b}$. If we regard the acceptability $\alpha(a)$ of an assertion a as a sort of subjective truth value relative to a given agent then we can describe the situation as follows. The logic is truth-functional for all connectives in the case of a confident classical agent, but only for the linear connectives in the case of a confident Bayesian agent. It is not truth-functional even for the linear connectives in the case of an uncertain (classical or Bayesian) agent, but this doesn't matter, as we shall see below. It is for this reason that the lattice connectives are harder to deal with than the linear connectives.

6   Further Developments

In this final section a brief discussion is given of some further developments in the logic of assertions. We start by considering the question of providing satisfactory foundations for this logic.

In introducing the logic of assertions in this paper various assumptions were made in order to simplify the presentation. In particular, in §4 we introduced, under the guise of "agents" of various types, a number of kinds of "uncertain belief". Although in each case the behaviour described could be considered rational, no justification was given for the claim that all reasonable behaviours had been covered. In addition, as presented, the theory appeared to depend on the notions of Bayesian statistics and decision theory, and in particular on probability and utility — concepts which, although plausible, seem inappropriate as a foundation for logic.

We shall now see that the assumptions made are not as arbitrary as they seem. In fact, the structure they lead to follows from certain very simple and primitive axioms, axioms which can (appropriately used) provide a foundation simultaneously for the logic of assertions and for decision theory. In the process of doing this we shall extend to the logic of assertions the concept of *logical consequence*, familiar in classical logic (*CL*). We start by considering, first from the point of view of *CL*, the problem faced by an agent who wishes to describe his state of belief.

In §4 two kinds of "classical agent" were introduced, and in §5 we related these notions to classical logic. A *confident classical agent* is one who knows (or thinks he knows) the exact value ω of the current world state, and hence the truth value (TRUE or FALSE) of every sentence, while an *uncertain classical agent* is one who believes that the actual world state is some unknown member of a known subset Δ of the set Ω of all world states. The state of belief of a confident agent can be represented by the corresponding world state ω. This state determines (and may, for practical purposes, be identified with) the mapping that assigns to each sentence a the truth value $\alpha(\omega)$, where $\alpha(\cdot)$ is the truth function of the sentence a. Note that this mapping is a *valuation* in that it preserves all the classical connectives. Using this interpretation of a world state, the relation $\models$ of logical consequence in classical logic can be defined: one says a sentence a is a logical consequence of a set of sentences Γ, and writes $\Gamma \models a$, if a is true in every world state in which every sentence in Γ is true; in other words, a is a logical consequence of Γ if a is true in the opinion of every confident classical agent who believes that every sentence in Γ is true.

Classical logic can also represent the beliefs of other kinds of classical agents. In fact, this is the purpose of the machinery of connectives. For instance, by asserting $a \rightarrow b$ to be true (a and b being sentences) an agent declares his belief that either b is true or a is false (perhaps both). Such an assertion is useful only in the case of an uncertain agent; there would be no point in making it if the agent already knew the truth values of the component sentences involved. The agent can express other aspects of his belief by making further assertions. In fact, as far as classical logic

is concerned, the complete *state of belief* of an uncertain agent may be
determined by giving the set of all sentences that he believes to be true.
Let us call a set of sentences that arises in this way a *belief set*. Note that
the belief set of a confident classical agent is just the set of all sentences
that are true in the corresponding world state ω. Thus to say $\Gamma \models a$ is
just to say that the sentence a lies in S whenever $S \supseteq \Gamma$ and S is the belief
set of a confident classical agent. For convenience. we shall describe a set
which is the belief set of a confident classical agent as a "confident classical
belief set". Similarly, the terms, "uncertain classical belief set", "confident
Bayesian belief set", *etc.*, refer to belief sets of an agent of the corresponding
type.

For an idiot, a belief set could be quite arbitrary. However, classical
logic considers only "rational" agents, where for classical logic an agent is
deemed *rational* if and only if his belief set is closed under the taking of
logical consequences: for every sentence a and set of sentences Γ, if $\Gamma \subseteq S$
and $\Gamma \models a$ then $a \in S$; a set S with this property is often called a *theory*.
Now, it is easy to show that this condition for rationality is equivalent to
the following: an agent is rational if he behaves as though he believes that
the actual world state is one of a certain set Δ of world states, but does
not know which one; in the sense that he declares a sentence a to be true if
and only if it is true in every world state belonging to the set Δ. It follows
that the agents that are considered rational in ordinary classical logic are
just those that we have previously described as "uncertain classical agents".
Moreover, (since each point in Δ corresponds to a confident classical agent)
every uncertain classical belief set is an intersection of confident classical
belief sets; and conversely, every such intersection is an uncertain classical
belief set.

By following the same approach in the logic of assertions (LOA), we can
obtain analogues there of the concepts of belief set and logical consequence.
In discussing CL we talked about the two types of classical agents; for LOA
we must consider instead confident and uncertain Bayesian agents. A confident Bayesian agent (see §4) is represented not by a specific world state
ω but rather by a specific probability measure μ on the set Ω of all world
states. Just as, in the classical case, the practical function of the world state
ω was to assign to each sentence a a truth value $a(\omega)$, so the function of
the probability measure μ is to assign to each assertion a a specific *expected
payoff* $\mu(a)$; and — just as the truth value of a sentence determines when it
can be correctly asserted — so the expected payoff has the property that a
is acceptable iff $\mu(a) \geq 0$. Unlike the situation in the classical case, however,

the map $a \mapsto \mu(a)$ does not preserve all the connectives but only the linear connectives. Thus the acceptability of a compound assertion is not in general determined by the acceptabilities of its components. In this practical sense *the logic of assertions* is not *truth-functional*. This fact is particularly evident in the case of $(0, 1)$-normalized crisp assertions, where, as we saw in §5, the expected payoff coincides with the probability of truth.

In spite of this complication of the logic of assertions, we can define the relation $\models$ of logical consequence in the same way as before: an assertion a is a logical consequence of a set of assertions Γ, written $\Gamma \models a$, if a is acceptable in the opinion of every confident Bayesian agent who believes that every assertion in Γ is acceptable. If in the *LOA* we now define the belief set of any agent to be the set of all acceptable assertions, *i.e.*, assertions that he would be willing to make, then this can be expressed as follows:

(9)   An assertion a is a logical consequence of Γ iff a belongs to every confident Bayesian belief set that contains Γ.

Now consider an uncertain Bayesian agent as defined in §4. Such an agent behaves as though he has a team of confident Bayesian advisors and regards an assertion as acceptable if and only if it is acceptable to all of them. From this it follows that the belief set of an uncertain Bayesian agent is the intersection of the belief sets of his (confident Bayesian) advisors; and conversely, every intersection of confident Bayesian belief sets is an uncertain Bayesian belief set. Also (9) now gives:

(10)   An assertion a is a logical consequence of Γ iff a belongs to every uncertain Bayesian belief set that contains Γ.

Classical logic is truth-functional: the truth value, and hence the "assertability", of any compound sentence is a function of the truth values of its components. Because of this the properties of the logic can be derived directly from the truth tables for the connectives. The logic of assertions is, as we have seen, not truth-functional in this sense. As a result, the rules governing the use of the language can not be so directly obtained from the definitions of the connectives. However, the connections established above show that they may instead be derived from the properties of belief sets. Let us therefore look at the structure of these sets. In this connection remember that an assertion is, for present purposes, identified with its payoff function. A belief set is therefore a set of real-valued functions on the set Ω of all world states.

Consider first the belief set S of an arbitrary confident Bayesian agent characterized by a probability measure μ on Ω. S consists of all assertions a for which the expected payoff $\mu(a)$ is nonnegative. From this we easily obtain the following properties:

    (I) S is *upclosed*: if $a \geq b \in S$ then $a \in S$.

    (II) S is *additive*: if $a \in S$ and $b \in S$ then $a+b \in S$.

    (III) S is *positively homogeneous*: $\mathbf{0} \in S$, and if $a \in S$ and $k \geq 0$ then $ka \in S$.

    (IV) S is (topologically) *closed*: if $\{a_n\}$ is a sequence of assertions in S and $a_n(\omega) \to a(\omega)$ uniformly for all ω in Ω then $a \in S$.

    (V) S is *definite*: if $a \notin S$ then $-a \in S$.

Now, an arbitrary uncertain Bayesian belief set is an intersection of confident Bayesian belief sets. Using this fact we deduce easily that, because a confident Bayesian belief set has the property (I), so does an uncertain Bayesian belief set. The same applies to properties (II), (III), (IV). However, simple examples show that an uncertain Bayesian belief set need not have the property (V).

Notice that the properties (I) — (V) have very simple meanings: (I) says if a has, for every world state, at least as large a payoff as b and b is acceptable then so is a; (II) says that if a and b are acceptable then the assertion $a+b$ (which, because the payoff is additive, may be interpreted roughly as an assertion of both a and b) is also acceptable; (III) says that if a can be asserted without danger of loss then it can also be asserted *emphatically* without danger. (II) and (III) can be criticized. See below. (IV) is a typical *closure* or *Archimedean* axiom: if each of a sequence of assertions is acceptable then so is the limit of the sequence. (V) is a little more specialized; it says that if a is not acceptable then its "reverse" $-a$ must be. This is plausible for a confident Bayesian agent: if he would lose in asserting a he would equally gain in asserting $-a$. But an uncertain agent might be afraid of losing in making either of the assertions a and $-a$ and so consider neither acceptable.

The plausibility, for a general agent, of properties (I, II, III, IV) suggests the possibility of taking them not as derived results but as axioms. This gives rise to a new formulation of the logic which is in many respects more satisfactory. The reformulation can be done in two ways. In the first way we start as here with the notion, derived from decision theory, of the payoff function of an assertion. As in decision theory, this is a real-valued function on the set Ω of all world states. Then we introduce the notion of a *belief set* as a set satisfying (I) — (IV), these now being taken as axioms and justified by their plausibility with reference to the understood meaning of a belief set. In this way a foundation for the logic is obtained in which the notion of subjective probability is never used. Nevertheless, it can be proved (surprisingly) that (*a*) every belief set is an intersection of "maximal belief sets" and (*b*) every maximal belief set can be represented uniquely as a "confident Bayesian belief set" given by a probability measure on Ω as described above. In this way we obtain the same structure as described here, in a way which is more satisfactory as a foundation for the logic in that it depends on a smaller number of more fundamental concepts.

The second way of reformulating the theory represents a further step in the same direction. An examination of the axiomatic structure of the first formulation reveals a great deal of similarity to modern formulations of utility and decision theory [Fishburn81]. This is not surprising, since the basic problem of the logic of assertions, whether or not to make a given assertion, is just a special case of the decision problem, which of a given set of possible acts to carry out. As a result, it is possible to give a formulation of the foundations of the logic which, by itself containing the necessary foundations, remains independent of any prior account of decision theory. Work in this direction is currently in progress.

This second approach offers the possibility of overcoming a certain difficulty which was briefly noted above. Of the axioms (I) — (IV) the least well justified are (II) and (III). We shall call these the *homogeneous* axioms, in view of the nature of the mathematical structure which they induce, and the logic of assertions described in this paper will accordingly be called the *homogeneous logic of assertions*. The justification offered above for axioms (II) and (III) can be criticized: in practice it is certainly not the case that an agent who is willing to make an assertion is necessarily willing to make it with an arbitrarily large emphasis; the risk involved in doing so may be too great. In the same way, one may be prepared to place a small bet on some event but unwilling to place a large bet. A similar criticism may be applied to (III). By dropping the homogeneous axioms, or more precisely by replacing them by a weaker "convexity" axiom

   if a and b are acceptable then so is $(a+b)/2$

a more general form, the *convex logic of assertions*, is obtained. In this alternative logic more general states of belief can be described than those allowed in the homogeneous case. This means that more general beliefs can be conveyed, so that the resulting language is *richer*. Normally, one would expect that as a result the mathematical structure would be more complicated and the processes of reasoning more difficult. It turns out, however, that the theory is still quite manageable, in fact very little is changed. Roughly speaking, where the homogeneous theory is dominated by convex cones (in linear spaces) the convex theory has convex sets and convex functions. The convex theory is outlined in [Giles88]. This paper also contains a demonstration of the power of *linear logic*, by which I mean the logic of assertions *without* the lattice connectives ∧ and ∨. In particular, a number of practical examples are given, indicating the richness of linear logic when the convex language is used.

Now, the difficulty, mentioned above, affecting the convex theory arises when one attempts to give an decision-theoretic foundation for it. Conventional decision theory (expected utility theory) corresponds to the *homogeneous* rather than to the *convex* case. As a result, to serve as a foundation for the convex logic of assertions a generalization of standard expected utility theory is required. A suitable generalization has recently been given [Giles], but its application to a complete decision-theoretic treatment of the logic has yet to be worked out.

Other work that remains to be done in the development of these logics includes the extension to a first order language, and the development of a system of deduction. As indicated above, in the latter direction it is relatively easy to describe a system of deduction for *linear logic*. An outline of such a system was given in [Giles85]. Owing to the dominance of convex sets and functions the process of reasoning reduces there essentially to solving a problem in *linear programming*. It is to be hoped that the powerful techniques developed in this field will prove valuable in the practical applications of the logic of assertions.

Acknowlegements. This work was supported by a grant from the National Science and Engineering Research Council of Canada.

7 Bibliography

Dunford, N. and J. Schwartz. *Linear Operators, Part I*, Interscience, 1958.

Fishburn, P. "Subjective expected utility: a review of normative theories," *Theory and Decision 13*, 139–199, 1981.

Giles, R. "A resolution logic for fuzzy reasoning," *Proceedings of the Fifteenth International Symposium on Multiple-Valued Logic 60–67*, 1985.

Giles, R. "A utility-valued logic for decision making," *International Journal of Approximate Reasoning 2*, pp. 113–141, 1988.

Giles, R. "A generalization of the theory of subjective probability and expected utility," to appear in *Synthese*.

James, W. *Pragmatism*, Longmans Green, 1907.

Luce, R. and H. Raiffa. *Games and Decisions*, Wiley, 1957.

Raiffa, H. *Decision Analysis*, Addison-Wesley, 1968.

Rescher, N. *Many-Valued Logic*, McGraw-Hill, 1969.

1131304

A New Normative Theory of
Probabilistic Logic

Romas Aleliunas 3-SFR-C

Every rational decision-making procedure is founded on some theory of probabilistic logic (also called a theory of rational belief). This article proposes practical and logically correct theories of rational belief that are more general than the probability theory we learn in school, yet remain capable of many of the inferences of this latter theory. We also show why recent attempts to devise novel theories of rational belief usually end up being either incorrect or reincarnations of the more familiar theories we learned in school.

1 What is a Probabilistic Logic?

Following [Keynes21], I take probabilistic logic to be any scheme for relating a body of evidence to a potential conclusion (a hypothesis) in a rational way. We assign *degrees of belief* (which we also call *probabilities*) to the possible relationships between hypotheses and pieces of evidence. These relationships are called *conditionals*. We will use the expression "$f(P \mid Q)$" to stand for "the conditional probability of P given the evidence Q as given by the probability assignment f." We have chosen to encode the potential hypothesis, P, and the collected evidence, Q, as finite sentences of some language L. We take *probabilistic logic* to be synonymous with *theory of rational belief*, *probability* to be identical to *degree of belief*, and *probability assignment* to be the same as *belief function*. Normative theories of rational belief have had a long history [Keynes21], [Carnap50], [Fine73].

Let the set of probabilities be P. We begin by regarding this as a set of *uninterpreted formal marks*. A theory of probabilistic logic is chiefly concerned with identifying the characteristics of a family F of functions from $L \times L$ to P. F is the *set of permissible belief functions* (also called the *set of possible probability assignments*) from which a rational agent is permitted to choose. Our convention is that for any f in F, $f(P \mid Q)$ represents the probability assigned to f by the hypothesis P given the evidence Q. P and Q can be any statements in L — no distinction is made between hypothesis statements and evidence statements in probabilistic logic.

H.E. Kyburg, Jr. et al. (eds.), Knowledge Representation and Defeasible Reasoning, 387–403.
© 1990 Kluwer Academic Publishers. Printed in the Netherlands.

The set F of rational probability assignments clearly cannot be the set of all functions from $L \times L$ to P. Both F, and each individual element in it, must be subject to some constraints. Of course different theories of rational belief may vary in their choices for these constraints, but I believe they all share some in common. One such common constraint is: if "I believe P is certain when I see Q" then it cannot also be the case that "I believe $\neg P$ is possible when I see Q." Moreover, the correctness of these constraints — and therefore of the rules of inference they engender — cannot depend on the particular application that they are put to. Decision "theory" does not dictate the standards of correctness for inferences in probabilistic logic [Tukey60].

Does the set of probabilities P have any internal structure? We must, at the very least, be able to assert that some conditionals are more believable than others, or else there is no practical use for this theory. This implies that we have, at the very least, a partial ordering among conditionals. If we want to approach the subject algebraically, we can without loss of generality, introduce a new probability symbol into P for each pair of sentences drawn from the language L and assign whatever (partial) set of orderings between these symbols that we wish. In this way we can reproduce any partial ordering whatsoever between the conditionals as an ordering of the elements of P. A theory which adopts this approach is called a *weak comparative theory of probability* in [Fine73].

A theory of rational belief is not a substitute for a decision-making procedure. Probabilistic logic does not prescribe "rules of detachment," "rules of commitment," or other decision-making rules. The only judgements a theory of probabilistic logic tells you how to make are conditional judgements — how to assign a value to a conditional probability. Conditional judgements of probability are the only judgements that can be infallible. Moreover, conditional judgements are the natural inputs to a decision-making apparatus.

2   What is a Decision Procedure?

A *decision procedure* tells you how to bet. I refrain from using the term *decision theory* since it is not a theory in the usual sense. A decision procedure is, instead, a concrete thing — a particular set of rules describing the behaviour of a specific physical machine. Decisions sometimes have to be made with little or no evidence; decision procedures make mistakes.

Regardless how it may be implemented, a decision procedure can always be described in a certain way. To formulate this kind of description we must first identify the general principles that govern the procedure's behaviour. I find it convenient to divide such a description into two parts. The first part describes the principles of evidence — the probabilistic logic — that the decision-making machine (implicitly) employs. The second part describes how these principles are applied in this specific implementation. Ideally the only possible causes of bad decisions are misapplications of probabilistic logic.

The principles governing the application of probabilistic logic to decision-making fall into several subgroups. These concern the problems of statistics, utility assignment, and the formulation of decision rules.

Statistics is concerned with how probabilities are assigned and how the statistical model is built. Statistical problems include the choice of language for encoding evidence and hypothesis statements, the choice of a set of hypotheses, and the choice of simplifying independence assumptions.[1]

A *utility assignment* describes how the decision procedure ranks the costs and rewards of various outcomes. *Decision rules* describe how probabilities and utilities combine to affect decisions.

Suppose, for instance, that we have a decision procedure called Alpha that always decides in favour of the hypothesis with maximum likelihood [Good83]. Then we can describe Alpha as a procedure which (implicitly) assigns equal prior probabilities and equal utilities to all hypotheses (outcomes).

Suppose we have another procedure called Beta that merely scans down an ordered list of hypotheses and chooses the first one that is consistent with the current evidence. Then Beta's probabilistic logic simply judges hypotheses to be either possible (probability $\neq 0$) or impossible (probability $= 0$) on the given evidence — a matter of testing logical consistency. Beta (implicitly) assigns non-zero probability exactly to those hypotheses which appear on its list, and Beta (implicitly) uses utilities ordered in the same fashion as the list.

The standards of correctness of a probabilistic logic cannot be dictated by the application to which it is put [Tukey60]. But what many writers have failed to realize — and this is a novel feature of the theory presented here — is that many other aspects of a probabilistic logic can be tailored to suit the application. We have, for example, a great deal of latitude in choosing a convenient set of probabilities P. After all, if the decision-making pro-

---

[1] A *hypothesis* is merely a statement whose expected utility is relevant to the decision-making machinery.

cedure does not (implicitly) use numerical utilities, than why should it use numerical probabilities? There is no reason to use a probabilistic logic that makes fine discriminations between degrees of belief if these discriminations serve no practical end.

3   New Axioms for Probabilistic Logic

These axioms are flexible enough to permit one to tailor the set of probabilities to the application at hand. The probabilities are therefore treated as uninterpreted formal marks in the axiomatization given below. We will examine possible interpretations later — each interpretation will give rise to a probabilistic logic.

The axioms describe the constraints that are appropriate for any rational theory of belief. The axioms fall into three groups: (1) axioms about the domain and range of each probability assignment f in F, (2) axioms stating consistency constraints that each individual f in F must obey, and (3) axioms that say something about F itself. Finite additivity does not appear as an axiom since it essentially forces probabilities to be numbers.

The usual semantics for probabilistic logic uses "possible worlds."[2] We associate to each proposition P a set of *situations* or *possible worlds* $S(P)$ in which P holds.[3] When Q is given as evidence, the conditional probability $f(P \mid Q)$ is some measure of the fraction of the set $S(Q)$ that is occupied by the subset $S(P \ \& \ Q)$.[4] This fraction is given by a (possibly non-numerical) function $\mu^f(S(P \ \& \ Q), S(Q))$ whose values range over the set P.[5] The correctness of any axioms for probabilistic logic can be grasped by a semantics of this form.

Axioms for Propositional Logic

Axioms about the domain and range of each f in F.

1. The set of probabilities P, is a partially ordered set. The ordering relation is "$\leq$."

---

[2]Historically, the possible world semantics of probability theory seems to have inspired Kripke's semantics for modal logics [Kripke80; p. 16].

[3]"Possible world" is left as a primitive unanalyzed concept.

[4]The individual points in $S(Q)$ need not have equal weight. They need not even have any weight at all as is often the case in Lebesgue measure theory.

[5]The familiar numerical theory of probability relies on this same semantics except that the relative sizes of the fractions must be coded numerically in this case.

2. The set of sentences, L, is a free boolean algebra with operations &, $\vee$, and $\neg$, and it is equipped with the usual equivalence relation "$\approx$." The generators of the algebra are a countable set of *primitive propositions*. Every sentence in L is either a primitive proposition or a finite combination of them.[6]

3. If $P \approx X$ and $Q \approx Y$, then $f(P \mid Q) = f(X \mid Y)$.

Axioms that hold for all f in F, and for any P, Q, R in L.

4. If Q is absurd (*i.e.*, $Q \approx R \ \& \ \neg R$), then $f(P \mid Q) = f(P \mid P)$.

5. $f(P \ \& \ Q \mid Q) = f(P \mid Q) \leq f(Q \mid Q)$.

6. For any other g in F, $f(P \mid P) = g(P \mid P)$.

7. There is a monotone non-increasing total function, i, from P into P such that $f(\neg P \mid R) = i(f(P \mid R))$.

8. There is an order-preserving total function, h, from $P \times P$ into P such that $f(P \ \& \ Q \mid R) = h(f(P \mid Q \ \& \ R)), f(Q \mid R))$. Moreover, if $f(P \ \& \ Q \mid R) = 0^*$, then $f(P \mid Q \ \& \ R) = 0^*$, where we define $0^* = f(\neg R \mid R)$ as a function of f and R.

9. If $f(P \mid R) \leq f(P \mid \neg R)$ then $f(P \mid R) \leq f(P \mid R \vee \neg R) \leq f(P \mid \neg R)$.

Axioms about the richness of the set F.

Let $1 = P \vee \neg P$. For any *distinct primitive* propositions A, B, and C in L, and for any arbitrary probabilities a, b, and c in P, there is as probability assignment f in F (not necessarily the same one in each case) for which:

10. $f(A \mid 1) = a$, $f(B \mid A) = b$, and $f(C \mid A \ \& \ B) = c$.

11. $f(A \mid B) = f(A \mid \neg B) = a$ and $f(B \mid A) = f(B \mid \neg A) = b$.

12. $f(A \mid 1) = a$ and $f(A \ \& \ B \mid 1) = b$, whenever $b \leq a$.

---

[6]See [Burris *et al.*81] for more details about boolean algebra.

4   Commentary on the Axioms

1. You cannot do anything useful with a probabilistic logic if you cannot compare some degrees of belief with others. On the other hand not all applications require a total ordering for probabilities.

2 & 3. We clearly do not sacrifice generality by letting L be a free algebra.

The laws of boolean equivalence state, to pick one particular example, that the truth conditions of the sentence P & R are the same as those of R & P. In other words each sentence picks out the same set of situations: $S(P$ & $R) = S(R$ & $P)$. These two conjunctions must therefore have the same probability given Q since $f(P$ & $R \mid Q) = \mu^f(S(P$ & $R)$ & $Q), S(Q))$ $= \mu^f(S((R$ & $P)$ & $Q), S(Q))$.[7]

The *prior probability* of P, which we will write as $f(P)$, can be defined to be $f(P) = f(P \mid P \vee \neg P)$. This is correct since $\neg P \vee P$ is vacuous when taken as an evidence statement.

4. Absurd evidence (such as $\neg R$ & R) provides no basis for judging the probability of any hypothesis since $S(\neg R$ & $R)$ is the empty set. Assigning $f(P \mid \neg R$ & $R) = f(P \mid P)$ in these cases is a mathematically elegant way to treat this anomaly consistently [Morgan82].[8]

5 & 6. These axioms establish useful scaling conventions among probabilities and probability assignments.

7. R. Cox [Cox46,61] first used the idea that the probability of $\neg P$ given R can be determined from the probability of P given R as an axiom in his study of probabilistic logics using real numbers. He did not, however, assume that i was order inverting.

8. This is a weak form of the product rule of probabilities: $f(P$ & $Q) = f(P \mid Q) \cdot f(Q)$. We will call h the *product of probabilities*. R. Cox [46,61] also introduced this axiom, but without insisting that h be order preserving or that it have no non-trivial zeroes (see below).

The contrapositive form of the last part of Axiom 8 states that the

---

[7] Indeed, a weaker notion than boolean equivalence is sufficient for most of the results below.

[8] An equally acceptable, alternative, treatment is to restrict the domain of each f so that absurd evidence is always excluded. Adopting this second approach does not alter any of the results stated later, but it does complicate the statement of the axioms.

product of two non-zero probabilities is also not zero. This is to say that, given the evidence R, if P & Q is impossible given Q, or both. We say that *h has no non-trivial zeroes* when this condition holds.

9. A *finite additivity axiom* is an axiom that asserts the existence of a function h^* such that for any f, P, Q, and R: $f(P \vee Q \mid R) = h^*(f(P \mid R), f(P \& \neg Q \mid R))$. Finite additivity requires that the probability of $P \vee Q$ can be determined from the probabilities assigned to just the two mutually exclusive sentences P and $\neg P$ & Q [Aczel66].

Suppose P is statistically independent of R, which we write as $f(P \mid R) = f(P \mid \neg R)$. Then it should follow that $f(P) = f(P \mid R) = f(P \mid \neg R)$ since the probability of P does not depend on whether R holds or not. Axiom 9 permits this conclusion to be drawn. So does finite additivity, but we are avoiding this axiom in favor of the weaker Axiom 9.

Consider next the following argument conducted in English: "If this coin lands heads I will almost certainly end up winning the entire game. If it lands tails then it is still likely that I will win (because I'm so far ahead). So even before we toss the coin, it is clear right now that my chances of winning are somewhere between likely and almost certain." The probabilities mentioned in this argument are not numbers, so no addition formula is possible, yet the conclusion is compelling. Axiom 9 is sufficient to draw the conclusion from the premises in this argument also.

10, 11 & 12. These three axioms guarantee that the set F of probability assignments is rich enough to freely model: (1) any behaviour of growing chains of evidence, (2) statistically independent events, and (3) partial probability assignments to conjunctions of potential hypotheses.

Axiom 10 shows that the product of the probabilities is associative since $f(P \& Q \& R) = h(h(f(R \mid P \& Q), f(Q \mid P)), f(P)) = h(f(R \mid P \& Q), h(f(Q \mid P), f(P)))$.

Axiom 11 can be used to show that the product is commutative by using the equation $f(P \& Q) = h(f(P \mid Q), f(Q)) = h(f(Q \mid P), f(P))$. Axiom 9 is used in this proof to calculate $f(P)$ and $f(Q)$ from $f(P \mid \neg Q) = f(Q \mid \neg P) = f(Q \mid P)$.

Hence we see that (P, h) forms a commutative semigroup, so we may write $p \cdot q$ instead of $h(p, q)$ whenever this is convenient.

Axiom 12 is another way of stating our conviction that any conditional must, in principle, have a probability. If we know, for example, that

$f(March\ winds) = a$

$$f(\text{March winds \& April showers}) = b$$

then there must be some probability r such that

$$f(\text{April showers} \mid \text{March winds}) = r.$$

Of course we must have $b = f \cdot a$ (Axiom 8), and $b \leq a$ (Axiom 5) or else this probability assignment is inconsistent. [Fuchs63] calls any partially ordered semigroup *naturally ordered* just in case there always exists a solution r to the equation $q = r \cdot p$ whenever $q \leq p$. Axiom 12 only requires that a solution exist, not that it be unique.

5   Possible Interpretations of this Theory

These axioms do not presume the existence of probabilities called 0 and 1 in the set P. It easily follows from the axioms, however, that $f(P \mid P) = d(Q \mid Q) = g(Q \mid Q)$ for arbitrary f, g, P and Q, and therefore the convention $1 = f(P \mid P)$ leaves the probability 1 well-defined. Likewise $0 = f(\neg P \mid P)$ is a good definition of probability 0. Thus every P that is consistent with the above axioms must have a 0 and a 1. Probability 1 denotes complete certainty, and probability 0 denotes impossibility. If I say "Q is possible," I mean $f(Q) \neq 0$ for my choice of f.

The probabilities 0 and 1 are therefore special elements of every possible P. To give a mathematical model for a P which satisfies these axioms we must therefore give a consistent interpretation to each component of the structure $(P, \leq, h, i, 0, 1)$.

(Model 1) (0, 1)-Probabilistic Logic.

> $P(2) = \{0, 1\}$ and $0 \cdot 0 = 0 \cdot 1 = 0$, $1 \cdot 1 = 1$, $i(0) = 1$, $i(1) = 0$, and $0 \leq 1$.

(Model 2) Simple Real Probabilistic Logic.

> $P(R) = [0, 1]$, the closed interval of real numbers from 0 to 1. Let $p \cdot q$ be the ordinary numerical product, and let $i(p) = 1 - p$. Use the usual ordering relation.

For more examples suppose $(P, \leq)$ is a totally ordered set with n elements. Then the table below displays the number, $N(n)$, of non-isomorphic models consistent with this constraint:

n	2	3	4	5	6	7
$N(n)$	1	1	2	3	7	16

Yet another model of these axioms is the following one mimicking English probabilities. My aim here is not to claim that this is the correct model for English probabilities, but instead to show that a good approximation to English probabilities will not be ruled out by these axioms.

(Model 3) Simplified English Probabilistic Logic. Let $P(E)$ be the algebra of probabilities generated by the two formal symbols {LIKELY, UNLIKELY}, subject to the following additional constraints:

(C1) UNLIKELY $= i($LIKELY$)$

(C2) $0 <$ UNLIKELY $<$ LIKELY < 1.

The elements of $P(E)$ are strings of symbols generated by:

(G1) concatenating previously constructed strings in $P(E)$,

(G2) forming $i(s)$ where s is a string in $P(E)$,

(G3) introducing the formal symbol $s(p, q)$ for any pair of elements p and q in $P(E)$ whenever $p \leq q$ and there does not yet exist a solution, r, in $P(E)$ for the equation $p = q \cdot r$.

The only ordering relations are those that can be inferred from (C1), (C2), and the properties of the functions h and i. This set is not totally ordered.

The symbols introduced by (G3) do not, as far as I know, have English names. But not being able to name them in English does not mean they do not exist.

6   Is This Theory Useful?

This theory is useful for several reasons –

(U1)   The number of distinct degrees of probability is a feature left up to the user. This makes it possible to tailor the probabilistic logic to the goals of the decision procedure.

(U2)   Many useful inferences can still be carried out.

(U3)   Some statistical problems, like assigning prior probabilities, can be considerably simpler to solve in a non-numerical system. For example in the (unique) three-valued system you only have to decide if an event is certain, impossible, or neither.

To illustrate (U2) I will exhibit a calculation in the system $P(E)$ (Model 3). Let's start with the three premises:

(P1)   It is possible that it's cloudy.

(P2)   If it's cloudy, it's likely to rain.

(P3)   If it rains then the street will get wet.

The following conclusion can be drawn from these premises:

If it's cloudy, the chances are better than likely that the street will get wet.

Let us code these premises symbolically for convenience. They become:

(P1) $f(C) \neq 0.$

(P2) $f(R \mid C) = \text{LIKELY}.$

(P3) $f(W \mid R) = 1.$

Now by (P3) we have $f(\neg W \mid R) = 0$. Hence $0 = f(\neg W \mid R) \cdot f(R) = f(\neg W \& R) \geq 0$, and therefore $f(\neg W \& R \& C) = 0$ by Axiom 5. Now $0 = f(\neg W \& R \& C) = f(\neg W \mid R \& C) \cdot f(R \mid C) \cdot f(C)$, and because $f(R \mid C) \neq 0$ and $f(C) \neq 0$, it must be the ease that $f(\neg W|R \& C) = 0$ since products have no non-trivial zeroes. Thus $f(W \mid R \& C) = 1$. It's now easy to find $f(W \mid C) \geq f(W \& R \mid C) = f(W \mid R \& C) \cdot f(R \mid C) = 1 \cdot \text{LIKELY} = \text{LIKELY}$. Hence $f(W \mid C) \geq \text{LIKELY}$.

There are several points to note:

(1) We used the following trivial theorems:

$$0 \le p \le 1 \text{ for any probability } p,$$

$$p \cdot q \le q \text{ for any pair of probabilities } p \text{ and } q.$$

(2) Premise (P1) is needed in this particular derivation.

(3) The inequality is a necessary part of the conclusion. After all, maybe the street can get wet in some other way.

(4) This argument holds regardless of whether it is cloudy or not at the moment, and regardless of whether it ever rains or not. This argument is about the state the world could be in — it does not confine itself to the unique actual state the world is in now. Probabilistic logic treats all conditionals, counterfactual or not, in the same way.

(5) The conclusion is completely convincing even though LIKELY can have no numerical interpretation.

7 The Tar-Pit Theorem

Under what conditions does the familiar numerical theory of probability become the only possible theory of rational belief? Richard Cox [Cox46,61] first investigated this question under the assumption that probabilities were numbers. [Aczel66] reports stronger results under the assumption of finite additivity for probabilities. The following theorem is in the same vein, but it drops these two assumptions and even some of the axioms. I call it the Tar-Pit Theorem because it shows how easy it is to get stuck in stuff that has been lying around for a long time.

Definition. P is *archimedean-ordered* if, for any $p \ne 1$ and any $q \ne 0$ in P, the repeated product $p \cdot p \cdot \ldots \cdot p = p^n$ becomes smaller than q for some positive integer n.

The Tar-Pit Theorem. Under the conditions established by Axioms 1 through to 12, the following two statements are logically equivalent:

(1) the set of probabilities P is totally ordered and also archimedean-ordered.

(2) The algebraic structure $(P, \geq, h, i, 0, 1)$ is isomorphic to a subalgebra of the system $(P(R), \geq, \cdot, i, 0, 1)$ given as Model 2, namely Simple Real Probabilistic Logic. Dropping both Axiom 11 and the assumption that products have no non-trivial zeroes does not affect the result.

A short proof of this is given in the Appendix. The requirement for archimedean ordering appearing this theorem can be removed and replaced by either cancellativity (*i.e.*, for any p, q, $r \neq 0$ in P, if $p \cdot r = q \cdot r$ then $p = q$), or else by finite additivity (with some other minor adjustments in hypotheses). Space is too limited to state these results precisely.

8   On Reinventing the Wheel

Several theories of belief have been recently developed that have claimed some novelty over the familiar probability theory with real numbers. The Dempster-Shafer theory is one example, and the MYCIN theory is another[9] Both of these theories use numbers to measure degrees of uncertainty. In light of the Tar-Pit theorem it is no surprise, therefore, that [Kyburg87] has shown that the Dempster-Shafer theory can be reinterpreted and understood in the language of familiar probability theory, and that [Heckerman86] has done a similar thing for the MYCIN theory. In the process of uncovering the exact relationship, each author has exposed the general statistical assumptions that were surreptitiously imposed by each of these two systems. Whatever novelty these systems may have had rested on these questionable statistical assumptions.

[Kyburg87] showed that the Dempster-Shafer theory manipulates convex sets of probability assignments.[10]

[Heckerman86], on the other hand, found that a MYCIN "certainty factor" is a monotonic increasing function of the likelihood ratio $f(P \mid Q)/f(P \mid \neg Q)$.

---

[9] see [Buchanan&Shortliffe84] for a description of both.

[10] *A* set S of probability assignments is *convex* if for any two probability assignments f and g in C, and any number z between 0 and 1, the function $z \cdot f + (1 - z) \cdot g$ is also in C. As a consequence of this the range of values assumed by $f(P \mid Q)$ for fixed P and Q, when you let f range over all members of C, forms a closed interval.

Both Kyburg and Heckerman observed, in the respective systems they studied, that certain statistical assumptions about conditional independence were also built into the inference rules themselves. Heckerman, for example, showed how MYCIN's implicit assumptions made MYCIN incapable of correctly handling a statistical inference problem that involved three or more mutually exclusive and exhaustive possible outcomes.

Non-monotonic "logics," which originated with [Reiter80] and [McDermott&Doyle80], are another recent novelty. Given a set of premises, say Q_1 & Q_2 & ...& Q_n, a non-monotonic "logic" is a non-deterministic machine for deriving "plausible inferences." We will write "P **d** $Q_1 \& Q_2 \& \ldots \& Q_n$" if P is derivable from the stated premises by one of these machines.

At the very least a non-monotonic "logic" must tell me what the good bets are. If "P **d** $Q_1 \& Q_2 \& \ldots \& Q_n$" does not mean that P is a good bet given I have already seen $Q_1 \& Q_2 \& \ldots \& Q_n$, then I see no practical point to non-monotonic "logic." I am indebted to Charles Morgan for showing me why a non-monotonic "logic" cannot be a logic in the usual sense of the word. This still leaves open the possibility, however, that non-monotonic "logic" is some sort of betting system. Here are three possible explanations for "plausible inference" in terms betting rules — there are, of course, an endless number of possibilities:

(D1) P **d** Q if $u(P) \cdot f(P \mid Q) > c$,

(D2) P **d** Q if $min\{u(P) \cdot g(P \mid Q) \ s.t. \ g \in S\} > c$,

(D3) P **d** Q if $f(P \mid Q) > c \cdot f(P \mid \neg Q)$,

where $u(P)$ denotes the utility of outcome P, f is some fixed probability assignment, c is some fixed constant, and S is some special of F.

Suppose Q holds. P is a good bet, according to (D1), when ny expected utility from it exceeds some threshold. (D2) is more conservative: it says P is a good bet only when the minimum I expect to gain (over some set of probability assignments) is large enough. (D3) uses likelihoods to pick out good bets.

For example Reiter's system [Reiter80], to a first approximation, judges hypotheses only on the basis of consistency and it assumes an equal assignment of utilities to all outcomes. It is therefore no surprise that such a scheme is too simple to be very useful.[11]

Non-monotonic "logic" is further hampered by not manipulating probabilities and utilities explicitly. Suppose we adopt the criterion that any event with probability exceeding 0.80 is a good bet, and suppose I have built a non-monotonic "logic" that is sound by this criterion. Toss a fair die (with six faces). Let $L(i)$ code the event that face i shows. Let Q denote the background information about dice tossing. Then certainly $L(i)$ will not be a non-monotonic inference from Q for any i in this system. The disjoint event $L(1) \vee L(2) \vee L(3) \vee L(4) \vee L(5)$, however, is a good bet according to our chosen criterion. But how can an inference like this be made in general within a non-monotonic "logic" that excludes probabilities from its calculations?

Fuzzy "logic" [Zadeh65][Gupta *et al.*79] is another novelty. This theory leads to bad bets because, among other things, it is inconsistent with Axiom 8. Fuzzy "logic" replaces the functional equation $f(H \& T) = h(f(H \mid T), f(T))$ with $f(H \& T)=h(f(H), f(T))$ where h is still a function with no non-trivial zeroes.

To demonstrate the difficulties this alteration leads to, consider tossing a fair coin. By symmetry, fuzzy "logic" must assign equal "possibility levels" to the two outcomes so that $f(H) = f(T) = p$ for some $p \neq 0$. Now according to fuzzy "logic's" rules, $f(H \& T) = min(f(H), f(T)) = p \neq 0$. But the event $H \& T$ is impossible! Interpreted charitably, this means that 0 is not the only way of coding impossibility in fuzzy "logic." We have just seen that the value p also must code for impossibility. But then both possible outcomes of the coin toss are now marked impossible — an absurdity. I am quite prepared to bet money against this unrealistic "logic" since I do not expect to lose.

The onus is clearly on the inventor of a new theory of rational belief (or rational decision-making procedure) to demonstrate its novelty and its correctness. None of the theories mentioned in this section are, simultaneously, a new and a good guide to betting.

---

[11] To be precise, Reiter's system is based on "P d Q if $f(P \mid Q \& B) > 0$ & $f(Q \mid P$ & $B) = 1$," where B is some base set of facts that is never doubted — this is explained in [Poole *et al.*87]. This criterion can be simplified to "P d Q if $g(P \mid Q) > 0$ & $g(Q \mid P)$ $= 1$" because, for fixed B, the equation $g(X \mid Y)=f(X \mid Y \& B)$ defines g to be another valid probability assignment in F.

9 Appendix: Proof of The Tar-Pit Theorem

Actually, this proof continues to hold even if we omit Axiom 11 (independence) and the last part of Axiom 8 (h has no non-trivial zeroes). That (2) implies (1) is obvious. So we will concentrate on proving the converse, namely any archimedean totally ordered set P that satisfies the remaining axioms must be a set of real numbers under ordinary multiplication.

This proof relies on another theorem that was first found by O. Holder at the turn of the century, and later rediscovered by A. H. Clifford (see [Fuchs63; p. 165]). Holder and Clifford proved that any totally and naturally ordered archimedean semigroup must be isomorphic to a subsemigroup of one of the following three. The *non-zero* and *non-unit* elements of these three distinguished semigroups are isomorphic to:

(1) the open interval of reals $(0, 1)$ under ordinary multiplication,

(2) the half-open interval of reals $[1/e, 1)$, under the binary operation $max(x \cdot y, 1/e)$

(3) the interval $[1/e, 1)$ augmented by an artificial element δ under the following operation:

$$x \cdot y \quad \text{if} \quad x \cdot y \geq 1/e \, \delta \quad \text{if} \quad x \cdot y < 1/e$$

where e is the base of the natural logarithms, and $\delta < 1/e$.

According to our axioms $i(i(p)) = p$, and so the function i is an antiisomorphism of P which inverts P's ordering relation. The semigroups resulting from (2) and (3) can therefore be ruled out because no such i can ever be found for them. This leaves only possibility (1), which, after we restore the 0 and 1 elements, is the closed interval $[0, 1]$ under multiplication. This proves the theorem.

Acknowledgements The Natural Sciences and Engineering Research Council of Canada supported my work while I was at Waterloo. Some of this work was prepared for presentation while I was a Visiting Scientist at the IBM Canada Laboratory. The preparation costs of this particular paper have been met by a President's Research Grant from Simon Fraser University.

I have benefited from discussions with Harvey Abramson, Robert Hadley, Peter Ludeman, Charles Morgan, Len Schubert and my colleagues from the Logic Programming and AI Group at Waterloo, including Robin Cohen, Randy Goebel, Eric Neufeld, David Poole, and Maarten van Emden.

10   Bibliography

Aczel, J. *Lectures on Functional Equations and Their Applications*, New York, Academic Press, 1966.

Buchanan, B. and E. Shortliffe, eds. *Rule-Based Expert Systems: The MYCIN Experiments of The Stanford Heuristic Programming Project*, Addison–Wesley, 1984.

Burris, S. and H. Sankappanavar. *A Course in Universal Algebra*, New York, Springer–Verlag, 1981.

Carnap, R. *Logical Foundations of Probability*, University of Chicago Press, 1950.

Carnap, R. "The aim of inductive logic," *Logic, Methodology, and Philosophy of Science*, E. Nagel, P. Suppes, and A. Tarski, eds., Stanford, Stanford University Press, pp. 303–318, 1962.

Cox, R. "Probability, frequency, and reasonable expectation," *American Journal of Physics 14*, pp. 1–13, 1946.

Cox, R. *The Algebra of Probable Inference*, Johns Hopkins Press, 1961.

Fine, F. *Theories of Probability: An Examination of Foundations*, Academic Press, 1973.

French, S. "Fuzzy decision analysis: some criticisms," *Studies in The Management Sciences: Fuzzy Sets and Decision Analysis 20*, Elsevier, 1984.

Fuchs, L. *Partially Ordered Algebraic Systems*, Pergamon Press, 1963.

Good, I. *Good Thinking, The Foundations of Probability and Its Applications*, University of Minnesota, 1983.

Gupta, M., Ragade, R., and R. Yager., eds. *Advances in Fuzzy Set Theory*, Elsevier, 1979.

Heckerman, D. "Probabilistic interpretation for MYCIN's certainty factors," *Uncertainty in Artificial Intelligence*, L. Kanal and J. Lemmer, eds., Elsevier, pp. 167–196, 1986.

Keynes, J. *Treatise on Probability*, Macmillan, 1921.

Koopman, B. "The axioms and algebra of intuitive probability," *Annals of Mathematics 42*, 2, pp. 269–292, 1940.

Koopman, B. "Intuitive probabilities and sequences," *Annals of Mathemetics 42*, 1, pp. 169–187, 1941.

Kyburg, H. "Bayesian and non-Bayesian evidential updating," *Artificial Intelligence 31*, 3, pp. 271–293, 1987.

Kripke, S. *Naming and Necessity*, Harvard University Press, p. 16, 1980.

McDermott, D., and J. Doyle. "Non-monotonic logic I," *Artificial Intelligence 13*, pp. 27–39, 1980.

McDermott, D. "Non-monotonic logic II: non-monotonic modal theories," *Journal of the ACM 21*, 1, pp. 33–57, 1982.

Morgan, C. "There is a probabilistic semantics for every extension of classical sentence logic," *Journal of Philosophical Logic 11*, pp. 431–442, 1982.

Poole, D., Goebel, R., and R. Aleliunas. "Theorist: a logical reasoning system for defaults and diagnosis," *Knowledge Frontier*, N. Cercone, and G. McCalla, eds., Spring–Verlag, pp. 331–352, 1987.

Reiter, R. "A logic for default reasoning," *Artificial Intelligence 13*, pp. 81–132, 1980.

Tukey, J. "Conclusions vs. decisions," *Technometrics 2*, 4, 1960.

Zadeh, L. "Fuzzy sets," *Information and Control 8*, pp. 338–353, 1965.

Index of Names

Index of Subjects

409

STUDIES IN COGNITIVE SYSTEMS

Series Editor: James H. Fetzer, *University of Minnesota*

KLUWER ACADEMIC PUBLISHERS